The
FOOTE
ASSOCIATION
YEARBOOK
1989–1990

CW00432670

The Football Association

Patron
HER MAJESTY THE QUEEN

President
HRH THE DUKE OF KENT KG

The FOOTBALL ASSOCIATION YEARBOOK 1989–1990

LONDON

PELHAM BOOKS
Stephen Greene Press

PELHAM BOOKS   Stephen Greene Press

Published by the Penguin Group
27 Wrights Lane, London W8 5TZ, England
Viking Penguin Inc., 40 West 23rd Street, New York, New York 10010, USA
The Stephen Greene Press, 15 Muzzey Street, Lexington, Massachusetts 02173, USA
Penguin Books Australia Ltd, Ringwood, Victoria, Australia
Penguin Books Canada Ltd, 2801 John Street, Markham, Ontario, Canada L3R 1B4
Penguin Books (NZ) Ltd, 182-190 Wairau Road, Auckland 10, New Zealand

Penguin Books Ltd, Registered Offices: Harmondsworth, Middlesex, England
First published 1989

Made and printed in Great Britain by
Richard Clay Limited, Bungay, Suffolk
Typeset by Rowland Phototypesetting (London) Ltd.

ISBN 0 7207 1912 7

A CIP catalogue record for this book is available from the British Library

Photo credits
The Publishers are grateful to the following for permission to reproduce
copyright photographs in the book: Action Images pages 34, 82, 84, 99, 100,
107, 108, 128, 141, 151; Bob Thomas pages 6, 20, 21, 28, 40, 42, 43, 44, 46,
48, 49, 50, 53, 54, 55, 85, 86, 139, 143, 145.

The sale of advertisements in this
publication was carried out by
AIM Publications Ltd, London W1.

Contents

"The Pressures on our Game"
by Graham Kelly.................... 7
Cup Winners 9
FIFA World Cup 1990 12
"Soccer in the Middle Ages".......... 17
European Club Competitions
1988-89 20
England's Record 1872-1989.......... 23
England's Goalscorers 1946-89....... 24
England's Caps 1946-89............... 25
Senior Caps 1988-89 29
European Under-21 Championships
1988-90 30
Under-21 Matches 1976-89........... 33
Under-21 Caps 1988-89 35
Under-21 Caps 1976-89 36
'B' Caps 1978-89 39
England Match Reports 1988-89..... 41
League and Cup Attendances 60
England Teams 1946-89............... 62
International Matches 1872-1989 73
Giant Killers............................. 79
FA Charity Shield Winners 1908-88 81
FA Charity Shield 1988 82
FA Cup Winners 1872-1989........... 83
FA Cup 1988-89 85
FA Cup Exemptions 1989-90 98
FA Trophy 1988-89 99
FA Trophy Winners 1970-89.......... 106
FA Trophy Exemptions 1989-90..... 106
FA Vase 1988-89........................ 107

FA Vase Winners 1975-89............. 118
FA Vase Exemptions 1989-90 118
FA/GM National School Caps and
Results 1988-89...................... 119
FA Youth Cup Winners 1953-39..... 120
FA County Youth Cup Winners
1945-89 121
FA Youth Cup 1988-89................. 122
Youth Caps 1988-89.................... 128
Youth Matches 1947-89 129
Football League Champions
1888-1989 133
Review of the Barclays League
Season 1988-89 136
First Division 1988-89 138
Second Division 1988-89............... 140
Third Division 1988-89................. 142
Fourth Division 1988-89 144
Football League Cup Winners
1961-89 146
Littlewoods Cup 1988-89 146
Sherpa Van Trophy 1988-89 148
Simod Cup 1988-89 152
FA Sunday Cup Winners 1965-89 ... 153
FA Sunday Cup 1988-89 153
Other Leagues' Tables 1988-89....... 156
A Hundred Years of the Northern
League 158
Soccer Star Scheme 161
FA Fixture Programme 1989-90 162
League Fixtures 1989-90............... 164

Liverpool captain Ronnie Whelan holds aloft the F.A. Cup.

The Pressures on our Game

by Graham Kelly, Chief Executive of The Football Association

Football continues to enjoy a vast fund of goodwill and the period since 1986 has seen more people playing and watching the game. It is now up to us to capitalise on this base in the wake of Hillsborough, the awful tragedy at the FA Cup semi-final having propelled football once again into the uncomfortable glare of the national and international limelight.

The Times reported on 17th May 1989: "Everyone wants a simple, easy solution to the ills of English Football. There is none. The solution must address a complex combination of social and political issues and those of the game itself". The game has been beset by the twin problems of hooliganism and outdated facilities and it has attempted to tackle both.

Hooliganism has been contained by the deployment of huge resources, both in terms of manpower and money. Better intelligence, closed circuit television surveillance and blanket policing, backed by public order legislation, have substantially reduced the number of incidents inside football grounds.

Clubs have spent an estimated £50 million on safety measures since the Safety of Sports Grounds Act 1975 led to the establishment of The Football Grounds Improvement Trust. But safety work did not usually enhance amenities and in latter years clubs began to receive grants for ground improvements generally.

After Hillsborough, football needs a dynamic approach towards regenerating its image, with a clear lead being given in the areas of improved facilities and efficient crowd control, because what has been done so far is not perceived by those outside the game to be enough.

First, we need to get more seats into our major grounds. Seated customers are more safely controlled and the tendency to taunt and gesture is gradually lessened. Football grounds become more pleasant places to visit. Spectators can stand and watch in safety, but the ratio of seats to standing accommodation must be altered so that there is a preponderance of seats.

Second, we need to look at ways of improving the facilities at grounds. Action is needed to allow our existing major stadia to become safer, more wholesome arenas. And to supplement these we need new multipurpose grounds, on green field sites, ready and willing to stage important international tournaments like the World Cup, which requires a number of all-seater stadia. There are may clubs which would probably welcome the opportunity of moving to areas that would provide better communications, better parking and perhaps the shared use of facilities.

To provide the necessary stimulus for these improvements there is a strong case for the reduction in the pool betting tax from 42½% to 40%. This would release £16 million per annum which the Pool Promoters might be persuaded to allocate for ground improvements, thereby putting the game in receipt of over £30 million per year from pools sources.

The Treasury must also be persuaded that ground improvements should be tax-deductible. There is no point Ministers complaining that football wastes money on transfer fees when the cost of much-needed improvements is virtually doubled by the need to pay tax.

To sum up, football needs a far-reaching development plan. In the short term, hooliganism can be contained and suppressed. In the medium term, facilities and standards need to be improved.

But, most important is the long term. We must aim at hosting major tournaments such as the World Cup. We must further develop our educational programmes at the grass roots of the game, with increased emphasis on discipline and personal responsibility. We must harness the enthusiasm of our youngest supporters to the long-term interests of the game, hopefully by creating firm and lasting links with their local senior clubs through the community programmes. And, at every level of the game, we must seek to establish a technical excellence that will serve England well in international competition.

Only by concerted and unified action will English football be able to withstand the pressures on our game.

World Cup Winners 1930-86

Year	Winners		Runners-up		Venue
1930	Uruguay	4	Argentina	2	Montevideo
1934	*Italy	2	Czechoslovakia	1	Rome
1938	Italy	4	Hungary	2	Paris
1950	Uruguay	2	Brazil	1	Rio de Janeiro
1954	West Germany	3	Hungary	2	Berne
1958	Brazil	5	Sweden	2	Stockholm
1962	Brazil	3	Czechoslovakia	1	Santiago
1966	*England	4	West Germany	2	London
1970	Brazil	4	Italy	1	Mexico City
1974	West Germany	2	Holland	1	Munich
1978	*Argentina	3	Holland	1	Buenos Aires
1982	Italy	3	West Germany	1	Madrid
1986	Argentina	3	West Germany	2	Mexico City

*After extra time

European Football Championship
Henri Delaunay Cup Winners 1960-88

(formerly EUROPEAN NATIONS CUP)

Year	Winners		Runners-up		Venue
1960	U.S.S.R.	2	Yugoslavia	1	Paris
1964	Spain	2	U.S.S.R.	1	Madrid
1968	Italy	2	Yugoslavia	0	Rome
			(After 1-1 draw)		
1972	West Germany	3	U.S.S.R.	0	Brussels
1976	*Czechoslovakia	2	West Germany	2	Belgrade
1980	West Germany	2	Belgium	1	Rome
1984	France	2	Spain	0	Paris
1988	Holland	2	U.S.S.R.	0	Munich

*Won on penalty-kicks

UEFA Competition for Under-23 Teams
Winners 1972-76

(AGGREGATE SCORES)

Year	Winners		Runners-up	
1972	Czechoslovakia	5	U.S.S.R.	3
1974	Hungary	6	German Dem Rep.	3
1976	U.S.S.R.	3	Hungary	2

UEFA Competition for Under-21 Teams
Winners 1976-88

(AGGREGATE SCORES)

Year	Winners		Runners-up	
1978	Yugoslavia	5	German Dem. Rep.	4
1980	U.S.S.R.	1	German Dem. Rep.	0
1982	England	5	West Germany	4
1984	England	3	Spain	0
1986	*Spain	3	Italy	3
1988	France	3	Greece	0

*Won on penalty-kicks

European Champion Clubs' Cup
Winners 1956-89

Year	Winners		Runners-up		Venue
1956	Real Madrid	4	Stade de Rheims	3	Paris
1957	Real Madrid	2	A.C. Fiorentina	0	Madrid
1958	Real Madrid	3	A.C. Milan	2	Brussels
1959	Real Madrid	2	Stade de Rheims	0	Stuttgart
1960	Real Madrid	7	Eintracht Frankfurt	3	Glasgow
1961	Benfica	3	Barcelona	2	Berne
1962	Benfica	5	Real Madrid	3	Amsterdam
1963	A.C. Milan	2	Benfica	1	London
1964	Inter-Milan	3	Real Madrid	1	Vienna
1965	Inter-Milan	1	Benfica	0	Milan
1966	Real Madrid	2	Partizan Belgrade	1	Brussels
1967	Celtic	2	Inter-Milan	1	Lisbon
1968	Manchester United	4	Benfica	1	London
1969	A.C. Milan	4	Ajax Amsterdam	1	Madrid
1970	Feyenoord	2	Celtic	1	Milan
1971	Ajax Amsterdam	2	Panathinaikos	0	London
1972	Ajax Amsterdam	2	Inter-Milan	0	Rotterdam
1973	Ajax Amsterdam	1	Juventus	0	Belgrade
1974	Bayern Munich	4	Atletico Madrid	0	Brussels
		(After 1-1 draw in Brussels)			
1975	Bayern Munich	2	Leeds United	0	Paris
1976	Bayern Munich	1	St. Etienne	0	Glasgow
1977	Liverpool	3	Borussia Mönchengladbach	1	Rome
1978	Liverpool	1	Bruges	0	London
1979	Nottingham Forest	1	Malmo	0	Munich
1980	Nottingham Forest	1	S.V. Hamburg	0	Madrid
1981	Liverpool	1	Real Madrid	0	Paris
1982	Aston Villa	1	Bayern Munich	0	Rotterdam
1983	S.V. Hamburg	1	Juventus	0	Athens
1984	*Liverpool	1	Roma	1	Rome
1985	Juventus	1	Liverpool	0	Brussels
1986	*Steaua Bucharest	0	Barcelona	0	Seville
1987	Porto	2	Bayern Munich	1	Vienna
1988	*P.S.V. Eindhoven	0	Benfica	0	Stuttgart
1989	A.C. Milan	4	Steaua Bucharest	0	Barcelona

*Won on penalty-kicks

European Fairs' Cup Winners 1958-71
(formerly INTER-CITIES FAIRS' CUP)
(AGGREGATE SCORES)

Year	Winners		Runners-up		Venue
1958	Barcelona	8	London	2	
1960	Barcelona	4	Birmingham City	1	
1961	A.S. Roma	4	Birmingham City	2	
1962	Valencia	7	Barcelona	3	
1963	Valencia	4	Dynamo Zagreb	1	
1964	*Real Zaragoza	2	Valencia	1	Barcelona
1965	*Ferencvaros	1	Juventus	0	Turin
1966	Barcelona	4	Real Zaragoza	3	
1967	Dynamo Zagreb	2	Leeds United	0	
1968	Leeds United	1	Ferencvaros	0	
1969	Newcastle United	6	Ujpest Dozsa	2	
1970	Arsenal	4	Anderlecht	3	
1971	†Leeds United	3	Juventus	3	

*One leg only   †Won on away goals

European Cup Winners' Cup Winners 1962-89

Year	Winners		Runners-up		Venue
1962	Atletico Madrid	3	A.C. Fiorentina	0	Stuttgart
	(After 1-1 draw in Glasgow)				
1963	Tottenham Hotspur	5	Atletico Madrid	1	Rotterdam
1964	Sporting Club, Lisbon	1	M.T.K. Budapest	0	Antwerp
	(After 3-3 draw in Brussels)				
1965	West Ham United	2	T.S.V. Munich	0	London
1966	Borussia Dortmund	2	Liverpool	1	Glasgow
1967	Bayern Munich	1	Glasgow Rangers	0	Nuremberg
1968	A.C. Milan	2	S.V. Hamburg	0	Rotterdam
1969	Slovan Bratislava	3	Barcelona	2	Basle
1970	Manchester City	2	Gornik Zabrze	1	Vienna
1971	Chelsea	2	Real Madrid	1	Athens
	(After 1-1 draw in Athens)				
1972	Glasgow Rangers	3	Moscow Dynamo	2	Barcelona
1973	A.C. Milan	1	Leeds United	0	Salonika
1974	Magdeburg	2	A.C. Milan	0	Rotterdam
1975	Dinamo Kiev	3	Ferencvaros	0	Basle
1976	Anderlecht	4	West Ham United	2	Brussels
1977	S.V. Hamburg	2	Anderlecht	0	Amsterdam
1978	Anderlecht	4	Austria Vienna	0	Paris
1979	Barcelona	4	Fortuna Düsseldorf	3	Basle
1980	†Valencia	0	Arsenal	0	Brussels
1981	Dinamo Tbilisi	2	Carl Zeiss Jena	1	Düsseldorf
1982	Barcelona	2	Standard Liege	1	Barcelona
1983	Aberdeen	2	Real Madrid	1	Gothenburg
1984	Juventus	2	Porto	1	Basle
1985	Everton	3	Rapid Vienna	1	Rotterdam
1986	Dinamo Kiev	3	Atletico Madrid	0	Lyon
1987	Ajax Amsterdam	1	Lokomotiv Leipzig	0	Athens
1988	Mechelen	1	Ajax Amsterdam	0	Strasbourg
1989	Barcelona	2	Sampdoria	0	Berne

*Aggregate scores †Won on penalty-kicks

UEFA Cup Winners 1973-89

(AGGREGATE SCORES)

Year	Winners		Runners-up	
1973	Liverpool	3	Borussia Mönchengladbach	2
1974	Feyenoord	4	Tottenham Hotspur	2
1975	Borussia Mönchengladbach	5	Twente Enschede	1
1976	Liverpool	4	F.C. Bruges	3
1977	†Juventus	2	Atletico Bilbao	2
1978	P.S.V. Eindhoven	3	Bastia	0
1979	Borussia Mönchengladbach	2	Red Star Belgrade	1
1980	†Eintracht Frankfurt	3	Borussia Mönchengladbach	3
1981	Ipswich Town	5	AZ 67 Alkmaar	4
1982	I.F.K. Gothenburg	4	S.V. Hamburg	0
1983	Anderlecht	2	Benfica	1
1984	*Tottenham Hotspur	2	Anderlecht	2
1985	Real Madrid	3	Videoton	1
1986	Real Madrid	5	Cologne	3
1987	Gothenburg	2	Dundee United	1
1988	*Bayer Leverkusen	3	Español	3
1989	Naples	5	VfB Stuttgart	4

†Won on away goals. *Won on penalty-kicks

FIFA World Cup Finals 1990 – Match Schedule

Date	Venue	Match	Group	Date	Venue	Match	Group
8.6.90	Milan	5 v 6	B	16.6.90	Turin	9 v 11	C
9.6.90	Rome	1 v 2	A	16.6.90	Genoa	10 v 12	C
9.6.90	Bari	7 v 8	B	16.6.90	Cagliari	21 v 23	F
9.6.90	Bologna	15 v 16	D	17.6.90	Verona	17 v 19	E
10.6.90	Florence	3 v 4	A	17.6.90	Udine	18 v 20	E
10.6.90	Turin	9 v 10	C	17.6.90	Palermo	22 v 24	F
10.6.90	Milan	13 v 14	D	18.6.90	Naples	5 v 8	B
11.6.90	Genoa	11 v 12	C	18.6.90	Bari	6 v 7	B
11.6.90	Cagliari	21 v 22	F	19.6.90	Rome	1 v 4	A
12.6.90	Verona	17 v 18	E	19.6.90	Florence	2 v 3	A
12.6.90	Palermo	23 v 24	F	19.6.90	Milan	13 v 16	D
13.6.90	Naples	5 v 7	B	19.6.90	Bologna	14 v 15	D
13.6.90	Udine	19 v 20	E	20.6.90	Turin	9 v 12	C
14.6.90	Rome	1 v 3	A	20.6.90	Genoa	10 v 11	C
14.6.90	Bari	6 v 8	B	21.6.90	Verona	17 v 20	E
14.6.90	Bologna	14 v 16	D	21.6.90	Udine	18 v 19	E
15.6.90	Florence	2 v 4	A	21.6.90	Cagliari	21 v 24	F
15.6.90	Milan	13 v 15	D	21.6.90	Palermo	22 v 23	F

Date	Venue	Match	
23.6.90	Naples	B1 v A3/C3/D3	(Eighth-Final 1)
23.6.90	Bari	A2 v C2	(Eighth-Final 2)
24.6.90	Turin	C1 v A3/B3/F3	(Eighth-Final 3)
24.6.90	Milan	D1 v B3/E3/F3	(Eighth-Final 4)
25.6.90	Rome	A1 v C3/D3/E3	(Eighth-Final 5)
25.6.90	Genoa	F2 v B2	(Eighth-Final 6)
26.6.90	Bologna	F1 v E2	(Eighth-Final 7)
26.6.90	Verona	E1 v D2	(Eighth-Final 8)
30.6.90	Rome	Winner 6 v Winner 5	(Quarter-Final 1)
30.6.90	Florence	Winner 3 v Winner 8	(Quarter-Final 2)
1.7.90	Naples	Winner 1 v Winner 7	(Quarter-Final 3)
1.7.90	Milan	Winner 2 v Winner 4	(Quarter-Final 4)
3.7.90	Naples	Winner 2 v Winner 1	(Semi-Final)
4.7.90	Turin	Winner 4 v Winner 3	(Semi-Final)
7.7.90	Bari	Third Place Match	
8.7.90	Rome	FINAL	

FIFA World Cup 1990

Results and Fixtures in the Qualifying Competition

EUROPE

Group 1

19.10.88	Greece v Denmark	1-1
19.10.88	Bulgaria v Rumania	1-3
2.11.88	Rumania v Greece	3-0
2.11.88	Denmark v Bulgaria	1-1
26. 4.89	Greece v Rumania	0-0
26. 4.89	Bulgaria v Denmark	0-2
17. 5.89	Rumania v Bulgaria	1-0
17. 5.89	Denmark v Greece	7-1
11.10.89	Bulgaria v Greece	
11.10.89	Denmark v Rumania	
15.11.89	Greece v Bulgaria	
15.11.89	Rumania v Denmark	

	P	W	D	L	F	A	Pts
Rumania	4	3	1	0	7	1	7
Denmark	4	2	2	0	11	3	6
Greece	4	0	2	2	2	11	2
Bulgaria	4	0	1	3	2	7	1

Group 2

19.10.88	ENGLAND v Sweden	0-0
19.10.88	Poland v Albania	1-0
5.11.88	Albania v Sweden	1-2
8. 3.89	Albania v ENGLAND	0-2
26. 4.89	ENGLAND v Albania	5-0
7. 5.89	Sweden v Poland	2-1
3. 6.89	ENGLAND v Poland	3-0
6. 9.89	Sweden v ENGLAND	
8.10.89	Sweden v Albania	
11.10.89	Poland v ENGLAND	
25.10.89	Poland v Sweden	
15.11.89	Albania v Poland	

	P	W	D	L	F	A	Pts
ENGLAND	4	3	1	0	10	0	7
Sweden	3	2	1	0	4	2	5
Poland	3	1	0	2	2	5	2
Albania	4	0	0	4	1	10	0

Group 3

31. 8.88	Iceland v U.S.S.R.	1-1
12.10.88	Turkey v Iceland	1-1
19.10.88	U.S.S.R. v Austria	2-0
19.10.88	East Germany v Iceland	2-0
2.11.88	Austria v Turkey	3-2
30.11.88	Turkey v East Germany	3-1
12. 4.89	East Germany v Turkey	0-2
26. 4.89	U.S.S.R. v East Germany	3-0
10. 5.89	Turkey v U.S.S.R.	0-1
17. 5.89	East Germany v Austria	1-1
31. 5.89	U.S.S.R. v Iceland	1-1
14. 6.89	Iceland v Austria	
23. 8.89	Austria v Iceland	
6. 9.89	Austria v U.S.S.R.	
6. 9.89	Iceland v East Germany	
20. 9.89	Iceland v Turkey	
25.10.89	East Germany v U.S.S.R.	
25.10.89	Turkey v Austria	
8.11.89	U.S.S.R. v Turkey	
15.11.89	Austria v East Germany	

	P	W	D	L	F	A	Pts
U.S.S.R.	5	3	2	0	8	2	8
Turkey	5	2	1	2	8	6	5
Austria	3	1	1	1	4	5	3
Iceland	4	0	3	1	3	5	3
East Germany	5	1	1	3	4	9	3

Group 4

31. 8.88	Finland v West Germany	0-4
14. 9.88	Holland v Wales	1-0
19.10.88	Wales v Finland	2-2
19.10.88	West Germany v Holland	0-0
26. 4.89	Holland v West Germany	1-1
31. 5.89	Wales v West Germany	0-0
31. 5.89	Finland v Holland	0-1
6. 9.89	Finland v Wales	
4.10.89	West Germany v Finland	
11.10.89	Wales v Holland	
15.11.89	West Germany v Wales	
15.11.89	Holland v Finland	

	P	W	D	L	F	A	Pts
Holland	4	2	2	0	3	1	6
West Germany	4	1	3	0	5	1	5
Wales	3	0	2	1	2	3	2
Finland	3	0	1	2	2	7	1

Group 5

14. 9.88	Norway v Scotland	1-2
28. 9.88	France v Norway	1-0
19.10.88	Scotland v Yugoslavia	1-1
22.10.88	Cyprus v France	1-1
2.11.88	Cyprus v Norway	0-3
19.11.88	Yugoslavia v France	3-2
11.12.88	Yugoslavia v Cyprus	4-0
8. 2.89	Cyprus v Scotland	2-3
8. 3.89	Scotland v France	2-0
26. 4.89	Scotland v Cyprus	2-1
29. 4.89	France v Yugoslavia	0-0
16. 5.89	Norway v Cyprus	3-1
14. 6.89	Norway v Yugoslavia	
5. 9.89	Norway v France	
6. 9.89	Yugoslavia v Scotland	
11.10.89	Yugoslavia v Norway	
11.10.89	France v Scotland	
28.10.89	Cyprus v Yugoslavia	
15.11.89	Scotland v Norway	
18.11.89	France v Cyprus	

	P	W	D	L	F	A	Pts
Scotland	5	4	1	0	10	5	9
Yugoslavia	4	2	2	0	8	3	6
Norway	4	2	0	2	7	4	4
France	5	1	2	2	4	6	4
Cyprus	6	0	1	5	5	16	1

Group 6

21. 5.88	Northern Ireland v Malta	3-0
14. 9.88	Northern Ireland v Rep. Ireland	0-0
19.10.88	Hungary v Northern Ireland	1-0
16.11.88	Spain v Rep. Ireland	2-0
11.12.88	Malta v Hungary	2-2
21.12.88	Spain v Northern Ireland	4-0
22. 1.89	Malta v Spain	0-2
8. 2.89	Northern Ireland v Spain	0-2
8. 3.89	Hungary v Rep. Ireland	0-0
22. 3.89	Spain v Malta	4-0
12. 4.89	Hungary v Malta	1-1
26. 4.89	Malta v Northern Ireland	0-2
26. 4.89	Rep. Ireland v Spain	1-0
28. 5.89	Rep. Ireland v Malta	2-0
4. 6.89	Rep. Ireland v Hungary	2-0
6. 9.89	Northern Ireland v Hungary	
11.10.89	Hungary v Spain	
11.10.89	Rep. Ireland v Northern Ireland	
15.11.89	Spain v Hungary	
15.11.89	Malta v Rep. Ireland	

13

	P	W	D	L	F	A	Pts
Spain	6	5	0	1	14	1	10
Rep. Ireland	6	3	2	1	5	2	8
Hungary	5	1	3	1	4	5	5
Northern Ireland	6	2	1	3	5	7	5
Malta	7	0	2	5	3	16	2

Group 7

1. 9.88	Luxembourg v Switzerland		1-4
19.10.88	Luxembourg v Czechoslovakia		0-2
19.10.88	Belgium v Switzerland		1-0
16.11.88	Czechoslovakia v Belgium		0-0
16.11.88	Portugal v Luxembourg		1-0
15. 2.89	Portugal v Belgium		1-1
26. 4.89	Portugal v Switzerland		3-1
30. 4.89	Belgium v Czechoslovakia		2-1
9. 5.89	Czechoslovakia v Luxembourg		4-0
1. 6.89	Luxembourg v Belgium		0-5
7. 6.89	Switzerland v Czechoslovakia		
6. 9.89	Belgium v Portugal		
20. 9.89	Swizerland v Portugal		
6.10.89	Czechoslovakia v Portugal		
11.10.89	Luxembourg v Portugal		
11.10.89	Switzerland v Belgium		
25.10.89	Czechoslovakia v Switzerland		
25.10.89	Belgium v Luxembourg		
15.11.89	Portugal v Czechoslovakia		
15.11.89	Switzerland v Luxembourg		

	P	W	D	L	F	A	Pts
Belgium	5	3	2	0	9	2	8
Portugal	3	2	1	0	5	2	5
Czechoslovakia	4	2	1	1	7	2	5
Switzerland	3	1	0	2	5	5	2
Luxembourg	5	0	0	5	1	16	0

Winners and runners-up from groups 3, 5, 6 and 7 qualify for the finals along with the winners of groups 1, 2 and 4 plus the two runners-up from groups 1, 2, and 4 with the best comparative records.

AFRICA

ROUND 1

7. 8.88	Angola v Sudan		0-0
11.11.88	Sudan v Angola		1-2
	Angola 2-1 on agg		
	Zimbabwe w/o v Lesotho		
	Zambia w/o v Rwanda (withdrew)		
16. 7.88	Uganda v Malawi		1-0
30. 7.88	Malawi v Uganda		3-1
	Malawi 3-2 on agg		
3. 6.89	Libya v Burkino Faso		3-0
3. 7.89	Burkino Faso v Libya		2-0
	Libya 3-2 on agg		
7. 8.88	Ghana v Liberia		0-0
21. 8.88	Liberia v Ghana		2-0
	Liberia 2-0 on agg		
5. 8.88	Tunisia v Guinea		5-0
21. 8.88	Guinea v Tunisia		3-0
	Tunisia 5-3 on agg		
	Gabon w/o v Togo		

ROUND 2

Group A

6. 1.89	Algeria v Zimbabwe		3-0
8. 1.89	Ivory Coast v Libya		1-0
20. 1.89	Libya v Algeria		0-2
	(Libya withdrew: Algeria walk-over)		
22. 1.89	Zimbabwe v Ivory Coast		0-0
11. 6.89	Ivory Coast v Algeria		

11. 6.89	Zimbabwe v Libya		
23. 6.89	Libya v Ivory Coast		
25. 6.89	Zimbabwe v Algeria		
11. 8.89	Algeria v Libya		
13. 8.89	Ivory Coast v Zimbabwe		
25. 8.89	Algeria v Ivory Coast		
25. 8.89	Libya v Zimbabwe		

	P	W	D	L	F	A	Pts
Algeria	2	2	0	0	5	0	4
Ivory Coast	2	1	1	0	1	0	3
Zimbabwe	2	0	1	1	0	3	1
Libya	2	0	0	2	0	3	0

Group B

6. 1.89	Egypt v Liberia		2-0
7. 1.89	Kenya v Malawi		1-1
21. 1.89	Malawi v Egypt		1-1
22. 1.89	Liberia v Kenya		0-0
10. 6.89	Kenya v Egypt		
11. 6.89	Liberia v Malawi		
24. 6.89	Malawi v Kenya		
25. 6.89	Liberia v Egypt		
11. 8.89	Egypt v Malawi		
12. 8.89	Kenya v Liberia		
25. 8.89	Egypt v Kenya		
26. 8.89	Malawi v Liberia		

	P	W	D	L	F	A	Pts
Egypt	2	1	1	0	3	1	3
Malawi	2	0	2	0	2	2	2
Kenya	2	0	2	0	1	1	2
Liberia	2	0	1	1	0	2	1

Group C

7. 1.89	Nigeria v Gabon		1-0
8. 1.89	Cameroon v Angola		1-1
22. 1.89	Gabon v Cameroon		1-3
22. 1.89	Angola v Nigeria		2-2
10. 6.89	Nigeria v Cameroon		
10. 6.89	Angola v Gabon		
25. 6.89	Gabon v Nigeria		
12. 8.89	Nigeria v Angola		
13. 8.89	Cameroon v Gabon		
27. 8.89	Cameroon v Nigeria		
27. 8.89	Gabon v Angola		

	P	W	D	L	F	A	Pts
Cameroon	2	1	1	0	4	2	3
Nigeria	2	1	1	0	3	2	3
Angola	2	0	2	0	3	3	2
Gabon	2	0	0	2	1	4	0

Group D

8. 1.89	Morocco v Zambia		1-0
8. 1.89	Zaire v Tunisia		3-1
22. 1.89	Tunisia v Morocco		2-1
22. 1.89	Zambia v Zaire		4-2
11. 6.89	Zaire v Morocco		
11. 6.89	Zambia v Tunisia		
25. 6.89	Zambia v Morocco		
25. 6.89	Tunisia v Zaire		
13. 8.89	Morocco v Tunisia		
13. 8.89	Zaire v Tunisia		
25. 8.89	Tunisia v Zambia		
27. 8.89	Morocco v Zaire		

	P	W	D	L	F	A	Pts
Zambia	2	1	0	1	4	3	2
Zaire	2	1	0	1	5	5	3
Morocco	2	1	0	1	2	2	2
Tunisia	2	1	0	1	3	4	2

ROUND 3

Winners Gp 1 v Winners Gp 2; Winners Gp 3 v Winners Gp 4. Aggregate winning teams qualify for the finals.

14

ASIA

Group 1

6. 1.89	Qatar v Jordan	1-0
6. 1.89	Oman v Iraq	1-1
13. 1.89	Oman v Qatar	0-0
13. 1.89	Jordan v Iraq	0-1
20. 1.89	Jordan v Oman	2-0
20. 1.89	Qatar v Iraq	1-0
27. 1.89	Jordan v Qatar	1-1
27. 1.89	Iraq v Oman	3-1
3. 2.89	Qatar v Oman	3-0
3. 2.89	Iraq v Jordan	4-0
10. 2.89	Oman v Jordan	0-2
10. 2.89	Iraq v Qatar	2-2

	P	W	D	L	F	A	Pts
Qatar	6	3	3	0	8	3	9
Iraq	6	3	2	1	11	5	8
Jordan	6	2	1	3	5	7	5
Oman	6	0	2	4	2	11	2

Group 2(Bahrain withdrew)

10. 3.89	Yeman AR v Syria	0-1
15. 3.89	Saudi Arabia v Syria	5-4
20. 3.89	Yemen AR v Saudi Arabia	0-1
25. 3.89	Syria v Yemen AR	2-0
30. 3.89	Syria v Saudi Arabia	0-0
5. 4.89	Saudi Arabia v Yeman AR	1-0

	P	W	D	L	F	A	Pts
S. Arabia	4	3	1	0	7	4	7
Syria	4	2	1	1	7	5	5
Yemen AR	4	0	0	4	0	5	0

Group 3
(RP 'South' Yemen withdrew)

6. 1.89	Pakistan v Kuwait	0-1
13. 1.89	Kuwait v UAE	3-2
20. 1.89	UAE v Pakistan	5-0
27. 1.89	Kuwait v Pakistan	2-0
3. 2.89	UAE v Kuwait	1-0
10. 2.89	Pakistan v UAE	1-4

	P	W	D	L	F	A	Pts
UAE	4	3	0	1	12	4	6
Kuwait	4	3	0	1	6	3	6
Pakistan	4	0	0	4	1	2	0

Group 4
(India withdrew so Nepal switched from Group 5)

Following matches all in S. Korea:
23. 5.89	Malaysia v Nepal	
23. 5.89	Singapore v S. Korea	
25. 5.89	Malaysia v Singapore	
25. 5.89	Nepal v S. Korea	
27. 5.89	Singapore v Nepal	
27. 5.89	S. Korea v Malaysia	

Following matches all in Singapore:
3. 6.89	Singapore v Malaysia	
3. 6.89	S. Korea v Nepal	
5. 6.89	Malaysia v S. Korea	
5. 6.89	Nepal v Singapore	
7. 6.89	Singapore v S. Korea	
7. 6.89	Malaysia v Nepal	

Group 5

20. 2.89	Thailand v Bangladesh	1-0
23. 2.89	China v Bangladesh	2-0
23. 2.89	Thailand v Iran	0-3
27. 2.89	Bangladesh v Iran	1-2
28. 2.89	Thailand v China	0-3
4. 3.89	Bangladesh v China	0-2
8. 3.89	Bangladesh v Thailand	3-1
17. 3.89	Iran v Bangladesh	1-0
11. 6.89	China v Iran	
21. 6.89	Iran v China	
28. 6.89	China v Thailand	

	P	W	D	L	F	A	Pts
China	3	3	0	0	7	0	6
Iran	3	3	0	0	6	1	6
Bangladesh	6	1	0	5	4	9	2
Thailand	4	1	0	3	2	9	2

Group 6

21. 5.89	Indonesia v N. Korea	
21. 5.89	Hong Kong v Japan	
27. 5.89	Hong Kong v N. Korea	
28. 5.89	Indonesia v Japan	
4. 6.89	Hong Kong v Indonesia	
4. 6.89	Japan v N. Korea	
11. 6.89	N. Korea v Hong Kong	
11. 6.89	Japan v Indonesia	
18. 6.89	N. Korea v Indonesia	
18. 6.89	Japan v Hong Kong	
25. 6.89	Indonesia v Hong Kong	
25. 6.89	N. Korea v Japan	

Winners of all groups play off in a league system with top two teams qualifying for the finals.

NORTH/CENTRAL AMERICA

Round 1

19. 6.88	Antigua v Neth. Antilles	0-1
29. 7.88	Neth. Antilles v Antigua	3-1
	Neth. Antilles 4-1 on agg	
12. 5.88	Jamaica v Puerto Rico	1-0
29. 5.88	Puerto Rico v Jamaica	1-2
	Jamaica 3-1 on agg	
17. 4.88	Guyana v Trinidad/Tobago	0-4
8. 5.88	Trinidad/Tobago v Guyana	1-0
	Trinidad/Tobago 5-0 on agg	
17. 7.88	Costa Rica v Panama	1-1
31. 7.88	Panama v Costa Rica	0-2
	Costa Rica 3-1 on agg	
30. 4.88	Cuba v Guatemala	0-1
15. 5.88	Guatemala v Cuba	1-1
	Guatemala 2-1 on agg	

Round 2

1.10.88	Neth. Antilles v El Salvador	0-1
16.10.88	El Salvador v Neth. Antilles	5-0
	El Salvador 6-0 on agg	
30.10.88	Trinidad/Tobago v Honduras	0-0
13.11.88	Honduras v Trinidad/Tobago	1-1
	Trinidad/Tobago on away goal: 1-1 agg	
24. 7.88	Jamaica v United States	0-0
31. 7.88	United States v Jamaica	5-1
	United States 5-1 on agg	
9.10.88	Guatemala v Canada	1-0
15.10.88	Canada v Guatemala	3-2
	Guatemala on away goals: 3-3 agg	
	Costa Rica w/o v Mexico	

Round 3

19. 3.89	Guatemala v Costa Rica	1-0
2. 4.89	Costa Rica v Guatemala	2-1
16. 4.89	Costa Rica v United States	1-0
30. 4.89	United States v Costa Rica	1-0

13. 5.89	United States v Trin/Tobago	....	1-1
28. 5.89	Trinidad/Tobago v Costa Rica	....	
10. 6.89	United States v Guatemala	....	
11. 6.89	Costa Rica v Tobago	....	
25. 6.89	El Salvador v Costa Rica	....	
9. 7.89	El Salvador v United States	....	
16. 7.89	Costa Rica v El Salvador	....	
30. 7.89	Trinidad/Tobago v El Salvador	....	
13. 8.89	El Salvador v Trinidad/Tobago	....	
20. 8.89	Guatemala v Trinidad/Tobago	....	
3. 9.89	Trinidad/Tobago v Guatemala	....	
8.10.89	Guatemala v United States	....	
5.11.89	United States v El Salvador	....	
19.11.89	Trinidad/Tobago v United States	....	
19.11.89	Guatemala v El Salvador	....	
26.11.89	El Salvador v Guatemala	....	

Note: Top two qualify for finals

OCEANIA

Round 1

11.12.88	Taiwan v New Zealand	....	0-4
18.12.88	New Zealand v Taiwan	....	4-1
	New Zealand 8-1 on agg		
26.11.88	Fiji v Australia	....	1-0
3.12.88	Australia v Fiji	....	5-2
	Australia 5-3 on agg		

Round 2

5. 3.89	Israel v New Zealand	....	1-0
12. 3.89	Australia v New Zealand	....	4-1
19. 3.89	Israel v Australia	....	1-1
2. 4.89	New Zealand v Australia	....	2-0
9. 4.89	New Zealand v Israel	....	2-2
16. 4.89	Australia v Israel	....	1-1

	P	W	D	L	F	A	Pts
Israel	4	1	3	0	5	4	5
Australia	4	1	2	1	6	5	4
N. Zealand	4	1	1	2	5	7	3

Israel play winners of S. America Gp 2 for place in the finals.

SOUTH AMERICA

Group 1

20. 8.89	Bolivia v Peru	....
27. 8.89	Peru v Uruguay	....
3. 9.89	Bolivia v Uruguay	....
10. 9.89	Peru v Bolivia	....
17. 9.89	Uruguay v Bolivia	....
24. 9.89	Uruguay v Peru	....

Group 2

20. 8.89	Colombia v Ecuador	....
27. 8.89	Paraguay v Colombia	....
3. 9.89	Ecuador v Colombia	....
10. 9.89	Paraguay v Ecuador	....
24. 9.89	Colombia v Paraguay	....
1.10.89	Ecuador v Paraguay	....

Group 3

30. 7.89	Venezuela v Brazil	....
6. 8.89	Venezuela v Chile	....
13. 8.89	Chile v Brazil	....
20. 8.89	Brazil v Venezuela	....
27. 8.89	Chile v Venezuela	....
3. 8.89	Brazil v Chile	....

Winners of Groups 1 and 3 qualify for the finals. Winners of Group 2 play off against Oceania section winners for place in the finals.

"Soccer in the Middle Ages" or "Veterans' Football"

by Arthur Clark

There is little doubt that, over a decade or so in some parts of England, the establishment and development of competitions for Over-35 and Over-40 players has outstripped any other. I refer to "Veterans' Football" as it is becoming known.

I suppose such a development in football could be expected in line with a national awareness of the need for better health and fitness, and the greater interest in sports and the pursuit of leisure activities at all ages.

In Tyne and Wear, my local area, two leagues – one for Over-35s with eleven clubs and the other for Over-40s with twenty-eight clubs in two divisions – have been running for eight years with associated cup competitions and have a full programme. In the South over the last twenty years there have been various cup competitions for Over-35s, but the Amateur Football Alliance leads the way with sixty-six teams from several counties competing in their two major cup competitions. The teams are mainly from multi-team clubs, which have always given players the chance to continue progressing "backwards" to the Over-35s. The fixtures are mainly friendlies; the only league being a Veterans' Division of the Southern Olympian League with seven clubs. Overall the programme is unintensive. In Sheffield the three-year-old "Wragg Over-35 League" boasts nineteen clubs and is well established with a full Sunday programme. There may be other similar organised leagues of which I am not aware, and undoubtedly there are many "Old Boys"

friendlies and annual fixtures.

Like many others, I had seen on television the story of a Hampshire pensioner still playing regularly, and had sometimes listened disbelievingly to participating old friends (former Northern League players) boast of their current efforts and prowess. Inevitably, curiosity got the better of me last season and I wandered along to a couple of nearby grounds to see just how seriously these lads take this "born again" enterprise. They usually play on Saturday mornings, forty minutes each way, so none of my regular afternoon matches had to be sacrificed.

I had anticipated a preponderance of grey-haired, stiff, balding, pot-bellied exponents, all struggling to stay upright and probably gasping for breath at every move. I suppose I even half-expected the kiss-of-life to be administered at least once in each half. But not a bit of it! This was more serious stuff. Well, perhaps there were one or two on the rotund side, but they were only really there to make up the numbers – mostly as press-ganged substitutes. The commitment, the skill, the pace and especially the general fitness had to be seen to be believed. I watched 50-year-olds with the agility of schoolboys, old-style wingers moving with breathtaking speed (literally, because the recovery would often take a while) and five-man moves that could only be described as being of "geometrical precision". I saw fine goals too, goalkeepers who knew the meaning of positioning, and not once a shirking of physical contact.

We've often heard the cry: "We need an old head". Well, these were all old heads – twenty-two at one go. Here were strategy, tactics, covering and jockeying. And inevitably the encouraging voices, urging, warning, instructing, all helping the man with the ball. Lovely stuff! I even heard "sorry" and "well played ref" said to the youngest man on the park.

I stood with several enthusiasts. Most, like kids visiting playschool, waiting for the day when they would be old enough to join in. I was starting to enjoy it all when my eye fell on a bald, slim, wiry midfielder who somehow looked familiar, but I just couldn't put a name to that number six shirt. I got closer, then someone called out "Terry!" I should have known, of course, but it was the Alf Garnett grey moustache that had fooled me. The same unmistakeable spring in the walk, the same fighting weight, the control, the weighted pass with a peach of a left peg. He had graced the North-East senior leagues thirty years earlier (yes, thirty) and as always was the best man on the field. But to spare his embarrassment he will have to remain nameless.

After the games I hung around. The banter was worth waiting for, especially to be asked: "Want a game next week?" or to hear: "Who needs squash?" Reacting tongue-in-cheek I enquired about injuries, and cardiac arrests, and inclement weather. I even asked if the physio carried Phyllosan.

But injuries weren't a problem. There were no kids trying to make their name with "ball or man" follow-throughs. "We're here to kick the ball, not the bucket", said one old-timer. And the weather? "Well, there's the ref to decide on that", said

another. "It's great to be able to go on playing after 35, or even 40, and still compete as an equal", he went on, "I've never really stopped playing". He had got it exactly right. The medics say that the way to do it is to continue playing without a long break. To retire in the early thirties and then start up again after a few years of inactivity is almost asking for trouble.

These games are for those special guys whom we've all met – the loyal, dedicated clubman from 18 onwards. First there and last away for training, never in bother, play-anywhere devotees with a zest for the game, built up over the years by a ritual of two nights a week training and a Saturday match. The stay-fit brigade with a special love for playing a game that they never want to end; genuine sportsmen, keen, venerable I'd call them. A bit like the old cricketers who went to the colonies. They had really got something going and we hadn't noticed – not until now. None enjoy the game more.

Suddenly they all hurried away and I wondered why. Then I realised. They all had their second affiliations to go to – as managers, coaches, trainers, secretaries and the like at their regular afternoon games. Good for them, I thought, but found myself wondering how their wives coped with a seven-hour absence. After a few visits I was recognised and immediately made welcome. I was even accused of scouting for Newcastle United, and when I jokingly "admitted" to the charge, I became a regular for a free oxo at half-time. The good humour becomes infectious – and smiles are all too rare these days.

So where do the Veterans go from here? They certainly have an attitude and spirit that a few of the others lack, and they swell the 40,000-odd English clubs playing every weekend. They stand for what is best in the game, showing something of the old Corinthian spirit, and The Football Association is committed to promoting the game at all levels. These players want to be taken seriously, so we should at least give them every encouragement. They deserve no less. We have an F.A. Cup, a Trophy, a Vase, two Youth Cups and a Sunday Cup, so perhaps a "Veterans' Cup" might be considered one day – with the Final at Wembley! Well, maybe not, but a County Veterans' Cup is an idea. The AFA have shown the way and adjoining counties could get together.

Logically, the next step would be a "Geriatrics' Cup", and that's me and a few mates. Frankly, it's not for me – I'd better stick to table football with our Oliver who's just six and sometimes lets me win!

Wandsworth Borough F.C. Veterans XI had a successful 1988-89 season, winning the Southern Olympian League Veterans Division.

European Champion Clubs' Cup 1988-89

First Round		Second Round		Quarter-Final		Semi-Final		Final	

A.C. Milan 2:5 / Vitocha Sofia 0:2 } A.C. Milan 1:1 ... A.C. Milan 0:1 ...
Dundalk 0:0 / Red Star 5:3 } Red Star 0:1
Honved 1:0 / Celtic 0:4 } Celtic 0:0 ... Werder Bremen 0:0
Dynamo Berlin 3:0 / Werder Bremen 0:5 } Werder Bremen 1:0

A.C. Milan 1:5
A.C. Milan 4

P.S.V. Eindhoven bye — P.S.V. Eindhoven 5:0

Porto 3:0 / H.J.K. Helsinki 0:2 } Porto 0:2 ... P.S.V. Eindhoven 1:1
Gornik Zabrze 3:4 / Jeunesse D'Esch 0:1 } Gornik Zabrze 0:2 ... Real Madrid 1:2
Real Madrid 3:1 / Moss 0:0 } Real Madrid 1:3

Real Madrid 1:0

In Barcelona

Bruges 1:1* / Brondby 0:2 } Bruges 1:1 ... Monaco 0:1
Valur 1:0 / Monaco 0:2 } Monaco 0:6
Larissa 2:1 / Neuchatel Xamax 1:2† } Neuchatel Xamax 3:0 ... Galatasaray 1:1
Rapid Vienna 2:0 / Galatasaray 1:2 } Galatasaray 0:5

Galatasaray 0:1
Steaua 0

Hamrun Spartans 2:0 / 17 Nentori Tirana 1:2 } 17 Nentori Tirana 0:0 ... Gothenburg 1:1
Pezoporikos 1:1 / Gothenburg 2:5 } Gothenburg 3:1
Spartak Moscow 2:1 / Glentoran 0:1 } Spartak Moscow 0:1 ... Steaua 0:5
Sparta Prague 1:2 / Steaua 5:2 } Steaua 3:2

Steaua 4:1

*Won on away goals rule †Won on penalty-kicks

A.C. Milan – European Cup Winners 1989.

European Cup Winners' Cup 1988-89

Preliminary Round

Elore Spartacus...............3:1
Bryne Idrettslag 0:2

First Round		Second Round		Quarter-Final		Semi-Final		Final	

```
Barcelona            2:5 ┐
Fram Reykjavik       0:0 ┘ Barcelona        1:1* ┐
Flamurtari Vlora     2:0 ┐                        ├ Barcelona        1:0 ┐
Lech Poznan          3:1 ┘ Lech Poznan      1:1  ┘                       ├ Barcelona     4:2 ┐
Derry C.             0:0 ┐                                                │                   │
Cardiff City         0:4 ┘ Cardiff City     1:0  ┐                       │                   │
Glenavon             1:1 ┐                        ├ Aarhus           0:0 ┘                   │
Aarhus               4:3 ┘ Aarhus           2:4  ┘                                           ├ Barcelona   2 ┐
Inter Slovnaft       2:0 ┐                                                                    │              │
C.F.K.A. Sredetz     3:5 ┘ C.F.K.A. Sredetz 2:1  ┐                                           │              │
Omonia               0:0 ┐                        ├ C.F.K.A. Sredetz 2:1* ┐                  │              │
Panathinaikos        1:2 ┘ Panathinaikos    0:0  ┘                        ├ C.F.K.A. Sredetz 2:1            │
Roda                 2:0 ┐                                                 │                                 │
Vitoria Guimaraes    0:1 ┘ Roda             1:0  ┐                        │                                 │
Borac-Banja Luka     2:0 ┐                        ├ Roda             1:2  ┘                                 │
Metallist Kharkov    0:4 ┘ Metallist Kharkov 0:0 ┘                             In Berne                     │
Grasshopper          0:0 ┐                                                                                   │
Eintracht Frankfurt  0:1 ┘ Eintracht Frankfurt 3:3 ┐                                                        │
Sakaryaspor          2:0 ┐                          ├ Eintracht Frankfurt 0:0 ┐                             │
Elore Spartacus      0:1 ┘ Sakaryaspor      1:0    ┘                           ├ Mechelen         2:0 ┐     │
Mechelen             5:3 ┐                                                      │                      │     │
Avenir Beggen        0:1 ┘ Mechelen         1:2    ┐                           │                      │     │
Metz                 1:0 ┐                          ├ Mechelen         0:1     ┘                      │     │
Anderlecht           3:2 ┘ Anderlecht       0:0    ┘                                                   ├ Sampdoria   0 ┘
Floriana             0:0 ┐                                                                             │
Dundee United        0:1 ┘ Dundee United    0:1    ┐                                                  │
Dinamo Bucharest     3:3 ┐                          ├ Dinamo Bucharest 1:0     ┐                      │
Kuusysi Lahti        0:0 ┘ Dinamo Bucharest 1:1    ┘                           ├ Sampdoria        1:3 ┘
Carl Zeiss Jena      5:0 ┐                                                      │
Sparkasse Krems      0:1 ┘ Carl Zeiss Jena  1:1    ┐                           │
Norrkoping           2:0 ┐                          ├ Sampdoria        1:0†    ┘
Sampdoria            1:2 ┘ Sampdoria        1:3    ┘
```

*Won on penalty-kicks   †Won on away goals

Barcelona – Winners of the European Cup Winners' Cup 1989

21

UEFA Cup 1988-89

First Round

Groningen	1:1*	Rangers	1:4	Otelul Galati	1:0
Atletico Madrid	0:2	Katowice	0:2	Juventus	0:5
Aarau	0:0	Aberdeen	0:0	Velez Mostar	1:5
Loko. Leipzig	3:4	Dynamo Dresden	0:2	Apoel	0:2
St. Patrick's Ath.	0:0	Dnepr	1:1	A.E.K. Athens	1:0
Hearts	2:2	Girondins	1:2	Athletic Bilbao	0:2
Zhalgiris Vilnus	2:2	Oesters	2:0	Montpellier	0:1
F.K. Austria	0:5	Dunajska Streda	0:6	Benfica	3:3
Sporting Portugal	4:2	Turun Pall.	0:1*	Sliema Wands.	0:1
Ajax Amsterdam	2:1	Linfield	0:1	Victoria Bucharest	2:6
Real Sociedad	2:2*	Molde	0:1	Naples	1:1
Dukla Prague	1:3	Waregem	0:5	P.A.O.K. Salonika	0:1
US Luxembourg	1:0	Bayern Munich	3:7	Partizan Belgrade	5:5
R.F.C. Liege	7:4	Legia Warsaw	1:3	Slavia Sofia	0:0
VfB Stuttgart	2:1	Malmo	2:1	Roma	1:3
Tatabanyai	0:2	Torpedo Moscow	0:2	Nuremberg	2:1
Inter-Milan	2:2	Foto Nettig	1:1	Servette Geneva	1:0
Brage	1:1	Ikast	0:2	Sturm Graz	0:0
Royal Antwerp	2:1	Bayer Leverkusen	0:0	Trakia Plovdiv	1:0
Cologne	4:2	Belenenses	1:1	Dynamo Minsk	2:0
Akranes	0:1			Besiktas	1:0
Ujpest Dozsa	0:2			Dinamo Zagreb	0:2

Second Round		Third Round		Quarter-Final		Semi-Final		Final	
Naples	1:2								
Lok Leipzig	1:0	Naples	1:0						
Ujpest Dozsa	0:0			Naples	0:3				
Girondins	1:1	Girondins	0:0						
R.F.C. Liege	2:1					Naples	2:2		
Benfica	1:1	R.F.C. Liege	0:0						
Juventus	5:2			Juventus	2:0				
Athletic Bilbao	1:3	Juventus	1:1						
Hearts	0:1							Naples	2:3
F.K. Austria	0:0	Hearts	3:1						
Velez Mostar	0:0†			Hearts	1:0				
Belenenses	0:0	Velez Mostar	0:2						
Bayern Munich	3:2					Bayern Munich	0:2		
Dunajska Streda	1:0	Bayern Munich	0:3						
Malmo	0:1			Bayern Munich	0:2				
Inter-Milan	1:1	Inter-Milan	2:1					First leg	
Dynamo Minsk	2:0							in Naples	
Victoria Bucharest	1:1*	Victoria Bucharest	1:2					Second leg	
Foto Nettig	2:0			Victoria Bucharest	1:0			in Stuttgart	
Turun Palloseura	1:1*	Turun Pallosuera	0:3						
Dynamo Dresden	4:1					Dynamo Dresden	0:1		
Waregem	1:2	Dynamo Dresden	2:2						
Partizan Belgrade	4:0			Dyamo Dresden	1:4				
Roma	2:2*	Roma	0:0						
Sporting Portugal	1:0							VfB Stuttgart	1:3
Real Sociedad	2:0	Real Sociedad	1:2						
Cologne	2:1			Real Sociedad	0:1				
Rangers	0:1	Cologne	0:2						
Groningen	2:1					VfB Stuttgart	1:1		
Servette Geneva	0:1	Groningen	1:0						
Dinamo Zagreb	1:1			VfB Stuttgart	1:0†				
VfB Stuttgart	3:1	VfB Stuttart	3:2						

*Won on away goals   † Won on penalty-kicks

England's Full International Record 1872–1989

(Up to and including 7 June 1989)

	HOME P	W	D	L	Goals For	Agst	AWAY P	W	D	L	Goals For	Agst
Albania	1	1	0	0	5	0	1	1	0	0	2	0
Argentina......................	4	3	1	0	8	4	5	1	2	2	5	5
Australia.......................	—	—	—	—	—	—	4	2	2	0	4	2
Austria	5	3	1	1	18	9	10	5	2	3	36	16
Belgium	4	3	1	0	17	3	13	9	3	1	49	21
Bohemia	—	—	—	—	—	—	1	1	0	0	4	0
Brazil	5	1	3	1	7	6	9	1	2	6	5	14
Bulgaria	2	1	1	0	3	1	3	2	1	0	4	0
Canada	—	—	—	—	—	—	1	1	0	0	1	0
Chile	1	0	1	0	0	0	3	2	1	0	4	1
Colombia	1	0	1	0	1	1	1	1	0	0	4	0
Cyprus..........................	1	1	0	0	5	0	1	1	0	0	1	0
Czechoslovakia	4	3	1	0	9	4	6	3	1	2	10	7
Denmark	4	3	0	1	7	3	7	4	3	0	18	8
Ecuador........................	—	—	—	—	—	—	1	1	0	0	2	0
Egypt	—	—	—	—	—	—	1	1	0	0	4	0
F.I.F.A..........................	1	0	1	0	4	4	—	—	—	—	—	—
Finland	2	2	0	0	7	1	6	5	1	0	25	4
France	7	5	2	0	21	4	13	9	0	4	39	23
Germany, East................	2	2	0	0	4	1	2	1	1	0	3	2
Germany, West	7	5	0	2	15	8	11	4	3	4	20	16
Greece	2	1	1	0	3	0	3	3	0	0	7	1
Holland	5	2	2	1	12	6	4	2	1	1	4	4
Hungary	6	5	0	1	17	9	10	5	1	4	28	18
Iceland	—	—	—	—	—	—	1	0	1	0	1	1
Ireland, Northern	49	40	6	3	169	36	47	34	10	3	150	44
Ireland, Republic of	5	3	1	1	10	5	5	2	2	1	6	4
Israel............................	—	—	—	—	—	—	2	1	1	0	2	1
Italy.............................	5	3	1	1	9	5	10	3	3	4	15	15
Kuwait	—	—	—	—	—	—	1	1	0	0	1	0
Luxembourg	3	3	0	0	18	1	4	4	0	0	20	2
Malta	1	1	0	0	5	0	1	1	0	0	1	0
Mexico	2	2	0	0	10	0	4	1	1	2	4	3
Morocco	—	—	—	—	—	—	1	0	1	0	0	0
Norway.........................	2	2	0	0	8	0	4	3	0	1	17	4
Paraguay.......................	—	—	—	—	—	—	1	1	0	0	3	0
Peru.............................	—	—	—	—	—	—	2	1	0	1	5	4
Poland..........................	3	1	2	0	5	2	3	2	0	1	4	2
Portugal........................	6	5	1	0	12	4	9	3	4	2	23	13
Rest of Europe	1	1	0	0	3	0	—	—	—	—	—	—
Rest of the World............	1	1	0	0	2	1	—	—	—	—	—	—
Rumania	3	0	3	0	2	2	5	2	2	1	4	2
Saudi Arabia..................	—	—	—	—	—	—	1	0	1	0	1	1
Scotland........................	53	25	11	17	115	87	54	18	13	23	73	81
Spain............................	6	5	0	1	19	6	10	5	2	3	16	13
Sweden.........................	4	2	1	1	9	6	8	4	2	2	14	8
Switzerland....................	5	3	2	0	12	3	10	7	0	3	25	9
Turkey	2	2	0	0	13	0	2	1	1	0	8	0
U.S.A.	—	—	—	—	—	—	5	4	0	1	29	5
U.S.S.R.........................	3	1	1	1	7	4	7	3	2	2	9	8
Uruguay	2	1	1	0	2	1	5	1	1	3	5	9
Wales...........................	49	32	9	8	126	46	48	30	12	6	113	44
Yugoslavia	6	3	3	0	13	6	7	1	2	4	8	13
TOTAL	275	177	58	40	732	279	373	198	85	90	836	428

GRAND TOTAL

Played	Won	Drawn	Lost	Goals For	Against
648	375	143	130	1568	707

23

England's Full International Goalscorers 1946-89

(Up to and including 7 June 1989)

Charlton, R.	49	Kevan	8	Grainger	3	Astall	1
Greaves	44	Beardsley	7	Kennedy, R.	3	Beattie	1
Finney	30	Connelly	7	McDermott	3	Bowles	1
Lofthouse	30	Coppell	7	Matthews, S.	3	Bradford	1
Lineker	29	Paine	7	Morris	3	Bridges	1
Hurst	24	Charlton, J.	6	O'Grady	3	Bull	1
Robson, B.	24	Johnson	6	Peacock	3	Chamberlain	1
Mortensen	23	Macdonald	6	Ramsey	3	Crawford	1
Channon	21	Mullen	6	Sewell	3	Gascoigne	1
Keegan	21	Rowley	6	Steven	3	Goddard	1
Peters	20	Waddle	6	Webb	3	Hughes, E.	1
Haynes	18	Atyeo	5	Wilkins	3	Kay	1
Hunt, R.	18	Baily	5	Wright, W.	3	Kidd	1
Lawton	16	Brooking	5	Allen, R.	2	Langton	1
Taylor, T.	16	Carter	5	Anderson	2	Lawler	1
Woodcock	16	Edwards	5	Bradley	2	Lee, J.	1
Chivers	13	Hitchens	5	Broadbent	2	Mabbutt	1
Mariner	13	Latchford	5	Brooks	2	Marsh	1
Smith, R.	13	Neal	5	Cowans	2	Medley	1
Francis, T.	12	Pearson, Stan	5	Eastham	2	Melia	1
Douglas	11	Pearson, Stuart	5	Froggatt, J.	2	Mullery	1
Mannion	11	Pickering, F.	5	Froggatt, R.	2	Nicholls	1
Clarke, A.	10	Adams	4	Haines	2	Nicholson	1
Flowers	10	Barnes, P.	4	Hancocks	2	Parry	1
Lee, F.	10	Dixon	4	Hunter	2	Sansom	1
Milburn	10	Hassall	4	Lee, S.	2	Shackleton	1
Wilshaw	10	Revie	4	Moore	2	Stiles	1
Barnes, J	9	Robson, R.	4	Perry	2	Summerbee	1
Bell	9	Watson, D.	4	Pointer	2	Tambling	1
Bentley	9	Baker	3	Royle	2	Thompson, Phil	1
Hateley	9	Blissett	3	Taylor, P.	2	Viollet	1
Ball	8	Butcher	3	Tueart	2	Wallace	1
Broadis	8	Currie	3	Wignall	2	Walsh	1
Byrne, J.	8	Elliott	3	Worthington	2	Weller	1
Hoddle	8	Francis, G.	3	A'Court	1	Withe	1

England's Full International Caps 1946–89

(Up to and including 7 June 1989)
*Does not include pre-war caps

Player	Caps
A'Court, A. (Liverpool)	5
Adams. T. (Arsenal)	17
Allen, A. (Stoke)	3
Allen, C. (Q.P.R. and Tottenham)	5
Allen, R. (W.B.A)	5
Anderson, S. (Sunderland)	2
Anderson, V. (Nottm For., Arsenal and Manchester United)	30
Angus, J. (Burnley)	1
Armfield, J. (Blackpool)	43
Armstrong, D. (Middlesbrough and Southampton)	3
Armstrong, K. (Chelsea)	1
Astall, G. (Birmingham)	2
Astle, J. (W.B.A.)	5
Aston, J. (Manchester U.)	17
Atyeo, J. (Bristol C.)	6
Bailey, G. (Manchester U.)	2
Bailey, M. (Charlton)	2
Baily, E. (Tottenham)	9
Baker, J. (Hibernian and Arsenal)	8
Ball, A. (Blackpool, Everton and Arsenal)	72
Banks, G. (Leicester and Stoke)	73
Banks, T. (Bolton)	6
Barham, M. (Norwich City)	2
Barlow, R. (W.B.A.)	1
Barnes, J. (Watford and Liverpool)	47
Barnes, P. (Manchester C., W.B.A. and Leeds)	22
Barrass, M. (Bolton)	3
Baynham, R. (Luton)	3
Beardsley, P. (Newcastle and Liverpool)	34
Beattie, K. (Ipswich)	9
Bell, C. (Manchester C.)	48
Bentley, R. (Chelsea)	12
Berry, J. (Manchester U.)	4
Birtles, G. (Nottingham For. and Manchester U.)	3
Blissett, L. (Watford and AC Milan)	14
Blockley, J. (Arsenal)	1
Blunstone, F. (Chelsea)	5
Bonetti, P. (Chelsea)	7
Bowles, S. (Q.P.R.)	5
Boyer, P. (Norwich)	1
Brabrook, P. (Chelsea)	3
Bracewell, P. (Everton)	3
Bradford. G. (Bristol R.)	1
Bradley, W. (Manchester U.)	3
Bridges, B. (Chelsea)	4
Broadbent, P. (Wolves)	7

Player	Caps
Broadis, I. (Manchester C. and Newcastle)	14
Brooking, T. (West Ham)	47
Brooks, J. (Tottenham)	3
Brown, A. (W.B.A.)	1
Brown, K. (West Ham)	1
Bull, S. (Wolves)	2
Butcher, T. (Ipswich and Rangers)	63
Byrne, G. (Liverpool)	2
Byrne, J. (Crystal Palace and West Ham)	11
Byrne, R. (Manchester U.)	33
Callaghan, I. (Liverpool)	4
Carter, H. (Derby)	*7
Chamberlain, M. (Stoke)	8
Channon, M. (Southampton and Manchester C.)	46
Charlton, J. (Leeds)	35
Charlton, R. (Manchester U.)	106
Charnley, R. (Blackpool)	1
Cherry, T. (Leeds)	27
Chilton, A. (Manchester U.)	2
Chivers, M. (Tottenham)	24
Clamp, E. (Wolves)	4
Clapton, D. (Arsenal)	1
Clarke, A. (Leeds)	19
Clarke, H. (Tottenham)	1
Clayton, R. (Blackburn)	35
Clemence, R. (Liverpool and Tottenham)	61
Clement, D. (Q.P.R.)	5
Clough, B. (Middlesbrough)	2
Clough, N. (Nottingham For.)	1
Coates, R. (Burnley and Tottenham)	4
Cockburn, H. (Manchester U.)	13
Cohen, G. (Fulham)	37
Compton, L. (Arsenal)	2
Connelly, J. (Burnley and Manchester U.)	20
Cooper, T. (Leeds)	20
Coppell, S. (Manchester U.)	42
Corrigan, J. (Manchester C.)	9
Cottee, T. (West Ham and Everton)	7
Cowans, G. (Aston Villa and Bari)	9
Crawford, R. (Ipswich)	2
Crowe, C. (Wolves)	1
Cunningham, L. (W.B.A. and Real Madrid)	6
Currie, A. (Sheffield U. and Leeds)	17
Davenport, P. (Nottingham For.)	1
Deeley, N. (Wolves)	2

Player	Caps
Devonshire, A. (West Ham)	8
Dickinson, J. (Portsmouth)	48
Ditchburn, E. (Tottenham)	6
Dixon, K. (Chelsea)	8
Dobson, M. (Burnley and Everton)	5
Douglas, B. (Blackburn)	36
Doyle, M. (Manchester C.)	5
Duxbury, M. (Manchester U.)	10
Eastham, G. (Arsenal)	19
Eckersley, W. (Blackburn)	17
Edwards, D. (Manchester U.)	18
Ellerington, W. (Southampton)	2
Elliott, W. (Burnley)	5
Fantham, J. (Sheffield W.)	1
Fashanu, J. (Wimbledon)	2
Fenwick, T. (Q.P.R. and Tottenham)	20
Finney, T. (Preston)	76
Flowers, R. (Wolves)	49
Foster, S. (Brighton)	3
Foulkes, W. (Manchester U.)	1
Francis, G. (Q.P.R.)	12
Francis, T. (Birmingham, Nottingham Forest, Manchester City and Sampdoria)	52
Franklin, N. (Stoke)	27
Froggatt, J. (Portsmouth)	13
Froggatt, R. (Sheffield W.)	4
Garrett, T. (Blackpool)	3
Gascoigne, P. (Tottenham)	5
Gates, E. (Ipswich)	2
George, C. (Derby County)	1
Gidman, J. (Aston Villa)	1
Gillard, I. (Q.P.R.)	3
Goddard, P. (West Ham)	1
Grainger, C. (Sheffield United and Sunderland)	7
Greaves, J. (Chelsea and Tottenham)	57
Greenhoff, B. (Manchester U. and Leeds)	18
Gregory, J. (Q.P.R.)	6
Hagan, J. (Sheffield U.)	1
Haines, J. (W.B.A.)	1
Hall, J. (Birmingham)	17
Hancocks, J. (Wolves)	3
Hardwick, G. (Middlesbrough)	13
Harford, M. (Luton Town)	2
Harris, G. (Burnley)	1
Harris, P. (Portsmouth)	2
Harvey, C. (Everton)	1
Hassall, H. (Huddersfield and Bolton)	5
Hateley, M. (Portsmouth, AC Milan and Monaco)	31

Player	Caps
Haynes, J. (Fulham)	56
Hector, K. (Derby)	2
Hellawell, M. (Birmingham)	2
Henry, R. (Tottenham)	1
Hill, F. (Bolton)	2
Hill, G. (Manchester U.)	6
Hill, R. (Luton)	3
Hinton, A. (Wolves and N. Forest)	3
Hitchens, G. (Aston Villa and Internazionale Milan)	7
Hoddle, G. (Tottenham and Monaco)	53
Hodge, S. (Aston Villa, Tottenham and Nottingham For.)	16
Hodgkinson, A. (Sheffield U.)	5
Holden, D. (Bolton)	5
Holliday, E. (Middlesbrough)	3
Hollins, J. (Chelsea)	1
Hopkinson, E. (Bolton)	14
Howe, D. (W.B.A)	23
Howe, J. (Derby)	3
Hudson, A. (Stoke)	2
Hughes, E. (Liverpool and Wolves)	62
Hughes, L. (Liverpool)	3
Hunt, R. (Liverpool)	34
Hunt, S. (W.B.A.)	2
Hunter, N. (Leeds)	28
Hurst, G. (West Ham)	49
Jezzard, B. (Fulham)	2
Johnson, D. (Ipswich and Liverpool)	8
Johnston, H. (Blackpool)	10
Jones, M. (Sheffield U. and Leeds)	3
Jones, W. H. (Liverpool)	2
Kay, A. (Everton)	1
Keegan, K. (Liverpool, S.V. Hamburg and Southampton)	63
Kennedy, A. (Liverpool)	2
Kennedy, R. (Liverpool)	17
Kevan, D. (W.B.A.)	14
Kidd, B. (Manchester U.)	2
Knowles, C. (Tottenham)	4
Labone, B. (Everton)	26
Lampard, F. (West Ham)	2
Langley, J. (Fulham)	3
Langton, R. (Blackburn, Preston and Bolton)	11
Latchford, R. (Everton)	12
Lawler, C. (Liverpool)	4
Lawton, T. (Chelsea and Notts. County)	*15
Lee, F. (Manchester C.)	27
Lee, J. (Derby)	1
Lee, S. (Liverpool)	14
Lindsay, A. (Liverpool)	4

Player	Caps	Player	Caps
Lineker, G. (Leicester, Everton and Barcelona)...............	42	Paine, T. (Southampton).............	19
Little, B. (Aston Villa).................	1	Pallister, G. (Middlesbrough)........	2
Lloyd, L. (Liverpool)	4	Parker, P. (Q.P.R.)....................	3
Lofthouse, N. (Bolton)	33	Parkes, P. (Q.P.R.)....................	1
Lowe, E. (Aston Villa)	3	Parry, R. (Bolton)	2
		Peacock, A. (Middlesbrough and Leeds)...................................	6
Mabbutt, G. (Tottenham).............	13	Pearce, S. (Nottingham Forest)......	15
MacDonald, M. (Newcastle)	14	Pearson, Stanley (Manchester U.)	8
Madeley, P. (Leeds)....................	24	Pearson, Stuart (Manchester U.)....	15
Mannion, W. (Middlesbrough)	26	Pegg, D. (Manchester U.).............	1
Mariner, P. (Ipswich and Arsenal)	35	Pejic, M. (Stoke)	4
Marsh, R. (Q.P.R. and Manchester C.)	9	Perry, W. (Blackpool)	3
Martin, A. (West Ham)...............	17	Perryman, S. (Tottenham)............	1
Marwood, B. (Arsenal)...............	1	Peters, M. (West Ham and Tottenham)...........................	67
Matthews, R. (Coventry).............	5	Phillips, L. (Portsmouth).............	3
Matthews, S. (Stoke and Blackpool)	*37	Pickering, F. (Everton)	3
McDermott, T. (Liverpool)..........	25	Pickering, N. (Sunderland)	1
McDonald, C. (Burnley)	8	Pilkington, B. (Burnley)..............	1
McFarland, R. (Derby)...............	28	Pointer, R. (Burnley)	3
McGarry, W. (Huddersfield).........	4	Pye, J. (Wolves)	1
McGuinness, W. (Manchester U.)	2		
McMahon, S. (Liverpool)............	5	Quixall, A. (Sheffield W.)............	5
McNab, R. (Arsenal).................	4		
McNeil, M. (Middlesbrough).........	9	Radford, J. (Arsenal)	2
Meadows, J. (Manchester C.)........	1	Ramsey, A. (Southampton and Tottenham)...........................	32
Medley, L. (Tottenham)..............	6	Reaney, P. (Leeds)	3
Melia, J. (Liverpool)	2	Reeves, K. (Norwich and Manchester C.)	2
Merrick, G. (Birmingham)...........	23	Regis, C. (W.B.A. and Coventry) ..	5
Metcalfe, V. (Huddersfield)	2	Reid, P. (Everton)	13
Milburn, J. (Newcastle)...............	13	Revie, D. (Manchester C.)...........	6
Miller, B. (Burnley)	1	Richards, J. (Wolves)	1
Mills, M. (Ipswich)...................	42	Rickaby, S. (W.B.A.).................	1
Milne, G. (Liverpool)	14	Rimmer, J. (Arsenal)	1
Milton, A. (Arsenal)	1	Rix, G. (Arsenal)	17
Moore, R. (West Ham)...............	108	Robb, G. (Tottenham)................	1
Morley, A. (Aston Villa).............	6	Roberts, G. (Tottenham)	6
Morris, J. (Derby)	3	Robson, B. (W.B.A. and Manchester United)	79
Mortensen, S. (Blackpool)...........	25	Robson, R. (W.B.A.)..................	20
Mozley, B. (Derby)....................	3	Rocastle, D. (Arsenal)................	7
Mullen, J. (Wolves)...................	12	Rowley, J. (Manchester U.)	6
Mullery, A. (Tottenham).............	35	Royle, J. (Everton and Manchester City)....................	6
Neal, P. (Liverpool)	50		
Newton, K. (Blackburn and Everton).................................	27	Sadler, D. (Manchester U.)..........	4
Nicholls, J. (W.B.A.)	2	Sansom, K. (Crystal Palace and Arsenal)	86
Nicholson, W. (Tottenham)	1	Scott, L. (Arsenal)	17
Nish, D. (Derby)	5	Seaman, D. (Q.P.R.)	2
Norman, M. (Tottenham).............	23	Sewell, J. (Sheffield W.)..............	6
		Shackleton, L. (Sunderland)	5
O'Grady, M. (Huddersfield and Leeds)...................................	2	Shaw, G. (Sheffield U.)..............	5
Osgood, P. (Chelsea)...................	4	Shellito, K. (Chelsea)	1
Osman, R. (Ipswich)	11		
Owen, S. (Luton)	3		

Player	Caps	Player	Caps
Shilton, P. (Leicester, Stoke, Nottingham For., Southampton and Derby County)	109	Ufton, D. (Charlton)	1
Shimwell, E. (Blackpool)	1	Venables, T. (Chelsea)	2
Sillett, P. (Chelsea)	3	Viljoen, C. (Ipswich)	2
Slater, W. (Wolves)	12	Viollet, D. (Manchester U.)	2
Smith, A. (Arsenal)	4		
Smith, L. (Arsenal)	6	Waddle, C. (Newcastle U. and Tottenham)	44
Smith, R. (Tottenham)	15	Waiters, A. (Blackpool)	5
Smith, T. (Liverpool)	1	Walker, D. (Nottingham For.)	9
Smith, T. (Birmingham)	2	Wallace, D. (Southampton)	1
Spink, N. (Aston Villa)	1	Walsh, P. (Luton)	5
Springett, R. (Sheffield W.)	33	Ward, P. (Brighton)	1
Staniforth, R. (Huddersfield)	8	Ward, T. (Derby)	2
Statham, D. (W.B.A.)	3	Watson, D. (Sunderland, Manchester C., Werder Bremen, Southampton and Stoke)	65
Stein, B. (Luton)	1		
Stepney, A. (Manchester U.)	1		
Sterland, M. (Sheffield W.)	1	Watson, D. (Norwich City and Everton)	12
Steven, T. (Everton)	25		
Stevens, G. (Tottenham)	7	Watson, W. (Sunderland)	4
Stevens, G. (Everton and Rangers)	33	Webb, N. (Nottingham Forest)	18
Stiles, N. (Manchester U.)	28	Weller, K. (Leicester)	4
Storey, P. (Arsenal)	19	West, G. (Everton)	3
Storey-Moore, I. (Nottingham For.)	1	Wheeler, J. (Bolton)	1
Streten, B. (Luton)	1	Whitworth, S. (Leicester)	7
Summerbee, M. (Manchester C.)	8	Whymark, T. (Ipswich)	1
Sunderland, A. (Arsenal)	1	Wignall, F. (Nottingham For.)	2
Swan, P. (Sheffield W.)	19	Wilkins, R. (Chelsea, Manchester U. and AC Milan)	84
Swift, F. (Manchester C.)	19	Williams, B. (Wolves)	24
		Williams, S. (Southampton)	6
Talbot, B. (Ipswich)	6	Willis, A. (Tottenham)	1
Tambling, R. (Chelsea)	3	Wilshaw, D. (Wolves)	12
Taylor, E. (Blackpool)	1	Wilson, R. (Huddersfield and Everton)	63
Taylor, J. (Fulham)	2		
Taylor, P. (Liverpool)	3	Withe, P. (Aston Villa)	11
Taylor, P. (Crystal Palace)	4	Wood, R. (Manchester U.)	3
Taylor, T. (Manchester U.)	19	Woodcock, T. (Nottingham For., Cologne and Arsenal)	42
Temple, D. (Everton)	1		
Thomas, D. (Coventry City)	2	Woods, C. (Norwich and Rangers)	14
Thomas, D. (Q.P.R.)	8		
Thomas, M. (Arsenal)	1	Worthington, F. (Leicester)	8
Thompson, Peter (Liverpool)	16	Wright, M. (Southampton and Derby County)	22
Thompson, Phil (Liverpool)	42		
Thompson, T. (Aston Villa and Preston)	2	Wright, T. (Everton)	11
		Wright, W. (Wolves)	105
Thomson, R. (Wolves)	8		
Todd, C. (Derby)	27	Young. G. (Sheffield W.)	1
Towers, A. (Sunderland)	3		
Tueart, D. (Manchester City)	6		

England Senior Caps 1988-89

	Denmark	Sweden	Saudi Arabia	Greece	Albania	Albania	Chile	Scotland	Poland	Denmark
P. Shilton (Derby County)	1	1		1	1	1	1	1	1	1
G. Stevens (Rangers)	2	2		2	2	2		2	2	
S. Pearce (Nottingham Forest)	3	3	3	3	3	3	3	3	3	3
D. Rocastle (Arsenal)	4		8	8	8	8			*8	8
T. Adams (Arsenal)	5	5	5							
T. Butcher (Rangers)	6	6		6	6	6	6	6	6	6
B. Robson (Manchester United)	7	7	7	7	7	7	7	7	7	7
N. Webb (Nottingham Forest)	8	4		4	4	4	4	4	4	4
M. Harford (Luton Town)	9									
P. Beardsley (Liverpool)	10	8	9	*9	*9	9			9	9
S. Hodge (Nottingham Forest)	11									
C. Woods (Rangers)	*1									
D. Walker (Nottingham Forest)	*5	*5		5	5	5	5	5	5	5
T. Cottee (Everton)	*9	*11					*10	10		
P. Gascoigne (Tottenham Hotspur)	*10		*4				*8	8	*10	
C. Waddle (Tottenham Hotspur)		9	11		9	11	11	11	8	*11
G. Lineker (Barcelona)		10	10	10	10	10			10	10
J. Barnes (Liverpool)		11		11	11				11	11
D. Seaman (Queens Park Rangers)			1							*1
M. Sterland (Sheffield Wednesday)			2							
M. Thomas (Arsenal)			4							
G. Pallister (Middlesbrough)			6							
A. Smith (Arsenal)			*9	9	*10				*9	
B. Marwood (Arsenal)			*11							
P. Parker (Queens Park Rangers)						*2	2			2
N. Clough (Nottingham Forest)							9			
J. Fashanu (Wimbledon)							10	9		
T. Steven (Everton)								8		
S. Bull (Wolverhampton Wanderers)								*9		*9
S. McMahon (Liverpool)										*4

*Substitute

European Championship for Under-21 Teams 1988-90

Qualifying Competition

GROUP 1

18.10.88	Greece............................ 2	Denmark........................... 2
18.10.88	Bulgaria......................... 2	Rumania 1
1.11.88	Denmark.......................... 1	Bulgaria........................... 3
1.11.88	Rumania 2	Greece.............................. 0
25.4.89	Bulgaria......................... 6	Denmark........................... 0
25.4.89	Greece............................ 1	Rumania 0
16.5.89	Denmark.......................... 3	Greece.............................. 0
16.5.89	Rumania 2	Bulgaria........................... 1
10.10.89	Denmark..........................	Rumania ....
10.10.89	Bulgaria.........................	Greece..............................
14.11.89	Rumania	Denmark...........................
14.11.89	Greece............................	Bulgaria...........................

	P	W	D	L	F	A	Pts
Bulgaria	4	3	0	1	12	4	6
Rumania	4	2	0	2	5	4	4
Greece	4	1	1	2	3	7	3
Denmark	4	1	1	2	6	11	3

GROUP 2

18.10.88	England 1	Sweden 1
18.10.88	Poland............................ 0	Albania............................ 0
4.11.88	Albania........................... 1	Sweden 2
7.3.89	Albania........................... 0	England 2
25.4.89	England 2	Albania............................ 0
6.5.89	Sweden 4	Poland............................. 0
2.6.89	England 2	Poland............................. 1
5.9.89	Sweden	England ....
7.10.89	Sweden	Albania............................
10.10.89	Poland............................	England ....
24.10.89	Poland............................	Sweden ....
14.11.89	Poland............................	Sweden ....

	P	W	D	L	F	A	Pts
England	4	3	1	0	7	3	7
Sweden	3	2	1	0	7	1	5
Albania	4	0	1	3	1	6	1
Poland	3	0	1	2	1	6	1

GROUP 3

18.10.88	U.S.S.R. 2	Austria 2
1.11.88	Austria 3	Turkey.............................. 0
29.11.88	Turkey............................ 3	East Germany 2
11.4.89	East Germany 0	Turkey.............................. 0
25.4.89	U.S.S.R. 1	East Germany 0
9.5.89	Turkey............................ 0	U.S.S.R. 3
19.5.89	East Germany 2	Austria 0
5.9.89	Austria	U.S.S.R. ....
7.10.89	East Germany	U.S.S.R. ....
24.10.89	Turkey............................	Austria ....
7.11.89	U.S.S.R.	Turkey..............................
14.11.89	Austria	East Germany ....

	P	W	D	L	F	A	Pts
U.S.S.R.	3	2	1	0	6	2	5
Austria	3	1	1	1	5	4	3
East Germany	4	1	1	2	4	4	3
Turkey	4	1	1	2	3	8	3

GROUP 4

30.8.88	Finland 0	West Germany 3
13.9.88	Iceland 1	Holland 1
28.9.88	Finland 2	Iceland 1
18.10.88	West Germany 2	Holland 0
25.4.89	Holland 0	West Germany 1
30.5.89	Finland 1	Holland 1
30.5.89	Iceland 1	West Germany 1
5.9.89	Iceland	Finland ....
3.10.89	West Germany	Finland ....
10.10.89	Holland	Iceland ....
25.10.89	West Germany	Iceland ....
14.11.89	Holland	Finland ....

	P	W	D	L	F	A	Pts
West Germany	4	3	1	0	7	1	7
Finland	3	1	1	1	3	5	3
Iceland	2	0	2	0	2	2	2
Holland	4	0	2	2	2	5	2

GROUP 5

13.9.88	Norway........................... 1	Scotland........................... 1
27.9.88	France 2	Norway........................... 0
18.10.88	Scotland........................... 0	Yugoslavia...................... 2
18.11.88	Yugoslavia...................... 2	France 2
7.3.89	Scotland........................... 2	France 3
24.4.89	France 0	Yugoslavia...................... 1
13.6.89	Norway...........................	Yugoslavia......................
5.9.89	Norway...........................	France ....
5.9.89	Yugoslavia......................	Scotland...........................
10.10.89	Yugoslavia......................	Norway...........................
10.10.89	France	Scotland...........................
14.11.89	Scotland...........................	Norway...........................

	P	W	D	L	F	A	Pts
Yugoslavia	3	2	1	0	5	2	5
France	4	2	1	1	7	5	5
Norway	2	0	1	1	1	3	1
Scotland	3	0	1	2	3	6	1

GROUP 6

11.12.88	Cyprus........................... 0	Hungary........................... 0
22.3.88	Cyprus........................... 0	Spain............................... 1
12.4.89	Hungary........................... 1	Cyprus........................... 0
31.5.89	Spain............................... 1	Cyprus........................... 0
10.10.89	Hungary...........................	Spain...............................
14.11.89	Spain...............................	Hungary...........................

	P	W	D	L	F	A	Pts
Spain	2	2	0	0	2	0	4
Hungary	2	1	1	0	1	0	3
Cyprus	4	0	1	3	0	3	1

GROUP 7

15.11.88	Czechoslovakia................ 0	Belgium.......................... 3
14.2.89	Portugal.......................... 1	Belgium.......................... 1
5.4.89	Czechoslovakia................ 4	Luxembourg.................... 0
25.4.89	Portugal.......................... 1	Luxembourg.................... 0
29.4.89	Belgium.......................... 1	Czechoslovakia................ 1
26.5.89	Luxembourg.................... 0	Belgium.......................... 0
5.9.89	Belgium..........................	Portugal..........................
5.10.89	Czechoslovakia................	Portugal..........................
9.10.89	Luxembourg....................	Portugal..........................
24.10.89	Belgium..........................	Luxembourg....................
14.11.89	Portugal..........................	Luxembourg....................
29.11.89	Luxembourg....................	Czechoslovakia................

	P	W	D	L	F	A	Pts
Belgium	4	1	3	0	5	2	5
Czechoslovakia	3	1	1	1	5	4	3
Portugal	2	1	1	0	2	1	3
Luxembourg	3	0	1	2	0	6	1

GROUP 8

26.4.89	Switzerland...................... 0	Italy................................ 0
6.6.89	San Marino...................... 0	Switzerland...................... 5
4.10.89	San Marino......................	Italy................................
25.10.89	Italy................................	Switzerland......................
14.11.89	Switzerland......................	San Marino......................
29.11.89	Italy................................	San Marino......................

	P	W	D	L	F	A	Pts
Switzerland	2	1	1	0	5	0	3
Italy	1	0	1	0	0	0	1
San Marino	1	0	0	1	0	5	0

Under-21 International Matches 1976-89

EC European Under-21 Championship

ENGLAND v. ALBANIA

				Goals	
Year	Date		Venue	Eng	Alb
EC1989	Mar.	7	Shkoder	2	1
EC1989	Apr.	25	Ipswich	2	0

ENGLAND v. BULGARIA

				Eng	Bulg
EC1979	June	5	Pernik	3	1
EC1979	Nov.	20	Leicester	5	0
1989	June	5	Toulon	2	3

ENGLAND v. DENMARK

				Eng	Den
EC1978	Sep.	19	Hvidovre	2	1
EC1979	Sep.	11	Watford	1	0
EC1982	Sep.	21	Hvidovre	4	1
EC1983	Sep.	20	Norwich	4	1
EC1986	Mar.	12	Copenhagen	1	0
EC1986	Mar.	26	Manchester City	1	1
1988	Sep.	13	Watford	0	0

ENGLAND v. FINLAND

				Eng	Fin
EC1977	May	26	Helsinki	1	0
EC1977	Oct.	12	Hull	8	1
EC1984	Oct.	16	Southampton	2	0
EC1985	May	21	Mikkeli	1	3

ENGLAND v. FRANCE

				Eng	Fra
EC1984	Feb.	28	Sheffield Weds.	6	1
EC1984	Mar.	28	Rouen	1	0
1987	June	11	Toulon	0	2
EC1988	Apr.	13	Besancon	2	4
EC1988	Apr.	27	Highbury	2	2
1988	June	12	Toulon	2	4

ENGLAND v. GERMANY D.R.

				Eng	GDR
EC1980	April	16	Sheffield United	1	2
EC1980	April	23	Jena	0	1

ENGLAND v. GERMANY F.R.

				Eng	GFR
EC1982	Sep.	21	Sheffield United	3	1
EC1982	Oct.	12	Bremen	2	3
1987	Sep.	8	Lüdenscheid	0	2

ENGLAND v. GREECE

				Eng	Gre
EC1982	Nov.	16	Piraeus	0	1
EC1983	Mar.	29	Portsmouth	2	1
1989	Feb.	7	Patras	0	1

ENGLAND v. HUNGARY

				Eng	Hun
EC1981	June	5	Keszthely	2	1
EC1981	Nov.	17	Nottingham Forest	2	0
EC1983	April	26	Newcastle	1	0
EC1983	Oct.	11	Nyiregyhaza	2	0

ENGLAND v. ISRAEL

				Eng	Isr
1985	Feb.	27	Tel Aviv	2	1

ENGLAND v. ITALY

				Goals	
Year	Date		Venue	Eng	Italy
EC1978	Mar.	8	Manchester City	2	1
EC1978	April	5	Rome	0	0
EC1984	April	18	Manchester City	3	1
EC1984	May	2	Florence	0	1
EC1986	April	9	Pisa	0	2
EC1986	April	23	Swindon	1	1

ENGLAND v. MEXICO

				Eng	Mex
1988	June	5	Toulon	2	1

ENGLAND v. MOROCCO

				Eng	Mor
1987	June	7	Toulon	2	0
1988	June	9	Toulon	1	0

ENGLAND v. NORWAY

				Eng	Nor
EC1977	June	1	Bergen	2	1
EC1977	Sep.	6	Brighton	6	0
1980	Sep.	9	Southampton	3	0
1981	Sep.	8	Drammen	0	0

ENGLAND v. POLAND

				Eng	Pol
EC1982	Mar.	17	Warsaw	2	1
EC1982	April	7	West Ham	2	2
EC1989	June	2	Plymouth	2	1

ENGLAND v. PORTUGAL

				Eng	Por
1987	June	13	Sollies-Pont	0	0

ENGLAND v. REPUBLIC OF IRELAND

				Eng	Rep of Ire
1981	Feb.	25	Liverpool	1	0
1985	Mar.	25	Portsmouth	3	2
1989	June	9	Six-Fours	0	0

ENGLAND v. RUMANIA

				Eng	Rum
EC1980	Oct.	14	Ploesti	0	4
EC1981	April	28	Swindon	3	0
EC1985	April	30	Brasov	0	0
EC1985	Sep.	9	Ipswich	3	0

ENGLAND v. SCOTLAND

				Eng	Scot
1977	April	27	Sheffield United	1	0
EC1980	Feb.	12	Coventry	2	1
EC1980	Mar.	4	Aberdeen	0	0
EC1982	April	19	Glasgow	1	0
EC1982	April	28	Manchester City	1	1
EC1988	Feb.	16	Aberdeen	1	0
EC1988	Mar.	22	Nottingham	1	0

ENGLAND v. SENEGAL

				Eng	Sen
1989	June	7	Sainte-Maxime	6	1

ENGLAND v. SPAIN

Year	Date		Venue	Goals Eng	Spa
EC1984	May	17	Seville	1	0
EC1984	May	24	Sheffield United..........	2	0
1987	Feb.	18	Burgos	2	1

ENGLAND v. SWEDEN

				Eng	Swe
1979	June	9	Vasteras	2	1
1986	Sep.	9	Oestersund	1	1
EC1988	Oct.	18	Coventry	1	1

ENGLAND v. SWITZERLAND

				Eng	Swit
EC1980	Nov.	18	Ipswich......................	5	0
EC1981	May	31	Neuenburg................	0	0
1988	May	28	Lausanne..................	1	1

ENGLAND v. TURKEY

				Eng	Turk
EC1984	Nov.	13	Bursa	0	0
EC1985	Oct.	15	Bristol City................	3	0
EC1987	April	28	Izmir.........................	0	0
EC1987	Oct.	13	Sheffield	1	1

ENGLAND v. U.S.A.

Year	Date		Venue	Goals Eng	USA
1989	June	11	Toulon	0	2

ENGLAND v. U.S.S.R.

				Eng	USSR
1987	June	9	La Ciotat	0	0
1988	June	7	Six-Fours..................	1	0

ENGLAND v. WALES

				Eng	Wales
1976	Dec.	15	Wolverhampton..........	0	0
1979	Feb.	6	Swansea	1	0

ENGLAND v. YUGOSLAVIA

				Eng	Yugo
EC1978	April	19	Novi Sad...................	1	2
EC1978	May	2	Manchester City.........	1	1
EC1986	Nov.	11	Peterborough	1	1
EC1987	Nov.	10	Zemun	5	1

England Under-21s prior to the match in Shkoder.

England Under-21 Caps 1988-89

	Denmark	Sweden	Greece	Albania	Albania	Poland	Bulgaria	Senegal	Rep. of Ireland	U.S.A.
N. Martyn (Bristol Rovers)	1	1	1	1	1					
C. Cooper (Middlesbrough)	2	3	2							
A. Hinchcliffe (Manchester City)	3									
P. Lake (Manchester City)	4			2	2	2				
S. Redmond (Manchester City)	5	5	4	5	5	5				
S. Chettle (Nottingham Forest)	6	6	5	6	6	6				
V. Samways (Tottenham Hotspur)	7	10								
I. Brightwell (Manchester City)	8				8					
P. Merson (Arsenal)	9		10			*7				
D. Hirst (Sheffield Wednesday)	10						*11	10	10	10
D. Smith (Coventry City)	11	11		11	11	11				
K. Pressman (Sheffield Wednesday)	*1									
B. Statham (Tottenham Hotspur)	*3	2								
S. Sedgley (Coventry City)	*4	4	7	10	10	10				
D. Yates (Notts County)	*6						4	4	4	4
S. Ripley (Middlesbrough)	*11	8	11	7	7					
D. Burrows (W.B.A. and Liverpool)		*2	3	3	3	3				
D. White (Manchester City)		7								
J. Dozzell (Ipswich Town)		9	*10							
D. Oldfield (Luton Town)		*9								
M. Thomas (Arsenal)			6	4	4	4				
R. Beardsmore (Manchester United)			8	*3		8	6			6
L. Sharpe (Manchester United)			9							
B. Horne (Millwall)			*1			1	1		1	1
L. Martin (Manchester United)			*2	*3						
D. Holdsworth (Watford)			*4							
D. Batty (Leeds United)			*8				8	8	8	8
P. Ince (West Ham United)				8						
S. Bull (Wolverhampton Wanderers)				9	9	9				
A. Mutch (Wolverhampton Wanderers)						7				
Ray Wallace (Southampton)							2	*2	2	
T. Dobson (Coventry City)							3	3	3	3
G. Butters (Tottenham Hotspur)							5	*4	*5	
C. Palmer (Sheffield Wednesday)							7	7	7	7
Rodney Wallace (Southampton)							9		*9	9
P. Williams (Charlton Athletic)							10	11	11	*11
M. Gabbiadini (Sunderland)							11			11
N. Ruddock (Southampton)							*5	5	5	5
A. Miller (Arsenal)								1		
G. Charles (Nottingham Forest)								2		2
J. Ebbrell (Everton)								6	6	*6
P. Mortimer (Charlton Athletic)								9	9	

*Substitute

England Under-21 Caps 1976-89

(Up to and including 11th June 1989)

Player	Caps	Player	Caps
Ablett, G. (Liverpool)	1	Clough, N. (Nottingham Forest)	15
Adams, N. (Everton)	1	Coney, D. (Fulham)	4
Adams, T. (Arsenal)	5	Connor, T. (Brighton & H.A.)	1
Allen, C. (Q.P.R. and C. Palace)	3	Cooke, R. (Tottenham Hotspur)	1
Allen, M. (Queens Park Rangers)	2	Cooper, C. (Middlesbrough)	8
Allen, P. (West Ham and		Corrigan, J. (Manchester City)	3
Tottenham Hotspur)	3	Cottee, T. (West Ham United)	10
Anderson, V. (Nottingham For.)	1	Cowans, G. (Aston Villa)	5
Andrews, I. (Leicester City)	1	Cranson, I. (Ipswich Town)	5
		Crooks, G. (Stoke City)	4
Bailey, G. (Manchester United)	14	Cunningham, L. (W.B.A.)	6
Baker, G. (Southampton)	2	Curbishley, A. (Birmingham City)	1
Bannister, G. (Sheffield Wed.)	1		
Barker, S. (Blackburn Rovers)	4	Daniel, P. (Hull City)	7
Barnes, J. (Watford)	3	Davis, P. (Arsenal)	11
Barnes, P. (Manchester City)	9	D'Avray, M. (Ipswich Town)	2
Batty, D. (Leeds United)	6	Deehan, J. (Aston Villa)	7
Beagrie, P. (Sheffield United)	2	Dennis, M. (Birmingham City)	3
Beardsmore, R. (Manchester		Dickens, A. (West Ham United)	1
United)	5	Digby, F. (Swindon Town)	4
Beeston, C. (Stoke City)	1	Dillon, K. (Birmingham City)	1
Bertschin, K. (Birmingham City)	3	Dixon, K. (Chelsea)	1
Birtles, G. (Nottingham Forest)	2	Dobson, T. (Coventry City)	4
Blissett, L. (Watford)	4	Donowa, L. (Norwich City)	3
Bracewell, P. (Stoke, Sunderland		Dorigo, T. (Aston Villa and	
and Everton)	13	Chelsea)	11
Bradshaw, P. (Wolverhampton)	4	Dozzell, J. (Ipswich Town)	8
Breacker, T. (Luton Town)	2	Duxbury, M. (Manchester United)	7
Brennan, M. (Ipswich Town)	5	Dyson, P. (Coventry City)	4
Brightwell, I. (Manchester City)	2		
Brock, K. (Oxford United)	4	Ebbrell, J. (Everton)	3
Bull, S. (Wolverhampton)	3	Elliott, P. (Luton and Aston Villa)	3
Burrows, D. (W.B.A. and			
Liverpool)	5	Fairclough, C. (Nottingham Forest	
Butcher, T. (Ipswich Town)	7	and Tottenham Hotspur)	7
Butters, G. (Tottenham Hotspur)	3	Fairclough, D. (Liverpool)	1
Butterworth, I. (Coventry and		Fashanu, J. (Norwich and	
Nottingham Forest)	8	Nottingham Forest)	11
		Fenwick, T. (Queen's Park	
Caesar, G. (Arsenal)	3	Rangers)	11
Callaghan, N. (Watford)	9	Fereday, W. (Q.P.R.)	5
Carr, C. (Fulham)	1	Flowers, T. (Southampton)	3
Carr, F. (Nottingham Forest)	9	Forsyth, M. (Derby County)	1
Caton, T. (Man. C. and Arsenal)	14	Foster, S. (Brighton & H.A.)	1
Chamberlain, M. (Stoke City)	4	Futcher, P. (Luton and Man. C.)	11
Chapman, L. (Stoke City)	1		
Charles, G. (Nottingham Forest)	2	Gabbiadini, M. (Sunderland)	2
Chettle, S. (Nottingham Forest)	10	Gale, A. (Fulham)	1
		Gascoigne, P. (Newcastle United)	13

Player	Caps
Gayle, H. (Birmingham City)	3
Gernon, I. (Ipswich Town)............	1
Gibbs, N. (Watford)....................	5
Gibson, C. (Aston Villa)	1
Gilbert, W. (Crystal Palace)	11
Goddard, P. (West Ham United)	8
Gordon, D. (Norwich City)...........	4
Gray, A. (Aston Villa).................	2
Haigh, P. (Hull City)	1
Hardyman, P. (Portsmouth)..........	2
Hateley, M. (Coventry and	
Portsmouth)	10
Hayes, M. (Arsenal)....................	3
Hazell, R. (Wolverhampton).........	1
Heath, A. (Stoke City).................	8
Hesford, I. (Blackpool)...............	7
Hilaire, V. (Crystal Palace)	9
Hinchcliffe, A. (Manchester City) ..	1
Hinshelwood, P. (Crystal Palace)...	2
Hirst, D. (Sheffield Wednesday).....	7
Hoddle, G. (Tottenham Hotspur)...	12
Hodge, S. (Nottingham Forest	
and Aston Villa)......................	8
Hodgson, D. (Middlesbrough and	
Liverpool).............................	7
Holdsworth, D. (Watford)............	1
Horne, B. (Millwall)....................	5
Hucker, P. (Queens Park Rangers)	2
Ince, P. (West Ham United)	1
Johnston, C. (Middlesbrough)	2
Jones, C. (Tottenham Hotspur)......	1
Jones, D. (Everton)	1
Keegan, G. (Oldham Athletic)	1
Keown, M. (Aston Villa)..............	8
Kerslake, D. (Q.P.R.)	1
Kilcline, B. (Notts. County)	2
King, A. (Everton)	2
Knight, A. (Portsmouth)	2
Knight, I. (Sheffield Wednesday) ...	2
Lake, P. (Manchester City)	4
Langley, T. (Chelsea)..................	1
Lee, R. (Charlton Athletic)...........	2
Lee, S. (Liverpool)	6
Lowe, D. (Ipswich Town)	2
Lukic, J. (Leeds United)	7
Lund, G. (Grimsby Town)	1

Player	Caps
McCall, S. (Ipswich Town)............	6
McDonald, N. (Newcastle United)	5
McGrath, L. (Coventry City).........	1
McLeary, A. (Millwall)................	1
McMahon, S. (Everton and	
Aston Villa)	6
Mabbutt, G. (Bristol R. and	
Tottenham Hotspur).................	6
Mackenzie, S. (W.B.A.)..............	3
Martin, L. (Mancheser United)......	2
Martyn, N. (Bristol Rovers)	10
May, A. (Manchester City)	1
Merson, P. (Arsenal)...................	3
Middleton, J. (Nottingham Forest	
and Derby County)	3
Miller, A. (Arsenal)	2
Mills, G. (Nottingham Forest)	2
Mimms, R. (Rotherham and	
Everton)................................	3
Moran, S. (Southampton).............	2
Morgan, S. (Leicester City)...........	2
Mortimer, P. (Charlton Athletic) ...	2
Mountfield, D. (Everton)	1
Moses, R. (W.B.A. and Man. U.)...	8
Mutch, A. (Wolverhampton).........	1
Newell, M. (Luton Town)	4
Oldfield, D. (Luton Town)...........	1
Osman, R. (Ipswich Town)	7
Owen, G. (Man. C. and W.B.A.) ...	22
Painter, I. (Stoke City)................	1
Palmer, C. (Sheffield Wednesday)	4
Parker, G. (Hull City and	
Nottingham Forest)..................	6
Parker, P. (Fulham)	8
Parkes, P. (Q.P.R.)	1
Parkin, S. (Stoke City)................	6
Peach, D. (Southampton)	8
Peake, A. (Leicester City)	1
Pearce, S. (Nottingham Forest)......	1
Pickering, N. (Sunderland and	
Coventry)	15
Platt, D. (Aston Villa)	3
Porter, G. (Watford)	12
Pressman, K. (Sheffield	
Wednesday)	1
Proctor, M. (Middlesbrough and	
Nottingham Forest).................	5

Player	Caps	Player	Caps
Ranson, R. (Manchester City)	11	Stewart, P. (Manchester City)........	1
Redmond, S. (Manchester City).....	12	Suckling, P. (Coventry, Man. City	
Reeves, K. (Norwich and Man. C.)	10	and Crystal Palace)	10
Regis, C. (W.B.A.)	6	Sunderland, A. (Wolverhampton)	1
Reid, N. (Manchester City)...........	6	Swindlehurst, D. (Crystal Palace)...	1
Reid, P. (Bolton Wanderers)	6		
Richards, J. (Wolverhampton).......	2	Talbot, B. (Ipswich Town)	1
Rideout, P. (Aston Villa and Bari)	6	Thomas, D. (Coventry and	
Ripley, S. (Middlesbrough)...........	7	Tottenham Hotspur).................	7
Ritchie, A. (Brighton & H.A.)	1	Thomas, M. (Arsenal)	11
Rix, G. (Arsenal)	7	Thomas, M. (Luton Town)...........	3
Robson, B. (W.B.A.)	7	Thompson, G. (Coventry City)	6
Robson, S. (Arsenal and		Thorn, A. (Wimbledon)..............	5
West Ham United)	8		
Rocastle, D. (Arsenal).................	14	Venison, B. (Sunderland)	10
Rodger, G. (Coventry City)	4		
Rosario, R. (Norwich City)...........	4	Waddle, C. (Newcastle United)......	1
Rowell, G. (Sunderland)	1	Walker, D. (Nottingham Forest)	7
Ruddock, N. (Southampton).........	4	Wallace, D. (Southampton)	14
Ryan, J. (Oldham Athletic)...........	1	Wallace, Ray (Southampton).........	3
		Wallace, Rodney (Southampton)....	3
Samways, V. (Tottenham Hotspur)	5	Walsh, G. (Manchester United)	2
Sansom, K. (Crystal Palace)..........	8	Walsh, P. (Luton Town)	7
Seaman, D. (Birmingham City)......	10	Walters, M. (Aston Villa)	9
Sedgley, S. (Coventry City)...........	10	Ward, P. (Brighton & H.A.)..........	2
Sellars, S. (Blackburn Rovers).......	3	Watson, D. (Norwich City)	7
Sharpe, L. (Manchester United).....	1	Webb, N. (Portsmouth and	
Shaw, G. (Aston Villa).................	7	Nottingham Forest).................	3
Shelton, G. (Sheffield Wednesday)	1	White, D. (Manchester City).........	5
Sheringham, T. (Millwall).............	1	Whyte, C. (Arsenal)...................	4
Simpson, P. (Manchester City)	5	Wicks, S. (Q.P.R.)......................	1
Sims, S. (Leicester City)...............	10	Wilkins, R. (Chelsea)	1
Sinnott, L. (Watford)...................	1	Wilkinson, P. (Grimsby Town and	
Smith, D. (Coventry City)	8	Everton)................................	4
Smith, M. (Sheffield Wednesday) ...	5	Williams, P. (Charlton Athletic).....	4
Snodin, I. (Doncaster Rovers		Williams, S. (Southampton)	14
and Leeds United)	4	Winterburn, N. (Wimbledon)........	1
Statham, B. (Tottenham Hotspur)	3	Wise, D. (Wimbledon).................	1
Statham, D. (W.B.A.)	6	Woodcock, A. (Nottingham Forest)	2
Stein, B. (Luton Town)	3	Woods, C. (Nottingham Forest,	
Sterland, M. (Sheffield Wednesday)	7	Q.P.R. and Norwich)	6
Steven, T. (Everton)....................	2	Wright, M. (Southampton)	4
Stevens, G. (Everton)..................	1	Wright, W. (Everton)	6
Stevens, G. (Brighton & H.A. and			
Tottenham Hotspur).................	7	Yates, D. (Notts County)	5

England 'B' Caps 1978-89

(Up to and including 22nd May 1989)

Player	Caps
Anderson, V. (Nottingham Forest)	7
Armstrong, D. (Middlesbrough)............	2
Bailey, G. (Manchester United)	2
Bailey, J. (Everton)	1
Barnes, P. (W.B.A.)............................	1
Batson, B. (W.B.A.)............................	3
Beasant, D. (Chelsea)	3
Birtles, G. (Nottingham Forest)............	1
Blissett, L. (Watford)............................	1
Bond, K. (Norwich and Man. City)........	2
Brock, K. (Q.P.R.)............................	1
Bruce, S. (Norwich City)......................	1
Bull, S. (Wolves)................................	3
Butcher, T. (Ipswich Town)..................	1
Callaghan, N. (Watford)......................	1
Corrigan, J. (Manchester City)	10
Cowans, G. (Aston Villa)......................	1
Crook, I. (Norwich City)......................	1
Cunningham, L. (W.B.A.)	1
Daley, S. (Wolves)	6
Davenport, P. (Nottingham Forest)........	1
Devonshire, A. (West Ham United)	1
Dorigo, T. (Chelsea)............................	3
Elliott, S. (Sunderland)	3
Eves, M. (Wolves)................................	3
Fairclough, C. (Tottenham)..................	1
Fairclough, D. (Liverpool)	1
Fashanu, J. (Nottingham Forest)	1
Flanagan, M. (Charlton and Palace)	3
Ford, T. (W.B.A.)............................	3
Gallagher, J. (Birmingham)..................	1
Gascoigne, P. (Tottenham)	2
Geddis, D. ((Ipswich)	1
Gibson, C. (Aston Villa)	1
Gidman, J. (Aston Villa)......................	2
Goddard, P. (West Ham United)	1
Greenhoff, B. (Manchester United)	1
Harford, M. (Luton Town)	1
Hazell, R. (Wolves)	1
Heath, A. (Everton)	1
Hilaire, V. (Crystal Palace)..................	1
Hill, G. (Manchester United and Derby)..	6
Hoddle, G. (Tottenham)......................	2
Hodge, S. (Nottingham Forest)	1
Hollins, J. (Q.P.R.)	5
Hurlock, T. (Millwall)	3
Johnston, C. (Liverpool)......................	1
Kennedy, A. (Liverpool)	7
Langley, T. (Chelsea)..........................	3
Lineker, G. (Leicester City)..................	1
Lyons, M. (Everton)	1

Player	Caps
McCall, S. (Ipswich Town)	1
McDermott, T. (Liverpool)	1
McLeary, A. (Millwall)	2
McMahon, S. (Aston Villa and Liverpool)......................................	2
Mabbutt, G. (Tottenham)	4
Mackenzie, S. (Man. City and Charlton)	2
Mariner, P. (Ipswich Town)	7
Martin, A. (West Ham United)..............	2
Money, R. (Liverpool)	1
Morley T. (Aston Villa)	2
Mortimer, D. (Aston Villa)	3
Mountfield, D. (Everton)......................	1
Mowbray, T. (Middlesbrough)	3
Mutch, A. (Wolves)............................	3
Naylor, S. (W.B.A.)	3
Needham, D. ((Nottingham Forest)	6
Osman, R. (Ipswich Town)..................	2
Owen, G. (Manchester City)................	7
Pallister, G. (Middlesbrough)	3
Parker, P. (Q.P.R.)	2
Parkes, P. (West Ham United)	2
Peach, D. (Southampton)	1
Platt, D. (Aston Villa)	3
Power, P. (Mancheser City)	1
Preece, D. (Luton Town)	3
Reeves, K. (Manchester City)	3
Regis, C. ((W.B.A.)	3
Richards, J. (Wolves)............................	3
Rix, G. (Arsenal)	3
Roberts, G. (Tottenham)	1
Robson, B. (W.B.A.)	2
Roeder, G. (Orient and Q.P.R.)............	6
Sansom, K. (Crystal Palace)..................	2
Seamon, D. ((Q.P.R.)..........................	1
Sims, S. (Leicester City)......................	1
Snodin, I. (Everton)............................	1
Speight, M. (Sheffield United)..............	4
Statham, D. (W.B.A.)	2
Sterland, M. (Sheffield Wednesday)	1
Stevens, G. (Everton)	1
Stewart, P. (Tottenham)	3
Sunderland, A. (Arsenal)......................	7
Talbot, B. (Ipswich and Arsenal)	8
Thomas, M. (Tottenham)......................	1
Thompson, P. (Liverpool)....................	1
Waldron, M. (Southampton)	1
Ward, P. (Nottingham Forest)..............	2
Williams, S. (Southampton)..................	4
Woodcock, T. (Cologne)	1
Woods, C. (Norwich City)	1
Wright, B. (Everton)............................	2

England on World Cup duty in Tirana.

40

England's International Matches 1988-89

England 0   Denmark 0
(Under-21)
13th September 1988, Watford

England, so strong at this level that they have lost only once at home in twelve years of Under-21 matches (to East Germany in 1980), seemed to run out of ideas in this friendly fixture at Vicarage Road. Manchester City midfielder Paul Lake was probably the only England player to impress a gathering of top managers including Dalglish, Graham and Souness – and he was withdrawn at half-time.

Striker Paul Merson, winning his first cap, was clearly determined not to be over-shadowed by five Arsenal team-mates who had been called into the senior squad and now formed part of the 3,500 crowd. He created two perfect first-half openings for David Hirst and Vinny Samways that unfortunately came to nothing.

John Molby, cousin of Liverpool's Jan, made his presence felt in midfield and ensured that the Danes were always "level on points" in a match that ended with a disappointing goalless scoreline. There was plenty of endeavour from both teams, but neither possessed the subtle skill to break down the opposing defence.

England: Martyn (Pressman), Cooper, Hinchliffe (B. Statham), Lake (Sedgley), Redmond, Chettle (Yates), Samways, Brightwell, Merson, Hirst, D. Smith (Ripley).

Denmark: Kjaer, Sorensen, Reiper, Larsen, Christiansen, Molby, Uldbjerg (Nielsen), Risom, Svinggaard, Strudal, Frank.

Referee: H. King of Wales.

England 1   Denmark 0
14th September 1988, Wembley

The 27,000 loyal Wembley supporters saw a promising debut by 21-year-old Arsenal midfielder David Rocastle and the team regain some degree of confidence after the disappointment of the summer's European Championship. Manager Bobby Robson had been under pressure to give more new recruits their chance, but his more cautious approach – Rocastle was the only debutant to start – was vindicated to a large extent as the recalled Neil Webb scored the goal that won the match on 28 minutes.

The contribution of England's captain, Bryan Robson, was outstanding again, and much of the credit for the goal was due to him. On a slippery pitch he lost his footing as Lars Olsen challenged but, having regained possession, he lifted the ball into the Danish goalmouth. Rasmussen flapped at it as Mick Harford moved in and Webb rushed up to drill the ball home from twelve yards.

Neither Peter Shilton nor his second-half deputy Chris Woods were particularly troubled by the Danish visitors, who showed clever ball control at times but lacked any real punch in attack. Their best opportunity came in the 75th minute, when Terry Butcher lost the ball to Elstrup who then switched it to the dangerous Laudrup. Fortunately the experienced England defender was quickly able to make amends with a timely tackle to deny the lively Juventus striker a shooting chance.

Des Walker and Tony Cottee were introduced as substitutes with England well in command midway

England's David Rocastle and Gary Stevens leave Denmark striker Elstrup grounded.

through the second period, and Tottenham's Paul Gascoigne (a £2 million summer signing from Newcastle) came on for the last few minutes. England got their victory to start the process of restoring the public's faith in the team.

England: Shilton (Woods), Stevens, Pearce, Rocastle, Adams (Walker), Butcher, Robson, Webb, Harford (Cottee), Beardsley (Gascoigne), Hodge.

Denmark: Rasmussen, Jensen (Heintze), Nielsen, Olsen, Bartram (Kristensen), Molby, Helt, Hansen, Vilfort (Jorgensen), Elstrup, Laudrup.

Referee: A. Ponnet of Belgium.

England 1   Sweden 1
(Under-21)
18th October 1988, Coventry

Dave Sexton's team began their European Championship qualifying campaign with a hard-earned point at Highfield Road. Goalkeeper Nigel Martyn, the only Third Division player in the side and one of the two over-age players allowed, made three outstanding saves as the lively young Swedes gave an indication to the watching 4,000 of what England's World Cup seniors might expect at Wembley.

England began tentatively and could easily have gone 2-0 behind in the first 25 minutes, Martyn touching over Jansson's close-range shot and Andersson just failing to control a through-ball when clear in the penalty area. With the Swedes' quick passing movements causing considerable problems for England's defence on an increasingly slippery surface, it came as a surprise when the home team went ahead on the half-hour. Sweden strangely made no real attempt to clear Vinny Samways' cross and David White stabbed the ball in from six yards.

Stuart Ripley had two clear chances to put England further ahead and White then thumped a 25-yarder against a post as the visitors began to look ragged. But they equalised on 67 minutes through Ingesson, following a misunderstanding between Chettle and Sedgley.

England: Martyn, B. Statham (Burrows), Cooper, Sedgley, Redmond, Chettle, White, Ripley, Dozzell (Oldfield), Samways, D. Smith.

Sweden: Eriksson, Nilsson, J. Eriksson, Carlsson, Kamark, Vaattovaara, Andersson, Ingesson, Schwartz, Jansson, Dahlin (Eklund).

Referee: K. Sorensen of Denmark.

England 0   Sweden 0
19th October 1988, Wembley

England began their journey towards the World Cup Finals in Italy two years on by dropping a point at home, a result that naturally delighted their Swedish opponents.

A home team that, by way of an innovation, had Chris Waddle supporting Gary Lineker and thereby allowing Peter Beardsley a freer role, appeared capable of unsettling the Swedes in the early stages of the match. Beardsley went close from Bryan Robson's free-kick and Lineker, largely kept on a tight rein by the excellent Swedish captain, Hysen, might have done better with a close-range header from John Barnes' pass.

Most of the 65,000 crowd must have sensed that there would be no

Chris Waddle plays the ball past Swedish defender Hysen.

John Barnes evades Prytz's sliding tackle as Robson and Lineker look on.

happy autumn ending to the England team's summer story of tribulation, following an incident five minutes into the second half. Robson played Waddle through the middle, and his run and pass to Lineker looked like producing a precious winning goal – but the World Cup's top scorer in Mexico in 1986 shot high and wide from England's best chance of the night.

With the defence stiffened by Terry Butcher's return and Robson driving on remorselessly in midfield, it was failings in attack that once again cost England victory and the best possible start to their six-match qualifying campaign. Sweden's central defensive pairing of Hysen and Larsson, arguably one of the most effective and dominating in world football, had a lot to do with that, although Waddle did come desperately close to scoring two minutes

from time. He might even have been fouled as he stretched for the loose ball with goalkeeper Ravelli squirming on the ground. It just wasn't England's night.

Bobby Robson sent on the speedier Des Walker for Adams, when Sweden played their final ace to bring on the lanky Ekstrom, and England also brought on £2 million striker Tony Cottee for the last ten minutes in a vain attempt to snatch a goal.

England: Shilton, Stevens, Pearce, Webb, Adams (Walker), Butcher, Robson, Beardsley, Waddle, Lineker, Barnes (Cottee).

Sweden: Ravelli, R. Nilsson (Schiller), Hysen, Larsson, Ljung, Thern, Stromberg, Prytz, J. Nilsson, Holmqvist (Ekstrom), Pettersson.

Referee: G. Biguet of France.

Saudi Arabia 1   England 1
16th November 1988, Riyadh

A national team inexperienced in world terms but which had played well recently against Argentina and Brazil held England to a draw, thereby proving that the concept of an "easy" international match no longer existed. Football in the Middle East has made dramatic progress in the last few years and the Saudis displayed technique, pace and sound organisation.

But England, once again, were short of luck. They had three goals disallowed for offside – one of those decisions a blatant injustice to Gary Lineker – and struck the bar through Peter Beardsley. Even the move which led to the Saudis' goal had an element of good fortune about it, Stuart Pearce's kick striking the referee and bouncing neatly into the stride of Al-Musaibeih.

He then delivered a defence-splitting pass for Abdullah to run on to, cut inside a flat-footed Mel Sterland and shoot under David Seaman's dive. This goal was a prelude to a period in which England's desperation clearly showed, as skipper Bryan Robson was miles wide with a long-range effort and defender Gary Pallister, winning his second cap, was equally as inaccurate from Chris Waddle's free-kick.

It did take England only six minutes to find a way past the substitute Saudi goalkeeper Subiyani – a half-time replacement for Al-Daye who had damaged a hand – Adams rising powerfully at the far post to head home from Arsenal team-mate David Rocastle's free-kick. It was the big defender's fourth goal for his country and probably the most valuable.

The Saudis were understandably delighted by the result, but England's total haul of nine goals from twelve internationals during the year was a cause for concern.

Saudi Arabia: Al-Daye (Subiyani), Al-Naema, Jameel, Jawad, Saleh, Al-Mutlaq, Al-Musaibeih, Al-Jamaan (Mussaj), Suwaid (Al-Thiniyan), Abdullah, Mubarak.

England: Seaman, Sterland, Pearce, Thomas (Gascoigne), Adams, Pallister, Robson, Rocastle, Beardsley (A. Smith), Lineker, Waddle (Marwood).

Referee: J. Mandi of Bahrain.

Greece 1   England 0
(Under-21)
7th February 1989, Patras

A controversial penalty awarded against the England "wall" at a free-kick gave Greece, beaten finalists in the last European Championship, a deserved victory over England in this Under-21 friendly. A fierce shot from Kavassis struck Burrows or Redmond (it was difficult to tell whom) after they had turned away, but the local referee signalled a spot-kick which Moustakidis converted on 33 minutes.

Greece ought to have won by more than a single goal. Vaitsis was just wide with two half-volleys and England substitute Holdsworth had to clear off the goal-line from Savidis in the second half. Skipper Michael Thomas was England's most influential player, but the team hardly created a worthwhile chance throughout, although Karkamanis had to dive smartly to snatch the ball away from the lurking Stuart Ripley.

Manchester United's Lee Sharpe,

who had become the youngest player to have worn an England Under-21 shirt at 17 years and eight months, had a good debut in midfield.

Greece: Karkamanis, Kavassis, Hatzinikolaou, Agelinas, Papoulidis, Alexandris, Ouzounidis, Savidis, Nolis, Moustakidis, Vaitsis.

England: Martyn (Horne), Cooper (Martin), Burrows, Redmond (Holdsworth), Chettle, Thomas, Sedgley, Beardsmore (Batty), Sharpe, Merson (Dozzell), Ripley.

Referee: L. Fillipidis of Greece.

Greece 1   England 2
8th February 1989, Athens

After recovering from the worst possible start – they conceded a goal in the first minute – England seemed to be destined to gain only a draw until Bryan Robson's timely intervention. England's captain had scored many spectacular goals in his long and glittering career, but his winner in the Olympic Stadium could have been one of his most important. Bobby Robson's team were desperate for a victory after a previous record of one win in six matches.

Only 52 seconds had elapsed on the stadium clock when Gary Stevens was dispossessed by Saravakos and England became instantly in trouble of their own making as Samaras broke through a gap between Walker and Butcher. The latter caught the centre-forward's ankle and the result was a penalty, converted by Saravakos for Greece's first goal in the five internationals played against England so far.

Thankfully, England did not have too long to dwell on this early disappointment. Seven minutes later John Barnes silenced the home fans

England defender Terry Butcher joins the attack at a corner-kick in Athens.

with an equaliser from a 20-yard free-kick. His looping left-foot shot cannoned off the underside of the bar and the ball finished up in the net via unlucky Ikonomopoulos' back. England had had some good fortune at last.

There could have been a glut of goals after that. Lineker just failed to make contact as Butcher headed a free-kick back from the far post, Barnes put one chance wide and another over the top, and Robson was off target with a free header. Then it all came right following Peter Beardsley's introduction on 78 minutes. Within seconds he was starting the move that ended with Lineker nodding the ball down and Robson driving home an unstoppable shot.

Greece: Ikonomopoulos, Hatziathanasiou (Manolas), Koutoulas, Mavridis, Kalintzakis, Tsalouhidis, Saravakos, Lagonidis (Borbokis), Samaras (Kalogeropoulos), Nioblias, Tsiantiakis.

England: Shilton, Stevens, Pearce, Webb, Walker, Butcher, Robson, Rocastle, Smith (Beardsley), Lineker, Barnes.

Referee: H. Holzmann of Austria.

Albania 1   England 2
(Under-21)
7th March 1989, Shkoder

In a provincial town under the picturesque Cukal mountains, the England Under-21 team found the going hard on an uneven and almost grassless pitch, but they ultimately reaped the reward of two Championship points for their perseverance.

England suffered the worst possible start by falling a goal behind in 20 minutes, after Forest's Steve Chettle

had played the Albanian striker Riza onside. He cleverly controlled Leskaj's pass and shot in off Martyn in the England goal.

It was only after the break that the England team's superior strength and stamina began to tell. The Albanians had obviously done their homework on Steve Bull, the prolific Wolves scorer included as an over-age player, and he consequently found himself very closely marked (and often fouled) every time he challenged for the ball. But he continued to battle away, despite the buffeting, and was involved in the build-up to an equaliser that finally came when Keci put through his own goal.

The Albanians lost heart after that, as expected, and six minutes from time England grabbed the winner. Stuart Ripley dispossessed Xhumba on the right, cut into the box and shot into the far corner of the net – the ball gently rolling in.

Albania: Shkurti, Keci (Ziu), Xhumba, Lutaj, Vata, Pashaj, Leskaj, Bilali, Kacaj, Riza, Kalaci (Tahiri).

England: Martyn, Lake, Burrows (Martin) (Beardsmore), Thomas, Redmond, Chettle, Ripley, Ince, Bull, Sedgley, D. Smith.

Referee: . V. Zonchev of Bulgaria.

Albania 0   England 2
8th March 1989, Tirana

England had never met Albania in a full international before, but their journey into the unknown brought two precious World Cup points and left the team sitting on top of Group 2.

The key was always going to be

Alan Smith strides away from Albania's Gega.

scoring the first goal – before the skilful and awkward Albanians could establish any superiority. In their previous two matches in a tight group, in which the margin for error was slim, Albania had visibly faded after conceding a goal. This proved to be the case again, as England took the lead on 16 minutes.

David Rocastle, winning his fourth cap and operating with some aplomb on the right flank, crossed for Chris Waddle to chest the ball down inside the box. In the ensuing confusion Gary Lineker couldn't get his foot to it, but John Barnes kept his cool to shoot along the ground past Mersini. It was Barnes' second goal in consecutive matches, following a barren spell for the double "Footballer of the Year" in 1988.

England's second and decisive goal arrived on the hour, with Barnes the architect his time. A typical charge down the left by full-back Stuart Pearce was halted illegally and Bryan Robson nodded Barnes' curling free-kick wide of Mersini's left hand. After that it was only a matter of how many England would add to their tally. That they failed to boost their goal difference was due to a mixture of indifferent finishing and desperate goal-line clearances by the Albanians. But no one in the England camp was complaining about the result.

Albania: Mersini, Zmijani, Josa, Hodja, Gega, Jera, Shehu, Lekbello, Millo (Majaci), Minga, Demollari.

England's Peter Beardsley is pursued by Albanian defender Zmijani.

England: Shilton, Stevens, Pearce, Webb, Walker, Butcher, Robson, Rocastle, Waddle (Beardsley), Lineker (Smith), Barnes.

Referee: J. Blankenstein of Holland.

England 2   Albania 0
(Under-21)
25th April 1989, Ipswich

England Under-21s' "old-fashioned" centre-forward Steve Bull, winning his second cap as an over-age player, demonstrated that his amazing goal-scoring touch does not desert him when he pulls on an international jersey. England's second goal at Portman Road – Bull's 47th of the season – clinched a workmanlike victory that took Dave Sexton's team to pole position in the group.

The home side's intentions were made clear as early as in the first minute, when Bull rose to head just over the bar from David Smith's long cross. But after half an hour's play, all they had to show for their superiority was a speculative cross from Stuart Ripley, touched over by Kela in the Albanian goal, and an overhead kick from the same player that went just wide.

Then, on 34 minutes, Ian Brightwell sneaked in behind Ripley to head Bull's cross in off the near post to give England the lead. Bull's goal on the hour was a prelude to England's enjoying their best spell of the match, with Ripley and Sedgley both narrowly missing the target with headers as the play was opened up in

(*Left*) Terry Butcher seems to be sharing a joke with Albanian defenders prior to a corner-kick. (*Right*) Chris Waddle, shadowed by Albanian defender Gega at Wembley.

the space down the flanks. Suddenly it started to seem like a practice match.

England: Martyn, Lake, Burrows, Thomas, Redmond, Chettle, Ripley, Brightwell, Bull, Sedgley, Smith.

Albania: Kela, Lufi, Teqini, Keci, Reci, Pashaj, Ismailati, Dilali, Ziu, Lutaj, Xhumba.

Referee: Costantin of Belgium.

England 5 Albania 0
26th April 1989, Wembley

Five England strikes savoured by a 60,000 Wembley crowd gave Bobby Robson's team, still unbeaten since the European Finals, a two-point leadership of their qualifying group and a significant goal difference as insurance against Sweden getting maximum points from their game in hand.

There was great personal relief for Gary Lineker, when his close-range header in the sixth minute finally put an end to a seven-match run without an international goal. It was his 27th in 36 England starts.

The striking partnership of Lineker and Peter Beardsley, so productive in past seasons, bore the fruit of a simple goal for the latter a further six minutes into the match. Then Albania's precocious young goalkeeper Nallbani, only a couple of weeks past his 17th birthday, did his duty by saving well from Lineker, Robson and Waddle. It was still 2-0 at the break.

Lineker's pass allowed Beardsley to carefully steer in his second goal – making it his first England brace in 27 starts – in the 63rd minute. Chris Waddle, in sparkling form on the left wing, deservedly got on the scoresheet nine minutes later with a header from two yards out after Nallbani had been slow to come for Paul Gascoigne's centre from the right.

Making his longest England appearance (24 minutes), "Gazza" delighted the home crowd with his clever dribbling and stylish passing and sent everyone home happy, bar about 25 Albanian sympathisers, as he ran through a retreating defence and shot left-footed into the far corner with two minutes left.

England: Shilton, Stevens (Parker), Pearce, Webb, Walker, Butcher, Robson, Rocastle (Gascoigne), Beardsley, Lineker, Waddle.

Albania: Nallbani, Zmijani, Bubeqi, Hodja, Gega, Jera, Shehu, Lekbello, Millo, Hasanpapa (Noga), Demollari.

Referee: Halle of Norway.

Switzerland 'B' 0   England 'B' 2
16th May 1989, Winterthur

England's first 'B' match for two years was played out at the home of a Swiss Second Division club on a grey evening before a crowd of under a thousand. But Paul Gascoigne livened up the proceedings with a brilliant goal to set England on their way to an ultimately comfortable victory.

The gifted Spurs midfielder had curbed his natural instinct to take on the whole opposing team until ten minutes into the second half. Then, set up by Gary Pallister's ball-winning tackle, he set off on a mazy dribble that took him past three Swiss defenders and the goalkeeper and ended with his sliding the ball into an empty net. It was just the touch of individual flair that a rather stale game had needed and it immediately brought back memories of the goal he had scored as a World Cup substitute at Wembley three weeks earlier.

England sealed the match in the 74th minute when the Swiss defender Schepull turned David Preece's probing cross from the left into his own goal. Any lingering possibility of a Swiss comeback was thereby extinguished.

Switzerland: Lehmann, Rey F., Baumann H., Schepull, Fischer, Rey O. (Hottiger), Hausermann (Baumann A.), Burri, Lorenz, Baumgartner (Sutter), Nadig.

England: Beasant (Naylor), Mabbutt, Dorigo, Hurlock, Mowbray, Pallister (McLeary), Mutch (Stewart), Gascoigne, Bull (Ford), Platt, Preece.

Referee: Wiesel of West Germany.

Iceland 0   England 'B' 2
19th May 1989, Reykjavik

The weather in Reykjavik was hardly conducive to good football – a biting wind, freezing temperatures and heavy rain – and less than 800 people saw Dave Sexton's England 'B' team gain their second victory on tour against the Icelandic World Cup side.

Millwall's Terry Hurlock, tasting international football for the first time at the age of 30, was the unlikely hero of this difficult match and broke the deadlock in the 71st minute with a superb shot from all of 25 yards. Ten minutes later Wolves' scoring machine Steve Bull notched a typically opportunist goal to make the result safe for a very professional England team. It was his 53rd in competitive matches and came after good work by his Wolves colleague Andy Mutch.

England included the influential Paul Gascoigne again in midfield, though he was destined to miss the final tour match in Norway and fly back to join Bobby Robson's Chile squad. He had gone close to opening the scoring in Reykjavik, heading Tony Dorigo's free-kick inches over the bar. Then his Spurs team-mate Gary Mabbutt endured similar misfortune with another header as England attempted to translate their obvious superiority into goals.

Iceland: Sigurosson, Arnporsson (Porkelsson), Edvaldsson, Podarson, Jonsson, Gislason, Bergsson, Askelsson, Margeirsson, Torfason G., Torfason O.

England: Naylor (Beasant), Parker, Dorigo, Hurlock, Mabbutt, Pallister (Mowbray), Stewart (Mutch), Gascoigne (Ford), Bull, Platt, Preece.

Referee: Nielsen of Denmark.

Norway 'B' 0   England 'B' 1
22nd May 1989, Stavanger

Steve Bull ensured that the England 'B' team returned home with a 100 per cent record of success in their three-match tour by scoring the goal that sunk the Norwegians – and then walked straight into Bobby Robson's senior squad for the Rous Cup match against Scotland. Not bad for a Third Divison player!

Without the ebullient Gascoigne, England were lacking any real inspiration in the first half. But when Bull arrived to replace Paul Stewart at half-time, it brought a new sense of urgency in attack. The Wolves striker's battling presence was

enough to unnerve the Norwegians, though his goal actually came from a 60th-minute penalty. Ford's shot looked certain to count until Hansen handled on the goal-line and Bull's ensuing spot-kick was typically ferocious.

Norway had three opportunities to go ahead before Bull struck. Fjetland volleyed narrowly over the bar inside the first minute and both Ingebrightsen and Bjornebye went close. A well-organised England team was generally in command in the second half, without really threatening to score a second.

Norway: Rice (Olsen), Hansen, Tangen, Bjerkeland (Halvorsen), Bjornebye, Pedersen J., Ingebrightsen, Torvanger (Klepp), Fjetland, Amundsen, Haberg (Pedersen E.).

England: Naylor (Beasant), Mabbutt, Dorigo, Hurlock (Platt), Mowbray (Pallister), McLeary, Mutch, Ford, Stewart (Bull), Mackenzie, Preece.

Referee: Horrsted of Denmark.

England 0 Chile 0
23rd May 1989, Wembley

The first fixture in the fifth series of Rous Cup matches brought Chile, losing finalists in the last South American Championship (1987) to Wembley for the first time. The attendance of 15,628 was undoubtedly so low because of a strike by underground staff.

Bobby Robson was unable to call up Liverpool or Arsenal players, both clubs being involved in crucial League matches during the week, but gave senior debuts to Nigel Clough and John Fashanu in attack. Paul

The aerial power of John Fashanu causes problems for Chile defenders Reyes and Contreras.

with the important World Cup qualifier with Poland only a few days away, it was important to retain morale. England had all of the chances but found Robert Rojas in top form in the Chilean goal as he saved two dangerous Gascoigne free-kicks and tipped Clough's delicate header over the bar as he twisted backwards. The 31-year-old Rojas, who now plays for Sao Paulo in Brazil, had defied England once before – in Santiago in 1984.

England: Shilton, Parker, Pearce, Webb, Walker, Butcher, Robson, Gascoigne, Clough, Fashanu (Cottee), Waddle.

Chile: Rojas, Reyes, Contreras, Gonzalez, Pizarro, Rubio, Ormeno, Covarrubias (Letelier), Astengo, Espinoza, Hurtado (Vera).

Referee: Fredriksson of Sweden.

Parker, at right-back, and Paul Gascoigne in midfield started an England match for the first time.

The Chileans did not endear themselves to the Wembley crowd with some questionable tactics. Very aware that their lack of height put them at a definite disadvantage against the likes of Fashanu, they subjected the Wimbledon striker to all kinds of buffeting as high balls floated across. Whenever a Chilean was tackled in the second half (or, sometimes, even when he wasn't), he would invariably fall theatrically to the ground and then have four or so trainers sprint onto the pitch to administer to him. In the last few minutes the play-acting reached farcical proportions.

England did at least stretch their unbeaten run to seven matches and,

Scotland 0   England 2
27th May 1989, Glasgow

England were still without the unavailable Lineker, Barnes and Beardsley for their second match in the Rous Cup and the 107th meeting all told between international football's two oldest rivals. Everton's Trevor Steven was included for the first time since the Eurpean Championship Finals and Tony Cottee started his first England match after no fewer than six appearances as substitute.

Scotland were on a high after gaining nine points out of a possible ten in their World Cup group, but they were no match for Bobby Robson's more adventurous England team in front of a 63,282 crowd at Hampden Park. At the final whistle, with two Rous Cup points safely in

(*Left*) Nigel Clough with his marker, Chile's Astengo. (*Right*) Neil Webb holds off the challenge of Scottish captain Roy Aitken.

the bag, England could point to three encouraging statistics – they had remained unbeaten in the season's eight matches played to date, they had conceded just two goals in those matches and they had kept a clean sheet for nearly seven and a half hours.

John Fashanu had recovered suficiently from his bruising debut against the Chileans to feature once again in attack. But another knock to his damaged knee caused him to leave the action after 30 minutes in favour of Steve Bull, the prolific Wolves striker thereby becoming the fifth Third Division player in history to win a full England cap. By the time of Fashanu's withdrawal England were already a goal ahead, Chris Waddle having stolen behind the Scottish defence in the 20th minute to head Gary Stevens' curling cross firmly past Leighton.

Bull had already proved during a remarkable season (54 goals in 62 competitive matches after this one) that he could find the net at Under-21 and 'B' level for England, and he made his mark at senior level with a stunning 80th-minute strike at Hampden. The ball hit him on the back as he tangled with McPherson on the edge of the box, but he was the quicker to react as it bounced down and slammed an unstoppable shot into the bottom left-hand corner of Leighton's goal.

Scotland: Leighton, McKimmie, Malpas, Aitken, McLeish, McPherson, Nevin, McStay, McCoist, Connor (Grant), Johnston.

England: Shilton, Stevens, Pearce, Webb, Walker, Butcher, Robson, Steven, Fashanu (Bull), Cottee (Gascoigne), Waddle.

Referee: Vautrot of France.

54

England 2 Poland 1
(Under-21)
2nd June 1989, Plymouth

England Under-21s assumed pole position in the European Championship qualifying group, fittingly after victory against the Poles, and should make the quarter-finals for the seventh tournament running, barring a disaster in Sweden.

It took England just ten minutes to go in front before a 10,000 crowd at Home Park that included several hundred Steve Bull fans from Wolverhampton. Russell Beardsmore's precise cross found the head of the unmarked Steve Sedgley and Matysek was left to pick the ball out of the net.

Beardsmore, one of the exciting new crop of Old Trafford youngsters, prompted most of England's best attacking moves and when his pass was only half-cleared a minute before the break, Michael Thomas curled in a left-footer from 25 yards that had Matysek twisting in vain.

Jegor's speculative effort in the 62nd minute was deflected past Horne to give the Poles hope that they could salvage a point. But in the end Burrows' miss from the penalty-spot in the first half did not have a bearing on the result as England held on to 2-1.

England: Horne, Lake, Burrows, Thomas, Redmond, Chettle, Mutch (Merson), Beardsmore, Bull, Sedgley, Smith.

Poland: Matysek, Kryger, Szewczyk, Jqzwiak, Jegor, Gesior, Cyzio, Skrzypszak, Dziudinski (Szcwczyk), Kubisztal, Trszeciak (Jelonek).

Referee: Houden of Holland.

Steve Bull, the prolific Wolves marksman, enjoyed a scoring debut at Hampden Park.

England 3 Poland 0
3rd June 1989, Wembley

Gary Lineker's hat-trick against the Poles in Monterrey had done wonders for his career and the Barcelona striker's opening goal in this World Cup qualifier – his 28th in 41 internationals – helped to put England firmly in control of Group 2 going into the summer break.

Poland's goalkeeper, the giant Bako, was said to have been discovered by Tomaszewski, the "clown" who kept England out of the Munich finals. But he had no hope of defying England as his mentor had done sixteen years earlier. On 24 minutes he was scrambling helplessly on the ground as Lineker angled a shot into the net to finish off a pass by John Barnes. Before that, he had earned a yellow card (and the boos of the crowd) for slamming into Lineker just outside the penalty-area to prevent a certain goal.

The score stayed at 1-0 for three-quarters of an hour, during which time Urban missed with a free header from five yards and Des Walker got in the way of a Lesniak header that looked a likely equaliser. But England were worthy winners in the end, with two further goals arising from enterprising play down the right flank.

Chris Waddle was at his mesmerising best, ghosting past two or three defenders each time he received the ball out wide, and he was linking up well with Gary Stevens, in an adventurous mood at right-back. Stevens' cross to the far post in the 70th minute was thumped home by Barnes and a similar ball from substitute David Rocastle on 83 minutes eluded several sprawling Polish defenders – but not the perfectly-placed

Neil Webb who made it 3-0 to send England fans home singing: "We're going to It-a-ly".

England: Shilton, Stevens, Pearce, Webb, Walker, Butcher, Robson, Waddle (Rocastle), Beardsley (Smith), Lineker, Barnes.

Poland: Bako, Wijas, Wojcicki, Wdowczyk, Lukasik, Matysik, Prusik, Urban (Tarasiewicz), Furtok, Warzycha, Lesniak (Kosecki).

Referee: Agnolin of Italy.

Bulgaria 3   England 2
(Under-21)
5th June 1989, Toulon

England reached the Final of the Toulon International Tournament last year but began this time with a defeat against the rugged Bulgarians. Dave Sexton's team had fallen behind in only the fourth minute, when Mitharski chipped the ball over Brian Horne.

Seven minutes after this early setback Rodney Wallace equalised on his Under-21 debut and England stayed level until the 34th minute, when Kalaydjiev's shot took a deflection off the unlucky Beardsmore and finished in the net.

Charlton striker Paul Williams was almost wrestled to the ground by Stoyanov after he had broken through early in the second half. The Bulgarian goalkeeper got a yellow card for his indiscretion and Williams got his revenge on 51 minutes by shooting home from ten yards to make it 2-2.

With matches in this tournament lasting just 80 minutes, England had ten minutes in which to respond after Bulgarian midfielder Trendafilov scrambled the ball in following Ray Wallace's misdirected clearance. It proved not to be long enough.

England: Horne, Ray Wallace, Dobson, Yates, Butters (Ruddock), Beardsmore, Palmer, Batty, Rodney Wallace, Williams, Gabbiadini (Hirst).

Bulgaria: Stoyanov (Ivanov), Velkov (Pavlov), Dartilov, Petkov, Ouroukov, Slavtchev, Tzvetanov, Stoyanov, Kalaydjiev, Mitharski, Trendafilov.

Referee: Egbertzen of Holland.

Denmark 1   England 1
7th June 1989, Copenhagen

England preserved their unbeaten record for the season with this hard-fought draw in the Idraetspark. It had not been achieved since 1974-75 when two fewer matches were played. More history was made on the night because Peter Shilton's 109th appearance beat Bobby Moore's total to leave him the most-capped England player of all time.

This match to mark the Centenary of the Danish FA was useful preparation for England's next visit to Scandinavia – to face the Swedes in that vital World Cup qualifier – and Bobby Robson's team began as though they meant business. Gary Lineker might have had a penalty in the second minute when Kent Nielsen's challenge bordered on the illegal, but Lineker exacted his own retribution on 26 minutes with his 29th England goal. It was a strange affair, Neil Webb easily side-stepping Andersen to find himself totally in the clear inside the box and rolling the ball across for Lineker to sweep it into an unguarded net. It was a ridiculously easy goal.

Shilton had kept a clean sheet for over 9½ hours of international football when his goal was finally breached by Lars Elstrup after 56 minutes. The Danish striker was allowed too much room in the corner of the penalty-area and, having looked up and taken careful aim, he watched his left-footer fly past an unsighted "Shilts".

Denmark: Schmeichel, Risom, Nielsen K., Olsen L., Nielsen I. (Larsen), Bartram, Helt, Andersen (Vilfort), Elstrup, Laudrup M., Laudrup B. (Rasmussen).

England: Shilton (Seaman), Parker, Pearce, Webb (McMahon), Walker, Butcher, Robson, Rocastle, Beardsley (Bull), Lineker, Barnes (Waddle).

Referee: Uilenberg of Holland.

Senegal 1   England 6
(Under-21)
7th June 1989, Sainte-Maxime

The Charlton pair of Paul Williams and Paul Mortimer scored two goals each to help England to an emphatic victory against the little-known Africans. But Bulgaria's 2-0 win over Ireland on the same night left England knowing that Senegal would have to beat Bulgaria to give them a chance of reaching the Final.

About a thousand people packed into the small ground saw England take the lead when Mortimer scored with a close-range header and then Senegal equalise within two minutes from Kome's penalty-kick. Then Williams, who had scored on his Under-21 debut in the previous match, beat the offside trap to convert Charles' free-kick before the interval. And a minute later he chipped in a second following Dobson's free-kick.

Seven minutes into the second half Hirst netted from Batty's cross to give

England enough breathing space at 4-1. Then the Charlton duo combined again with Williams' pass putting Mortimer through for the fifth on 65 minutes and the impressive Batty completed the rout with four minutes left.

Senegal: Diouf, Saar, Cisse, Dacosta, Kabou, Ndiaye M., Sagna, Kome, Diatta, Thiam, Ndiaye S.

England: Miller, Charles (Ray Wallace), Dobson, Yates (Butters), Ruddock, Ebbrell, Palmer, Batty, Mortimer, Hirst, Williams.

Referee: Santos of Portugal

Rep. of Ireland 0   England 0
(Under-21)
9th June 1989, Six-Fours
Bulgaria's 4-1 win over Senegal had put paid to England's chances of earning a place in the Tournament Final and this frustrating goalless draw against the Irish just added to the feeling of disappointment in the England camp.

Ruddock's airborne collision with Kelly, for which the Southampton defender was booked, was an isolated problem for the Irish goalkeeper, with England rarely threatening throughout. Ireland had dominated the first half and free-kicks floated accurately in by Fleming continued to cause Horne some discomfort, particularly with Quinn and Dolan jumping in to try for flick-ons.

Brazil's strike was disallowed for offside and a header from West Ham striker Dolan was cleared off the line by Yates. England responded with a Williams effort that Kelly deflected onto the bar and the team's superior goal difference took them into the match for third place.

Rep. of Ireland: Kelly, Fleming, Scully, Daish, Kenna, Poutch, Brazil, Staunton, McGee, Dolan, Quinn.

England: Horne, Ray Wallace, Dobson, Yates, Ruddock (Butters), Ebbrell, Palmer, Batty, Mortimer (Rodney Wallace), Hirst, Williams.

Referee: Harrel of France.

United States 2   England 0
(Under-21)
11th June 1989, Toulon
There were shades of 1950 as England suffered the embarrassment of defeat against the college students of the USA at the Stade Mayol. It meant that they finished the tournament in fourth place and the team likely to form the nucleus of the American World Cup squad when they host the Finals in five years' time were third.

England had two good scoring opportunities in the first half, Keller smothering Gabbiadini's shot in the third minute and Rod Wallace going close after that. Balboa put the US amateurs in front nine minutes after the break with a looping shot from thirty yards and Gutierrez completed the victory with two minutes left, much to the delight of a large number of American sailors based in Toulon who were among the 1,000 crowd.

United States: Keller, Benedetti (Santel), Balboa, Gosslein, Agoos, Grimes, Covone, Gutierrez, Henderson, Thompson, Wynalda (Palic).

England: Horne, Charles, Dobson, Yates, Ruddock, Beardsmore (Ebbrell), Palmer, Batty, Rodney Wallace, Hirst, Gabbiadini (Williams).

Referee: Dante of Portugal.

England Under-21s pictured before the first match in Toulon.

Paul Gascoigne and Chris Waddle give the thumbs up to a successful season for the England senior team. Ten matches played and no defeats!

Attendances at Football League Matches

Season	Matches Played	Total (Millions)	Div. 1	Div. 2	Div. 3 (S)	Div. 3 (N)
1946-47	1848	35·6	15·0	11·1	5·7	3·9
1947-48	1848	40·3	16·7	12·3	6·7	4·6
1948-49	1848	41·3	17·9	11·4	7·0	5·0
1949-50	1848	40·5	17·3	11·7	7·1	4·4
1950-51	2028	39·6	16·7	10·8	7·4	4·8
1951-52	2028	39·0	16·1	11·1	7·0	4·9
1952-53	2028	37·1	16·1	9·7	6·7	4·7
1953-54	2028	36·2	16·2	9·5	6·3	4·2
1954-55	2028	34·1	15·1	9·0	6·0	4·1
1955-56	2028	33·2	14·1	9·1	5·7	4·3
1956-57	2028	32·7	13·8	8·7	5·6	4·6
1957-58	2028	33·6	14·5	8·7	6·1	4·3
1958-59	2028	33·6	14·7	8·6	5·9	4·3
1959-60	2028	32·5	14·4	8·4	5·7	4·0
1960-61	2028	28·6	12·9	7·0	4·8	3·9
1961-62	2015	28·0	12·1	7·5	5·2	3·3
1962-63	2028	28·9	12·5	7·8	5·3	3·3
1963-64	2028	28·5	12·5	7·6	5·4	3·0
1964-65	2028	27·6	12·7	7·0	4·4	3·5
1965-66	2028	27·2	12·5	6·9	4·8	3·0
1966-67	2028	28·9	14·2	7·3	4·4	3·0
1967-68	2028	30·1	15·3	7·5	4·0	3·4
1968-69	2028	29·4	14·6	7·4	4·3	3·1
1969-70	2028	29·6	14·9	7·6	4·2	2·9
1970-71	2028	28·2	14·0	7·1	4·4	2·8
1971-72	2028	28·7	14·5	6·8	4·7	2·7
1972-73	2028	25·4	14·0	5·6	3·7	2·1
1973-74	2027	25·0	13·1	6·3	3·4	2·2
1974-75	2028	25·6	12·6	7·0	4·1	2·0
1975-76	2028	24·9	13·1	5·8	3·9	2·1
1976-77	2028	26·2	13·6	6·3	4·2	2·1
1977-78	2028	25·4	13·3	6·5	3·3	2·3
1978-79	2028	24·5	12·7	6·2	3·4	2·3
1979-80	2028	24·6	12·2	6·1	4·0	2·3
1980-81	2028	21·9	11·4	5·2	3·6	1·7
1981-82	2028	20·0	10·4	4·8	2·8	2·0
1982-83	2028	18·8	9·3	5·0	2·9	1·6
1983-84	2028	18·3	8·7	5·3	2·7	1·5
1984-85	2028	17·8	9·8	4·0	2·7	1·4
1985-86	2028	16·5	9·0	3·6	2·5	1·4
1986-87	2028	17·4	9·1	4·2	2·4	1·7
1987-88	2030	18·0	8·1	5·3	2·8	1·8
1988-89	2036	18·5	7·8	5·8	3·0	1·8

NOTE: *From Season 1958-1959 onwards for Div. 3 (S) read Div. 3 and for Div. 3 (N) read Div. 4.*

F.A. Cup Attendances 1967-89

	1st Round	2nd Round	3rd Round	4th Round	5th Round
1988-89	212,775	121,326	690,199	421,255	206,781
1987-88	204,411	104,561	720,121	443,133	281,461
1986-87	209,290	146,769	593,520	349,342	263,550
1985-86	171,142	130,034	486,838	495,526	311,833
1984-85	174,604	137,078	616,229	320,772	269,232
1983-84	192,276	151,647	625,965	417,298	181,832
1982-83	191,312	150,046	670,503	452,688	260,069
1981-82	236,220	127,300	513,185	356,987	203,334
1980-81	246,824	194,502	832,578	534,402	320,530
1979-80	267,121	204,759	804,701	507,725	364,039
1978-79	243,773	185,343	880,345	537,748	243,683
1977-78	258,248	178,930	881,406	540,164	400,751
1976-77	379,230	192,159	942,523	631,265	373,330
1975-76	255,533	178,099	867,880	573,843	471,925
1974-75	283,956	170,466	914,994	646,434	393,323
1973-74	214,236	125,295	840,142	747,909	346,012
1972-73	259.432	169,114	938,741	735,825	357,386
1971-72	277,726	236,127	986,094	711,399	486,378
1970-71	329,687	230,942	956,683	757,852	360,687
1969-70	345,229	195,102	925,930	651,374	319,893
1968-69	331,858	252,710	1,094,043	883,675	464,915
1967-68	322,121	236,195	1,229,519	771,284	563,779

	6th Round	Semi-Finals & Final	Total	No. of matches	Average per match
1988-89	176,629	167,353	1,966,318	164	12,173
1987-88	119,313	177,585	2,050,585	155	13,229
1986-87	119,396	195,533	1,877,400	165	11,378
1985-86	184,262	192,316	1,971,951	168	11,738
1984-85	148,690	242,754	1,909,359	157	12,162
1983-84	185,382	187,000	1,941,400	166	11,695
1982-83	193,845	291,162	2,209,625	154	14,348
1981-82	124,308	279,621	1,840,955	160	11,506
1980-81	288,714	339,250	2,756,800	169	16,312
1979-80	157,530	355,541	2,661,416	163	16,328
1978-79	263,213	249,897	2,604,002	166	15,687
1977-78	137,059	198,020	2,594,578	160	16,216
1976-77	205,379	258,216	2,982,102	174	17,139
1975-76	206,851	205,810	2,759,941	161	17,142
1974-75	268,361	291,369	2,968,903	172	17,261
1973-74	233,307	273,051	2,779,952	167	16,646
1972-73	241,934	226,543	2,928,975	160	18,306
1971-72	230,292	248,546	3,158,562	160	19.741
1970-71	304,937	279,644	3,220,432	162	19,879
1969-70	198,537	390,700	3,026,765	170	17,805
1968-69	188,121	216,232	3,431,554	157	21,857
1967-68	240,095	223,831	3,586,824	160	22,418

England's Full International Teams 1946–89

(Up to and including 7th June 1989)

* Captain † Own goal

Season 1946-47 versus	Result	1	2	3	4	5	6	7	8	9	10	11	Substitutes
Ireland	7-2	Swift	Scott	Hardwick*	Wright, W.	Franklin	Cockburn	Finney[1]	Carter[1]	Lawton[1]	Mannion[3]	Langton[1]	
Republic of Ireland	1-0	Swift	Scott	Hardwick*	Wright, W.	Franklin	Cockburn	Finney[1]	Carter	Lawton[1]	Mannion[2]	Langton	
Wales	3-0	Swift	Scott	Hardwick*	Wright, W.	Franklin	Cockburn	Finney[1]	Carter	Lawton[1]	Mannion[1]	Langton	
Netherlands	8-2	Swift	Scott	Hardwick*	Wright, W.	Franklin	Johnston	Matthews S.	Carter[2]	Lawton[4]	Mannion[1]	Langton	
Scotland	1-1	Swift	Scott	Hardwick*	Wright, W.	Franklin	Johnston	Finney[1]	Carter[1]	Lawton	Mannion	Mullen	
France	3-0	Swift	Scott	Hardwick*	Wright, W.	Franklin	Lowe	Matthews S.	Carter	Lawton	Mannion[1]	Langton	
Switzerland	0-1	Swift	Scott	Hardwick*	Wright, W.	Franklin	Lowe	Matthews, S.[1]	Carter	Lawton	Mannion	Langton	
Portugal	10-0	Swift	Scott	Hardwick*	Wright, W.	Franklin	Cockburn	Matthews, S.[1]	Mortensen[4]	Lawton[4]	Mannion	Finney[1]	Mullen (7)[1]
1947–48													
Belgium	5-2	Swift	Scott	Hardwick*	Ward	Franklin	Wright, W.	Matthews, S.	Mortensen[1]	Lawton[2]	Mannion	Finney[2]	
Wales	3-0	Swift	Scott	Hardwick*	Taylor, P.	Franklin	Wright, W.	Matthews, S.	Mortensen[1]	Lawton[1]	Mannion	Finney[1]	
Ireland	2-2	Swift	Scott	Hardwick*	Taylor, P.	Franklin	Wright, W.	Matthews, S.	Mortensen	Lawton[1]	Mannion[1]	Finney	
Sweden	4-2	Swift	Scott	Hardwick*	Taylor, P.	Franklin	Wright, W.	Finney	Mortensen[3]	Lawton[1]	Mannion	Langton	
Scotland	2-0	Swift	Scott	Hardwick*	Wright, W.	Franklin	Cockburn	Matthews, S.	Mortensen[1]	Lawton[1]	Pearson	Finney[1]	
Italy	4-0	Swift*	Scott	Howe, J.	Wright, W.	Franklin	Cockburn	Matthews, S.	Mortensen[1]	Lawton[1]	Mannion	Finney[2]	
1948–49													
Denmark	0-0	Swift*	Scott	Aston	Wright, W.	Franklin	Cockburn	Matthews, S.[1]	Hagan	Lawton	Shackleton	Lawton	
Ireland	6-2	Swift	Scott	Howe, J.	Wright, W.*	Franklin	Cockburn	Matthews, S.[1]	Mortensen[3]	Milburn	Pearson[1]	Finney	
Wales	1-0	Swift	Scott	Aston	Ward	Franklin	Wright, W.*	Matthews, S.	Shackleton	Milburn[1]	Shackleton	Finney[1]	
Switzerland	6-0	Ditchburn	Ramsey	Aston	Wright, W.*	Franklin	Cockburn	Matthews, S.	Rowley J.[1]	Milburn[1]	Haines[2]	Hancocks[2]	
Scotland	1-3	Swift	Aston	Howe, J.	Wright, W.*	Franklin	Cockburn	Matthews, S.	Mortensen	Milburn[1]	Pearson	Finney	
Sweden	1-3	Ditchburn	Aston	Aston	Wright, W.*	Franklin	Cockburn	Finney[1]	Mortensen	Bentley	Rowley, J.	Langton	
Norway	4-1	Swift	Ellerington	Aston	Wright, W.*	Franklin	Dickinson	Finney[1]	Morris[1]	Bentley	Mannion	Mullen[1]	
France	3-1	Williams	Ellerington	Aston	Wright, W.*	Franklin	Dickinson	Finney	Morris[2]	Mortensen	Mannion	Mullen	†
1949–50													
Republic of Ireland	0-2	Williams	Mozley	Aston	Wright, W.*	Franklin	Dickinson	Harris, P.	Morris	Pye	Mannion	Finney	
Wales	4-1	Williams	Mozley	Aston	Wright, W.*	Franklin	Dickinson	Finney	Mortensen[1]	Milburn[3]	Shackleton	Hancocks	
Ireland	9-2	Streten	Mozley	Aston	Watson, W.	Franklin	Wright, W.*	Finney	Mortensen[2]	Rowley, J.[4]	Pearson[2]	Froggatt, J.[1]	
Italy	2-0	Williams	Ramsey	Aston	Watson, W.	Franklin	Wright, W.*[1]	Finney	Mortensen	Rowley, J.[1]	Pearson[1]	Froggatt, J.	
Scotland	1-0	Williams	Ramsey	Aston	Wright, W.*	Franklin	Dickinson	Finney	Mannion	Mortensen	Bentley[1]	Langton	
Portugal	5-3	Williams	Ramsey	Aston	Wright, W.*	Jones, W. H.	Dickinson	Milburn	Mortensen[1]	Bentley[1]	Mannion	Finney[4]	
Belgium	4-1	Williams	Ramsey	Aston	Wright, W.*	Jones, W. H.	Dickinson	Milburn	Mortensen[1]	Bentley[1]	Mannion[1]	Finney	
Chile	2-0	Williams	Ramsey	Aston	Wright, W.*	Hughes, L.	Dickinson	Finney	Mannion	Bentley	Mortensen[1]	Mullen	
U.S.A.	0-1	Williams	Ramsey	Aston	Wright, W.*	Hughes, L.	Dickinson	Finney	Mannion	Bentley	Mortensen	Mullen	
Spain	0-1	Williams	Ramsey	Eckersley	Wright, W.*	Hughes, L.	Dickinson	Matthews, S.	Mortensen	Milburn	Baily, E.	Finney	
1950–51													
Ireland	4-1	Williams	Ramsey	Aston	Wright, W.*[1]	Chilton	Dickinson	Matthews S.	Mannion[1]	Lee, J.[1]	Baily, E.[2]	Langton	
Wales	4-2	Williams	Ramsey*	Smith, L.	Watson, W.	Compton, L.	Dickinson	Finney	Mannion[1]	Milburn[1]	Baily, E.[2]	Medley	
Yugoslavia	2-2	Williams	Ramsey*	Eckersley	Watson, W.	Compton, L.	Dickinson	Hancocks	Mannion	Lofthouse[2]	Baily, E.	Medley	
Scotland	2-3	Williams	Ramsey	Eckersley	Johnston	Froggatt, J.	Wright, W.*	Matthews, S.	Mannion	Mortensen	Hassall[1]	Finney[1]	
Argentina	2-1	Williams	Ramsey	Eckersley	Nicholson[1]	Taylor, J.	Cockburn	Finney	Mortensen[1]	Milburn[2]	Hassall[1]	Metcalfe	
Portugal	5-2	Williams	Ramsey*	Eckersley	Nicholson[1]	Taylor, J.	Cockburn	Finney[1]	Pearson	Milburn[2]	Hassall[1]	Metcalfe	

Small numerals goals scored — Number after sub. player replaced

62

Opponent	Score	GK	RB	LB	RH	CH	LH	OR	IR	CF	IL	OL	Notes
1951–52													†
France	2-2	Williams	Ramsey	Willis	Wright, W.*	Chilton	Cockburn	Finney	Mannion	Milburn	Hassall[1]	Medley[1]	
Wales	1-1	Williams	Ramsey	Smith, L.	Wright, W.*	Barrass	Dickinson	Finney	Thompson, T.	Lofthouse[2]	Baily, E.	Medley	
Ireland	2-0	Merrick	Ramsey	Smith, L.	Wright, W.*	Barrass	Dickinson	Finney	Sewell	Lofthouse[1]	Phillips	Medley	
Austria	2-2	Merrick	Ramsey*	Eckersley	Wright, W.*	Froggatt, J.[1]	Dickinson	Milton	Broadis[1]	Lofthouse	Pearson[2]	Medley	
Scotland	2-1	Merrick	Ramsey	Garrett	Wright, W.*	Froggatt, J.[1]	Dickinson	Finney	Broadis[1]	Lofthouse[2]	Pearson	Rowley, J.[1]	
Italy	1-1	Merrick	Ramsey	Garrett	Wright, W.*	Froggatt, J.[1]	Dickinson	Finney	Broadis[1]	Lofthouse	Baily, E.[1]	Elliott	
Austria	3-2	Merrick	Ramsey	Eckersley	Wright, W.*	Froggatt, J.	Dickinson	Finney	Sewell[1]	Lofthouse[2]	Baily, E.	Elliott	
Switzerland	3-0	Merrick	Ramsey	Eckersley	Wright, W.*	Froggatt, J.	Dickinson	Allen, R.	Sewell[1]	Lofthouse[1]	Baily, E.	Finney	
Ireland	2-2	Merrick	Ramsey	Eckersley	Wright, W.*	Froggatt, J.[1]	Dickinson	Finney	Sewell	Lofthouse[1]	Baily, E.	Elliot[1]	
Wales	5-2	Merrick	Ramsey	Smith, L.	Wright, W.*	Froggatt, J.[1]	Dickinson	Finney[1]	Froggatt, R.[1]	Lofthouse[2]	Bentley[1]	Elliott	
Belgium	5-0	Merrick	Ramsey	Eckersley	Wright, W.*	Froggatt, J.[1]	Dickinson	Finney	Bentley	Lofthouse[2]	Bentley	Elliot[2]	
Scotland	2-2	Merrick	Ramsey	Smith, L.	Wright, W.*	Barrass	Dickinson	Finney	Broadis[2]	Lofthouse	Froggatt, R.[1]	Froggatt, J.	
Argentina	0-0	Merrick	Ramsey	Eckersley	Wright, W.*	Johnston	Dickinson	Finney	Broadis	Lofthouse	Froggatt, R.	Berry	
Chile	2-1	Merrick	Ramsey	Eckersley	Wright, W.*	Johnston	Dickinson	Finney	Broadis	Lofthouse[1]	Taylor, T.[1]	Berry	
Uruguay	1-2	Merrick	Ramsey	Eckersley	Wright, W.*	Johnston	Dickinson	Finney[2]	Broadis	Lofthouse[2]	Taylor, T.[1]	Berry	
U.S.A.	6-3	Ditchburn	Ramsey	Eckersley	Wright, W.*	Johnston	Dickinson	Finney[2]	Broadis[1]	Lofthouse[1]	Froggatt, R.[1]	Froggatt, J.	
1953–54													
Wales	4-1	Merrick	Garrett	Eckersley	Wright, W.*	Johnston	Dickinson	Finney	Quixall	Lofthouse[2]	Wilshaw[2]	Mullen[1]	
F.I.F.A.	4-4	Merrick	Ramsey[1]	Eckersley	Wright, W.*	Ufton	Dickinson	Matthews, S.	Mortensen[1]	Lofthouse[1]	Quixall[1]	Mullen[2]	
Ireland	3-1	Merrick	Rickaby	Eckersley	Wright, W.*	Johnston	Dickinson	Matthews, S.	Quixall	Lofthouse[1]	Hassall[2]	Mullen	
Hungary	3-6	Merrick	Ramsey[1]	Byrne, R.	Wright, W.*	Johnston	Dickinson	Matthews, S.	Taylor, E.	Mortensen[1]	Sewell	Robb	
Scotland	4-2	Merrick	Staniforth	Byrne, R.	Wright, W.*	Clarke, H.	Dickinson	Finney	Broadis	Nicholls[1]	Nicholls	Allen, R.[1]	
Yugoslavia	0-1	Merrick	Staniforth	Byrne, R.	Wright, W.*	Owen	Dickinson	Finney	Broadis	Mortensen	Broadis	Mullen	
Hungary	1-7	Merrick	Staniforth	Byrne, R.	Wright, W.*	Owen	Dickinson	Harris, P.	Sewell	Broadis[1]	Broadis[1]	Finney	
Belgium	4-4	Merrick	Staniforth	Byrne, R.	Wright, W.*	Owen	Dickinson	Matthews, S.	Broadis[2]	Lofthouse[2]	Broadis[2]	Finney	
Switzerland	2-0	Merrick	Staniforth	Byrne, R.	McGarry	Wright, W.*	Dickinson	Finney	Broadis	Taylor, T.[1]	Taylor, T.[1]	Finney	
Uruguay	2-4	Merrick	Staniforth	Byrne, R.	McGarry	Wright, W.*	Dickinson	Matthews, S.	Broadis	Lofthouse	Wilshaw	Finney	
1954–55													
Ireland	2-0	Wood	Foulkes	Byrne, R.	Wheeler	Wright, W.*	Barlow	Matthews, S.	Revie[2]	Lofthouse	Haynes[1]	Pilkington	
Wales	3-2	Wood	Staniforth	Byrne, R.	Phillips	Wright, W.*	Slater	Matthews, S.	Bentley[3]	Allen, R.[1]	Shackleton	Blunstone	
West Germany	3-1	Williams	Staniforth	Byrne, R.	Phillips	Wright, W.*	Slater	Matthews, S.	Bentley[1]	Allen, R.[1]	Shackleton[1]	Finney	
Scotland	7-2	Williams	Williams	Byrne, R.	Armstrong	Wright, W.*	Edwards	Matthews, S.	Revie[1]	Lofthouse[2]	Wilshaw[4]	Blunstone	
France	0-1	Williams	Sillett, P.	Byrne, R.	Flowers	Wright, W.*	Edwards	Matthews, S.	Revie	Lofthouse	Wilshaw	Blunstone	
Spain	1-1	Williams	Sillett, P.	Byrne, R.	Dickinson	Wright, W.*	Edwards	Matthews, S.	Bentley[1]	Lofthouse	Quixall	Wilshaw	
Portugal	1-3	Williams	Sillett, P.	Byrne, R.	Dickinson	Wright, W.*	Edwards	Matthews, S.	Bentley[1]	Lofthouse	Wilshaw	Blunstone	Quixall (9)
1955–56													
Denmark	5-1	Baynham	Hall	Byrne, R.	McGarry	Wright, W.*	Dickinson	Milburn	Revie[2]	Lofthouse[2]	Bradford[1]	Finney	†
Wales	1-2	Williams	Hall	Byrne, R.	McGarry	Wright, W.*	Dickinson	Matthews, S.	Revie	Lofthouse	Wilshaw	Finney	
Ireland	3-0	Baynham	Hall	Byrne, R.	Clayton	Wright, W.*	Dickinson	Finney[1]	Haynes	Jezzard	Wilshaw[2]	Perry[2]	
Spain	4-1	Baynham	Hall	Byrne, R.	Clayton	Wright, W.*	Dickinson	Finney[1]	Atyeo[1]	Lofthouse	Haynes[1]	Perry[2]	
Scotland	1-1	Matthews, R.	Hall	Byrne, R.	Dickinson	Wright, W.*	Edwards	Finney	Taylor, T.	Lofthouse	Haynes[1]	Perry	
Brazil	4-2	Matthews, R.	Hall	Byrne, R.	Clayton	Wright, W.*	Edwards	Matthews, S.	Atyeo	Taylor, T.[2]	Haynes	Grainger[2]	
Sweden	0-0	Matthews, R.	Hall	Byrne, R.	Clayton	Wright, W.*	Edwards	Berry	Atyeo	Taylor, T.	Wilshaw[1]	Grainger	
Finland	5-1	Wood	Hall	Byrne, R.	Clayton	Wright, W.*	Edwards	Astall[1]	Haynes[1]	Taylor, T.	Wilshaw	Grainger	Lofthouse (9)[2]
West Germany	3-1	Matthews, R.	Hall	Byrne, R.	Clayton	Wright, W.*	Edwards[1]	Astall	Haynes[1]	Taylor, T.	Wilshaw	Grainger[1]	
1956–7													
Ireland	1-1	Matthews, R.	Hall	Byrne, R.	Clayton	Wright, W.*	Edwards	Matthews, S.[1]	Revie	Taylor, T.	Wilshaw	Grainger	
Wales	3-1	Ditchburn	Hall	Byrne, R.	Clayton	Wright, W.*	Dickinson	Matthews, S.	Brooks[1]	Finney[1]	Haynes[1]	Grainger	
Yugoslavia	3-0	Ditchburn	Hall	Byrne, R.	Clayton	Wright, W.*	Dickinson	Matthews, S.	Brooks*[1]	Finney[1]	Haynes	Blunstone	Taylor, T. (10)[2]

ENGLAND'S FULL INTERNATIONAL TEAMS 1946–89 (contd)

versus	Result	1	2	3	4	5	6	7	8	9	10	11	Substitutes
1956-7 (contd)													
Denmark	5-2	Ditchburn	Hall	Byrne, R.	Clayton	Wright, W.*	Dickinson[1]	Matthews, S.	Brooks	Taylor, T.[3]	Edwards[2]	Finney[1]	
Scotland	2-1	Hodgkinson	Hall	Byrne, R.	Clayton	Wright, W.*	Edwards[1]	Matthews, S.	Thompson, T.	Finney	Kevan[1]	Grainger	
Republic of Ireland	5-1	Hodgkinson	Hall	Byrne, R.	Clayton	Wright, W.*	Edwards	Matthews, S.	Atyeo[1]	Taylor, T.[2]	Haynes[1]	Finney	+
Denmark	4-1	Hodgkinson	Hall	Byrne, R.	Clayton	Wright, W.*	Edwards	Matthews, S.	Atyeo[2]	Taylor, T.[2]	Haynes[1]	Finney	
Republic of Ireland	1-1	Hodgkinson	Hall	Byrne, R.	Clayton	Wright, W.*	Edwards	Finney	Atyeo[1]	Taylor, T.	Haynes	Pegg	
1957-58													
Wales	4-0	Hopkinson	Howe, D.	Byrne, R.	Clayton	Wright, W.*	Edwards	Douglas	Kevan	Taylor, T.	Haynes[2]	Finney[1]	
Ireland	2-3	Hopkinson	Howe, D.	Byrne, R.	Clayton	Wright, W.*	Edwards[1]	Douglas	Kevan	Taylor, T.[1]	Haynes	A'Court[1]	
France	4-0	Hopkinson	Howe, D.	Langley	Clayton	Wright, W.*	Edwards[1]	Douglas[1]	Robson, R.[2]	Kevan[2]	Haynes	Finney	
Scotland	4-0	Hopkinson	Howe, D.	Langley	Clayton	Wright, W.*	Slater	Douglas[1]	Charlton, R.[2]	Kevan	Haynes	Finney	
Portugal	2-1	Hopkinson	Howe, D.	Langley	Clayton	Wright, W.*	Slater	Douglas	Charlton, R.[2]	Kevan	Haynes	Finney	
Yugoslavia	0-5	Hopkinson	Howe, D.	Langley	Clayton	Wright, W.*	Slater	Douglas	Charlton, R.	Kevan	Haynes	Finney	
U.S.S.R.	1-1	McDonald	Howe, D.	Banks, T.	Clamp	Wright, W.*	Slater	Douglas	Robson, R.	Kevan[1]	Haynes	Finney[1]	
U.S.S.R.	2-2	McDonald	Howe, D.	Banks, T.	Clamp	Wright, W.*	Slater	Douglas	Robson, R.	Kevan[1]	Haynes	Finney[1]	
Brazil	0-0	McDonald	Howe, D.	Banks, T.	Clamp	Wright, W.*	Slater	Douglas	Robson, R.	Kevan[1]	Haynes	A'Court	
Austria	2-2	McDonald	Howe, D.	Banks, T.	Clamp	Wright, W.*	Slater	Douglas	Robson, R.	Kevan[1]	Haynes[1]	A'Court	
U.S.S.R.	0-1	McDonald	Howe, D.	Banks, T.	Clayton	Wright, W.*	Slater	Brabrook	Broadbent	Kevan	Broadbent	A'Court	
1958-59													
Ireland	3-3	McDonald	Howe, D.	Banks, T.	Clayton	Wright, W.*	McGuinness	Brabrook	Broadbent	Charlton, R.[2]	Haynes[1]	Finney[1]	Flowers (6) Bradley (7)
U.S.S.R.	5-0	McDonald	Howe, D.	Shaw, G.	Clayton	Wright, W.*	Slater	Douglas	Charlton, R.[1]	Lofthouse	Haynes[3]	Finney	
Wales	2-2	McDonald	Howe, D.	Shaw, G.	Clayton	Wright, W.*	Flowers	Clapton	Broadbent[1]	Lofthouse	Charlton, R.	A'Court	
Scotland	1-0	Hopkinson	Howe, D.	Shaw, G.	Clayton	Wright, W.*	Flowers	Douglas	Broadbent	Charlton, R.[1]	Haynes	Holden	
Italy	2-2	Hopkinson	Howe, D.	Shaw, G.	Clayton	Wright, W.*	Flowers	Bradley[1]	Broadbent	Charlton, R.[1]	Haynes	Holden	
Brazil	0-2	Hopkinson	Howe, D.	Armfield	Clayton	Wright, W.*	Flowers	Deeley	Broadbent	Charlton, R.	Haynes	Holden	
Peru	1-4	Hopkinson	Howe, D.	Armfield	Clayton	Wright, W.*	Flowers	Deeley	Greaves[1]	Charlton, R.	Haynes	Holden	
Mexico	1-2	Hopkinson	Howe, D.	Armfield	Clayton	Wright, W.*	McGuinness	Holden	Greaves[1]	Kevan[1]	Haynes	Charlton, R.[3]	
U.S.A.	8-1	Hopkinson	Howe, D.	Armfield	Clayton	Wright, W.*	Flowers[2]	Bradley[1]	Greaves	Kevan[1]	Haynes[1]	Charlton, R.[3]	
1959-60													
Wales	1-1	Hopkinson	Howe, D.	Allen, A.	Clayton*	Smith, T.	Flowers	Connelly	Greaves	Clough	Charlton, R.[1]	Holliday	
Sweden	2-3	Hopkinson	Howe, D.	Allen, A.	Clayton*	Smith, T.	Flowers	Connelly	Greaves	Clough	Charlton, R.[1]	Holliday	
Ireland	2-1	Springett, R.	Howe, D.	Allen, A.	Clayton*	Brown, K.	Flowers	Connelly	Haynes	Baker[1]	Parry	Holliday	
Scotland	1-1	Springett, R.	Armfield	Wilson	Clayton*	Slater	Flowers	Connelly	Broadbent	Baker	Parry	Charlton, R.[1]	
Yugoslavia	3-3	Springett, R.	Armfield	Wilson	Robson, R.	Swan	Flowers	Douglas[1]	Haynes[1]	Baker	Greaves	Charlton, R.	
Spain	0-3	Springett, R.	Armfield	Wilson	Robson, R.	Swan	Flowers	Brabrook	Haynes*	Baker	Greaves	Charlton, R.	
Hungary	0-2	Springett, R.	Armfield	Wilson	Robson, R.	Swan	Flowers	Douglas	Haynes*	Baker	Viollet	Charlton, R.	
1960-61													
Ireland	5-2	Springett, R.	Armfield	McNeil	Robson, R.	Swan	Flowers	Douglas[1]	Greaves[2]	Smith, R.[1]	Haynes*	Charlton, R.[1]	
Luxembourg	9-0	Springett, R.	Armfield	McNeil	Robson, R.	Swan	Flowers	Douglas[1]	Greaves[3]	Smith, R.[2]	Haynes*[3]	Charlton, R.[3]	
Spain	4-2	Springett, R.	Armfield	McNeil	Robson, R.	Swan	Flowers	Douglas[1]	Greaves[1]	Smith, R.*	Haynes*[1]	Charlton, R.[1]	
Wales	5-1	Hodgkinson	Armfield	McNeil	Robson, R.[1]	Swan	Flowers	Douglas[1]	Greaves[3]	Smith, R.[2]	Haynes*[2]	Charlton, R.[1]	
Scotland	9-3	Springett, R.	Armfield	McNeil	Robson, R.[1]	Swan	Flowers	Douglas[1]	Greaves[3]	Smith, R.[2]	Haynes*[2]	Charlton, R.[3]	
Mexico	8-0	Springett, R.	Armfield	McNeil	Robson, R.[1]	Swan	Flowers[1]	Douglas[2]	Kevan	Smith, R.[1]	Haynes*	Charlton, R.[3]	
Portugal	1-1	Springett, R.	Armfield	McNeil	Robson, R.	Swan	Flowers[1]	Douglas	Greaves	Smith, R.	Haynes*	Charlton, R.	
Italy	3-2	Springett, R.	Armfield	McNeil	Robson, R.	Swan	Flowers	Douglas	Greaves[1]	Hitchens[2]	Haynes*	Charlton, R.	

Opponent	Score	Springett, R.	Armfield	Angus	Miller	Swan	Flowers	Douglas	Greaves[1]	Hitchens	Haynes*	Charlton, R.	
1961–62													
Austria	1-3	Springett, R.	Armfield*	McNeil	Robson, R.	Swan	Flowers	Douglas	Fantham	Pointer[1]	Viollet[1]	Charlton, R.[2]	
Luxembourg	4-1	Springett, R.	Armfield*	Wilson	Robson, R.	Swan	Flowers	Connelly	Douglas[1]	Pointer	Haynes*	Charlton, R.	
Wales	1-1	Springett, R.	Armfield	Wilson	Robson, R.	Swan	Flowers	Connelly[1]	Douglas	Pointer[1]	Haynes*	Charlton, R.	
Portugal	2-0	Springett, R.	Armfield	Wilson	Robson, R.	Swan	Flowers	Douglas	Byrne, J.	Crawford	Haynes*	Charlton, R.[1]	
Ireland	1-1	Springett, R.	Armfield	Wilson	Anderson	Swan	Flowers[1]	Connelly	Hunt[1]	Crawford[1]	Haynes*	Charlton, R.	
Austria	3-1	Springett, R.	Armfield	Wilson	Anderson	Swan	Flowers	Douglas	Greaves	Smith, R.	Haynes*	Charlton, R.	
Scotland	0-2	Springett, R.	Armfield	Wilson	Robson, R.	Swan	Flowers	Douglas	Greaves	Hitchens[1]	Haynes*	Charlton, R.	
Switzerland	3-1	Springett, R.	Armfield	Wilson	Moore	Norman	Flowers[1]	Connelly[1]	Greaves[3]	Hitchens	Haynes*	Charlton, R.	
Peru	4-0	Springett, R.	Armfield	Wilson	Moore	Norman	Flowers[1]	Douglas	Greaves[1]	Hitchens	Haynes*	Charlton, R.	
Hungary	1-2	Springett, R.	Armfield	Wilson	Moore	Norman	Flowers[1]	Douglas	Greaves[1]	Peacock	Haynes*	Charlton, R.[1]	
Argentina	3-1	Springett, R.	Armfield	Wilson	Moore	Norman	Flowers[1]	Douglas	Greaves[1]	Peacock	Haynes*	Charlton, R.[1]	
Bulgaria	0-0	Springett, R.	Armfield	Wilson	Moore	Norman	Flowers	Douglas	Greaves	Peacock	Haynes*	Charlton, R.	
Brazil	1-3	Springett, R.	Armfield	Wilson	Moore	Norman	Flowers	Douglas	Greaves	Hitchens[1]	Haynes*	Charlton, R.	
1962–63													
France	1-1	Springett, R.	Armfield*	Wilson	Moore	Norman	Flowers[1]	Hellawell	Crowe	Charnley	Greaves	Hinton, A.	
Ireland	3-1	Springett, R.	Armfield*	Wilson	Moore	Labone	Flowers	Hellawell	Hill, F.	Peacock[2]	Greaves[1]	O'Grady[2]	
Wales	4-0	Springett, R.	Armfield*	Shaw, G.	Moore	Labone	Flowers	Connelly[1]	Hill, F.	Peacock[2]	Greaves[1]	Tambling	
France	2-5	Springett, R.	Armfield*	Henry	Moore	Labone	Flowers	Connelly	Tambling[1]	Smith, R.	Greaves	Charlton, R.	
Scotland	1-2	Banks, G.	Armfield*	Byrne, G.	Moore	Norman	Flowers	Douglas[1]	Greaves	Smith, R.	Melia	Charlton, R.[1]	
Brazil	1-1	Banks, G.	Shellito	Wilson	Milne	Norman	Moore	Douglas[1]	Greaves	Smith, R.[1]	Eastham	Charlton, R.[1]	
Czechoslovakia	4-2	Banks, G.	Armfield*	Wilson	Milne	Norman	Moore*	Paine	Greaves[2]	Smith, R.	Eastham	Charlton, R.[1]	
German D. R.	2-1	Banks, G.	Armfield*	Wilson	Milne	Norman	Moore	Paine	Hunt[1]	Smith, R.	Eastham	Charlton, R.[1]	
Switzerland	8-1	Banks, G.	Armfield*	Wilson	Kay[1]	Moore	Flowers	Douglas[1]	Greaves	Byrne, J.[2]	Melia[1]	Charlton, R.[3]	
1963–64													
Wales	4-0	Banks, G.	Armfield*	Wilson	Milne	Norman	Moore	Paine	Greaves[1]	Smith, R.[2]	Eastham	Charlton, R.[1]	
Rest of the World	2-1	Banks, G.	Armfield*	Wilson	Milne	Norman	Moore	Paine[1]	Greaves[4]	Smith, R.[1]	Eastham	Charlton, R.	
Ireland	8-3	Banks, G.	Armfield*	Thomson, R.	Milne	Norman	Moore	Paine[3]	Hunt	Byrne, J.	Eastham	Charlton, R.	
Scotland	0-1	Banks, G.	Armfield*	Wilson	Milne	Norman	Moore	Paine	Hunt	Byrne, J.[2]	Eastham	Charlton, R.	
Uruguay	2-1	Banks, G.	Cohen	Wilson	Milne	Norman	Moore*	Paine	Greaves	Byrne, J.[1]	Eastham	Charlton, R.	
Portugal	4-3	Banks, G.	Cohen	Wilson	Milne	Norman	Moore*	Thompson, P.	Greaves	Byrne, J.[3]	Eastham	Charlton, R.[1]	
Republic of Ireland	3-1	Waiters	Cohen	Wilson	Milne	Flowers	Moore*	Thompson, P.	Greaves[1]	Byrne, J.[1]	Eastham	Charlton, R.	
U.S.A.	10-0	Banks, G.	Cohen	Thomson, R.	Bailey, M.	Norman	Flowers*	Paine[2]	Hunt[4]	Pickering[1]	Eastham	Thompson, P.	Charlton, R. (10)
Brazil	1-5	Waiters	Cohen	Wilson	Milne	Norman	Moore*	Thompson, P.	Greaves[1]	Byrne, J.	Eastham	Charlton, R.	
Portugal	1-1	Waiters	Thomson, R.	Wilson	Flowers	Norman	Moore*	Paine	Greaves	Byrne, J.	Hunt[1]	Thompson, P.	
Argentina	0-1	Banks, G.	Thomson, R.	Wilson	Milne	Charlton, J.	Moore*	Thompson, P.	Greaves	Byrne, J.	Eastham	Charlton, R.	
1964–65													
Ireland	4-3	Banks, G.	Cohen	Thomson, R.	Milne	Norman	Moore*	Paine	Greaves[3]	Pickering[1]	Charlton, R.	Thompson, P.	
Belgium	2-2	Waiters	Cohen	Thomson, R.	Milne	Norman	Moore*	Thompson, P.	Greaves	Pickering[1]	Venables	Hinton, A.	†
Wales	2-1	Waiters	Cohen	Thomson, R.	Bailey, M.	Flowers*	Young	Thompson, P.	Hunt	Wignall[2]	Byrne, J.	Hinton, A.	
Netherlands	1-1	Waiters	Cohen	Thomson, R.	Mullery	Norman	Flowers*	Thompson, P.	Greaves[1]	Wignall	Venables	Charlton, R.[1]	
Scotland	2-2	Banks, G.	Cohen	Wilson	Stiles	Charlton, J.	Moore*	Paine	Greaves[1]	Bridges	Byrne, J.[1]	Charlton, R.[1]	
Hungary	1-0	Banks, G.	Cohen	Wilson	Stiles	Charlton, J.	Moore*	Paine	Greaves[1]	Bridges[1]	Eastham	Connelly	
Yugoslavia	1-1	Banks, G.	Cohen	Wilson	Stiles	Charlton, J.	Moore*	Paine[1]	Greaves	Bridges[1]	Ball	Connelly	
West Germany	1-0	Banks, G.	Cohen	Wilson	Flowers	Charlton, J.	Moore*	Paine[1]	Ball[1]	Jones, M.	Eastham	Temple	
Sweden	2-1	Banks, G.	Cohen	Wilson	Stiles	Charlton, J.	Moore*	Paine	Ball[1]	Jones, M.	Eastham	Connelly[1]	
1965–66													
Wales	0-0	Springett, R.	Cohen	Wilson	Stiles	Charlton, J.	Moore*	Paine	Greaves	Peacock	Charlton, R.[1]	Connelly[1]	
Austria	2-3	Springett, R.	Cohen	Wilson	Stiles	Charlton, J.	Moore*	Paine	Greaves	Bridges	Charlton, R.[1]	Connelly[1]	

65

ENGLAND'S FULL INTERNATIONAL TEAMS 1946–89 (*contd*)

versus	Result	1	2	3	4	5	6	7	8	9	10	11	Substitutes
Ireland	2-1	Banks, G.	Cohen	Wilson	Stiles	Charlton, J.	Moore*	Thompson, P.	Baker[1]	Peacock[1]	Charlton, R.	Connelly	
Spain	2-0	Banks, G.	Cohen	Wilson	Stiles	Charlton, J.	Moore*	Ball	Hunt	Baker[1]	Eastham	Charlton, R.	Hunter (9)
Poland	1-1	Banks, G.	Cohen	Wilson	Stiles	Charlton, J.	Moore*[1]	Ball	Hunt	Baker	Eastham	Harris, G.	
West Germany	1-0	Banks, G.	Cohen	Newton, K.	Moore*	Charlton, J.	Hunter	Ball	Hunt	Stiles[1]	Hurst, G.[1]	Charlton, R.	Wilson (3)
Scotland	4-3	Banks, G.	Cohen	Newton, K.	Stiles	Charlton, J.	Moore*	Ball	Hunt[2]	Charlton, R.[1]	Hurst, G.[1]	Connelly	
Yugoslavia	3-0	Banks, G.	Armfield*	Wilson	Stiles	Charlton, J.	Moore*	Paine	Greaves[1]	Charlton, R.	Hurst, G.[1]	Tambling	
Finland	6-1	Banks, G.	Armfield*	Wilson	Peters[1]	Charlton, J.[1]	Hunter	Callaghan	Hunt[1]	Charlton, R.	Hurst, G.	Ball	
Norway	6-1	Springett, R.	Cohen	Byrne, G.	Stiles	Flowers	Hunter	Paine	Greaves[4]	Charlton, R.	Hunt	Connelly[1]	
Denmark	2-0	Bonetti	Cohen	Wilson	Stiles	Charlton, J.[1]	Moore*	Ball	Greaves	Hurst, G.	Eastham[1]	Connelly	
Poland	1-0	Banks, G.	Cohen	Wilson	Stiles	Charlton, J.	Moore*	Ball	Greaves	Charlton, R.	Hunt[1]	Peters	
Uruguay	0-0	Banks, G.	Cohen	Wilson	Stiles	Charlton, J.	Moore*	Ball	Greaves	Charlton, R.	Hunt	Connelly	
Mexico	2-0	Bonetti	Cohen	Wilson	Stiles	Charlton, J.	Moore*	Paine	Greaves	Charlton, R.[1]	Hunt[1]	Peters	
France	2-0	Banks, G.	Cohen	Wilson	Stiles	Charlton, J.	Moore*	Callaghan	Greaves	Charlton, R.	Hunt[2]	Peters	
Argentina	1-0	Banks, G.	Cohen	Wilson	Stiles	Charlton, J.	Moore*	Ball	Hurst, G.[1]	Charlton, R.	Hunt	Peters	
Portugal	2-1	Banks, G.	Cohen	Wilson	Stiles	Charlton, J.	Moore*	Ball	Hurst, G.	Charlton, R.[2]	Hunt	Peters	
West Germany	4-2	Banks, G.	Cohen	Wilson	Stiles	Charlton, J.	Moore*	Ball	Hurst, G.[3]	Charlton, R.	Hunt	Peters[1]	
1966–67													
Ireland	2-0	Banks, G.	Cohen	Wilson	Stiles	Charlton, J.	Moore*	Ball	Hurst, G.	Charlton, R.	Hunt[1]	Peters[1]	
Czechoslovakia	0-0	Banks, G.	Cohen	Wilson	Stiles	Charlton, J.	Moore*	Ball	Hurst, G.	Charlton, R.	Hunt	Peters	
Wales	5-1	Banks, G.	Cohen	Wilson	Stiles	Charlton, J.[1]	Moore*	Ball	Hurst, G.[2]	Charlton, R.	Hunt[1]	Peters[1]	
Scotland	2-3	Banks, G.	Cohen	Wilson	Stiles	Charlton, J.[1]	Moore*	Ball	Greaves	Charlton, R.	Hurst, G.[1]	Peters	†
Spain	2-0	Bonetti	Cohen	Newton, K.	Mullery	Labone	Moore*	Ball	Greaves[1]	Hurst, G.	Hunt[1]	Hollins	
Austria	1-0	Bonetti	Newton, K.	Wilson	Mullery	Labone	Moore*	Ball[1]	Greaves	Hurst, G.	Hunt	Hunter	
1967–68													
Wales	3-0	Banks, G.	Cohen	Newton, K.	Mullery	Charlton, J.	Moore*	Ball[1]	Hunt	Charlton, R.[1]	Hurst, G.[1]	Peters[1]	
Ireland	2-0	Banks, G.	Cohen	Wilson	Mullery	Sadler	Moore*	Thompson, P.	Hunt	Charlton, R.[1]	Hurst, G.[1]	Peters[1]	
U.S.S.R.	2-2	Banks, G.	Knowles, C.	Wilson	Mullery	Sadler	Moore*	Ball[1]	Hunt	Charlton, R.	Hurst, G.	Peters[1]	
Scotland	1-1	Banks, G.	Knowles, C.	Wilson	Mullery	Labone	Moore*	Ball	Hurst, G.	Summerbee	Charlton, R.[1]	Peters[1]	
Spain	1-0	Banks, G.	Knowles, C.	Wilson	Mullery	Charlton, J.	Moore*	Ball	Hunt	Summerbee	Hunt	Peters	
Sweden	2-1	Bonetti	Newton, K.	Knowles, C.	Mullery	Labone	Moore*	Bell	Peters[1]	Charlton, R.	Hurst, G.	Hunter[1]	
West Germany	0-1	Stepney	Newton, K.	Knowles, C.	Hunter	Labone	Moore*	Ball	Bell	Summerbee	Hurst, G.	Hunter	Hurst, G. (9)
Yugoslavia	0-1	Banks, G.	Newton, K.	Wilson	Mullery	Labone	Moore*	Ball	Peters	Charlton, R.	Hunt	Thompson, P.	
U.S.S.R.	0-1	Banks, G.	Wright, T.	Wilson	Mullery	Labone	Moore*	Ball	Hunt	Charlton, R.[1]	Hurst, G.[1]	Hunter	
U.S.S.R.	2-0	Banks, G.	Wright, T.	Wilson	Stiles	Labone	Moore*	Hunter	Hunt	Charlton, R.	Hurst, G.	Peters	
1968–69													
Rumania	0-0	Banks, G.	Wright, T.	Newton, K.	Mullery	Labone	Moore*	Ball	Hunt	Charlton, R.	Hurst, G.[1]	Peters	McNab (2)
Bulgaria	1-1	West	Newton, K.	McNab	Mullery	Labone	Moore*	Lee, F.	Bell	Charlton, R.	Hurst, G.[1]	Ball	Reaney (2)
Rumania	1-1	Banks, G.	Newton, K.	McNab	Stiles	Charlton, J.[1]	Hunter	Radford	Hunt	Charlton, R.[1]	Hurst, G.	Ball	
France	5-0	Banks, G.	Newton, K.	Cooper	Mullery	Labone	Moore*	Lee, F.[1]	Bell	Hurst, G.[3]	Charlton, R.	O'Grady[1]	
Ireland	3-1	Banks, G.	Newton, K.	McNab	Mullery	Charlton, J.	Moore*	Ball	Ball	Astle	Charlton, R.[1]	Ball	
Wales	2-1	West	Newton, K.	Cooper	Moore*	Labone	Hunter	Lee, F.[1]	Ball	Charlton, R.	Hurst, G.[2]	Peters[2]	
Scotland	4-1	Banks, G.	Newton, K.	Cooper	Mullery	Labone	Moore*	Lee, F.	Bell	Charlton, R.	Hurst, G.	Peters	
Mexico	0-0	West	Newton, K.	Newton, K.	Mullery	Labone	Moore*	Lee, F.	Bell	Hurst, G.	Ball	Peters	
Uruguay	2-1	Banks, G.	Wright, T.	Newton, K.	Mullery	Labone	Moore*	Lee, F.[1]	Bell	Hurst, G.[1]	Ball	Peters	
Brazil	1-2	Banks, G.	Wright, T.	Newton, K.	Mullery	Labone	Moore*	Ball	Bell[1]	Charlton, R.	Hurst, G.	Peters	Wright, T. (2)

Opponent	Score	1	2	3	4	5	6	7	8	9	10	11	Substitutes
1969–70													
Netherlands	1–0	Bonetti	Wright, T.	Hughes, E.	Mullery	Charlton, J.	Moore*	Lee, F.	Bell	Charlton, R.	Hurst, G.	Peters	Thompson, P. (7)
Portugal	1–0	Bonetti	Reaney	Hughes, E.	Mullery	Charlton, J.[1]	Moore*	Lee, F.	Bell	Astle	Charlton, R.	Ball	Peters (8)
Netherlands	0–0	Banks, G.	Newton, K.	Cooper	Peters	Charlton, J.	Hunter	Lee, F.	Ball	Jones, M.	Charlton, R.*	Storey-Moore	Mullery (7) Hurst, G. (9)
Belgium	3–1	Banks, G.	Wright, T.	Cooper	Moore*	Labone	Hughes, E.	Lee, F.	Ball[2]	Osgood	Hurst, G.	Peters	
Wales	1–1	Banks, G.	Wright, T.	Hughes, E.	Mullery	Labone	Stiles	Coates	Kidd	Charlton, R.[1]	Hurst, G.[1]	Peters[1]	Bell (2)
Ireland	3–1	Banks, G.	Newton, K.	Hughes, E.	Mullery	Labone	Moore*	Thompson, P.	Ball	Astle	Hurst, G.	Peters[1]	Mullery (7)
Scotland	0–0	Banks, G.	Newton, K.	Hughes, E.	Stiles	Labone	Moore*	Lee, F.	Ball[1]	Charlton, R.[1]	Hurst, G.[1]	Peters[2]	
Columbia	4–0	Banks, G.	Newton, K.	Cooper	Mullery	Labone	Moore*	Lee, F.	Ball	Charlton, R.[1]	Hurst, G.	Peters	Kidd (7)[1] Sadler (9)
Ecuador	2–0	Banks, G.	Newton, K.	Cooper	Mullery	Labone	Moore*	Lee, F.	Ball	Charlton, R.	Hurst, G.[1]	Peters	Wright, T. (2) Osgood (7)
Rumania	1–0	Banks, G.	Newton, K.	Cooper	Mullery	Labone	Moore*	Lee, F.	Ball	Charlton, R.	Hurst, G.[1]	Peters	Astle (7) Bell (9)
Brazil	0–1	Banks, G.	Wright, T.	Cooper	Mullery	Labone	Moore*	Bell	Ball	Astle	Clarke, A.[1]	Peters	Ball (8) Osgood (9)
Czechoslovakia	1–0	Banks, G.	Newton, K.	Cooper	Mullery	Charlton, J.	Moore*	Lee, F.	Ball	Charlton, R.	Clarke, A.[1]	Peters	Bell (9) Hunter (11)
West Germany	2–3	Bonetti	Newton, K.	Cooper	Mullery[1]	Labone	Moore*	Lee, F.	Ball	Charlton, R.	Hurst, G.	Peters[1]	
1970–71													
German D.R.	3–1	Shilton	Hughes, E.	Cooper	Mullery	Sadler	Moore*	Lee, F.[1]	Ball	Hurst, G.	Clarke, A.[1]	Peters[1]	
Malta	1–0	Banks, G.	Reaney	Hughes, E.	Mullery*	McFarland	Hunter	Ball	Chivers	Royle	Harvey	Peters	Coates (8)
Greece	3–0	Banks, G.	Storey	Hughes, E.	Mullery	McFarland	Moore*	Lee, F.[1]	Ball	Chivers[2]	Hurst, G.[1]	Peters[1]	Ball (11)
Malta	5–0	Banks, G.	Lawler[1]	Cooper	Moore*	McFarland	Hughes, E.	Lee, F.[1]	Coates	Chivers[2]	Clarke, A.[1]	Peters[1]	
Ireland	1–0	Banks, G.	Madeley	Cooper	Storey	McFarland	Moore*	Lee, F.	Ball	Chivers	Clarke, A.[1]	Peters*[1]	
Wales	0–0	Shilton	Lawler	Cooper	Smith, T.	Lloyd	Hughes, E.	Lee, F.	Brown, A.	Hurst, G.[2]	Coates	Peters	Clarke, A. (8)
Scotland	3–1	Banks, G.	Lawler	Cooper	Storey	McFarland	Moore*	Lee, F.	Ball	Chivers[2]	Hurst, G.	Peters[1]	Clarke, A. (7)
1971–72													
Switzerland	3–2	Banks, G.	Lawler	Cooper	Mullery	McFarland	Moore*	Lee, F.	Madeley	Chivers[1]	Hurst, G.[1]	Peters[1]	Radford (10)
Switzerland	1–1	Shilton	Madeley	Cooper	Storey	Lloyd	Moore*	Summerbee[1]	Ball	Hurst, G.[1]	Lee, F.	Hughes, E.	Chivers (7) Marsh (10)
Greece	2–0	Banks, G.	Madeley	Hughes, E.	Bell	McFarland	Hunter	Lee, F.[1]	Ball	Chivers[1]	Hurst, G.	Peters	
West Germany	1–3	Banks, G.	Madeley	Hughes, E.	Storey	Moore*	Moore*	Lee, F.[1]	Ball	Chivers	Marsh	Hunter	Marsh (10)
West Germany	0–0	Banks, G.	Madeley	Hughes, E.	Storey	McFarland	Moore*	Ball	Bell[1]	Chivers	Marsh[1]	Hunter	Summerbee (10) Peters (11)
Wales	3–0	Banks, G.	Madeley	Hughes, E.[1]	Storey	McFarland	Hunter	Lee, F.	Bell*	Marsh[1]	Marsh	Currie	
Ireland	0–1	Shilton	Todd	Hughes, E.	Storey	Lloyd	Moore*	Ball	Summerbee	MacDonald	MacDonald	Hunter	Peters (11) Chivers (9)
Scotland	1–0	Banks, G.	Madeley	Hughes, E.	Storey	McFarland	Moore*	Ball[1]	Bell	Chivers	Marsh	Hunter	MacDonald (10)
1972–73													
Yugoslavia	1–1	Shilton	Mills, M.	Lampard	Storey	Blockley	Moore*	Ball	Channon	Royle[1]	Bell	Marsh	
Wales	1–0	Clemence	Storey	Hughes, E.	Hunter	McFarland	Moore*	Keegan	Bell[1]	Chivers	Marsh	Ball	
Wales	1–1	Clemence	Storey	Hughes, E.	Hunter[1]	McFarland	Moore*	Keegan	Bell	Chivers	Marsh	Ball	MacDonald (10) Hunter (11)
Scotland	5–0	Shilton	Storey	Hughes, E.	Bell	Madeley	Moore*	Ball	Channon[1]	Chivers[2]	Clarke, A.[2]	Peters	Summerbee (8)
Ireland	2–1	Shilton	Nish	Nish	Bell	McFarland	Moore*	Ball	Channon[1]	Chivers[1]	Richards	Peters[1]	
Wales	3–0	Shilton	Storey	Hughes, E.	Bell	McFarland	Moore*	Ball	Channon	Chivers	Clarke, A.	Peters[1]	
Scotland	1–0	Shilton	Storey	Hughes, E.	Bell	McFarland	Moore*	Ball	Channon	Chivers	Clarke, A.[1]	Peters[1]	
Czechoslovakia	1–1	Shilton	Madeley	Storey	Madeley	McFarland	Moore*	Ball	Channon	Chivers	Clarke, A.	Peters[1]	
Poland	0–2	Shilton	Madeley	Hughes, E.	Storey	McFarland	Moore*	Ball	Bell	Chivers[1]	Clarke, A.	Peters	
U.S.S.R.	2–1	Shilton	Madeley	Hughes, E.	Storey	McFarland	Hunter	Currie	Channon	Chivers[1]	Clarke, A.	Peters†	
Italy	0–2	Shilton	Madeley	Hughes, E.	Storey	McFarland	Moore*	Currie	Channon	Chivers	Clarke, A.	Peters	
1973–74													
Austria	7–0	Shilton	Madeley	Hughes, E.	Bell[1]	McFarland	Hunter	Currie[1]	Channon[2]	Chivers[1]	Clarke, A.[2]	Peters*	Hector (9)
Poland	1–1	Shilton	Madeley	Hughes, E.	Bell	McFarland	Hunter	Currie	Channon	Chivers	Clarke, A.[1]	Peters*	Hector (10)
Italy	0–1	Shilton	Madeley	Hughes, E.	Bell	McFarland	Moore*	Currie	Osgood	Osgood	Clarke, A.	Peters*	Ball (9)
Portugal	0–0	Parkes	Nish	Pejic	Dobson	Watson	Todd	Bowles	MacDonald	MacDonald	Brooking	Peters*	
Wales	2–0	Shilton	Nish	Pejic	Hughes, E.*	McFarland	Todd	Keegan[1]	Channon	Channon	Weller[1]	Bowles[1]	Hughes, E.*

67

ENGLAND'S FULL INTERNATIONAL TEAMS 1946–89 (contd)

versus	Result	1	2	3	4	5	6	7	8	9	10	11	Substitutes
1973–74 (contd)													
Ireland	1-0	Shilton	Nish	Pejic	Hughes, E.*	McFarland	Todd	Keegan	Bell	Channon	Weller[1]	Bowles	Hunter (5) Worthington (11)
Scotland	0-2	Shilton	Nish	Pejic	Hughes, E.*	Hunter	Todd	Channon	Bell	Worthington[1]	Weller	Peters	Watson (5) MacDonald (9)
Argentina	2-2	Shilton	Hughes, E.*	Lindsay	Todd	Watson	Dobson	Keegan	Channon[1]	Worthington[1]	Bell	Brooking	
German D. R.	1-1	Clemence	Hughes, E.*	Lindsay	Todd	Watson	Dobson	Keegan	Channon[1]	Worthington[1]	Bell	Brooking	
Bulgaria	1-0	Clemence	Hughes, E.*	Lindsay	Todd	Watson	Dobson	Keegan	Channon[1]	Worthington[1]	Bell	Brooking	
Yugoslavia	2-2	Clemence	Hughes, E.*	Lindsay	Todd	Watson	Dobson	Keegan[1]	Channon[1]	Worthington[1]	Bell	Brooking	MacDonald (9)
1974–75													
Czechoslovakia	3-0	Clemence	Madeley	Cooper	Dobson	Watson	Hunter	Bell[2]	Channon[1]	Worthington	Keegan	Francis, G.	Brooking (4) Thomas (9)
Portugal	0-0	Clemence	Madeley	Gillard	Brooking	Watson	Hughes, E.*	Bell	Channon	Francis, G.[1]	Clarke, A.	Thomas	Todd (3) Worthington (10)
West Germany	2-0	Clemence	Whitworth	Beattie	Bell[1]	Watson	Todd	Ball*	Channon	MacDonald[1]	Hudson	Keegan	Thomas (8)
Cyprus	5-0	Shilton	Whitworth	Beattie	Bell	Watson	Todd	Ball*	Channon	MacDonald[5]	Hudson	Keegan	Hughes, E. (3) Tueart (11)
Cyprus	1-0	Clemence	Whitworth	Whitworth	Bell	Watson	Todd	Ball*	Channon	MacDonald	Keegan[1]	Thomas	Channon (9)
Ireland	0-0	Clemence	Whitworth	Gillard	Bell	Watson	Todd	Ball*	Channon	MacDonald	Keegan	Tueart	
Wales	2-2	Clemence	Whitworth	Hughes, E.	Francis, G.	Watson	Todd	Ball*	Channon	Johnson[2]	Viljoen	Thomas	Little (8)
Scotland	5-1	Clemence	Beattie[1]	Beattie[1]	Bell[1]	Watson	Todd	Ball*	Channon	Johnson[1]	Francis, G.[2]	Keegan	Thomas (11)
1975–76													
Switzerland	2-1	Clemence	Whitworth	Gillard	Francis, G.*	Watson	Todd	Keegan[1]	Channon[1]	Johnson	Currie	Bell	MacDonald (9)
Czechoslovakia	1-2	Clemence	Madeley	Gillard	Francis, G.*	McFarland	Todd	Keegan	Channon[1]	MacDonald	Clarke, A.	Bell	Watson (5) Thomas (8)
Portugal	1-1	Clemence	Whitworth	Beattie	Madeley	Madeley	Todd	Keegan	Channon[1]	MacDonald	Francis, G.*	Brooking	Clarke, A. (9) Thomas (4)
Wales	2-1	Clemence	Cherry	Neal	Doyle	Doyle	Mills, M.	Keegan	Channon	MacDonald	Kennedy, R.[1]	Brooking	Clement (2) Taylor, P. (8)
Wales	1-0	Clemence	Clement	Mills, M.	Thompson, P.	Thompson, P.	Kennedy, R.	Keegan*	Francis, G.*	Boyer	Towers	Taylor, P.[1]	
N. Ireland	4-0	Clemence	Todd	Mills, M.	Thompson, P.	Greenhoff, B.	Kennedy, R.	Keegan	Channon[1]	Pearson, S.	Francis, G.[*1]	Taylor, P.	Towers (11) Royle (7)
Scotland	1-2	Clemence	Todd	Mills, M.	Thompson, P.	Greenhoff, B.	Kennedy, R.	Keegan	Channon[1]	Pearson, S.	Taylor, P.	Taylor, P.	Cherry (9) Doyle (5)
Brazil	0-1	Clemence	Todd	Mills, M.	Thompson, P.[1]	Doyle	Cherry	Keegan	Channon	Pearson, S.	Brooking	Francis, G.*	
Italy	3-2	Rimmer	Clement	Neal	Thompson, P.[1]	Doyle	Towers	Wilkins	Channon	Royle	Brooking	Hill, G.	
Finland	4-1	Clemence	Todd	Mills, M.	Thompson, P.	Madeley	Cherry	Keegan[2]	Channon[1]	Pearson, S.[1]	Brooking	Francis, G.*	Corrigan (1) Mills, M. (3)
1976–77													
Republic of Ireland	1-1	Clemence	Todd	Beattie	Greenhoff, B.	McFarland	Madeley	Keegan*	Wilkins	Pearson, S.[1]	Brooking	George	Hill, G. (11)
Finland	2-1	Clemence	Todd	Beattie	Thompson, B.	Thompson, P.	Wilkins	Keegan*	Channon	Royle[1]	Brooking	Tueart[1]	Mills, M. (10) Hill, G. (11)
Italy	0-2	Clemence	Clement	Mills, M.	Greenhoff, B.	McFarland	Bell	Keegan*	Channon	Bowles	Cherry	Brooking	Beattie (2)
Netherlands	0-2	Clemence	Clement	Beattie	Kennedy, R.[1]	Watson	Madeley	Keegan*	Francis, T.[1]	Greenhoff, B.	Bowles	Brooking	Todd (9) Pearson, S. (6)
Luxembourg	5-0	Clemence	Gidman	Cherry	Greenhoff, B.	Watson	Todd	Keegan[1]	Channon[1]	Royle	Francis, T.[1]	Hill, G.	Mariner (9)
N. Ireland	2-1	Shilton	Neal	Mills, M.	Greenhoff, B.	Watson	Todd	Keegan*	Channon[1]	Mariner	Brooking	Tueart[1]	Talbot (7)
Wales	0-1	Clemence	Neal	Mills, M.	Greenhoff, B.	Watson	Hughes, E.*	Francis, T.[1]	Channon[1]	Pearson, S.	Brooking	Kennedy, R.	Tueart (10)
Scotland	1-2	Clemence	Neal	Cherry	Greenhoff, B.	Watson	Hughes, E.*	Keegan*	Francis, T.	Pearson, S.	Talbot	Kennedy, R.	Cherry (4) Tueart (11)
Brazil	0-0	Clemence	Neal	Cherry	Greenhoff, B.	Watson	Hughes, E.*	Keegan*	Channon	Pearson, S.	Wilkins	Talbot	Channon (9) Kennedy, R. (10)
Argentina	1-1	Clemence	Neal	Cherry	Greenhoff, B.	Watson	Hughes, E.*	Keegan*	Francis, T.	Pearson, S.	Wilkins	Talbot	Kennedy, R. (4)
Uruguay	0-0	Clemence	Neal	Cherry	Greenhoff, B.	Watson	Hughes, E.*	Keegan*	Channon	Mariner	Wilkins	Talbot	
1977–78													
Switzerland	0-0	Clemence	Neal	Cherry	McDermott	Watson	Hughes, E.*	Keegan	Channon	Francis, T.[1]	Francis, T.[1]	Callaghan	Hill, G. (8) Wilkins (11)
Luxembourg	2-0	Clemence	Cherry	Hughes, E.*	Watson	Kennedy, R.[1]	Callaghan	McDermott	Wilkins	Mariner[1]	Francis, T.[1]	Hill, G.	Whymark (7) Beattie (4)
Italy	2-0	Clemence	Neal	Neal	Wilkins	Watson	Hughes, E.*	Keegan	Coppell	Latchford, R.[1]	Brooking	Barnes	Pearson, S. (9) Francis, T. (7)
West Germany	1-2	Clemence	Neal	Mills, M.	Wilkins	Watson	Hughes, E.*	Keegan	Coppell	Pearson, S.[1]	Brooking	Barnes	Francis, T. (7)
Brazil	1-1	Shilton	Mills, M.*	Cherry	Greenhoff, B.	Watson	Currie	Keegan*	Francis, T.	Latchford, R.[1]	Brooking	Barnes	
Wales	3-1	Clemence	Neal[1]	Cherry	Greenhoff, B.	Watson	Wilkins	Coppell	Coppell	Pearson, S.	Francis, T.	Barnes[1]	Currie (3)[1] Mariner (9)
N. Ireland	1-0	Clemence	Neal	Mills, M.	Wilkins	Watson	Hughes, E.*	Coppell[1]	Wilkins	Pearson, S.	Currie	Woodcock	
Scotland	1-0	Clemence	Neal	Mills, M.	Wilkins	Watson	Hughes, E.*	Coppell[1]	Currie	Mariner	Francis, T.	Barnes.	Greenhoff, B. (6) Brooking (9)

Opponent	Result	1	2	3	4	5	6	7	8	9	10	11	Substitutes
Hungary	4-1	Shilton	Neal[1]	Mills, M.	Wilkins	Watson	Hughes, E.*	Keegan[2]	Coppell	Francis, T.[1]	Brooking	Barnes[1]	Greenhoff, B. (5) Currie (8)[1]
1978-79													
Denmark	4-3	Clemence	Neal[1]	Mills, M.	Wilkins	Watson	Hughes, E.*	Keegan	Coppell	Latchford, R.[1]	Brooking[1]	Barnes	Thompson, P. (5) Woodcock (11)
Republic of Ireland	1-1	Clemence	Neal[1]	Mills, M.	Wilkins	Watson	Hughes, E.*	Keegan*	Coppell[1]	Latchford, R.[1]	Brooking	Barnes	Latchford, R. (9)
Czechoslovakia	1-0	Shilton	Anderson	Cherry	Thompson, P.	Watson[1]	Wilkins	Keegan[1]	Coppell[1]	Woodcock	Currie	Barnes	Coppell (9) Brooking (4)
Northern Ireland	4-0	Clemence	Neal	Mills, M.*	Currie	Watson[1]	Currie	Coppell[1]	Coppell	Latchford, R.[2]	Currie	Barnes	Francis, T. (9) Woodcock (11)
Northern Ireland	2-0	Clemence	Cherry	Mills, M.	Thompson, P.	Watson[1]	Wilkins	Keegan	Wilkins	Latchford, R.	McDermott	Cunningham	Wilkins, R. (4) Thompson, P. (5) Brooking (10)
Wales	0-0	Corrigan	Neal	Sansom	Currie	Watson[1]	Wilkins	Keegan*[1]	Coppell	Latchford, R.	Brooking	Barnes[1]	Clemence (1) Francis, T. (9) Cunningham (11)
Scotland	3-1	Clemence	Neal	Cherry	Thompson, P.	Watson[1]	Hughes, E.*	Keegan	Coppell[1]	Latchford, R.	Brooking	Barnes[1]	McDermott (10)
Bulgaria	3-0	Clemence	Mills, M.	Mills, M.	Mills, M.	Watson	Wilkins	Keegan	Francis, T.	Woodcock	Currie	Cunningham	Coppell (9)
Sweden	0-0	Shilton	Anderson	Cherry	Cherry	Watson	Wilkins	Keegan	Woodcock	Latchford, R.[1]	Brooking	Barnes	Hughes (2) Cunningham (9)
Austria	3-4	Shilton	Neal	Mills, M.	Thompson, P.	Watson	Wilkins	Keegan*[1]	Coppell[1]	Latchford, R.	Brooking	Barnes	
1979-80													
Denmark	1-0	Clemence	Neal	Mills, M.	Thompson, P.	Watson	Wilkins	Keegan*[1]	Coppell[1]	McDermott	Brooking	Barnes	Cherry (2) Birtles (9)
Northern Ireland	5-1	Shilton	Neal	Sansom	Thompson, P.	Watson	Wilkins	Keegan*	Coppell[1]	Francis[1]	Brooking	Woodcock[2]	Sansom (2) Wilkins (5)
Bulgaria	2-0	Clemence	Anderson	Sansom	Thompson, P.*	Watson[1]	Wilkins	Reeves	Hoddle[1]	Francis	Kennedy, R.	Woodcock	Mariner (10)
Republic of Ireland	2-0	Clemence	Cherry	Mills, M.	Thompson, P.	Watson	Robson	Keegan*[2]	McDermott	Johnson	Woodcock	Cunningham	Hughes (10)
Spain	2-0	Shilton	Neal	Sansom	Thompson, P.	Watson	Wilkins	Keegan*	Coppell[1]	Francis[1]	Kennedy, R.	Woodcock[1]	Greenhoff (7) Ward (10) Devonshire (11)
Argentina	3-1	Clemence	Neal	Cherry	Thompson, P.	Watson	Wilkins	Keegan*[1]	Coppell[1]	Johnson[2]	Woodcock	Kennedy, R.	McDermott (8) Kennedy, R. (9)
Wales	1-4	Clemence	Cherry	Sansom	Thompson, P.*	Lloyd	Kennedy, R.	Coppell	Hoddle	Mariner[1]	Brooking	Barnes	Mariner (9)
Northern Ireland	1-1	Corrigan	Cherry	Sansom	Brooking	Watson	Hughes'*	McDermott	Wilkins	Johnson[1]	Reeves	Devonshire[1]	Cherry (2) Mariner (8)
Scotland	2-0	Clemence	Cherry	Sansom	Thompson, P.*	Watson	Wilkins	Coppell[1]	McDermott	Johnson	Mariner	Brooking[1]	Cunningham (9) Coppell (11)
Australia	2-1	Corrigan	Cherry*	Lampard	Talbot	Osman	Butcher	Robson	Hoddle[1]	Mariner[1]	Sunderland	Armstrong	Rix (10)
Belgium	1-1	Clemence	Neal	Sansom	Thompson, P.	Watson	Wilkins[1]	Keegan*	Coppell	Johnson	Brooking	Woodcock	Barnes (8) Wilkins (10)
Italy	0-1	Shilton	Neal	Sansom	Thompson, P.	Watson	Wilkins	Keegan*	Coppell	Birtles	Kennedy, R.	Woodcock	McDermott (10)
Spain	2-1	Clemence	Anderson	Mills, M.	Thompson, P.	Watson	Wilkins	Keegan*	Hoddle	McDermott	Brooking[1]	Woodcock[1]	Woodcock (9)
1980-81													
Norway	4-0	Shilton	Anderson	Sansom	Thompson*	Watson	Gates	Gates	McDermott[2]	Mariner[1]	Woodcock[1]	Rix	Martin (5) Francis (11)
Rumania	1-2	Clemence	Neal	Sansom	Thompson*	Robson	Robson	Rix	McDermott	Birtles	Woodcock[1]	Gates	McDermott (11)[1] Barnes (5)
Switzerland	2-1	Shilton	Neal	Sansom	Robson	Watson	Mills*	Keegan*	McDermott	Mariner[1]	Brooking	Woodcock[1]	Wilkins (10)
Spain	1-2	Clemence	Anderson	Sansom	Robson	Osman	Butcher	Coppell	Francis	Mariner	Brooking	Hoddle[1]	Withe (9) Barnes (10)
Rumania	0-0	Shilton	Neal	Sansom	Robson	Butcher	Osman	Coppell	Wilkins	Francis	Brooking	Woodcock	Morley (8)
Brazil	0-1	Clemence*	Anderson	Sansom	Robson	Martin	Wilkins	Coppell	McDermott	Withe	Rix	Rix	Regis (9) Woodcock (11)
Wales	0-1	Corrigan	Anderson	Mills	Robson	Watson*	Robson	Keegan*[1]	Hoddle	Withe	Rix	Barnes	McDermott (8) Regis (10)
Scotland	0-1	Corrigan	Mills	Mills	Wilkins	Robson	Osman	Keegan*[1]	Hoddle	Withe	Rix	Woodcock	Rix (8) Barnes (9)
Switzerland	1-1	Clemence	Neal	Mills	Wilkins	Watson*	Robson	Keegan*	Coppell	Mariner	Robson	Francis	
Hungary	3-1	Clemence	Neal	Sansom	Thompson	Watson	Robson	Keegan*[1]	Coppell	Mariner	Brooking[2]	McDermott	
1981-82													
Norway	1-2	Clemence	Neal	Mills	Thompson	Osman	Robson[1]	Keegan*	Francis	Mariner[1]	Hoddle	McDermott	
Hungary	1-0	Shilton	Neal	Mills	Thompson	Martin	Robson	Keegan*[1]	Coppell[1]	Francis	Brooking[1]	McDermott	
Northern Ireland	4-0	Clemence	Anderson	Sansom	Wilkins[1]	Watson	Foster	Keegan[1]	Robson[1]	Withe	Hoddle[1]	Morley	
Wales	1-0	Corrigan	Neal	Sansom	Thompson[1]	Butcher	Robson	Wilkins	Francis[1]	Withe	Hoddle	Morley	
Holland	2-0	Shilton*	Neal	Sansom	Thompson	Foster	Robson	Keegan*	Devonshire	Mariner[1]	McDermott	Woodcock[1]	
Scotland	1-0	Shilton*	Mills	Sansom	Thompson	Butcher	Robson	Keegan*	Coppell	Mariner[1]	Brooking	Wilkins	McDermott (7) Francis (9)
Iceland	1-1	Corrigan	Neal*	Neal*	Watson	Osman	McDermott	Hoddle	Devonshire	Withe	Regis	Morley	Perryman (8) Goddard (10)[1]

ENGLAND'S FULL INTERNATIONAL TEAMS 1946–89 (contd)

versus	Result	1	2	3	4	5	6	7	8	9	10	11	Substitutes
1981-82 (contd)													
Finland	4-1	Clemence	Mills	Sansom	Thompson	Martin	Robson[2]	Keegan*	Coppell	Mariner[2]	Brooking	Wilkins	Rix (6) Francis (8) Woodcock (10)
France	3-1	Shilton	Mills*	Sansom	Thompson	Butcher	Robson[2]	Coppell	Francis	Mariner[1]	Rix	Wilkins	Neal (3)
Czechoslovakia	2-0	Shilton	Mills*	Sansom	Thompson	Butcher	Robson	Coppell	Francis[1]	Mariner	Rix	Wilkins†	Hoddle (6)
Kuwait	1-0	Shilton	Neal	Mills*	Thompson	Foster	Hoddle	Coppell	Francis[1]	Mariner	Rix	Wilkins	
West Germany	0-0	Shilton	Mills*	Sansom	Thompson	Butcher	Robson	Coppell	Francis	Mariner	Rix	Wilkins	Woodcock (8)
Spain	0-0	Shilton	Mills*	Sansom	Thompson	Butcher	Robson	Rix	Francis	Mariner	Woodcock	Wilkins	Brooking (7) Keegan (10)
1982-83													
Denmark	2-2	Shilton	Neal	Sansom	Wilkins*	Osman	Robson*	Morley	Robson	Mariner	Francis[2]	Rix	Hill (7)
West Germany	1-2	Shilton	Mabbutt	Sansom	Thompson	Butcher	Wilkins*	Hill	Regis	Mariner	Armstrong	Mariner	Woodcock (8)[1] Blissett (9) Rix (10)
Greece	3-0	Shilton	Neal	Sansom	Thompson	Martin	Robson*	Lee[1]	Mabbutt	Mariner	Woodcock[2]	Morley	
Luxembourg	9-0	Clemence	Neal[1]	Sansom	Robson*	Martin	Butcher	Coppell[1]	Lee	Woodcock[1]	Blissett[3]	Mabbutt†	Chamberlain (7)[1] Hoddle (11)[1]
Wales	2-1	Shilton*	Neal[1]	Statham	Lee	Martin	Butcher	Mabbutt	Blissett	Mariner	Cowans	Devonshire	
Greece	0-0	Shilton*	Neal	Sansom	Lee	Martin	Butcher	Coppell	Mabbutt	Francis	Woodcock	Devonshire	Blissett (10) Rix (11)
Hungary	2-0	Shilton*	Neal	Sansom	Lee	Martin	Butcher	Mabbutt	Francis[1]	Withe[1]	Blissett	Cowans	
Northern Ireland	0-0	Shilton*	Neal	Sansom	Hoddle	Roberts	Butcher	Mabbutt	Francis	Withe	Blissett	Cowans	Barnes J. (10)
Scotland	2-0	Shilton	Thomas	Statham	Lee	Roberts	Butcher	Barham	Francis	Withe	Hoddle	Cowans[1]	Mabbutt (7) Blissett (9)
Australia	0-0	Shilton*	Neal	Statham	Williams	Osman	Butcher	Gregory	Gregory	Blissett	Francis	Cowans[1]	Barnes(3) Walsh(9)
Australia	1-0	Shilton*	Neal	Statham	Barham	Osman	Butcher	Gregory	Blissett	Walsh[1]	Cowans	Cowans	Williams(3)
Australia	1-1	Shilton*	Neal	Pickering	Lee	Osman	Butcher	Gregory	Francis[1]	Walsh	Cowans	Barnes	Spink(1) Thomas(2) Blissett(9)
1983-84													
Denmark	0-1	Shilton	Neal	Sansom	Lee	Osman	Butcher	Wilkins*	Gregory	Mariner	Francis	Barnes	Blissett(4) Chamberlain(11)
Hungary	3-0	Shilton	Gregory	Sansom	Lee[1]	Martin	Butcher	Robson*[2]	Hoddle	Mariner[1]	Blissett	Mabbutt	Withe(10)
Luxembourg	4-0	Clemence	Duxbury	Sansom	Lee[1]	Martin	Butcher[1]	Robson*[2]	Hoddle	Mariner[1]	Woodcock	Devonshire	Barnes(10)
France	0-2	Shilton	Duxbury	Sansom	Lee	Roberts	Butcher	Robson*	Stein	Walsh	Hoddle	Williams	Barnes(4) Woodcock (8)
Northern Ireland	1-0	Shilton	Anderson	Kennedy	Lee	Roberts	Butcher	Robson*	Wilkins	Woodcock[1]	Francis	Rix	
Wales	0-1	Shilton	Duxbury	Kennedy	Lee	Martin	Wright	Wilkins*	Gregory	Walsh	Woodcock	Barnes	Fenwick(5) Blissett(11)
Scotland	1-1	Shilton	Duxbury	Sansom	Wilkins	Roberts	Fenwick	Robson*	Robson*	Woodcock[1]	Blissett	Barnes	Hunt(7) Lineker(9)
U.S.S.R.	0-2	Shilton	Duxbury	Sansom	Wilkins	Roberts	Fenwick	Chamberlain	Robson*	Francis	Francis	Barnes[1]	Hateley(9) Hunt(11)
Brazil	2-0	Shilton	Duxbury	Sansom	Wilkins	Watson	Fenwick	Chamberlain	Chamberlain	Hateley	Woodcock	Barnes[1]	Allen (10)
Uruguay	0-2	Shilton	Duxbury	Sansom	Wilkins	Watson	Fenwick	Robson*	Chamberlain	Hateley	Allen	Barnes	Woodcock (10)
Chile	0-0	Shilton	Duxbury	Sansom	Wilkins	Watson	Fenwick	Robson*	Chamberlain	Hateley	Allen	Barnes	Lee (8)
1984-85													
East Germany	1-0	Shilton	Duxbury	Sansom[1]	Williams	Wright	Butcher	Robson*[1]	Wilkins	Mariner	Woodcock[1]	Barnes	Hateley (9) Francis (10)
Finland	5-0	Shilton	Duxbury	Sansom[1]	Williams	Wright	Butcher	Robson*[1]	Wilkins	Hateley[2]	Woodcock[1]	Barnes[2]	Stevens (2) Chamberlain (7)
Turkey	8-0	Shilton	Anderson	Sansom	Williams	Wright	Butcher	Robson*[3]	Wilkins	Withe	Woodcock[2]	Barnes[2]	Stevens (4) Francis (10)
Northern Ireland	1-0	Shilton	Anderson	Sansom	Stevens	Martin	Butcher	Steven	Wilkins*	Hateley[1]	Woodcock	Barnes	Francis (10)
Republic of Ireland	2-1	Bailey	Anderson	Sansom	Steven[1]	Wright	Butcher	Robson*	Wilkins	Hateley	Lineker[1]	Waddle	Hoddle (7) Davenport (9)
Rumania	0-0	Shilton	Anderson	Sansom	Steven	Wright	Butcher	Robson*	Wilkins	Mariner	Francis	Barnes	Lineker (9) Waddle (11)
Finland	1-1	Shilton	Anderson	Sansom	Steven	Fenwick	Butcher	Robson*	Wilkins	Hateley[1]	Francis	Barnes	Waddle (4)
Scotland	0-1	Shilton	Anderson	Sansom	Hoddle	Fenwick	Butcher	Robson*	Wilkins	Hateley	Francis	Barnes	Lineker (4) Waddle (11)
Italy	1-2	Shilton	Stevens	Sansom	Steven	Wright	Butcher	Robson*	Wilkins	Hateley[1]	Francis	Waddle	Hoddle (4) Lineker (10)
Mexico	0-1	Bailey	Anderson	Sansom	Hoddle	Fenwick	Watson	Robson*	Wilkins	Hateley	Francis	Barnes	Dixon (4) Reid (8) Waddle (11)
West Germany	3-0	Shilton	Stevens	Sansom	Hoddle	Wright	Butcher	Robson*[1]	Reid	Dixon[2]	Lineker	Waddle	Bracewell (7) Barnes (10)

Table: England international match line-ups, 1985–86 to 1988–89. Columns correspond to the positions Woods, Anderson, Sansom, Hoddle, Fenwick, Butcher, Robson*, Bracewell, Dixon, Lineker, Waddle (superscript numerals denote goals scored; * denotes captain). The final column lists substitutes/scorers with the shirt number replaced in brackets.

Opponent	Score	1	2	3	4	5	6	7	8	9	10	11	Substitutes
U.S.A.	5-0	Woods	Anderson	Sansom	Hoddle	Fenwick*	Butcher	Robson*	Bracewell	Dixon²	Lineker²	Waddle	Watson (3) Steven (4)¹ Reid (7) Barnes (11)
1985–86													
Rumania	1-1	Shilton	Stevens	Sansom	Reid	Wright	Fenwick	Robson*¹	Hoddle¹	Hateley	Lineker	Waddle	Woodcock(10) Barnes(11)
Turkey	5-0	Shilton	Stevens	Sansom	Hoddle	Wright	Fenwick	Bracewell	Wilkins	Hateley	Lineker³	Waddle¹	Steven(7) Woodcock(9)
Northern Ireland	0-0	Shilton	Stevens	Sansom	Hoddle	Wright	Fenwick	Steven¹	Wilkins*	Dixon	Lineker	Waddle	Woods(1) Hill(7)
Egypt	4-0	Shilton	Stevens	Sansom	Cowans¹	Wright	Fenwick	Robson*²	Wilkins*	Hateley	Lineker	Wallace¹†	Beardsley(10)
Israel	2-1	Shilton	Stevens	Sansom	Hoddle	Martin	Butcher	Robson*²	Wilkins	Dixon	Beardsley	Waddle	Woods(1) Woodcock(9) Barnes(11)
U.S.S.R.	1-0	Shilton	Anderson	Sansom	Hoddle	Wright	Butcher¹	Wilkins*	Wilkins*¹	Beardsley	Lineker	Waddle¹	Hodge(7) Steven(11)
Scotland	2-1	Shilton	Stevens	Sansom	Hoddle¹	Watson	Butcher¹	Robson*	Francis	Hateley²	Hodge	Waddle	Reid(7) Stevens(10)
Mexico	3-0	Shilton	Anderson	Sansom	Hoddle	Fenwick	Butcher	Hodge	Wilkins	Hateley¹	Beardsley¹	Waddle	Stevens(7) Steven(8)
Canada	1-0	Shilton	Stevens	Sansom	Hoddle	Martin	Butcher	Hodge	Wilkins*	Hateley¹	Lineker	Waddle	Dixon(9) Barnes(11)
Portugal	0-1	Shilton	Stevens	Sansom	Hoddle	Fenwick	Butcher	Robson*¹	Wilkins	Hateley	Lineker	Waddle	Woods(1) Reid(8)
Morocco	0-0	Shilton	Stevens	Sansom	Hoddle	Fenwick	Butcher	Robson*	Wilkins	Hateley	Lineker	Waddle	Beardsley(10) Barnes(11)
Poland	3-0	Shilton*	Stevens	Sansom	Hoddle	Fenwick	Butcher	Hodge	Reid	Beardsley	Lineker³	Steven	Hodge(7) Beardsley(11)
Paraguay	3-0	Shilton*	Stevens	Sansom	Hoddle	Martin	Butcher	Hodge	Reid	Beardsley¹	Lineker²	Steven	Hodge(7) Stevens(9)
Argentina	1-2	Shilton*	Stevens	Sansom	Hoddle	Fenwick	Butcher	Hodge	Reid	Beardsley	Lineker¹	Steven	Waddle(9) Dixon(10) Stevens(8) Hateley (9) Waddle(8) Barnes(11)
1986–87													
Sweden	0-1	Shilton*	Anderson	Sansom	Hoddle	Martin	Butcher	Steven	Wilkins	Dixon	Hodge²	Barnes	Cottee(7) Waddle(11)
Northern Ireland	3-0	Shilton	Anderson	Sansom	Hoddle	Watson	Butcher	Robson*¹	Hodge	Beardsley	Lineker²	Waddle¹	Cottee(9)
Yugoslavia	2-0	Woods	Anderson¹	Sansom	Hoddle	Wright	Butcher*	Mabbutt¹	Hodge	Beardsley	Lineker	Waddle	Wilkins(8) Steven(11)
Spain	4-2	Shilton	Anderson	Sansom	Hoddle	Adams	Butcher	Robson*¹	Hodge	Beardsley*	Lineker⁴	Waddle¹	Woods(1) Steven(1)
Northern Ireland	2-0	Shilton	Anderson	Sansom	Hoddle	Wright	Mabbutt	Robson*¹	Hodge	Beardsley	Lineker	Waddle	Woods(1)
Turkey	0-0	Woods	Anderson	Pearce	Mabbutt	Adams	Butcher	Robson*	Hodge	Beardsley	Lineker	Waddle	Barnes(8) Hateley(9)
Brazil	1-1	Shilton	Stevens	Sansom	Reid	Adams	Butcher	Robson*	Barnes	Allen	Lineker¹	Waddle	Hateley(10)
Scotland	0-0	Woods	Stevens	Pearce	Hoddle	Wright	Butcher	Robson*	Hodge	Beardsley	Hateley	Waddle	
1987–88													
West Germany	1-3	Shilton*	Anderson	Sansom	Hoddle	Adams	Mabbutt	Reid	Barnes	Beardsley¹	Lineker¹	Waddle	Pearce(3) Webb(4) Hateley(11)
Turkey	8-0	Shilton	Stevens	Sansom	Steven	Adams¹	Butcher	Robson*¹	Webb¹	Beardsley¹	Lineker³	Barnes²	Hoddle(4) Regis(9)
Yugoslavia	4-1	Shilton	Stevens	Sansom	Steven	Adams¹	Butcher	Robson*¹	Webb	Beardsley*	Lineker	Barnes¹	Reid(7) Hoddle(8)
Israel	0-0	Woods	Stevens	Pearce	Webb	Watson	Wright	Allen	McMahon	Beardsley*	Barnes	Waddle	Fenwick(6) Harford(7)
Holland	2-2	Shilton	Stevens	Sansom	Steven	Adams¹	Watson	Robson*	Webb	Beardsley	Lineker¹	Barnes	Wright(6) Hoddle(8) Hateley(9)
Hungary	0-0	Woods	Anderson	Pearce	Steven	Adams	Pallister	Robson*	McMahon	Beardsley	Lineker	Waddle	Stevens(3) Hateley(9) Cottee(10)
Scotland	1-0	Shilton	Stevens	Sansom	Webb	Watson	Adams	Robson*	Steven	Beardsley¹	Lineker	Barnes	Hoddle(11)
Colombia	1-1	Shilton	Anderson	Sansom	McMahon	Wright	Adams	Robson*	Waddle	Beardsley	Lineker¹	Barnes	Waddle(8)
Switzerland	1-0	Shilton	Stevens	Sansom	Webb	Wright	Adams	Robson*	Steven	Beardsley	Lineker¹	Barnes	Hoddle(8) Hateley(9)
Rep. of Ireland	0-1	Shilton*	Stevens	Sansom	Webb	Wright	Adams	Robson*¹	Waddle	Beardsley	Lineker	Barnes	Woods(1) Watson(6) Reid (7) Waddle(8)
Holland	1-3	Shilton*	Stevens	Sansom	Hoddle	Wright	Adams¹	Robson*¹	Steven	Beardsley	Lineker	Barnes	Hoddle(4) Hateley(9)
U.S.S.R.	1-3	Woods	Stevens	Sansom	Hoddle	Watson	Adams¹	Robson*	Steven	McMahon	Lineker	Barnes	Waddle(8) Hateley(9) Webb(9) Hateley(10)
1988–89													
Denmark	1-0	Shilton	Stevens	Pearce	Rocastle	Adams	Butcher	Robson*	Webb¹	Harford	Beardsley	Hodge	Woods (1) Walker (5) Cottee (9) Gascoigne (10)
Sweden	0-0	Shilton	Stevens	Pearce	Webb	Adams	Butcher	Robson*	Beardsley	Waddle	Lineker	Barnes	Walker (5) Cottee (11)

ENGLAND'S FULL INTERNATIONAL TEAMS 1946–89 (contd)

versus	Result	1	2	3	4	5	6	7	8	9	10	11	Substitutes
Saudi Arabia	1-1	Seaman	Sterland	Pearce	Thomas	Adams[1]	Pallister	Robson*	Rocastle	Beardsley	Lineker	Waddle	Gascoigne (4) Smith (9) Marwood (11)
Greece	2-1	Shilton	Stevens	Pearce	Webb	Walker	Butcher	Robson*[1]	Rocastle	Smith	Lineker	Barnes[1]	Beardsley (9)
Albania	2-0	Shilton	Stevens	Pearce	Webb	Walker	Butcher	Robson*[1]	Rocastle	Waddle	Lineker	Barnes[1]	Beardsley (9) Smith (10)
Albania	5-0	Shilton	Stevens	Pearce	Webb	Walker	Butcher	Robson*	Rocastle	Beardsley[2]	Lineker[1]	Waddle[1]	Parker (2) Gascoigne (8)[1]
Chile	0-0	Shilton	Parker	Pearce	Webb	Walker	Butcher	Robson*	Gascoigne	Clough	Fashanu	Waddle[1]	Cottee (10)
Scotland	2-0	Shilton	Stevens	Pearce	Webb[1]	Walker	Butcher	Robson*	Steven	Fashanu	Cottee	Waddle[1]	Bull (9)[1] Gascoigne (10)
Poland	3-0	Shilton	Stevens	Pearce	Webb	Walker	Butcher	Robson*	Waddle	Beardsley	Lineker[1]	Barnes[1]	Rocastle (8) Smith (9)
Denmark	1-1	Shilton	Parker	Pearce	Webb	Walker	Butcher	Robson*	Rocastle	Beardsley	Lineker[1]	Barnes	Seaman (1) McMahon (4) Bull (9) Waddle (11)

International Matches 1872–1989

(Up to and including 7th June 1989)

wc World Cup   ENC European Nations' Cup   BJT Brazilian Jubilee Tournament
EC European Championship   SFAC Scottish F.A. Centenary   FAWC F.A. of Wales Centenary
USABCT United States of America Bi-Centenary Tournament   RC Rous Cup

ENGLAND v. ALBANIA

			Goals	
Year	Date	Venue	Eng	Alb
wc1989	Mar. 8	Tirana	2	0
wc1989	April 26	Wembley	5	0

ENGLAND v. ARGENTINA

			Eng	Arg
1951	May 9	Wembley	2	1
wc1962	June 2	Rancagua	3	1
BJT1964	June 6	Rio de Janeiro	0	1
wc1966	July 23	Wembley	1	0
1974	May 22	Wembley	2	2
1977	June 12	Buenos Aires	1	1
1980	May 13	Wembley	3	1
wc1986	June 22	Mexico City	1	2

ENGLAND v. AUSTRIA

			Eng	Aust
1908	June 6	Vienna	6	1
1908	June 8	Vienna	11	1
1909	June 1	Vienna	8	1
1930	May 14	Vienna	0	0
1932	Dec. 7	Chelsea	4	3
1936	May 6	Vienna	1	2
1951	Nov. 28	Wembley	2	2
1952	May 25	Vienna	3	2
wc1958	June 15	Boras	2	2
1961	May 27	Vienna	1	3
1962	April 4	Wembley	3	1
1965	Oct. 20	Wembley	2	3
1967	May 27	Vienna	1	0
1973	Sept. 26	Wembley	7	0
1979	June 13	Vienna	3	4

ENGLAND v. AUSTRALIA

			Eng	Aus
1980	May 31	Sydney	2	1
1983	June 12	Sydney	0	0
1983	June 15	Brisbane	1	0
1983	June 19	Melbourne	1	1

ENGLAND v. BELGIUM

			Eng	Belg
1921	May 21	Brussels	2	0
1923	Mar. 19	Highbury	6	1
1923	Nov. 1	Antwerp	2	2
1924	Dec. 8	West Bromwich	4	0
1926	May 24	Antwerp	5	3
1927	May 11	Brussels	9	1
1928	May 19	Antwerp	3	1
1929	May 11	Brussels	5	1
1931	May 16	Brussels	4	1
1936	May 9	Brussels	2	3
1947	Sept. 21	Brussels	5	2
1950	May 18	Brussels	4	1
1952	Nov. 26	Wembley	5	0
wc1954	June 17	Basle	4	4
1964	Oct. 21	Wembley	2	2
1970	Feb. 20	Brussels	3	1
EC1980	June 12	Turin	1	1

ENGLAND v. BOHEMIA

			Eng	Boh
1908	June 13	Prague	4	0

ENGLAND v. BRAZIL

			Eng	Brazil
1956	May 9	Wembley	4	2
wc1958	June 11	Gothenburg	0	0
1959	May 13	Rio de Janeiro	0	2
wc1962	June 10	Vina Del Mar	1	3
1963	May 8	Wembley	1	1
BJT1964	May 30	Rio de Janeiro	1	5

ENGLAND v. BRAZIL (contd)

			Goals	
Year	Date	Venue	Eng	Brazil
1969	June 12	Rio de Janeiro	1	2
wc1970	June 7	Guadalajara	0	1
USABCT1976	May 23	Los Angeles	0	1
1977	June 8	Rio de Janeiro	0	0
1978	April 19	Wembley	1	1
1981	May 12	Wembley	0	1
1984	June 10	Rio de Janeiro	2	0
RC1987	May 19	Wembley	1	1

ENGLAND v. BULGARIA

			Eng	Bulg
wc1962	June 7	Rancagua	0	0
1968	Dec. 11	Wembley	1	1
1974	June 1	Sofia	1	0
EC1979	June 6	Sofia	3	0
EC1979	Nov. 22	Wembley	2	0

ENGLAND v. CANADA

			Eng	Can
1986	May 24	Vancouver	1	0

ENGLAND v. CHILE

			Eng	Chile
wc1950	June 25	Rio de Janeiro	2	0
1953	May 24	Santiago	2	1
1984	June 17	Santiago	0	0
RC1989	May 23	Wembley	0	0

ENGLAND v. COLOMBIA

			Eng	Col
1970	May 20	Bogota	4	0
RC1988	May 24	Wembley	1	1

ENGLAND v. CYPRUS

			Eng	Cyp
EC1975	April 16	Wembley	5	0
EC1975	May 11	Limassol	1	0

ENGLAND v. CZECHOSLOVAKIA

			Eng	Czech
1934	May 16	Prague	1	2
1937	Dec. 1	Tottenham	5	4
1963	May 29	Bratislava	4	2
1966	Nov. 2	Wembley	0	0
wc1970	June 11	Guadalajara	1	0
1973	May 27	Prague	1	1
EC1974	Oct. 30	Wembley	3	0
EC1975	Oct. 30	Bratislava	1	2
1978	Nov. 29	Wembley	1	0
wc1982	June 20	Bilbao	2	0

ENGLAND v. DENMARK

			Eng	Den
1948	Sept. 26	Copenhagen	0	0
1955	Oct. 2	Copenhagen	5	1
wc1956	Dec. 5	Wolverhampton	5	2
wc1957	May 15	Copenhagen	4	1
1966	July 3	Copenhagen	2	0
EC1978	Sept. 20	Copenhagen	4	3
EC1979	Sept. 12	Wembley	1	0
EC1982	Sept. 22	Copenhagen	2	2
EC1983	Sept. 21	Wembley	0	1
1988	Sept. 14	Wembley	1	0
1989	June 7	Copenhagen	1	1

ENGLAND v. ECUADOR

Year	Date		Venue	Goals Eng	Ecua
1970	May	24	Quito	2	0

ENGLAND v. EGYPT

				Eng	Egy
1986	Jan	29	Cairo	4	0

ENGLAND v. F.I.F.A.

				Eng	FIFA
1953	Oct.	21	Wembley	4	4

ENGLAND v. FINLAND

				Eng	Fin
1937	May	20	Helsinki	8	0
1956	May	20	Helsinki	5	1
1966	June	26	Helsinki	3	0
wc1976	June	13	Helsinki	4	1
wc1976	Oct.	13	Wembley	2	1
1982	June	3	Helsinki	4	1
wc1984	Oct.	17	Wembley	5	0
wc1985	May	22	Helsinki	1	1

ENGLAND v. FRANCE

				Eng	Fr
1923	May	10	Paris	4	1
1924	May	17	Paris	3	1
1925	May	21	Paris	3	2
1927	May	26	Paris	6	0
1928	May	17	Paris	5	1
1929	May	9	Paris	4	1
1931	May	14	Paris	2	5
1933	Dec.	6	Tottenham	4	1
1938	May	26	Paris	4	2
1947	May	3	Highbury	3	0
1949	May	22	Paris	3	1
1951	Oct.	3	Highbury	2	2
1955	May	15	Paris	0	1
1957	Nov.	27	Wembley	4	0
ENC1962	Oct.	3	Sheffield	1	1
ENC1963	Feb.	27	Paris	2	5
wc1966	July	20	Wembley	2	0
1969	Mar.	12	Wembley	5	0
wc1982	June	16	Bilbao	3	1
1984	Feb.	29	Paris	0	2

ENGLAND v. GERMANY D.R.

				Eng	D.R.
1963	June	2	Leipzig	2	1
1970	Nov.	25	Wembley	3	1
1974	May	29	Leipzig	1	1
1984	Sept.	12	Wembley	1	0

ENGLAND v. GERMANY F.R.

				Eng	F.R.
1930	May	10	Berlin	3	3
1935	Dec.	4	Tottenham	3	0
1938	May	14	Berlin	6	3
1954	Dec.	1	Wembley	3	1
1956	May	26	Berlin	3	1
1965	May	12	Nuremberg	1	0
1966	Feb.	23	Wembley	1	0
wc1966	July	30	Wembley	4	2
1968	June	1	Hanover	0	1
wc1970	June	14	Leon	2	3
EC1972	April	29	Wembley	1	3
EC1972	May	13	Berlin	0	0
1975	Mar.	12	Wembley	2	0
1978	Feb.	22	Munich	1	2
wc1982	June	29	Madrid	0	0
1982	Oct.	13	Wembley	1	2
1985	June	12	Mexico City	3	0
1987	Sept.	9	Düsseldorf	1	3

ENGLAND v. GREECE

Year	Date		Venue	Goals Eng	Gr
EC1971	April	21	Wembley	3	0
EC1971	Dec.	1	Athens	2	0
EC1982	Nov.	17	Salonika	3	0
EC1983	Mar.	30	Wembley	0	0
1989	Feb.	8	Athens	2	1

ENGLAND v. HUNGARY

				Eng	Hun
1908	June	10	Budapest	7	0
1909	May	29	Budapest	4	2
1909	May	31	Budapest	8	2
1934	May	10	Budapest	1	2
1936	Dec.	2	Highbury	6	2
1953	Nov.	25	Wembley	3	6
1954	May	23	Budapest	1	7
1960	May	22	Budapest	0	2
wc1962	May	31	Rancagua	1	2
1965	May	5	Wembley	1	0
1978	May	24	Wembley	4	1
wc1981	June	6	Budapest	3	1
wc1981	Nov.	18	Wembley	1	0
EC1983	Apr.	27	Wembley	2	0
EC1983	Oct.	12	Budapest	3	0
1988	Apr.	27	Budapest	0	0

ENGLAND v. ICELAND

				Eng	Ice
1982	June	2	Reykjavik	1	1

ENGLAND v. IRELAND

				Eng	Ire
1882	Feb.	18	Belfast	13	0
1883	Feb.	24	Liverpool	7	0
1884	Feb.	23	Belfast	8	1
1885	Feb.	28	Manchester	4	0
1886	Mar.	13	Belfast	6	1
1887	Feb.	5	Sheffield	7	0
1888	Mar.	31	Belfast	5	1
1889	Mar.	2	Everton	6	1
1890	Mar.	15	Belfast	9	1
1891	Mar.	7	Wolverhampton	6	1
1892	Mar.	5	Belfast	2	0
1893	Feb.	25	Birmingham	6	1
1894	Mar.	3	Belfast	2	2
1895	Mar.	9	Derby	9	0
1896	Mar.	7	Belfast	2	0
1897	Feb.	20	Nottingham	6	0
1898	Mar.	5	Belfast	3	2
1899	Feb.	18	Sunderland	13	2
1900	Mar.	17	Dublin	2	0
1901	Mar.	9	Southampton	3	0
1902	Mar.	22	Belfast	1	0
1903	Feb.	14	Wolverhampton	4	0
1904	Mar.	12	Belfast	3	1
1905	Feb.	25	Middlesborough	1	1
1906	Feb.	17	Belfast	5	0
1907	Feb.	16	Everton	1	0
1908	Feb.	15	Belfast	3	1
1909	Feb.	13	Bradford	4	0
1910	Feb.	12	Belfast	1	1
1911	Feb.	11	Derby	2	1
1912	Feb.	10	Dublin	6	1
1913	Feb.	15	Belfast	1	2
1914	Feb.	14	Middlesborough	0	3
1919	Oct.	25	Belfast	1	1
1920	Oct.	23	Sunderland	2	0
1921	Oct.	22	Belfast	1	1
1922	Oct.	21	West Bromwich	2	0
1923	Oct.	20	Belfast	1	2
1924	Oct.	22	Everton	3	1
1925	Oct.	24	Belfast	0	0
1926	Oct.	20	Liverpool	3	3
1927	Oct.	22	Belfast	0	2
1928	Oct.	22	Everton	2	1
1929	Oct.	19	Belfast	3	0
1930	Oct.	20	Sheffield	5	1

ENGLAND v. IRELAND *(contd)*

				Goals	
Year	Date		Venue	Eng	Ire
1931	Oct.	17	Belfast	6	2
1932	Oct.	17	Blackpool	1	0
1933	Oct.	14	Belfast	3	0
1935	Feb.	6	Everton	2	1
1935	Oct.	19	Belfast	3	1
1936	Nov.	18	Stoke	3	1
1937	Oct.	23	Belfast	5	1
1938	Nov.	16	Manchester	7	0
1946	Sept.	28	Belfast	7	2
1947	Nov.	5	Everton	2	2
1949	Oct.	9	Belfast	6	2
wc1949	Nov.	16	Manchester	9	2
1950	Oct.	7	Belfast	4	1
1951	Nov.	14	Aston Villa	2	0
1952	Oct.	4	Belfast	2	2
wc1953	Nov.	11	Liverpool	3	1
1954	Oct.	2	Belfast	2	0
1955	Nov.	2	Wembley	3	0
1956	Oct.	6	Belfast	1	1
1957	Nov.	6	Wembley	2	3
1958	Oct.	4	Belfast	3	3
1959	Nov.	18	Wembley	2	1
1960	Oct.	8	Belfast	5	2
1961	Nov.	22	Wembley	1	1
1962	Oct.	20	Belfast	3	1
1963	Nov.	20	Wembley	8	3
1964	Oct.	3	Belfast	4	3
1965	Nov.	10	Wembley	2	1
ec1966	Oct.	22	Belfast	2	0
ec1967	Nov.	22	Wembley	2	0
1969	May	3	Belfast	3	1
1970	April	21	Wembley	3	1
1971	May	15	Belfast	1	0
1972	May	23	Wembley	0	1
1973	May	12	Everton	2	1
1974	May	15	Wembley	1	0
1975	May	17	Belfast	0	0
1976	May	11	Wembley	4	0
1977	May	28	Belfast	2	1
1978	May	16	Wembley	1	0
ec1979	Feb.	7	Wembley	4	0
1979	May	19	Belfast	2	0
ec1979	Oct.	17	Belfast	5	1
1980	May	20	Wembley	1	1
1982	Feb.	23	Wembley	4	0
1983	May	28	Belfast	0	0
1984	April	4	Wembley	1	0
wc1985	Feb.	27	Belfast	1	0
wc1985	Nov.	13	Wembley	0	0
ec1986	Oct.	15	Wembley	3	0
ec1987	Apr.	1	Belfast	2	0

ENGLAND v. REPUBLIC OF IRELAND

				Eng	Rep of Ire
1946	Sept.	30	Dublin	1	0
1949	Sept.	21	Everton	0	2
wc1957	May	8	Wembley	5	1
wc1957	May	19	Dublin	1	1
1964	May	24	Dublin	3	1
1976	Sept.	8	Wembley	1	1
ec1978	Oct.	25	Dublin	1	1
ec1980	Feb.	6	Wembley	2	0
1985	Mar.	26	Wembley	2	1
ec1988	June	12	Stuttgart	0	1

ENGLAND v. ISRAEL

				Eng	Isr
1986	Feb.	26	Tel Aviv	2	1
1988	Feb.	17	Tel Aviv	0	0

ENGLAND v. ITALY

				Goals	
Year	Date		Venue	Eng	Italy
1933	May	13	Rome	1	1
1934	Nov.	14	Highbury	3	2
1939	May	13	Milan	2	2
1948	May	16	Turin	4	0
1949	Nov.	30	Tottenham	2	0
1952	May	18	Florence	1	1
1959	May	6	Wembley	2	2
1961	May	24	Rome	3	2
1973	June	14	Turin	0	2
1973	Nov.	14	Wembley	0	1
usabct1976	May	28	New York	3	2
wc1976	Nov.	17	Rome	0	2
wc1977	Nov.	16	Wembley	2	0
ec1980	June	15	Turin	0	1
1985	June	6	Mexico City	1	2

ENGLAND v. KUWAIT

				Eng	Kuw
wc1982	June	25	Bilbao	1	0

ENGLAND v. LUXEMBOURG

				Eng	Lux
1927	May	21	Luxembourg	5	2
wc1960	Oct.	19	Luxembourg	9	0
wc1961	Sept.	28	Highbury	4	1
wc1977	Mar.	30	Wembley	5	0
wc1977	Oct.	12	Luxembourg	2	0
ec1982	Dec.	15	Wembley	9	0
ec1983	Nov.	16	Luxembourg	4	0

ENGLAND v. MALTA

				Eng	Malta
ec1971	Feb.	3	Valletta	1	0
ec1971	May	12	Wembley	5	0

ENGLAND v. MEXICO

				Eng	Mex
1959	May	24	Mexico City	1	2
1961	May	10	Wembley	8	0
wc1966	July	16	Wembley	2	0
1969	June	1	Mexico City	0	0
1985	June	9	Mexico City	0	1
1986	May	17	Los Angeles	3	0

ENGLAND v. MOROCCO

				Eng	Mor
wc1986	June	6	Monterrey	0	0

ENGLAND v. NETHERLANDS

				Eng	Neth
1935	May	18	Amsterdam	1	0
1946	Nov.	27	Huddersfield	8	2
1964	Dec.	9	Amsterdam	1	1
1969	Nov.	5	Amsterdam	1	0
1970	Jan.	14	Wembley	0	0
1977	Feb.	9	Wembley	0	2
1982	May	25	Wembley	2	0
1988	Mar.	23	Wembley	2	2
ec1988	June	15	Düsseldorf	1	3

ENGLAND v. NORWAY

				Eng	Nor
1937	May	14	Oslo	6	0
1938	Nov.	9	Newcastle	4	0
1949	May	18	Oslo	4	1
1966	June	29	Oslo	6	1
wc1980	Sept.	10	Wembley	4	0
wc1981	Sept.	9	Oslo	1	2

ENGLAND v. PARAGUAY

				Goals	
Year	Date		Venue	Eng	Par
wc1986	June	18	Mexico City	3	0

ENGLAND v. PERU

				Eng	Peru
1959	May	17	Lima	1	4
1962	May	20	Lima	4	0

ENGLAND v. POLAND

				Eng	Pol
1966	Jan	5	Everton	1	1
1966	July	5	Chorzow	1	0
wc1973	June	6	Chorzow	0	2
wc1973	Oct.	17	Wembley	1	1
wc1986	June	11	Monterrey	3	0
wc1989	June	3	Wembley	3	0

ENGLAND v. PORTUGAL

				Eng	Port
1947	May	25	Lisbon	10	0
1950	May	14	Lisbon	5	3
1951	May	19	Everton	5	2
1955	May	22	Oporto	1	3
1958	May	7	Wembley	2	1
wc1961	May	21	Lisbon	1	1
wc1961	Oct.	25	Wembley	2	0
1964	May	17	Lisbon	4	3
BJT1964	June	4	Sao Paulo	1	1
wc1966	July	26	Wembley	2	1
1969	Dec.	10	Wembley	1	0
1974	April	3	Lisbon	0	0
EC1974	Nov.	20	Wembley	0	0
EC1975	Nov.	19	Lisbon	1	1
wc1986	June	3	Monterrey	0	1

ENGLAND v. REST OF EUROPE

				Eng	RoE
1938	Oct.	26	Highbury	3	0

ENGLAND v. REST OF THE WORLD

				Eng	RoW
1963	Oct.	23	Wembley	2	1

ENGLAND v. RUMANIA

				Eng	Rum
1939	May	24	Bucharest	2	0
1968	Nov.	6	Bucharest	0	0
1969	Jan.	15	Wembley	1	1
wc1970	June	2	Guadalajara	1	0
wc1980	Oct.	15	Bucharest	1	2
wc1981	April	29	Wembley	0	0
wc1985	May	1	Bucharest	0	0
wc1985	Sept.	11	Wembley	1	1

ENGLAND v. SAUDI ARABIA

				Eng	Saud
1986	Nov	16	Riyadh	1	1

ENGLAND v. SCOTLAND

				Eng	Scot
1872	Nov.	30	Glasgow	0	0
1873	Mar.	8	Kennington Oval	4	2
1874	Mar.	7	Glasgow	1	2
1875	Mar.	6	Kennington Oval	2	2
1876	Mar.	4	Glasgow	0	3
1877	Mar.	3	Kennington Oval	1	3
1878	Mar.	2	Glasgow	2	7
1879	April	5	Kennington Oval	5	4
1880	Mar.	13	Glasgow	4	5
1881	Mar.	12	Kennington Oval	1	6
1882	Mar.	11	Glasgow	1	5
1883	Mar.	10	Sheffield	2	3
1884	Mar.	15	Glasgow	0	1
1885	Mar.	21	Kennington Oval	1	1

ENGLAND v. SCOTLAND *(contd)*

				Eng	Scot
1886	Mar.	31	Glasgow	1	1
1887	Mar.	19	Blackburn	2	3
1888	Mar.	17	Glasgow	5	0
1889	April	13	Kennington Oval	2	3
1890	April	5	Glasgow	1	1
1891	April	6	Blackburn	2	1
1892	April	2	Glasgow	4	1
1893	April	1	Richmond	5	2
1894	April	7	Glasgow	2	2
1895	April	6	Everton	3	0
1896	April	4	Glasgow	1	2
1897	April	3	Crystal Palace	1	2
1898	April	2	Glasgow	3	1
1899	April	8	Birmingham	2	1
1900	April	7	Glasgow	1	4
1901	Mar.	30	Crystal Palace	2	2
1902	Mar.	3	Birmingham	2	2
1903	April	4	Sheffield	1	2
1904	April	9	Glasgow	1	0
1905	April	1	Crystal Palace	1	0
1906	April	7	Glasgow	1	2
1907	April	6	Newcastle	1	1
1908	April	4	Glasgow	1	1
1909	April	3	Crystal Palace	2	0
1910	April	2	Glasgow	0	2
1911	April	1	Everton	1	1
1912	Mar.	23	Glasgow	1	1
1913	April	5	Chelsea	1	0
1914	April	14	Glasgow	1	3
1920	April	10	Sheffield	5	4
1921	April	9	Glasgow	0	3
1922	April	8	Aston Villa	0	1
1923	April	14	Glasgow	2	2
1924	April	12	Wembley	1	1
1925	April	4	Glasgow	0	2
1926	April	17	Manchester	0	1
1927	April	2	Glasgow	2	1
1928	Mar.	31	Wembley	1	5
1929	April	13	Glasgow	0	1
1930	April	5	Wembley	5	2
1931	Mar.	28	Glasgow	0	2
1932	April	9	Wembley	3	0
1933	April	1	Glasgow	1	2
1934	April	14	Wembley	3	0
1935	April	6	Glasgow	0	2
1936	April	4	Wembley	1	1
1937	April	17	Glasgow	1	3
1938	April	9	Wembley	0	1
1939	April	15	Glasgow	2	1
1947	April	12	Wembley	1	1
1948	April	10	Glasgow	2	0
1949	April	9	Wembley	1	3
wc1950	April	15	Glasgow	1	0
1951	April	14	Wembley	2	3
1952	April	5	Glasgow	2	1
1953	April	18	Wembley	2	2
wc1954	April	3	Glasgow	4	2
1955	April	2	Wembley	7	2
1956	April	14	Glasgow	1	1
1957	April	6	Wembley	2	1
1958	April	19	Glasgow	4	0
1959	April	11	Wembley	1	0
1960	April	9	Glasgow	1	1
1961	April	15	Wembley	9	3
1962	April	14	Glasgow	0	2
1963	April	6	Wembley	1	2
1964	April	11	Glasgow	0	1
1965	April	10	Wembley	2	2
1966	April	2	Glasgow	4	3
EC1967	April	15	Wembley	2	3
EC1968	Feb.	24	Glasgow	1	1
1969	May	10	Wembley	4	1
1970	April	25	Glasgow	0	0
1971	May	22	Wembley	3	1
1972	May	27	Glasgow	1	0
SFAC1973	Feb.	14	Glasgow	5	0
1973	May	19	Wembley	1	0

76

ENGLAND v. SCOTLAND *(contd)*

Year	Date		Venue	Eng	Scot
1974	May	18	Glasgow	0	2
1975	May	24	Wembley	5	1
1976	May	15	Glasgow	1	2
1977	June	4	Wembley	1	2
1978	May	20	Glasgow	1	0
1979	May	26	Wembley	3	1
1980	May	24	Glasgow	2	0
1981	May	23	Wembley	0	1
1982	May	29	Glasgow	1	0
1983	June	1	Wembley	2	0
1984	May	26	Glasgow	1	1
RC1985	May	25	Glasgow	0	1
RC1986	April	23	Wembley	2	1
RC1987	May	23	Glasgow	0	0
RC1988	May	21	Wembley	1	0
RC1989	May	27	Glasgow	2	0

ENGLAND v. SPAIN

				Eng	Spain
1929	May	15	Madrid	3	4
1931	Dec.	9	Highbury	7	1
wc1950	July	2	Rio de Janeiro	0	1
1955	May	18	Madrid	1	1
1955	Nov.	30	Wembley	4	1
1960	May	15	Madrid	0	3
1960	Oct.	26	Wembley	4	2
1965	Dec.	8	Madrid	2	0
1967	May	24	Wembley	2	0
EC1968	April	3	Wembley	1	0
EC1968	May	8	Madrid	2	1
1980	Mar.	26	Barcelona	2	0
EC1980	June	18	Naples	2	1
1981	Mar.	25	Wembley	1	2
wc1982	July	5	Madrid	0	0
1987	Feb.	18	Madrid	4	2

ENGLAND v. SWEDEN

				Eng	Swe
1923	May	21	Stockholm	4	2
1923	May	24	Stockholm	3	1
1937	May	17	Stockholm	4	0
1947	Nov.	19	Highbury	4	2
1949	May	13	Stockholm	1	3
1956	May	16	Stockholm	0	0
1959	Oct.	28	Wembley	2	3
1965	May	16	Gothenburg	2	1
1968	May	22	Wembley	3	1
1979	June	10	Stockholm	0	0
1986	Sept.	10	Stockholm	0	1
wc1988	Oct.	19	Wembley	0	0

ENGLAND v. SWITZERLAND

				Eng	Swit
1933	May	29	Berne	4	0
1938	May	21	Zurich	1	2
1947	May	18	Zurich	0	1
1948	Dec.	2	Highbury	6	0
1952	May	28	Zurich	3	0
wc1954	June	20	Berne	2	0
1962	May	9	Wembley	3	1
1963	June	5	Basle	8	1
EC1971	Oct.	13	Basle	3	2
EC1971	Nov.	10	Wembley	1	1
1975	Sept.	3	Basle	2	1
1977	Sept.	7	Wembley	0	0
wc1980	Nov.	19	Wembley	2	1
wc1981	May	30	Basle	1	2
1988	May	28	Lausanne	1	0

ENGLAND v. TURKEY

				Eng	Turk
wc1984	Nov.	14	Istanbul	8	0
wc1985	Oct.	16	Wembley	5	0
EC1987	Apr.	29	Izmir	0	0
EC1987	Oct.	14	Wembley	8	0

ENGLAND v. U.S.A.

Year	Date		Venue	Eng	USA
wc1950	June	20	Belo Horizonte	0	1
1953	June	8	New York	6	3
1959	May	28	Los Angeles	8	1
1964	May	27	New York	10	0
1985	June	16	Los Angeles	5	0

ENGLAND v. U.S.S.R.

				Eng	USSR
1958	May	18	Moscow	1	1
wc1958	June	8	Gothenburg	2	2
wc1958	June	17	Gothenburg	0	1
1958	Oct.	22	Wembley	5	0
1967	Dec.	6	Wembley	2	2
EC1968	June	8	Rome	2	0
1973	June	10	Moscow	2	1
1984	June	2	Wembley	0	2
1986	Mar.	26	Tbilisi	1	0
EC1988	June	18	Frankfurt	1	3

ENGLAND v. URUGUAY

				Eng	Uru
1953	May	31	Montevideo	1	2
wc1954	June	26	Basle	2	4
1964	May	6	Wembley	2	1
wc1966	July	11	Wembley	0	0
1969	June	8	Montevideo	2	1
1977	June	15	Montevideo	0	0
1984	June	13	Montevideo	0	2

ENGLAND v. WALES

				Eng	Wales
1879	Jan.	18	Kennington Oval	2	1
1880	Mar.	15	Wrexham	3	2
1881	Feb.	26	Blackburn	0	1
1882	Mar.	13	Wrexham	3	5
1883	Feb.	3	Kennington Oval	5	0
1884	Mar.	17	Wrexham	4	0
1885	Mar.	14	Blackburn	1	1
1886	Mar.	29	Wrexham	3	1
1887	Feb.	26	Kennington Oval	4	0
1888	Feb.	4	Crewe	5	1
1889	Feb.	23	Stoke	4	1
1890	Mar.	15	Wrexham	3	1
1891	Mar.	7	Sunderland	4	1
1892	Mar.	5	Wrexham	2	0
1893	Mar.	13	Stoke	6	0
1894	Mar.	12	Wrexham	5	1
1895	Mar.	18	Queen's Club, Kensington	1	1
1896	Mar.	16	Cardiff	9	1
1897	Mar.	29	Sheffield	4	0
1898	Mar.	28	Wrexham	3	0
1899	Mar.	20	Bristol	4	0
1900	Mar.	26	Cardiff	1	1
1901	Mar.	18	Newcastle	6	0
1902	Mar.	3	Wrexham	0	0
1903	Mar.	2	Portsmouth	2	1
1904	Feb.	29	Wrexham	2	2
1905	Mar.	27	Liverpool	3	1
1906	Mar.	19	Cardiff	1	0
1907	Mar.	18	Fulham	1	1
1908	Mar.	16	Wrexham	7	1
1909	Mar.	15	Nottingham	2	0
1910	Mar.	14	Cardiff	1	0
1911	Mar.	13	Millwall	3	0
1912	Mar.	11	Wrexham	2	0
1913	Mar.	17	Bristol	4	3
1914	Mar.	16	Cardiff	2	0
1920	Mar.	15	Highbury	1	2
1921	Mar.	14	Cardiff	0	0
1922	Mar.	13	Liverpool	1	0
1923	Mar.	5	Cardiff	2	2
1924	Mar.	3	Blackburn	1	2
1925	Feb.	28	Swansea	2	1
1926	Mar.	1	Crystal Palace	1	3

77

ENGLAND v. WALES *(contd)*

Year	Date		Venue	Goals Eng	Wales
1927	Feb.	12	Wrexham	3	3
1927	Nov.	28	Burnley	1	2
1928	Nov.	17	Swansea	3	2
1929	Nov.	20	Chelsea	6	0
1930	Nov.	22	Wrexham	4	0
1931	Nov.	18	Liverpool	3	1
1932	Nov.	16	Wrexham	0	0
1933	Nov.	15	Newcastle	1	2
1934	Sept.	29	Cardiff	4	0
1936	Feb.	5	Wolverhampton	1	2
1936	Oct.	17	Cardiff	1	2
1937	Nov.	17	Middlesborough	2	1
1938	Oct.	22	Cardiff	2	4
1946	Nov.	13	Manchester	3	0
1947	Oct.	18	Cardiff	3	0
1948	Nov.	10	Aston Villa	1	0
wc1949	Oct.	15	Cardiff	4	1
1950	Nov.	15	Sunderland	4	2
1951	Oct.	20	Cardiff	1	1
1952	Nov.	12	Wembley	5	2
wc1953	Oct.	10	Cardiff	4	1
1954	Nov.	10	Wembley	3	2
1955	Oct.	22	Cardiff	1	2
1956	Nov.	14	Wembley	3	1
1957	Oct.	19	Cardiff	4	0
1958	Nov.	26	Aston Villa	2	2
1959	Oct.	17	Cardiff	1	1
1960	Nov.	23	Wembley	5	1
1961	Oct.	14	Cardiff	1	1
1962	Nov.	21	Wembley	4	0
1963	Oct.	12	Cardiff	4	0
1964	Nov.	18	Wembley	2	1
1965	Oct.	2	Cardiff	0	0
EC1966	Nov.	16	Wembley	5	1
EC1967	Oct.	21	Cardiff	3	0
1969	May	7	Wembley	2	1

ENGLAND v. WALES *(contd)*

Year	Date		Venue	Goals Eng	Wales
1970	April	18	Cardiff	1	1
1971	May	19	Wembley	0	0
1972	May	20	Cardiff	3	0
wc1972	Nov.	15	Cardiff	1	0
wc1973	Jan.	24	Wembley	1	1
1973	May	15	Wembley	3	0
1974	May	11	Cardiff	2	0
1975	May	21	Wembley	2	2
FAWC1976	Mar.	24	Wrexham	2	1
1976	May	8	Cardiff	1	0
1977	May	31	Wembley	0	1
1978	May	13	Cardiff	3	1
1979	May	23	Wembley	0	0
1980	May	17	Wrexham	1	4
1981	May	20	Wembley	0	0
1982	April	27	Cardiff	1	0
1983	Feb.	23	Wembley	2	1
1984	May	2	Wrexham	0	1

ENGLAND v. YUGOSLAVIA

Year	Date		Venue	Eng	Yugo
1939	May	18	Belgrade	1	2
1950	Nov.	22	Highbury	2	2
1954	May	16	Belgrade	0	1
1956	Nov.	28	Wembley	3	0
1958	May	11	Belgrade	0	5
1960	May	11	Wembley	3	3
1965	May	9	Belgrade	1	1
1966	May	4	Wembley	2	0
EC1968	June	5	Florence	0	1
1972	Oct.	11	Wembley	1	1
1974	June	5	Belgrade	2	2
EC1986	Nov.	12	Wembley	2	0
EC1987	Nov.	11	Belgrade	4	1

Giant Killers

Football "Giant Killers" were in the news again during Season 1988-89 as Sutton United of the GM Vauxhall Conference defeated First Division Coventry City 2-1 at the former's Gander Green Lane ground in the third round of the F.A. Challenge Cup. Barry Williams' team thereby became the sixth from outside the League to beat First Division opponents since the last war. The others were: Colchester United (1-0 v Huddersfield Town in 1948), Yeovil Town (2-1 v Sunderland in 1949), Hereford United (2-1 v Newcastle United in 1972), Wimbledon (1-0 v Burnley in 1975) and Altrincham (2-1 v Birmingham City in 1986).

It is this type of match which affords the chance of the most genuine "giant-killing" act, and the "giants" of Liverpool, Manchester United, Arsenal and the like enter the Challenge Cup at their peril. They are there to be shot down by the "minnows" and it is this which, in part, gives the competition its special appeal. But most levels of football have their relative "giants" and so many "giant-killing" feats receive little or no publicity. One match which certainly should have hit the headlines took place on the evening of 24th March 1971 – at Wembley Stadium of all places!

A Great Britain team has not played in the Olympic football finals since 1960. The team failed to make the finals in Tokyo (1964) and Mexico City (1968), as qualifying matches became more and more difficult with even the smallest footballing nations taking the game and its preparations more seriously than ever. Britain once again received a difficult draw as they attempted to qualify for Munich four years later. Bulgaria had been silver medallists in Mexico and, because there were officially no full-time professional players in their country, they would be bringing their full international team to Wembley.

On paper, Britain had no chance against such highly experienced visitors, although anyone who had followed the preparations organised for the British party by team manager Charles Hughes must have been impressed by the team's performances.

The results of the trial matches, played against professional clubs, testified to the quality of a British

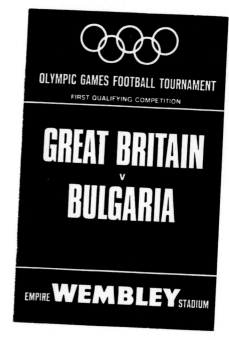

OLYMPIC GAMES FOOTBALL TOURNAMENT
FIRST QUALIFYING COMPETITION

GREAT BRITAIN
v
BULGARIA

EMPIRE **WEMBLEY** STADIUM

team which played attractive and progressive football. Perhaps the highlight of these matches was the outstanding display given at Southampton, when six First Division regulars were included in the home side that was soundly beaten 4-0.

So the best amateur representative side seen in Britain prepared to do battle with the accomplished Bulgarians. The visitors were in for a few shocks even before the day of the match. They had assumed that a crowd of some 70-80,000 would be present to watch the match at Wembley and that the British team would include the likes of Gordon Banks, Bobby Moore and Geoff Hurst.

The team which actually took the field was as follows: John Swannell (Hendon), Paul Fuschillo (Wycombe), Bill Currie (Albion Rovers), Ted Powell (Wycombe), Derek Gamblin (Leatherhead), John Payne (Enfield), Roger Day (Slough), Rod Haider (Hendon), Peter Hardcastle (Skelmersdale), Ken Gray (Enfield) and Joe Adams (Slough).

Thanks to their clubs' training schedules, and the special coaching sessions adopted by their manager, this British side was fitter and more tactically aware than any of its predecessors. But they were now up against the best footballers in Bulgaria, their First Division stars who had played in the World Cup, and surely it would be a case of lambs to the slaughter. An equivalent match today might have the England semi-professional team – with players from clubs like Maidstone, Telford and Runcorn – taking on Franz Beckenbauer's West Germany.

On a dismally wet evening, about 2,000 people lost in the Wembley stands saw the impossible happen. Skipper Ted Powell was everywhere, prompting and encouraging his troops, and Joe Adams' 15th-minute header won the match for Britain.

The World Cup tournament, and international football in general, has produced its share of staggering results over the years – as one would expect. Particularly memorable have been England's defeat against the American part-timers in Belo Horizonte in 1950 (the 1-0 scoreline was originally taken to be a mis-print), North Korea's humiliation of Italy in 1966 and Algeria's victory over West Germany in 1982. But these upsets were achieved by full international teams, in matches where teams of the same level were playing each other. What made Britain's Wembley win so remarkable was the fact that they beat a team of a much higher level. It has to go down as one of the greatest "giant-killings" in football history.

If you have an inquiry about Cellphones, ask us. The Japanese did.

THE CELLPHONE NETWORK

To find out more call 0800 424 323.

AFTER A GAME
OF TWO HALVES

THERE'S NO SUBSTITUTE

TENNENT'S ARE PROUD TO SPONSOR THE F.A. CHARITY SHIELD.

ANOTHER WINNER FROM LUTON TOWN.

THE NEW VAUXHALL CAVALIER

 VAUXHALL. ONCE DRIVEN, FOREVER SMITTEN.

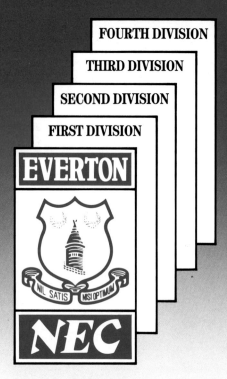

F.A. Charity Shield Winners 1908–88

Year	Winners	Runners-up	Score
1908	Manchester United	Queen's Park Rangers	4-0 after 1-1 draw
1909	Newcastle United	Northampton Town	2-0
1910	Brighton and Hove Albion	Aston Villa	1-0
1911	Manchester United	Swindon Town	8-4
1912	Blackburn Rovers	Queen's Park Rangers	2-1
1913	Professionals	Amateurs	7-2
1920	West Bromwich Albion	Tottenham Hotspur	2-0
1921	Tottenham Hotspur	Burnley	2-0
1922	Huddersfield Town	Liverpool	1-0
1923	Professionals	Amateurs	2-0
1924	Professionals	Amateurs	3-1
1925	Amateurs	Professionals	6-1
1926	Amateurs	Professionals	6-3
1927	Cardiff City	Corinthians	2-1
1928	Everton	Blackburn Rovers	2-1
1929	Professionals	Amateurs	3-0
1930	Arsenal	Sheffield Wednesday	2-1
1931	Arsenal	West Bromwich Albion	1-0
1932	Everton	Newcastle United	5-3
1933	Arsenal	Everton	3-0
1934	Arsenal	Manchester City	4-0
1935	Sheffield Wednesday	Arsenal	1-0
1936	Sunderland	Arsenal	2-1
1937	Manchester City	Sunderland	2-0
1938	Arsenal	Preston North End	2-1
1948	Arsenal	Manchester United	4-3
1949	Portsmouth	Wolverhampton Wanderers	1-1*
1950	World Cup Team	Canadian Touring Team	4-2
1951	Tottenham Hotspur	Newcastle United	2-1
1952	Manchester United	Newcastle United	4-2
1953	Arsenal	Blackpool	3-1
1954	Wolverhampton Wanderers	West Bromwich Albion	4-4*
1955	Chelsea	Newcastle United	3-0
1956	Manchester United	Manchester City	1-0
1957	Manchester United	Aston Villa	4-0
1958	Bolton Wanderers	Wolverhampton Wanderers	4-1
1959	Wolverhampton Wanderers	Nottingham Forest	3-1
1960	Burnley	Wolverhampton Wanderers	2-2*
1961	Tottenham Hotspur	F.A. XI	3-2
1962	Tottenham Hotspur	Ipswich Town	5-1
1963	Everton	Manchester United	4-0
1964	Liverpool	West Ham United	2-2*
1965	Manchester United	Liverpool	2-2*
1966	Liverpool	Everton	1-0
1967	Manchester United	Tottenham Hotspur	3-3*
1968	Manchester City	West Bromwich Albion	6-1
1969	Leeds United	Manchester City	2-1
1970	Everton	Chelsea	2-1
1971	Leicester City	Liverpool	1-0
1972	Manchester City	Aston Villa	1-0
1973	Burnley	Manchester City	1-0
1974	Liverpool	Leeds United	1-1†
1975	Derby County	West Ham United	2-0
1976	Liverpool	Southampton	1-0
1977	Liverpool	Manchester United	0-0*
1978	Nottingham Forest	Ipswich Town	5-0
1979	Liverpool	Arsenal	3-1
1980	Liverpool	West Ham United	1-0
1981	Aston Villa	Tottenham Hotspur	2-2*
1982	Liverpool	Tottenham Hotspur	1-0
1983	Manchester United	Liverpool	2-0
1984	Everton	Liverpool	1-0
1985	Everton	Manchester United	2-0
1986	Everton	Liverpool	1-1*
1987	Everton	Coventry City	1-0
1988	Liverpool	Wimbledon	2-1

* Each Club retained Shield for six months
† Liverpool won 6-5 on penalty-kicks

F.A. Charity Shield 1988

Liverpool 2 Wimbledon 1

Liverpool, League champions for a record seventeenth time, edged out Wimbledon, romantic F.A. Cup winners three months earlier, in the annual curtain-raiser to the new season at Wembley on 20th August. Liverpool's 2-1 victory in a repeat of the Cup Final was watched by 54,000 fans.

With only six of Wimbledon's Cup-winning team on parade, and former captain and goalkeeper Beasant, the heroic saver of a penalty from Aldridge, watching from the stands with his former Plough Lane (then Newcastle) team-mate Thorn, the prospects of a repeat performance from Bobby Gould's team did not look bright. Yet the Merseysiders, though their revenge mission proved ultimately successful, were far from outclassing their opponents. In fact, Wimbledon were close to equalising towards the end when Grobbelaar was almost bowled over backwards by the force of Cawley's shot.

Liverpool were without their influential skipper Hansen (who was not expected to play again for at least two months after injuring a knee pre-season in Spain), but they started the Charity Shield match as if they wanted to beat the opposition into submission as quickly as possible. Beasant's replacement Tracey, playing in only his second first team match, leapt acrobatically to keep out Barnes' effort for an early confidence-booster and then set up John Fashanu's 18th-minute headed goal with a well-controlled clearance upfield.

It was John Aldridge, who had finished the Cup Final a very unhappy man, who scored a brace to win the Shield for Liverpool. His place in their attack had been thought to be at risk, following the sensational return of Ian Rush from Italy, but he put paid to some of the doubts with smartly-taken goals in the 23rd and 69th minutes.

Liverpool have now featured in ten Charity Shield matches since the fixture was brought to Wembley on Ted Croker's initiative in 1974.

Liverpool: Grobbelaar, Gillespie, Venison, Ablett, Whelan, Watson, Beardsley, Aldridge, Houghton, Barnes, McMahon.

Wimbledon: Tracey, Scales (Clement), Phelan, Ryan, Young, Cawley, Gibson, Fairweather, Fashanu (Turner), Sanchez, Wise.

Referee: J. Martin of Alton.

Winning captain Ronnie Whelan holds the Shield.

F.A. Challenge Cup Winners 1872-1989

1872 & 1874-92	Kennington Oval
1873	Lillie Bridge
1893	Fallowfield, Manchester
1894	Everton
1895-1914	Crystal Palace
1915	Old Trafford, Manchester
1920-22	Stamford Bridge
1923 to date	Wembley

Year	Winners	Runners-up	Score
1872	Wanderers	Royal Engineers	1-0
1873	Wanderers	Oxford University	2-0
1874	Oxford University	Royal Engineers	2-0
1875	Royal Engineers	Old Etonians	2-0 after 1-1 draw
1876	Wanderers	Old Etonians	3-0 after 0-0 draw
1877	Wanderers	Oxford University	2-0 after extra time
1878	*Wanderers	Royal Engineers	3-1
1879	Old Etonians	Clapham Rovers	1-0
1880	Clapham Rovers	Oxford University	1-0
1881	Old Carthusians	Old Etonians	3-0
1882	Old Etonians	Blackburn Rovers	1-0
1883	Blackburn Olympic	Old Etonians	2-1 after extra time
1884	Blackburn Rovers	Queen's Park, Glasgow	2-1
1885	Blackburn Rovers	Queen's Park, Glasgow	2-0
1886	†Blackburn Rovers	West Bromwich Albion	2-0 after 0-0 draw
1887	Aston Villa	West Bromwich Albion	2-0
1888	West Bromwich Albion	Preston North End	2-1
1889	Preston North End	Wolverhampton Wanderers	3-0
1890	Blackburn Rovers	Sheffield Wednesday	6-1
1891	Blackburn Rovers	Notts. County	3-1
1892	West Bromwich Albion	Aston Villa	3-0
1893	Wolverhampton Wanderers	Everton	1-0
1894	Notts. County	Bolton Wanderers	4-1
1895	Aston Villa	West Bromwich Albion	1-0
1896	Sheffield Wednesday	Wolverhampton Wanderers	2-1
1897	Aston Villa	Everton	3-2
1898	Nottingham Forest	Derby County	3-1
1899	Sheffield United	Derby County	4-1
1900	Bury	Southampton	4-0
1901	Tottenham Hotspur	Sheffield United	3-1 after 2-2 draw
1902	Sheffield United	Southampton	2-1 after 1-1 draw
1903	Bury	Derby County	6-0
1904	Manchester City	Bolton Wanderers	1-0
1905	Aston Villa	Newcastle United	2-0
1906	Everton	Newcastle United	1-0
1907	Sheffield Wednesday	Everton	2-1
1908	Wolverhampton Wanderers	Newcastle United	3-1
1909	Manchester United	Bristol City	1-0
1910	Newcastle United	Barnsley	2-0 after 1-1 draw
1911	Bradford City	Newcastle United	1-0 after 0-0 draw
1912	Barnsley	West Bromwich Albion	1-0 after 0-0 draw
1913	Aston Villa	Sunderland	1-0
1914	Burnley	Liverpool	1-0
1915	Sheffield United	Chelsea	3-0
1920	Aston Villa	Huddersfield Town	1-0 after extra time
1921	Tottenham Hotspur	Wolverhampton Wanderers	1-0
1922	Huddersfield Town	Preston North End	1-0
1923	Bolton Wanderers	West Ham United	2-0
1924	Newcastle United	Aston Villa	2-0
1925	Sheffield United	Cardiff City	1-0
1926	Bolton Wanderers	Manchester City	1-0
1927	Cardiff City	Arsenal	1-0
1928	Blackburn Rovers	Huddersfield Town	3-1
1929	Bolton Wanderers	Portsmouth	2-0
1930	Arsenal	Huddersfield Town	2-0
1931	West Bromwich Albion	Birmingham	2-1
1932	Newcastle United	Arsenal	2-1
1933	Everton	Manchester City	3-0
1934	Manchester City	Portsmouth	2-1
1935	Sheffield Wednesday	West Bromwich Albion	4-2
1936	Arsenal	Sheffield United	1-0
1937	Sunderland	Preston North End	3-1
1938	Preston North End	Huddersfield Town	1-0 after extra time
1939	Portsmouth	Wolverhampton Wanderers	4-1
1946	Derby County	Charlton Athletic	4-1 after extra time
1947	Charlton Athletic	Burnley	1-0 after extra time

Year	Winners	Runners-up	Score
1948	Manchester United......................	Blackpool	4-2
1949	Wolverhampton Wanderers...........	Leicester City.............................	3-1
1950	Arsenal	Liverpool..................................	2-0
1951	Newcastle United........................	Blackpool	2-0
1952	Newcastle United........................	Arsenal	1-0
1953	Blackpool	Bolton Wanderers	4-3
1954	West Bromwich Albion	Preston North End	3-2
1955	Newcastle United........................	Manchester City	3-1
1956	Manchester City	Birmingham City	3-1
1957	Aston Villa................................	Manchester United.......................	2-1
1958	Bolton Wanderers	Manchester United.......................	2-0
1959	Nottingham Forest	Luton Town	2-1
1960	Wolverhampton Wanderers...........	Blackburn Rovers	3-0
1961	Tottenham Hotspur	Leicester City.............................	2-0
1962	Tottenham Hotspur	Burnley	3-1
1963	Manchester United.......................	Leicester City.............................	3-1
1964	West Ham United	Preston North End	3-2
1965	Liverpool..................................	Leeds United	2-1 after extra time
1966	Everton	Sheffield Wednesday....................	3-2
1967	Tottenham Hotspur	Chelsea	2-1
1968	West Bromwich Albion	Everton	1-0 after extra time
1969	Manchester City	Leicester City.............................	1-0
1970	Chelsea	Leeds United	2-1 after 2-2 draw both games extra time
1971	Arsenal	Liverpool..................................	2-1 after extra time
1972	Leeds United	Arsenal	1-0
1973	Sunderland................................	Leeds United	1-0
1974	Liverpool..................................	Newcastle United........................	3-0
1975	West Ham United	Fulham.....................................	2-0
1976	Southampton..............................	Manchester United.......................	1-0
1977	Manchester United.......................	Liverpool..................................	2-1
1978	Ipswich Town.............................	Arsenal	1-0
1979	Arsenal	Manchester United.......................	3-2
1980	West Ham United	Arsenal	1-0
1981	Tottenham Hotspur	Manchester City	3-2 after 1-1 draw after extra time
1982	Tottenham Hotspur	Queen's Park Rangers	1-0 after 1-1 draw after extra time
1983	Manchester United.......................	Brighton & Hove Albion................	4-0 after 2-2 draw after extra time
1984	Everton	Watford....................................	2-0
1985	Manchester United.......................	Everton	1-0 after extra time
1986	Liverpool..................................	Everton	3-1
1987	Coventry City	Tottenham Hotspur......................	3-2 after extra time
1988	Wimbledon	Liverpool..................................	1-0
1989	Liverpool..................................	Everton	3-2 after extra time

* Won outright, but restored to the Association
† A special trophy was awarded for third consecutive win

Liverpool – F.A. Cup Winners 1989.

F.A. Challenge Cup – Final Tie 1989

Liverpool 3   Everton 2

Liverpool striker John Aldridge made up for the disappointment of his Cup Final penalty miss a year earlier to give the "Reds" a fourth-minute lead that they held until the last few seconds of normal time. His 72nd-minute replacement, Ian Rush, became the first player to score twice in two Cup Finals – he got a double in the 3-1 victory over Everton in 1986 – and at the end of a thrilling extra half-hour Liverpool's dream of winning a Final that had become a memorial to the supporters who perished at Hillsborough had come true.

Liverpool, also just two points away from clinching the League championship for the eighteenth time, were superior in most departments to their Merseyside rivals and, having survived one early scare when Steve McMahon had to boot clear from his own goal-line following a corner, they achieved the important breakthrough after only four minutes. McMahon moved perfectly into space to receive Steve Nicol's high pass upfield and, as two Everton defenders moved in to stop his progress, he slipped the ball across to give Aldridge plenty of time in which to guide his shot high into the net to Southall's left.

Aldridge missed two chances in the first half that were at least as easy as the one from which he had scored, but with Everton always finding it difficult to get behind the Liverpool defence (and the diminutive Cottee probably wondering why so many high balls were being played in his direction), the early goal looked to be enough to being the precious Cup

back to Anfield. Then perhaps less than ten seconds before the ninety minutes were up Pat Nevin flicked the ball out to Dave Watson and his hard-driven centre slipped out of the diving Grobbelaar's hands to allow substitute Stuart McCall to lunge forward and poke the ball in. With the perimeter fencing at Wembley now removed, a hundred or so Everton fans spilled onto the pitch to celebrate their team's dramatic reprieve.

The excitement of the first fifteen minutes of extra time possibly equalled anything in Cup Final history and two big-money signings who had suffered indifferent seasons were the key players involved. Ian Rush, still

Everton's Neil McDonald in a tussle with John Barnes.

85

Trevor Steven pushes the ball forward to avoid Peter Beardsley's challenge.

Liverpool's favourite son, turned on a cross from Nicol, now switched to left back, and lashed the ball high into the net to give his Welsh team-mate Southall no chance at all (95 minutes). Hansen's headed clearance from a crowded box fell in front of Everton's McCall in space and he chested the ball down before driving a shot just inside the unsighted Grobbelaar's left-hand post (102 minutes).

Within two mintues Rush had restored Liverool's one-goal advantage by turning a centre from England man John Barnes inside a post with a glancing header. Liverpool were in no mood to give up the lead for a third time and both Rush and Houghton were close to making it 4-2.

In the chaotic scenes after the Cup had been presented by HRH The Duchess of Kent to Liverpool captain Ronnie Whelan, the traditional winning team group photograph was thought to have featured several hundred more than usual.

Liverpool: Grobbelaar, Ablett, Staunton (Venison), Nicol, Whelan, Hansen, Beardsley, Aldridge (Rush), Houghton, Barnes, McMahon.

Everton: Southall, McDonald, Van den Hauwe, Ratcliffe, Watson, Bracewell (McCall), Nevin, Steven, Sharp, Cottee, Sheedy (Wilson).

Referee: J. Worrall of Warrington.

F.A. Challenge Cup Competition 1988-89

Preliminary Round		Result				Attendance		
Saturday 3rd September 1988	1st Tie	1st Rep	2nd Rep	3rd Rep	1st Tie	1st Rep	2nd Rep	3rd Rep
Esh Winning v Ryhope CA	1-1				30			
Ryhope CA v Esh Winning		2-3				42		
Cleator Moor Celtic v Bridlington Town	0-0				600			
Bridlington Town v Cleator Moor Celtic		4-1				247		
Evenwood Town v Bedlington Terriers	2-0				20			
Farsley Celtic v Netherfield	2-2				152			
Netherfield v Farsley Celtic		0-3				132		
Workington v Murton	1-1				180			
Murton v Workington		2-4				200		
Crook Town v Ferryhill Athletic	0-4				96			
Leyland Motors v Bridlington Trinity	0-1				77			
Stockton v Harrogate Town	1-1				325			
Harrogate Town v Stockton		2-1				506		
Durham City v Guiseley	1-2				77			
Norton & Stockton Ancients v Darwen	1-0				39			
Shildon v Willington	6-2				105			
Annfield Plain v Denaby United	1-0				62			
Ashington v Rossendale United	2-4				127			
Wren Rovers v Whitley Bay	0-3				65			
Ossett Albion v Northallerton Town	2-2				60			
Northallerton Town v Ossett Albion		2-1				62		
West Auckland Town v South Bank	0-0				74			
South Bank v West Auckland Town		2-0				95		
Clitheroe v Lancaster City	2-2				150			
Lancaster City v Clitheroe		1-0				191		
Armthorpe Welfare v Darlington CB	3-1				74			
Emley v Langley Park Welfare	4-1				228			
Peterlee Newtown v Droylsden	1-2				44			
Formby v Congleton Town	0-7				82			
St Helens Town v Ashton United	0-1				127			
Irlam Town v Oakham United	3-1				64			
Harworth CI v Belper Town	0-0				105			
Belper Town v Harworth CI		1-5				193		
Radcliffe Borough v Ilkeston Town	2-1				92			
Glossop v Prescot Cables	0-0				120			
Prescot Cables v Glossop		1-0				85		
Arnold v Bootle	1-0				92			
Bilston Town v Alfreton Town	4-0				96			
Leek Town v Heanor Town	3-0				261			
Long Eaton United v Bridgnorth Town	0-5				66			
Warrington Town v Curzon Ashton	3-2				106			
Hinckley Athletic v Winsford United	3-0				147			
Grantham v Borrowash Victoria	2-1				366			
Boston v Sutton Town	2-0				68			
Hednesford Town v Eastwood Town	1-3				301			
Harrisons v Dudley Town	0-2				65			
Walsall Wood v Louth United	0-0				74			
Louth United v Walsall Wood		1-3				85		
Rothwell Town v Mile Oak Rovers & Youth	1-5				73			
Hinckley Town v Stourbridge	2-0				72			
Gresley Rovers v Paget Rangers	2-0				272			
Brackley Town v Spalding United	1-0				168			
Highgate United v Rushden Town	0-4				30			
Desborough Town v Witney Town	2-2				101			
Witney Town v Desborough Town		1-0					253		
Tividale v Rushall Olympic	1-4				61			
Northampton Spencer v Irthlingboro Diamonds	0-1				106			
Wednesfield Social v Chasetown	2-3				45			
Chatteris Town v Racing Club Warwick	2-2				82			

Match								
Racing Club Warwick v Chatteris Town	6-0			125				
Leighton Town v Wolverton Town (MK)	2-0	105						
Evesham United v Kings Lynn	3-0	127						
Histon v Wisbech Town	0-1	110						
Holbeach United v Banbury United	1-4	123						
Berkhamsted Town v March Town United	2-2	66						
March Town United v Berkhamsted Town			4-2	200				
Saffron Walden Town v Ely City	2-0	95						
Bourne Town v Baker Perkins	1-1	130						
Baker Perkins v Bourne Town			0-1	182				
Ware v Lowestoft Town	2-0	83						
Edgware Town v Hitchin Town	1-4	125						
Wivenhoe Town v Clacton Town	3-0	283						
Basildon United v Braintree Town	2-4	122						
Soham Town Rangers v Watton United	0-1	60						
Heybridge Swifts v Gorleston	3-1	108						
Barkingside v Uxbridge	1-2	70						
Thetford Town v Harlow Town	2-2	98						
Harlow Town v Thetford Town			4-1	117				
Potton United v Welwyn GC	2-0	78						
Aveley v Halstead Town	2-2	85						
Aveley v Halstead Town			1-4					130
Leatherhead v Hounslow	1-1	159						
Hounslow v Leatherhead			1-2	180				
Tiptree United v Dunstable	1-1	96						
Dunstable v Tiptree United			1-1	82				
Tiptree United v Dunstable					0-0	80		
Dunstable v Tiptree United							0-1	107
Kempston Rovers v Beckenham Town	0-1	150						
Canvey Island v Stowmarket Town	2-3	70						
Staines Town v Newmarket Town	3-0	163						
Finchley v Wootton Blue Cross	1-0	35						
Billericay Town v Haverhill Rovers	0-1	165						
Purfleet v Metropolitan Police	0-1	65						
Felixstowe Town v Baldock Town	1-1	85						
Baldock Town v Felixstowe Town			4-0	210				
Chesham United v Hornchurch	1-1	200						
Hornchurch v Chesham United			5-6	149				
Arlesey Town v Hoddesdon Town	1-1	75						
Hoddesdon Town v Arlesey Town			1-3	87				
Merstham v Clapton	3-3	73						
Clapton v Mertsham			2-1	120				
Corinthian Casuals v Hanwell Town	0-4	55						
Burgess Hill Town v Harefield United	2-1	99						
Gravesend & Northfleet v Tunbridge Wells	2-1	328						
Flackwell Heath v Camberley Town	3-2	75						
Redhill v Malden Vale	0-1	160						
Darenth Heathside v Hertford Town	0-1	33						
Ruislip v Crockenhill	2-0	16						
Stevenage Borough v Rayners Lane	6-1	168						
Collier Row v Rainham Town	0-3	156						
Sheppey United v Maidenhead United	1-1	152						
Maidenhead United v Sheppey United			0-1	91				
Cray Wanderers v Tilbury	1-4	96						
Hailsham Town v Ruislip Manor	0-0	102						
Ruislip Manor v Hailsham Town			0-2	115				
Yeading v Haywards Heath	2-3	53						
Chatham Town v Dorking	1-5	78						
Sittingbourne v Hastings Town	2-3	189						
Shoreham v Eastbourne United	1-3	201						
Peacehaven & Telescombe v Ramsgate	0-1	89						
Feltham v Hythe Town	1-1	66						
Hythe Town v Feltham			2-5	300				
Folkestone v Ringmer	2-0	197						
Whyteleafe v Arundel	6-0	90						
Molesey v Herne Bay	7-0	26						
Tonbridge AFC v Canterbury City	2-3	238						
Horndean v Banstead Athletic	2-3	77						

Corinthian *v* Wick	2-1	60	
Whitehawk *v* Lancing	2-0	92	
Salisbury *v* Newbury Town	4-2	202	
Chichester City *v* Petersfield United	2-1	56	
Abingdon Town *v* Havant Town	4-2	121	
Oxford City *v* Pagham	(walkover for Pagham)		
Calne Town *v* Thatcham Town	0-1	135	
Hungerford Town *v* Eastleigh	0-0	110	
Eastleigh *v* Hungerford Town	0-1		168
Chippenham Town *v* Andover	4-0	140	
Trowbridge Town *v* Romsey Town	2-0	301	
Taunton Town *v* Poole Town	1-1	241	
Poole Town *v* Taunton Town	1-0		168
Devizes Town *v* Sholing Sports	3-2	77	
Cwmbran Town *v* Radstock Town	2-2	78	
Radstock Town *v* Cwmbran Town	1-0		121
Tiverton Town *v* Bridgend Town	7-2	201	
Minehead *v* Sharpness	0-4	124	
Bristol Manor Farm *v* Barry Town	0-1	109	
Bideford *v* Shortwood United	1-1	276	
Shortwood United *v* Bideford	2-1		163
Frome Town *v* St Blazey	4-1	177	
Paulton Rovers *v* Barnstaple Town	2-1	75	
Clandown *v* Yate Town	0-2	52	
Welton Rovers *v* Exmouth Town	0-5	92	

First Round Qualifying	Result				Attendance			
Saturday 17th September 1988	1st Tie	1st Rep	2nd Rep	3rd Rep	1st Tie	1st Rep	2nd Rep	3rd Rep
North Shields *v* Bridlington Town	1-1				293			
Bridlington Town *v* North Shields		1-1				416		
Bridlington Town *v* North Shields			2-1				706	
Bishop Auckland *v* Evenwood Town	4-0				232			
Guisborough Town *v* Alnwick Town	3-0				142			
Esh Winning *v* Farsley Celtic	1-1				32			
Farsley Celtic *v* Esh Winning		2-1				160		
Horden CW *v* Ferryhill Athletic	0-2				71			
Spennymoor United *v* Bridlington Trinity	3-0				179			
Tow Law Town *v* Consett	2-0				103			
Workington *v* Gateshead	0-0				266			
Gateshead *v* Workington		1-0				229		
Billingham Town *v* Guiseley	1-0				117			
Newcastle BS *v* Norton & Stockton Ancients	4-0				81			
Seaham Red Star *v* Accrington Stanley	0-0				160			
Accrington Stanley *v* Seaham Red Star		2-1				505		
Harrogate Town *v* Billingham Synthonia	1-3				344			
Brandon United *v* Annfield Plain	2-0				91			
Blyth Spartans *v* Rossendale United	1-0				480			
Gretna *v* Chester-le-Street Town	5-0				109			
Shildon *v* Whitley Bay	1-5				156			
Shotton Comrades *v* South Bank	1-1				32			
South Bank *v* Shotton Comrades		3-1				138		
Barrow *v* Lancaster City	3-1				701			
Morecambe *v* Skelmersdale United	3-3				271			
Skelmersdale United *v* Morecambe		1-2				263		
Northallerton Town *v* Easington Colliery	2-0				59			
Burscough *v* Emley	0-1				196			
Horwich RMI *v* Droylsden	3-3				174			
Droylsden *v* Horwich RMI		1-2				217		
Marine *v* Thackley	5-0				202			
Armthorpe Welfare *v* Fleetwood Town	2-2				102			
Fleetwood Town *v* Armthorpe Welfare		5-0				404		
Colwyn Bay *v* Ashton United	0-0				262			
Ashton United *v* Colwyn Bay		2-1				153		
Bangor City *v* Irlam Town	2-2				291			

89

Match	Score	Score (replay)	Attendance	Attendance	
Irlam Town v Bangor City	1-4			244	
Southport v Penrith	1-0		228		
Congleton Town v Harworth CI	1-1		146		
Harworth CI v Congleton Town	1-0			295	
Eastwood Hanley v Prescot Cables	2-0		88		
Northwich Victoria v Arnold	5-0		445		
Stalybridge Celtic v Chadderton	1-4		344		
Radcliffe Borough v Hyde United	0-2		260		
South Liverpool v Leek Town	1-1		144		
Leek Town v South Liverpool		2-1		433	
Mossley v Bridgnorth Town	2-0		150		
Rhyl v Ashtree Highfield	4-1		381		
Bilston Town v Warrington Town	0-0		83		
Warrington Town v Bilston Town		3-2		94	
North Ferriby United v Grantham	3-2		144		
Witton Albion v Boston	0-0		315		
Boston v Witton Albion		0-2		98	
Frickley Athletic v Boldmere St Michaels	2-1		296		
Hinckley Athletic v Buxton	1-3		162		
Oldbury United v Dudley Town	2-3		220		
Matlock Town v Walsall Wood	2-3		227		
Worksop Town v Sutton Coldfield Town	1-2		274		
Eastwood Town v Brigg Town	3-1		130		
Lye Town v Hinckley Town	0-3		170		
Gainsborough Trinity v Gresley Rovers	2-2		232		
Gresley Rovers v Gainsborough Trinity		3-1		640	
Boston United v Coventry Sporting	8-1		1617		
Mile Oak Rovers & Youth v Goole Town	3-1		95		
Leicester United v Rushden Town	4-1		225		
Shepshed Charterhouse v Witney Town	3-2		246		
Stafford Rangers v Halesowen Harriers	2-0		661		
Brackley Town v Rushall Olympic	1-2		116		
Wellingborough Town v Chasetown	1-2		67		
Tamworth v Racing Club Warwick	3-0		851		
Willenhall Town v Malvern Town	3-3		115		
Malvern Town v Willenhall Town		0-0		116	
Willenhall Town v Malvern Town		0-2			183
Irthlingborough Diamonds v Moor Green	1-1		104		
Moor Green v Irthlingborough Diamonds		4-3		275	
Redditch United v Evesham United	2-1		278		
Atherstone United v Wisbech Town	4-0		380		
Nuneaton Borough v Stamford	2-0		533		
Leighton Town v Banbury United	0-0		163		
Banbury United v Leighton Town		2-1		251	
Barton Rovers v Saffron Walden United	1-0		117		
Bedworth United v Bourne Town	1-1		147		
Bourne Town v Bedworth United		3-4		109	
Bromsgrove Rovers v Chalfont St Peter	1-1		627		
Chalfont St Peter v Bromsgrove Rovers		0-3		253	
March Town United v Alvechurch	1-2		195		
Boreham Wood v Hitchin Town	2-0		156		
Bury Town v Wivenhoe Town	0-0		350		
Wivenhoe Town v Bury Town		0-2		363	
Great Yarmouth Town v Milton Keynes Boro	3-0		164		
Ware v Kettering Town	0-3		383		
Witham Town v Watton United	2-1		115		
Bishops Stortford v Heybridge Swifts	3-1		360		
Hendon v Harwich & Parkeston	5-1		206		
Braintree Town v Corby Town	2-0		320		
Sudbury Town v Harlow Town	3-1		345		
Cambridge City v Potton United	5-1		455		
Leyton-Wingate v Hampton	1-1		93		
Hampton v Leyton-Wingate		0-1		235	
Uxbridge v Halstead Town	0-2		137		
Grays Athletic v Tiptree United	5-0		261		
Barking v Beckenham Town	0-0		116		
Beckenham Town v Barking		0-1		106	
Barnet v Epsom & Ewell	7-0		1156		

Leatherhead v Stowmarket Town	1-0	154	
Buckingham Town v Finchley	0-3	130	
Wycombe Wanderers v Haverhill Rovers	4-1	1012	
Letchworth GC v Cheshunt	1-2	63	
Staines Town v Harrow Borough	2-0	341	
Hemel Hempstead v Baldock Town	5-1	106	
Hayes v Chesham United	1-0	221	
Wealdstone v Vauxhall Motors (Beds)	2-1	365	
Metropolitan Police v Arlesey Town	1-1	53	
Arlesey Town v Metropolitan Police	2-0		150
Erith & Belvedere v Hanwell Town	0-1	92	
Wembley v Burgess Hill Town	3-1	82	
Horsham v Walton & Hersham	1-5	130	
Clapton v Leytonstone Ilford	0-1	171	
Dartford v Flackwell Heath	7-1	579	
St Albans City v Malden Vale	1-0	249	
Wokingham Town v Kingsbury Town	2-1	488	
Gravesend & Northfleet v Hertford Town	1-3	321	
Royston Town v Stevenage Borough	0-1	277	
Burnham v Rainham Town	2-2	105	
Rainham Town v Burnham	1-1		40
Burnham v Rainham Town	3-1		131
Dulwich Hamlet v Three Bridges	1-0	128	
Ruislip v Marlow	1-1	52	
Marlow v Ruislip	3-0		256
Tring Town v Tilbury	2-1	62	
Crawley Town v Hailsham Town	2-1	408	
Carshalton Athletic v Lewes	3-1	171	
Sheppey United v Bromley	1-4	199	
Ashford Town v Dorking	2-1	147	
Croydon v Hastings Town	1-2	170	
Dover Athletic v Egham Town	2-0	589	
Haywards Heath v Eastbourne United	3-2	108	
Chertsey Town v Feltham	0-0	121	
Feltham v Chertsey Town	1-0		168
Kingstonian v Folkestone	4-1	189	
Thanet United v Portfield	1-0	200	
Ramsgate v Fisher Athletic	0-2	210	
Horsham YMCA v Molesey	1-2	13	
Woking v Canterbury City	3-0	280	
Southwick v Littlehampton Town	5-0	141	
Whyteleafe v Tooting & Mitcham United	2-1	201	
Steyning Town v Corinthian	5-1	48	
Bracknell Town v Whitehawk	1-2	105	
Worthing v AFC Totton	3-2	291	
Banstead Athletic v Windsor & Eton	0-2	91	
Fareham Town v Chichester City	3-0	127	
Basingstoke Town v Abingdon Town	3-1	410	
Newport IOW v Bashley	1-1	409	
Bashley v Newport IOW	1-0		485
Salisbury v Pagham	2-3	175	
Abingdon United v Hungerford Town	1-2	80	
Waterlooville v Chippenham Town	2-0	219	
Thame United v Westbury United	3-1	81	
Thatcham Town v Gosport Borough	1-3	116	
Chard Town v Poole Town	0-3	141	
Forest Green Rovers v Devizes Town	5-0	159	
Wimborne Town v Weston-super-Mare	3-5	156	
Trowbridge Town v Weymouth	1-2	651	
Clevedon Town v Tiverton Town	1-2	106	
Merthyr Tydfil v Sharpness	3-0	1211	
Melksham Town v Gloucester City	0-5	175	
Radstock Town v Cheltenham Town	0-2	283	
Maesteg Park v Shortwood United	1-0	72	
Dorchester Town v Frome Town	3-1	247	
Mangotsfield United v Torrington	6-0	137	
Barry Town v Worcester City	0-2	284	
Swanage Town & Herston v Yate Town	2-1	164	

	Result				Attendance			
Ton Pentre v Exmouth Town.........................	0-1				240			
Falmouth Town v Glastonbury	3-0				225			
Paulton Rovers v Saltash United	1-4				120			

Second Round Qualifying

Saturday 1st October 1988

	1st Tie	*1st Rep*	*2nd Rep*	*3rd Rep*	*1st Tie*	*1st Rep*	*2nd Rep*	*3rd Rep*
Guisborough Town v Farsley Celtic	0-0				201			
Farsley Celtic v Guisborough Town		0-1				266		
Bridlington Town v Bishop Auckland..............	2-1				495			
Tow Law Town v Gateshead	3-2				172			
Ferryhill Athletic v Spennymoor United	0-2				212			
Accrington Stanley v Billingham Synthonia	1-1				419			
Billingham Synthonia v Accrington Stanley		5-1				427		
Billingham Town v Newcastle Blue Star	2-1				130			
Gretna v Whitley Bay	1-1				120			
Whitley Bay v Gretna		1-0				359		
Brandon United v Blyth Spartans	4-2				210			
Morecambe v Northallerton Town	3-2				237			
South Bank v Barrow	0-0				205			
Barrow v South Bank		1-0				1187		
Marine v Fleetwood Town	2-4				238			
Emley v Horwich RMI.................................	5-0				384			
Southport v Harworth CI	2-0				262			
Ashton United v Bangor City	1-3				271			
Chadderton v Hyde United............................	1-5				420			
Eastwood Hanley v Northwich Victoria	0-1				304			
Rhyl v Warrington Town	1-1				393			
Warrington Town v Rhyl..............................		2-0				228		
Leek Town v Mossley	2-0				316			
Frickley Athletic v Buxton............................	1-0				476			
North Ferriby United v Witton Albion.............	2-2				102			
Witton Albion v North Ferriby United..............		3-1				393		
Sutton Coldfield Town v Eastwood Town	1-0				247			
Dudley Town v Walsall-Wood	2-1				235			
Boston United v Mile Oak Rovers & Youth	5-0				1238			
Hinckley Town v Gresley Rovers	1-0				197			
Stafford Rangers v Rushall Olympic	1-0				553			
Leicester United v Shepshed Charterhouse	1-0				566			
Malvern Town v Moor Green	0-2				138			
Chasetown v Tamworth	0-1				659			
Nuneaton Borough v Banbury United	1-1				509			
Banbury United v Nuneaton Borough		1-0				394		
Redditch United v Atherstone United	2-1				264			
Bromsgrove Rovers v Alvechurch	2-2				932			
Alvechurch v Bromsgrove Rovers		3-3				970		
Bromsgrove Rovers v Alvechurch			2-0				1189	
Barton Rovers v Bedworth United	1-3				155			
Great Yarmouth Town v Kettering Town	0-3				521			
Boreham Wood v Bury Town	0-0				137			
Bury Town v Boreham Wood		1-4				503		
Hendon v Braintree Town	3-1				262			
Witham Town v Bishops Stortford..................	2-3				310			
Leyton-Wingate v Halstead Town	7-1				155			
Sudbury Town v Cambridge City....................	2-1				554			
Barnet v Leatherhead..................................	4-3				857			
Grays Athletic v Barking	1-1				357			
Barking v Grays Athletic..............................		0-3				184		
Cheshunt v Staines Town	1-2				140			
Finchley v Wycombe Wanderers	0-3				450			
Wealdstone v Arlesey Town..........................	1-0				362			
Hemel Hempstead v Hayes...........................	2-3				121			
Walton & Hersham v Leytonstone Ilford..........	3-2				129			
Hanwell Town v Wembley	0-1				135			
Wokingham Town v Hertford Town	3-1				400			
Dartford v St Albans City	1-1				707			

92

St Albans City *v* Dartford	2-4					329		
Dulwich Hamlet *v* Marlow	1-0				128			
Stevenage Borough *v* Burnham	3-2				261			

(match awarded to Burnham FC as Stevenage Borough FC played an ineligible player)

Carshalton Athletic *v* Bromley	1-1			282		
Bromley *v* Carshalton Athletic		4-2				428
Tring Town *v* Crawley Town	1-2			196		
Dover Athletic *v* Haywards Heath	5-2			609		
Ashford Town *v* Hastings Town	2-1			409		
Thanet United *v* Fisher Athletic	1-3			320		
Feltham *v* Kingstonian	0-0			216		
Kingstonian *v* Feltham		3-0				174
Southwick *v* Whyteleafe	0-1			102		
Molesey *v* Woking	1-1					
Woking *v* Molesey		1-0				357
Worthing *v* Windsor & Eton	0-4			285		
Steyning Town *v* Whitehawk	1-3			88		
Bashley *v* Pagham	4-3			244		
Fareham Town *v* Basingstoke Town	3-0			350		
Thame United *v* Gosport Borough	1-3			110		
Hungerford Town *v* Waterlooville	0-2			156		
Weston-super-Mare *v* Weymouth	0-1			453		
Poole Town *v* Forest Green Rovers	2-4			248		
Gloucester City *v* Cheltenham Town	3-0			1730		
Tiverton Town *v* Merthyr Tydfil	0-1			508		
Mangotsfield United *v* Worcester City	0-1			407		
Maesteg Park *v* Dorchester Town	0-2			50		
Falmouth Town *v* Saltash United	2-2			341		
Saltash United *v* Falmouth Town		5-0				427
Swanage Town & Herston *v* Exmouth Town	1-1			140		
Exmouth Town *v* Swanage Town & Herston		3-0				188

Third Round Qualifying

	Result				Attendance			

Saturday 15th October 1988

	1st Tie	1st Rep	2nd Rep	3rd Rep	1st Tie	1st Rep	2nd Rep	3rd Rep
Guisborough Town *v* Bridlington Town	1-1				716			
Bridlington Town *v* Guisborough Town		0-1				957		
Tow Law Town *v* Spennymoor United	2-2				268			
Spennymoor United *v* Tow Law Town		2-2				304		
Spennymoor United *v* Tow Law Town			1-2				353	
Billingham Synthonia *v* Billingham Town	3-0				772			
Whitley Bay *v* Brandon United	0-1				545			
Morecambe *v* Barrow	0-0				1156			
Barrow *v* Morecambe		5-1				1918		
Fleetwood Town *v* Emley	2-2				702			
Emley *v* Fleetwood Town		2-2				758		
Fleetwood Town *v* Emley			3-1				1026	
Southport *v* Bangor City	3-0				502			
Hyde United *v* Northwich Victoria	1-1				1090			
Northwich Victoria *v* Hyde United		3-0				1012		
Warrington Town *v* Leek Town	1-2				378			
Frickley Athletic *v* Witton Albion	3-1				548			
Sutton Coldfield Town *v* Dudley Town	0-1				313			
Boston United *v* Hinckley Town	3-4				1360			
Stafford Rangers *v* Leicester United	1-1				654			
Leicester United *v* Stafford Rangers		2-3				562		
Moor Green *v* Tamworth	1-1				794			
Tamworth *v* Moor Green		4-6				1387		
Banbury United *v* Redditch United	2-3				375			
Bromsgrove Rovers *v* Bedworth United	3-1				677			
Kettering Town *v* Boreham Wood	4-0				1549			
Hendon *v* Bishops Stortford	5-3				372			
Leyton-Wingate *v* Sudbury Town	1-2				239			
Barnet *v* Grays Athletic	0-1				1135			
Staines Town *v* Wycombe Wanderers	0-1				972			
Wealdstone *v* Hayes	1-2				680			

Match	1st Tie	1st Rep	2nd Rep	3rd Rep	1st Tie	1st Rep	2nd Rep	3rd Rep
Walton & Hersham v Wembley	2-1				168			
Wokingham Town v Dartford	1-2				651			
Dulwich Hamlet v Burnham	1-1				128			
Burnham v Dulwich Hamlet		2-3				219		
Bromley v Crawley Town	2-2				686			
Crawley Town v Bromley		1-0				1208		
Dover Athletic v Ashford Town	3-0				1055			
Fisher Athletic v Kingstonian	1-1				323			
Kingstonian v Fisher Athletic		1-4				411		
Whyteleafe v Woking	0-2				395			
Windsor & Eton v Whitehawk	1-1				329			
Whitehawk v Windsor & Eton		1-0				511		
Bashley v Fareham Town	1-2				460			
Gosport Borough v Waterlooville	0-1				650			
Weymouth v Forest Green Rovers	3-0				559			
Gloucester City v Merthyr Tydfil	0-1				1429			
Worcester City v Dorchester Town	1-1				946			
Dorchester Town v Worcester City		1-2				431		
Saltash United v Exmouth Town	2-2				221			
Exmouth Town v Saltash United		4-3				522		

Fourth Round Qualifying	Result				Attendance			
Saturday 29th October 1988	1st Tie	1st Rep	2nd Rep	3rd Rep	1st Tie	1st Rep	2nd Rep	3rd Rep
Frickley Athletic v Chorley	1-1				855			
Chorley v Frickley Athletic		0-1				811		
Southport v Tow Law Town	2-1				816			
Barrow v Whitby Town	1-1				2031			
Whitby Town v Barrow		1-3				615		
Fleetwood Town v Runcorn	1-3				913			
Caernarfon Town v Brandon United	1-1				317			
Brandon United v Caernarfon Town		2-0				482		
Northwich Victoria v Billingham Synthonia	2-0				1001			
Leek Town v Guisborough Town	0-0				1096			
Guisborough Town v Leek Town		0-0				1824		
Guisborough Town v Leek Town			1-0				2031	
Macclesfield Town v Altrincham	0-0				3014			
Altrincham v Macclesfield Town		4-0				2834		
Chelmsford City v Halesowen Town	1-3				1240			
Dagenham v Burton Albion	2-0				455			
Welling United v Hinckley Town	1-1				940			
Hinckley Town v Welling United		0-3				832		
Dudley Town v Grays Athletic	3-3				576			
Grays Athletic v Dudley Town		2-0				823		
Bromsgrove Rovers v Moor Green	2-0				1219			
Aylesbury United v Sudbury Town	1-1				1054			
Sudbury Town v Aylesbury United		0-1				1486		
Hayes v Redditch United	1-0				501			
Stafford Rangers v Kidderminster Harriers	2-1				1552			
Wycombe Wanderers v Kettering Town	1-2				4554			
VS Rugby v Hendon	1-1				834			
Hendon v VS Rugby		2-0				518		
Slough Town v Dartford	1-2				940			
Sutton United v Walton & Hersham	1-1				1179			
Walton & Hersham v Sutton United		0-3				1227		
Fareham Town v Dover Athletic	1-1				504			
Dover Athletic v Fareham Town		0-1				1590		
Crawley Town v Merthyr Tydfil	3-3				1649			
Merthyr Tydfil v Crawley Town		3-1				1920		
Bognor Regis Town v Whitehawk	2-2				678			
Whitehawk v Bognor Regis Town		0-2				2060		
Newport County v Weymouth	2-1				1614			
Exmouth Town v Woking	1-5				937			
Fisher Athletic v Dulwich Hamlet	3-3				911			
Dulwich Hamlet v Fisher Athletic		0-3				1011		
Worcester City v Yeovil Town	1-2				2145			
Farnborough Town v Waterlooville	2-3				547			

First Round Proper		Result				Attendance			
Saturday 19th November 1988	1st Tie	1st Rep	2nd Rep	3rd Rep		1st Tie	1st Rep	2nd Rep	3rd Rep
Grimsby Town v Wolverhampton Wanderers ...	1-0					7922			
Rotherham United v Barrow	3-1					5439			
Halifax Town v York City	1-0					2894			
Burnley v Chester City	0-2					8474			
Preston North End v Tranmere Rovers	1-1					7946			
Tranmere Rovers v Preston North End		3-0					7676		
Altrincham v Lincoln City	3-2					2169			
Scarborough v Stockport County	2-1					2939			
Darlington v Notts County	1-2					2110			
Frickley Athletic v Northwich Victoria	0-2					1292			
Mansfield Town v Sheffield United	1-1					9101			
Sheffield United v Mansfield Town		2-1					11556		
Telford United v Carlisle United	1-1					2163			
Carlisle United v Telford United		4-1					2833		
Blackpool v Scunthorpe United	2-1					3976			
Doncaster Rovers v Brandon United	0-0					2139			
Brandon United v Doncaster Rovers		1-2					1832		
Hartlepool United v Wigan Athletic	2-0					2491			
Bolton Wanderers v Chesterfield	0-0					4840			
Chesterfield v Bolton Wanderers		2-3					4168		
Runcorn v Wrexham	2-2					1910			
Wrexham v Runcorn		2-3					2705		
Guisborough Town v Bury	0-1					5990			
Southport v Port Vale	0-2					3424			
Stafford Rangers v Crewe Alexandra	2-2					4348			
Crewe Alexandra v Stafford Rangers		3-2					4492		
Huddersfield Town v Rochdale	1-1					6178			
Rochdale v Huddersfield Town		3-4					5645		
Brentford v Halesowen Town	2-0					4514			
Welling United v Bromsgrove Rovers	3-0					1555			
Bath City v Grays Athletic	2-0					995			
Bristol Rovers v Fisher Athletic	3-0					5161			
Bognor Regis Town v Exeter City	2-1					1903			
Gillingham v Peterborough United	3-3					4509			
Peterborough United v Gillingham		1-0					4494		
Fulham v Colchester United	0-1					4481			
Dagenham v Sutton United	0-4					1249			
Torquay United v Fareham Town	2-2					2432			
Fareham Town v Torquay United		2-3					1418		
Woking v Cambridge United	1-4					2614			
Kettering Town v Dartford	2-1					3024			
Newport County v Maidstone United	1-2					2148			
Swansea City v Northampton Town	3-1					4521			
Reading v Hendon	4-2					5096			
Cardiff City v Hereford United	3-0					4341			
Yeovil Town v Merthyr Tydfil	3-2					4079			
Enfield v Leyton Orient	1-1					4031			
Leyton Orient v Enfield		2-2					4862		
Leyton Orient v Enfield			0-1					6029	
Bristol City v Southend United	3-1					7027			
Waterlooville v Aylesbury United	1-4					846			
Aldershot v Hayes	1-0					2830			

Second Round Proper		Result				Attendance			
Saturday 10th December 1988	1st Tie	1st Rep	2nd Rep	3rd Rep		1st Tie	1st Rep	2nd Rep	3rd Rep
Northwich Victoria v Tranmere Rovers	1-2					2594			
Grimsby Town v Rotherham United	3-2					5676			
Bolton Wanderers v Port Vale	1-2					7499			
Hartlepool United v Notts County	1-0					3184			
Doncaster Rovers v Sheffield United	1-3					6556			

Match	1st Tie	1st Rep	2nd Rep	3rd Rep	1st Tie	1st Rep	2nd Rep	3rd Rep
Scarborough v Carlisle United	0-1				2849			
Runcorn v Crewe Alexandra	0-3				3509			
Huddersfield Town v Chester City	1-0				6295			
Blackpool v Bury	3-0				5324			
Altrincham v Halifax Town	0-3				3971			
Colchester United v Swansea City	2-2				2697			
Swansea City v Colchester United		1-3				4045		
Aldershot v Bristol City	1-1				3793			
Bristol City v Aldershot		0-0				7299		
Aldershot v Bristol City			2-2				3801	
Bristol City v Aldershot				1-0				6246
Reading v Maidstone United	1-1				5249			
Maidstone United v Reading		1-2				2821		
Bognor Regis Town v Cambridge United	0-1				3189			
Enfield v Cardiff City	1-4				3594			
Aylesbury United v Sutton United	0-1				2135			
Kettering Town v Bristol Rovers	2-1				4450			
Peterborough United v Brentford	0-0				5609			
Brentford v Peterborough United		3-2				5605		
Bath City v Welling United	0-0				1361			
Welling United v Bath City		3-2				3117		
Yeovil Town v Torquay United	1-1				5612			
Torquay United v Yeovil Town		1-0				3246		

Third Round Proper

	Result				Attendance			
Saturday 7th January 1989	1st Tie	1st Rep	2nd Rep	3rd Rep	1st Tie	1st Rep	2nd Rep	3rd Rep
Newcastle United v Watford	0-0				24217			
Watford v Newcastle United		2-2				16431		
Newcastle United v Watford			0-0				28498	
Watford v Newcastle United				1-0				15115
Carlisle United v Liverpool	0-3				18556			
Stoke City v Crystal Palace	1-0				12294			
Sutton United v Coventry City	2-1				8000			
Hartlepool United v Bristol City	1-0				4033			
Plymouth Argyle v Cambridge United	2-0				8648			
West Ham United v Arsenal	2-2				22017			
Arsenal v West Ham United		0-1				44124		
Crewe Alexandra v Aston Villa	2-3				5938			
Middlesbrough v Grimsby Town	1-2				19190			
Brighton & Hove Albion v Leeds United	1-2				10914			
Millwall v Luton Town	3-2				12504			
Walsall v Brentford	1-1				5375			
Brentford v Walsall		1-0				8163		
Cardiff City v Hull City	1-2				7128			
Derby County v Southampton	1-1				17178			
Southampton v Derby County		1-2				16323		
West Bromwich Albion v Everton	1-1				31186			
Everton v West Bromwich Albion		1-0				31753		
Barnsley v Chelsea	4-0				13241			
Tranmere Rovers v Reading	1-1				7799			
Reading v Tranmere Rovers		2-1				6574		
Sunderland v Oxford United	1-1				17074			
Oxford United v Sunderland		2-0				7237		
Charlton Athletic v Oldham Athletic	2-1				5060			
Manchester United v Queens Park Rangers	0-0				36222			
Queens Park Rangers v Manchester United		2-2				22246		
Manchester United v Queens Park Rangers			3-0				47257	
Nottingham Forest v Ipswich Town	3-0				20743			
Shrewsbury Town v Colchester United	0-3				3982			
Welling United v Blackburn Rovers	0-1				3850			
Huddersfield Town v Sheffield United	0-1				15543			
Sheffield Wednesday v Torquay United	5-1				11384			
Manchester City v Leicester City	1-0				23838			
Bradford City v Tottenham Hotspur	1-0				15917			
Blackpool v AFC Bournemouth	0-1				5317			

	1st Tie	1st Rep	2nd Rep	3rd Rep	1st Tie	1st Rep	2nd Rep	3rd Rep
Kettering Town v Halifax Town	1-1				5800			
Halifax Town v Kettering Town		2-3				5632		
Port Vale v Norwich City	1-3				15697			
Portsmouth v Swindon Town	1-1				10403			
Swindon Town v Portsmouth		2-0				11457		
Birmingham City v Wimbledon	0-1				10341			

Fourth Round Proper   Result   Attendance

Saturday 28th January 1989

	1st Tie	1st Rep	2nd Rep	3rd Rep	1st Tie	1st Rep	2nd Rep	3rd Rep
Bradford City v Hull City	1-2				13748			
Aston Villa v Wimbledon	0-1				25043			
Manchester United v Oxford United	4-0				47754			
Nottingham Forest v Leeds United	2-0				28107			
Swindon Town v West Ham United	0-0				18627			
West Ham United v Swindon Town		1-0				24723		
Stoke City v Barnsley	3-3				18592			
Barnsley v Stoke City		2-1				21086		
Plymouth Argyle v Everton	1-1				27566			
Everton v Plymouth Argyle		4-0				28542		
Grimsby Town v Reading	1-1				9401			
Reading v Grimsby Town		1-2				8541		
Norwich City v Sutton United	8-0				23073			
Hartlepool United v AFC Bournemouth	1-1				6240			
AFC Bournemouth v Hartlepool United		5-2				10142		
Blackburn Rovers v Sheffield Wednesday	2-1				16235			
Brentford v Manchester City	3-1				12100			
Watford v Derby County	2-1				20075			
Millwall v Liverpool	0-2				23615			
Sheffield United v Colchester United	3-3				14406			
Colchester United v Sheffield United		0-2				7638		
Charlton Athletic v Kettering Town	2-1				16001			

Fifth Round Proper   Result   Attendance

Saturday 18th February 1989

	1st Tie	1st Rep	2nd Rep	3rd Rep	1st Tie	1st Rep	2nd Rep	3rd Rep
Barnsley v Everton	0-1				32551			
Norwich City v Sheffield United	3-2				24139			
Charlton Athletic v West Ham United	0-1				18785			
Wimbledon v Grimsby Town	3-1				12959			
AFC Bournemouth v Manchester United	1-1				12708			
Manchester United v AFC Bournemouth		1-0				52422		
Hull City v Liverpool	2-3				19893			
Blackburn Rovers v Brentford	0-2				15280			
Watford v Nottingham Forest	0-3				18044			

Sixth Round   Result   Attendance

Saturday 18th March 1989

	1st Tie	1st Rep	2nd Rep	3rd Rep	1st Tie	1st Rep	2nd Rep	3rd Rep
Liverpool v Brentford	4-0				42376			
West Ham United v Norwich City	0-0				29119			
Norwich City v West Ham United		3-1				25785		
Everton v Wimbledon	1-0				24309			
Manchester United v Nottingham Forest	0-1				55040			

Semi-Final

Saturday 15th April 1989
Liverpool v Nottingham Forest ....
at Sheffield Wednesday FC (match abandoned after 6 mins)

Everton v Norwich City 1-0   46553
at Aston Villa FC

Liverpool *v* Nottingham Forest...................... 3-1   38000
at Manchester United FC

Final

Saturday 20th May 1989

Liverpool *v* Everton................................... 3-2   82800
at Wembley Stadium

F.A. Challenge Cup Competition 1989-90

Exemptions

44 Clubs to the Third Round Proper

Arsenal
Aston Villa
Barnsley
Blackburn Rovers
AFC Bournemouth
Bradford City
Brighton & Hove Albion
Charlton Athletic
Chelsea
Coventry City
Crystal Palace
Derby County
Everton
Hull City
Ipswich Town

Leeds United
Leicester City
Liverpool
Luton Town
Manchester City
Manchester United
Middlesbrough
Millwall
Newcastle United
Norwich City
Nottingham Forest
Oldham Athletic
Oxford United
Plymouth Argyle
Portsmouth

Port Vale
Queens Park Rangers
Sheffield United
Sheffield Wednesday
Southampton
Stoke City
Sunderland
Swindon Town
Tottenham Hotspur
Watford
West Bromwich Albion
West Ham United
Wimbledon
Wolverhampton Wanderers

52 Clubs to the First Round Proper

Aldershot
Birmingham City
Blackpool
Bolton Wanderers
Brentford
Bristol City
Bristol Rovers
Burnley
Bury
Cambridge United
Cardiff City
Carlisle United
Chester City
Chesterfield
Colchester United
Crewe Alexandra
Doncaster Rovers
Exeter City

Fulham
Gillingham
Grimsby Town
Halifax Town
Hartlepool United
Hereford United
Huddersfield Town
Kettering Town*
Leyton Orient
Lincoln City
Macclesfield Town†
Maidstone United
Mansfield Town
Northampton Town
Notts County
Peterborough United
Preston North End
Reading

Rochdale
Rotherham United
Scarborough
Scunthorpe United
Shrewsbury Town
Southend United
Stockport County
Sutton United*
Swansea City
Telford United†
Torquay United
Tranmere Rovers
Walsall
Wigan Athletic
Wrexham
York City

20 Clubs to the Fourth Round Qualifying

Altrincham
Aylesbury United
Bath City
Bognor Regis Town
Burton Albion
Chelmsford City
Chorley

Dagenham
Darlington
Enfield
Farnborough Town
Halesowen Town
Hayes
Kidderminster Harriers

Merthyr Tydfil
Northwich Victoria
Runcorn
VS Rugby
Welling United
Yeovil Town

† Trophy Finalists
* Two Clubs outside the Football League considered most appropriate

F.A. Challenge Trophy – Final Tie 1989

Telford United 1   Macclesfield Town 0

A repeat of the first Trophy Final of 1970 brought together the teams placed 7th (Macclesfield) and 16th (Telford) in the GM Vauxhall Conference final table. There was no score at the end of normal time for the third consecutive Final, but for once there was a Wembley winner – Ian Crawley's goal five minutes into extra time won the Trophy for Stan Storton's Shropshire outfit.

The 1988-89 season had seen high-profile exploits by Conference clubs in the FA Cup and yet the most notable "giantkillers", Sutton United and Kettering Town, failed even to make it into the last sixteen in a tough Trophy competition. Given such a high standard of competitor, it was perhaps to be expected that one with the all-round experience of Telford would be present on Final day. After all, seven of their players had already appeared in Wembley finals and four

The two captains, Lee (Telford) and Edwards (Macclesfield), shake hands prior to the kick-off.

had played in the England semi-professional team.

The story of the first ninety minutes was one of Macclesfield's dictating the play to such an extent that almost all of the game had been played in Telford's half. Aberdeen-born striker Steve Burr, who had notched 36 goals in the previous season, had clearly been identified by Telford as their most dangerous opponent and he was closely policed by at least two defenders throughout. Another "Macc" striker, John Timmons, took advantage of the additional space thereby afforded to him and looked a likely scorer with his pace and eye for a shooting opportunity. Ultimately, though, his nearest effort was a left-footer against the far post – which would not have counted anyway, as he was adjudged to have brought the ball under control with his hand.

Ian Crawley, who shot VS Rugby's Vase Final winner in 1983, had come on as 65th-minute substitute for Mayman and became a Wembley hero again after a mix-up in the "Macc" defence. Goalkeeper Zelem and defender Tobin left a high bouncing ball to each other and Crawley had time to almost walk it into the net.

Telford had done so much chasing in normal time – mostly after Burr and Timmons, but also after Derbyshire when he joined the fray as an orthodox right-winger – that they were expected to be the more tired of the two teams in the extra period. The sight of one Telford player after another collapsing with cramp tended to reinforce such a view. But they had that precious lead to give them the

Telford's Hancock seems to have everything under control, despite the presence of Macclesfield's danger man, Burr.

will to carry on and, despite the scare of Burr's lifting one shot over the top from five yards in a crowded box, they survived to experience joyous scenes at the final whistle.

Telford United: Charlton, Lee, Wiggins, Mayman (Crawley), Brindley, Hancock, Joseph, Grainger, Lloyd, Stringer (Griffiths), Nelson.

Macclesfield Town: Zelem, Roberts, Hardman, Edwards, Tobin, Hanlon, Askey (Derbyshire), Timmons, Lake, Burr, Imrie (Kendall).

Referee: T. Holbrook of Staffordshire.

Attendance: 18,106.

F.A. Challenge Trophy Competition 1988-89

First Round Qualifying	Result			Attendance		
Saturday 24th September 1988	1st Tie	1st Rep	2nd Rep	1st Tie	1st Rep	2nd Rep
Accrington Stanley *v* Fleetwood Town	1-1			452		
Fleetwood Town *v* Accrington Stanley		2-1			524	
Workington *v* Worksop Town	0-0			141		
Worksop Town *v* Workington		3-2			208	
Tow Law Town *v* Stockton	1-3			103		
Alfreton Town *v* North Shields	2-2			110		
North Shields *v* Alfreton Town		2-1			321	
Southport *v* Buxton	3-4			268		
Goole Town *v* Horwich RMI	3-0			219		
Chester-le-Street Town *v* Radcliffe Borough	0-0			127		
Radcliffe Borough *v* Chester-le-Street Town		1-0			88	
Ryhope CA *v* Gretna	0-1			55		
Stalybridge Celtic *v* Shildon	2-0			303		
Seaham Red Star *v* Guisborough Town	0-2			87		
Ferryhill Athletic *v* Brandon United	0-3			123		
South Liverpool *v* Mossley	4-1			105		
Easington Colliery *v* Crook Town	6-0			40		
Dudley Town *v* Congleton Town	4-1			201		
Winsford United *v* Coventry Sporting	1-4			108		
Grantham *v* Shepshed Charterhouse	2-1			356		
Sutton Coldfield Town *v* Colwyn Bay	2-3			124		
Matlock Town *v* Redditch United	3-1			271		
Moor Green *v* Eastwood Town	2-4			201		
Gainsborough Trinity *v* Halesowen Town	1-0			225		
VS Rugby *v* Atherstone United	1-3			463		
Willenhall Town *v* Leek Town	4-3			116		
Bedworth United *v* Stourbridge	1-0			131		
Staines Town *v* Dunstable	3-0			191		
Farnborough Town *v* Hampton	2-2			247		
Hampton *v* Farnborough Town		2-3			230	
Wivenhoe Town *v* Chalfont St Peter	0-0			137		
Chalfont St Peter *v* Wivenhoe Town		1-3			157	
Uxbridge *v* Witney Town	4-0			117		
Ashford Town *v* Burnham	2-0			141		
Basingstoke Town *v* Folkestone	1-0			326		
Erith & Belvedere *v* Dover Athletic	0-3			162		
Sheppey United *v* Banbury United	3-2			69		
Tonbridge AFC *v* Grays Athletic	0-3			167		
Billericay Town *v* Kingstonian	1-5			227		
Leatherhead *v* Kingsbury Town	2-1			138		
Metropolitan Police *v* Boreham Wood	2-1			58		
Gravesend & Northfleet *v* Bognor Regis Town	1-1			241		
Bognor Regis Town *v* Gravesend & Northfleet		1-1			203	
Gravesend & Northfleet *v* Bognor Regis Town			1-0			316
Woking *v* St Albans City	1-1			308		
St Albans City *v* Woking		1-4			318	
Barking *v* Basildon United	1-1			122		
Basildon United *v* Barking		2-3			112	
Wembley *v* Chelmsford City	2-1			141		
Hayes *v* Bracknell Town	4-2			136		
Thanet United *v* Hitchin Town	1-0			219		
Lewes *v* Dulwich Hamlet	2-2			127		
Dulwich Hamlet *v* Lewes		4-1			118	
Chesham United *v* Collier Row	2-0			146		
Croydon *v* Walton & Hersham	1-0			125		
Bridgend Town *v* Salisbury	1-6			57		
Frome Town *v* Cwmbran Town	0-0			140		
Cwmbran Town *v* Frome Town		2-4			94	
Barry Town *v* Bideford	4-1			133		

Match	Result 1st Tie	Result 1st Rep	Result 2nd Rep	Att 1st Tie	Att 1st Rep	Att 2nd Rep
Taunton Town v Dorchester Town	0-2			176		
Forest Green Rovers v Gloucester City	1-2			384		
Ton Pentre v Andover	3-3			189		
Andover v Ton Pentre		3-2			89	
Maesteg Park v Weston-super-Mare	0-2			50		
Worcester City v Waterlooville	4-0			562		
Gosport Borough v Trowbridge Town	2-0			187		

Second Round Qualifying	Result			Attendance		
Saturday 22nd October 1988	1st Tie	1st Rep	2nd Rep	1st Tie	1st Rep	2nd Rep
Worksop Town v Goole Town	0-1			331		
Stockton v Penrith	0-0			78		
Penrith v Stockton		4-5			148	
Fleetwood Town v Stalybridge Celtic	2-1			402		
Brandon United v Buxton	1-5			143		
North Shields v South Liverpool	3-3			307		
South Liverpool v North Shields		2-2			143	
South Liverpool v North Shields			2-1			154
Easington Colliery v Radcliffe Borough	2-2			33		
Radcliffe Borough v Easington Colliery		2-0			143	
Gretna v Guisborough Town	1-0			90		
Coventry Sporting v Eastwood Town	1-4			62		
Grantham v Alvechurch	1-1			503		
Alvechurch v Grantham		0-1			315	
Dudley Town v Willenhall Town	1-1			270		
Willenhall Town v Dudley Town		2-3			154	
Wellingborough Town v Matlock Town	0-1			125		
Colwyn Bay v Hednesford Town	2-1			351		
Leicester United v Gainsborough Trinity	0-0			165		
Gainsborough Trinity v Leicester United		2-4			260	
Atherstone United v Bedworth United	4-1			519		
Metropolitan Police v Carshalton Athletic	1-2			142		
Barking v Gravesend & Northfleet	0-1			144		
Dover Athletic v Kings Lynn	6-0			715		
Chesham United v Basingstoke Town	1-3			196		
Farnborough Town v Wivenhoe Town	1-2			348		
Sheppey United v Woking	0-2			205		
Oxford City v Hayes	(walkover for Hayes)					
Southwick v Uxbridge	0-4			75		
Croydon v Staines Town	2-1			138		
Ashford Town v Dulwich Hamlet	2-1			212		
Marlow v Grays Athletic	2-1			225		
Thanet United v Leatherhead	0-3			260		
Kingstonian v Wembley	2-0			121		
Gloucester City v Frome Town	3-2			524		
Weston-super-Mare v Worcester City	0-2			499		
Gosport Borough v Poole Town	4-0			280		
Andover v Salisbury	2-5			296		
Dorchester Town v Barry Town	1-0			218		

Third Round Qualifying	Result			Attendance		
Saturday 3rd December 1988	1st Tie	1st Rep	2nd Rep	1st Tie	1st Rep	2nd Rep
Whitby Town v Stockton	2-2			272		
Stockton v Whitby Town		3-0			228	
Spennymoor United v Gretna	0-0			169		
Gretna v Spennymoor United		3-0			153	
Morecambe v Fleetwood Town	1-1			336		
Fleetwood Town v Morecambe		4-0			404	

102

Match	1st Tie	1st Rep	2nd Rep	1st Tie	1st Rep	2nd Rep
South Bank v Radcliffe Borough	5-0			70		
Gateshead v South Liverpool	0-1			92		
Whitley Bay v Frickley Athletic	0-1			313		
Billingham Synthonia v Bishop Auckland	1-1			307		
Bishop Auckland v Billingham Synthonia		3-1			389	
Witton Albion v Nuneaton Borough	2-1			345		
Bangor City v Rhyl	2-0			315		
Corby Town v Colwyn Bay	2-2			188		
Colwyn Bay v Corby Town		2-1			221	
Northwich Victoria v Goole Town	2-0			784		
Dudley Town v Atherstone United	1-2			373		
Grantham v Matlock Town	2-2			487		
Matlock Town v Grantham		3-0			402	
Eastwood Town v Buxton	1-3			191		
Leicester United v Caernarfon Town	1-0			119		
Ashford Town v Slough Town	0-3			261		
Leyton-Wingate v Welling United	2-2			226		
Welling United v Leyton-Wingate		3-1			608	
Harrow Borough v Windsor & Eton	1-1			294		
Windsor & Eton v Harrow Borough		2-0			333	
Wivenhoe Town v Kingstonian	2-3			452		
Bishops Stortford v Gravesend & Northfleet	3-3			414		
Gravesend & Northfleet v Bishops Stortford		2-1			428	
Croydon v Dagenham	2-2			123		
Dagenham v Croydon		0-0			233	
Croydon v Dagenham			0-1			209
Carshalton Athletic v Leatherhead	2-1			228		
Leytonstone Ilford v Uxbridge	0-1			82		
Hendon v Hayes	3-3			230		
Hayes v Hendon		0-2			435	
Dover Athletic v Tooting & Mitcham United	3-2			430		
Wycombe Wanderers v Cambridge City	2-0			1272		
Merthyr Tydfil v Salisbury	5-0			862		
Saltash United v Gosport Borough	1-2			178		
Worcester City v Marlow	1-0			578		
Dorchester Town v Gloucester City	1-1			301		
Gloucester City v Dorchester Town		1-3			687	
Worthing v Basingstoke Town	1-2			286		
Crawley Town v Woking	3-4			528		

First Round Proper

Saturday 14th January 1989

Match	Result 1st Tie	1st Rep	2nd Rep	Attendance 1st Tie	1st Rep	2nd Rep
Bangor City v South Bank	2-3			325		
Matlock Town v Northwich Victoria	2-6			577		
Boston United v Stafford Rangers	2-0			1646		
Stockton v Hyde United	1-4			184		
Telford United v Witton Albion	3-0			1318		
Burton Albion v Chorley	4-1			1827		
Colwyn Bay v Frickley Athletic	1-1			329		
Frickley Athletic v Colwyn Bay		3-0			442	
Marine v Macclesfield Town	2-2			757		
Macclesfield Town v Marine		4-1			1350	
Buxton v Altrincham	0-2			1005		
Leicester United v Blyth Spartans	3-0			306		
Runcorn v Gretna	2-3			761		
Newcastle Blue Star v South Liverpool	1-0			267		
Fleetwood Town v Bishop Auckland	0-0			437		
Bishop Auckland v Fleetwood Town		5-1			605	
Atherstone United v Barrow	1-4			758		
Fisher Athletic v Cheltenham Town	0-1			296		
Dover Athletic v Worcester City	3-1			1050		
Bromsgrove Rovers v Woking	2-3			916		
Fareham Town v Yeovil Town	1-2			559		
Windsor & Eton v Gosport Borough	2-0			334		

Enfield *v* Hendon	4-1			803		
Barnet *v* Gravesend & Northfleet	1-1			1534		
Gravesend & Northfleet *v* Barnet		2-1			896	
Sutton United *v* Kingstonian	1-0			1321		
Kidderminster Harriers *v* Maidstone United	2-1			1313		
Bath City *v* Wycombe Wanderers	0-0			1174		
Wycombe Wanderers *v* Bath City		4-0			1177	
Dagenham *v* Aylesbury United	2-2			653		
Aylesbury United *v* Dagenham		4-0			971	
Uxbridge *v* Carshalton Athletic	1-1			286		
Carshalton Athletic *v* Uxbridge		5-2			338	
Wokingham Town *v* Merthyr Tydfil	2-2			844		
Merthyr Tydfil *v* Wokingham Town		1-0			1524	
Dartford *v* Dorchester Town	4-0			756		
Weymouth *v* Newport County	2-1			1019		
Welling United *v* Slough Town	4-0			1106		
Basingstoke Town *v* Kettering Town	1-1			1143		
Kettering Town *v* Basingstoke Town		5-3			2306	
Bromley *v* Wealdstone	1-2			544		

Second Round Proper	Result			Attendance		
Saturday 4th February 1989	1st Tie	1st Rep	2nd Rep	1st Tie	1st Rep	2nd Rep
Boston United *v* Northwich Victoria	3-2			2002		
Gravesend & Northfleet *v* Kettering Town	1-1			1119		
Kettering Town *v* Gravesend & Northfleet		1-2			2821	
Kidderminster Harriers *v* Burton Albion	1-1			3524		
Burton Albion *v* Kidderminster Harriers		0-1			4135	
Aylesbury United *v* Merthyr Tydfil	1-3			1402		
Sutton United *v* Bishop Auckland	1-1			1245		
Bishop Auckland *v* Sutton United		2-1			1742	
Wealdstone *v* Wycombe Wanderers	0-1			1469		
Cheltenham Town *v* Barrow	0-0			1375		
Barrow *v* Cheltenham Town		0-0			2310	
Barrow *v* Cheltenham Town			1-0			2223
Altrincham *v* Carshalton Athletic	2-0			1029		
Windsor & Eton *v* Enfield	1-0			865		
Woking *v* Weymouth	2-1			660		
South Bank *v* Macclesfield Town	0-3			489		
Hyde United *v* Gretna	1-1			837		
Gretna *v* Hyde United		2-3			640	
Newcastle Blue Star *v* Frickley Athletic	3-1			152		
Dover Athletic *v* Dartford	0-0			1415		
Dartford *v* Dover Athletic		2-0			1208	
Yeovil Town *v* Telford United	1-4			2714		
Leicester United *v* Welling United	1-3			376		

Third Round Proper	Result			Attendance		
Saturday 25th February 1989	1st Tie	1st Rep	2nd Rep	1st Tie	1st Rep	2nd Rep
Dartford *v* Bishop Auckland	2-0			1108		
Newcastle Blue Star *v* Woking	2-0			653		
Windsor & Eton *v* Hyde United	2-2			757		
Hyde United *v* Windsor & Eton		2-0			1074	
Kidderminster Harriers *v* Telford United	1-1			2867		
Telford United *v* Kidderminster Harriers		2-0			2941	
Welling United *v* Boston United	0-0			2062		
Boston United *v* Welling United		0-1			2829	
Wycombe Wanderers *v* Merthyr Tydfil	2-0			3434		
Altrincham *v* Barrow	5-3			1148		
Macclesfield Town *v* Gravesend & Northfleet	2-0			1344		

Fourth Round Proper	Result			Attendance		
Saturday 11th March 1989	*1st Tie*	*1st Rep*	*2nd Rep*	*1st Tie*	*1st Rep*	*2nd Rep*
Macclesfield Town *v* Welling United	1-0			2088		
Newcastle Blue Star *v* Telford United	1-4			1097		
Hyde United *v* Wycombe Wanderers............................	1-0			2341		
Dartford *v* Altrincham	1-0			1629		

Semi-Final

First Leg – Saturday 8th April 1989

Dartford *v* Macclesfield Town......................................	0-0			3771		
Hyde United *v* Telford United	0-1			3593		

Second Leg – Saturday 15th April 1989

Macclesfield Town *v* Dartford......................................	4-1			4000		
Telford United *v* Hyde United	3-0			3729		

Macclesfield Town won on aggregate 4-1
Telford United won on aggregate 4-0

Final

Saturday 13th May 1989

Telford United *v* Macclesfield Town..............................	1-0			18106		

at Wembley Stadium

105

F.A. Challenge Trophy Winners 1970-89

Year	Winners		Runners-up		Venue
1970	Macclesfield Town	2	Telford United	0	Wembley
1971	Telford United	3	Hillingdon Borough	2	Wembley
1972	Stafford Rangers	3	Barnet	0	Wembley
1973	*Scarborough	2	Wigan Athletic	1	Wembley
1974	Morecambe	2	Dartford	1	Wembley
1975	Matlock Town	4	Scarborough	0	Wembley
1976	*Scarborough	3	Stafford Rangers	2	Wembley
1977	Scarborough	2	Dagenham	1	Wembley
1978	Altrincham	3	Leatherhead	1	Wembley
1979	Stafford Rangers	2	Kettering Town	0	Wembley
1980	Dagenham	2	Mossley	1	Wembley
1981	Bishop's Stortford	1	Sutton United	0	Wembley
1982	*Enfield	1	Altrincham	0	Wembley
1983	Telford United	2	Northwich Victoria	1	Wembley
1984	†Northwich Victoria	2	Bangor City	1	Stoke
1985	Wealdstone	2	Boston United	1	Wembley
1986	Altrincham	1	Runcorn	0	Wembley
1987	§Kidderminster Harriers	2	Burton Albion	1	West Bromwich
1988	§Enfield	3	Telford United	2	West Bromwich
1989	*Telford United	1	Macclesfield Town	0	Wembley

*After extra time   †After 1-1 draw at Wembley   §After 0-0 draw at Wembley

F.A. Challenge Trophy Competition 1989-90

Exemptions

32 Clubs to the First Round Proper

Altrincham
Aylesbury United
Barnet
Barrow
Billingham Synthonia
Bishop Auckland
Boston United
Burton Albion
Cheltenham Town
Darlington
Dartford

Enfield
Farnborough Town
Fisher Athletic
Hyde United
Kettering Town
Kidderminster Harriers
Macclesfield Town
Merthyr Tydfil
Newcastle Blue Star
Northwich Victoria
Redbridge Forest

Runcorn
Sutton United
Telford United
Tow Law Town
Wealdstone
Welling United
Windsor & Eton
Wokingham Town
Wycombe Wanderers
Yeovil Town

32 Clubs to the Third Round Qualifying

Bangor City
Bath City
Blyth Spartans
Bromley
Bromsgrove Rovers
Buxton
Cambridge City
Carshalton Athletic
Chorley
Crawley Town
Dagenham

Dover Athletic
Fareham Town
Frickley Athletic
Gravesend & Northfleet
Gretna
Guisborough Town
Hendon
Leicester United
Leyton-Wingate
Marine
Rhyl

Slough Town
South Bank
South Liverpool
Spennymoor United
Stafford Rangers
VS Rugby
Weymouth
Witton Albion
Woking
Worcester City

F.A. Challenge Vase – Final Tie 1989

Tamworth 3   Sudbury Town 0
(After a 1-1 draw)

A record attendance by some margin for a Vase Final (26,487) saw an enthralling match in the Wembley sunshine involving two new finalists. Sudbury took a sixth-minute lead through Dave Hubbick. the former Ipswich and Colchester professional, and Martin Devaney's equaliser for Beazer Homes League Tamworth four minutes into the second half produced a 1-1 scoreline at the end of ninety minutes.

The extra half-hour, if anything, was even more exciting with close calls at both ends. But it was not without controversy, Sudbury full-back Mike Henry having been dismissed by referee Vickers at the end of the first period after appearing to strike Tamworth's Russell Gordon in the centre circle.

Sudbury had swept forward in the opening minutes, with 29-year-old Hubbick especially prominent in raids down the left. On six minutes, full-back Marty Thorpe's huge kick from the left touchline was allowed to drift over to the far post with no attempt at interception by the Tamworth defence and, when Bryan Klug flicked the ball back into the middle, the unmarked Hubbick was there to head a goal of stunning simplicity.

The Jewson League club definitely had the edge in the first half and Henry had been one of their mainstays with some gritty tackling whenever Tamworth threatened down the left flank. It was a shame, then, that a moment's hesitancy in front of goal by the 28-year-old decorator let Devaney in for a gentle shot into the

Tamworth's experienced striker, Ian Moores, disputes possession with Hunt of Sudbury.

bottom corner of Garnham's goal from eight yards (49 minutes).

There were chances galore in normal time, plus a suspicion that the ball had touched a Sudbury hand in their own box in the last few seconds, and then the fun continued in extra time. Mick Money, a 26-year-old insurance representative who substituted for Barton in the second half (of normal time), had brought more aerial power to the Sudbury attack and immediately made an impact with a couple of neat back-headers to put the ever-dangerous Hubbick into space on the left. But when Money's big moment came, put clean through with just two minutes of extra time left, his run and shot were those of a tired player and Belford succeeded in turning the latter round the post.

A 12th-minute headed goal from the former Tottenham and Stoke striker Ian Moores helped Tamworth win a fiercely contested replay at Peterborough four days later, watched by a crowd of 11,201. Two late goals from Mark Stanton (72 and 84 minutes) then finished off the gallant Suffolk team. Moores also put a penalty wide of the target a minute before half-time and Sudbury's Paul Smith hit one over the top in the 66th minute. All in all a highly eventful final tie!

Tamworth: Belford, Lockett, McCormack (sub'd by Heaton, replaced by Finn in replay), Atkins, Cartwright, Devaney, Myers, Finn (George in replay), Stanton, Gordon (sub'd by Heaton in replay), Moores (sub'd by Rathbone).

Sudbury Town: Garnham, Henry, Thorpe, Barker G., Boyland, Barker D., Oldfield (sub'd by Hunt, replaced by Money in replay), Klug, Hubbick, Smith P., Barton (sub'd by Money, replaced by Hunt in replay).

Referee: D. Vickers of Essex.

Tamworth – F.A. Vase Winners 1989.

F.A. Challenge Vase Competition 1988-89

Extra Preliminary Round	Result				Attendance			
Saturday 10th September 1988	*1st Tie*	*1st Rep*	*2nd Rep*	*3rd Rep*	*1st Tie*	*1st Rep*	*2nd Rep*	*3rd Rep*
Sunderland Vaux RCW *v* Hebburn Reyrolle.....	1-2				75			
Dunston FB *v* Marske United........................	4-2				82			
Boldon CA *v* Gosforth St Nicholas	(walkover for Boldon CA)							
Seaton Delaval ST *v* Washington....................	3-2				30			
Rowntree Mackintosh *v* Coundon TT.............	4-1				29			
Pickering Town *v* Prudhoe East End	3-2				60			
Ponteland United *v* Newtown Aycliffe............	3-2				30			
Harrogate RA *v* Marchon...........................	2-0				47			
Nelson *v* Eppleton CW	1-2				48			
South Shields *v* Blackpool Mechanics	1-0				106			
Flixton *v* Daisy Hill	1-2				100			
Ford Motors (Liverpool) *v* Merseyside Police....	1-6				10			
Atherton Collieries *v* St Dominics	1-3				40			
Linotype *v* Maine Road	0-1				35			
Salford *v* Rylands	3-1				15			
Hanley Town *v* Knypersley Victoria...............	0-3				83			
General Chemicals *v* Ellesmere Port Town	5-2				30			
Meir KA *v* Oldham Town	2-2				30			
Oldham Town *v* Meir KA		1-4				45		
Waterloo Dock *v* Redgate Clayton	2-1				41			
Poulton Victoria *v* Cheadle Town	1-1				65			
Cheadle Town *v* Poulton Victoria..................		1-2				45		
Friar Lane OB *v* Melton Town	0-2				50			
Bradley Rangers *v* Ossett Town	1-2				26			
Hall Road Rangers *v* Liversedge	1-4				41			
Wigston Fields *v* Skegness Town	2-0				25			
Pontefract Collieries *v* Eccleshill United	1-2				80			
Arnold Kingswell *v* Sheffield	0-4				20			
Maltby MW *v* Mickleover RBL......................	5-2				40			
Lutterworth Town *v* Stapenhill	2-3				50			
Frecheville Community *v* Staveley Works	2-3				39			
Derby Prims *v* Clipstone Welfare	4-3				40			
Solihull Borough *v* Westfields........................	2-1				18			
Cogenhoe United *v* Kings Heath	1-2				100			
Long Buckby *v* Princes End United.................	2-0				70			
Baker Perkins *v* Raunds Town	2-1				59			
Coleshill Town *v* Northfield Town	1-2				30			
West Midlands Police *v* Stratford Town	2-1				34			
St Ives Town *v* Leiston	4-2				60			
Coalite Yaxley *v* Eynesbury Rovers	0-1				50			
Mirrless Blackstone *v* Norwich United.............	2-4				55			
Burnham Ramblers *v* RSSC Ransomes.............	2-0				68			
Hadleigh United *v* LBC Ortonians	1-3				45			
Brightlingsea United *v* Huntingdon United	4-2				76			
Ramsey Town *v* Downham Town	0-1				38			
Somersham Town *v* Brantham Athletic	1-2				32			
Diss Town *v* Great Shelford	2-1				180			
Crown & Manor *v* Stotfold...........................	1-3				60			
Southgate Athletic *v* Waltham Abbey	5-0				18			
The 61 *v* Beaconsfield United	3-0				5			
Langford *v* Biggleswade Town.......................	2-0				90			
Amersham Town *v* J-M Sports.......................	2-1				21			
Selby *v* Mount Grace (Potters Bar)	6-3				30			
Norsemen *v* East Thurrock United	1-2				81			
Northwood *v* Electrolux..............................	3-1				140			
Sandridge Rovers *v* Arlesey Town	1-2				55			
London Colney *v* Winslow United	6-0				32			
Beckton United *v* Brimsdown Rovers..............	3-2				21			
Totternhoe *v* Eton Manor............................	2-0				42			

Park Street v Shillington............................ 1-4   42
Pennant v Wingate.................................... 1-5   18
Sun Sports v Rayners Lane 0-2   30
Pirton v Cockfosters.................................. 1-0   35
East Ham United v Ford United (London) 1-2   14
Deal Town v Metropolitan Police (Hayes)....... 5-2   63
BAE (Weybridge) v Oakwood ....(walkover for Oakwood)
Farnham Town v Greenwich Borough............. 2-0   67
Whitstable Town v Thames Polytechnic........... 1-0   127
Old Salesians v Cobham.............................. 2-0   15
Ash United v Southwark Sports 1-4   34
Langney Sports v Midland Bank..................... 3-2   106
Horley Town v Wandsworth & Northwood....... 0-4   32
Cove v West Wickham................................. 1-2   50
Chobham v Bexhill Town 1-0   30
East Grinstead v Bedfont 0-3   35
Selsey v Slade Green 1-1   89
Slade Green v Selsey   2-2   46
Slade Green v Selsey   3-1   38
Farleigh Rovers v Faversham Town 2-4   38
Chipstead v Godalming Town 3-0   40
Vale Recreation v Wallingford Town 5-3   175
First Tower United v Bournemouth 0-1   78
Portsmouth RN v Wantage Town 2-1   14
East Cowes Victoria Ath v Kintbury Rangers.... 1-1   75
Kintbury Rangers v East Cowes Victoria Ath   2-3   95
Wellington v Westland Sports........................ 4-3   100
Lawrence Weston Hallen v Flight Refuelling 1-0   44
Pegasus Juniors v Ellwood 4-1   46
Portishead v Penhill 0-2   10
Larkhall Athletic v Keynsham Town 2-1   53
St Austell v Odd Down 3-4   55
Patchway v Sherborne Town 0-0   46
Sherborne Town v Patchway   3-1   50
Backwell United v Yate Town 0-2   74
Port of Bristol v Chard Town 2-2   44
Chard Town v Port of Bristol   2-1   107
Cinderford Town v Almondsbury Picksons....... 1-4   52
Wotton Rovers v Fairford Town...................... 0-1   50
Harrow Hill v Cirencester Town..................... 2-1   32
Truro City v Supermarine............................. 2-0   92
Ilfracombe Town v DRG (FP) 2-3   101
Brislington v Ottery St Mary 2-0   63

	Preliminary Round	Result				Attendance			
Saturday 8th October 1988		1st Tie	1st Rep	2nd Rep	3rd Rep	1st Tie	1st Rep	2nd Rep	3rd Rep
South Shields v Eppleton CW		3-1				110			
Esh Winning v Rowntree Mackintosh		0-4				50			
Peterlee Newtown v Harrogate RA		1-3				48			
Alnwick Town v Horden CW		4-3				62			
Darlington CB v Northallerton Town		0-1				38			
Harrogate Town v Durham City		1-0				286			
Dunston FB v Lancaster City		2-0				152			
Norton & Stockton Anc v Seaton Delaval ST		0-1				32			
Ponteland United v Pickering Town		1-0				72			
Clitheroe v Ashington		3-2				107			
West Auckland Town v Annfield Plain		0-2				95			
Leyland Motors v Willington		4-1				131			
Bridlington Town v Wren Rovers		0-0				194			
Wren Rovers v Bridlington Town			0-3				61		
Darwen v Langley Park Welfare		3-2				66			
Cleator Moor Celtic v Shotton Comrades		2-1				100			
Netherfield v Bedlington Terriers		3-1				95			
Billingham Town v Bridlington Trinity		3-0				51			
Consett v Boldon CA		2-0				93			

110

Fixture						
Hebburn Reyrolle v Evenwood Town	3-0			80		
Burscough v St Dominics	3-1			87		
Poulton Victoria v Newton	2-0			86		
Merseyside Police v Heswall	3-3			30		
Heswall v Merseyside Police		0-1			80	
Droylsden v Prescot Cables	2-1			185		
Bootle v Waterloo Dock	4-1			81		
Daisy Hill v General Chemicals	1-2			36		
Maine Road v Eastwood Hanley	1-2			59		
Chadderton v Maghull	1-3			60		
Meir KA v Curzon Ashton	1-2			60		
Newcastle Town v Glossop	2-2			70		
Glossop v Newcastle Town		0-1			150	
Atherton LR v Salford	1-2			72		
Knypersley Vic v Vauxhall GM (Cheshire)	1-3			150		
Irlam v Skelmersdale United	4-3			42		
Formby v Ashton United	2-3			40		
Armthorpe Welfare v Stapenhill	0-5			83		
Kimberley Town v Belper Town	1-1			51		
Belper Town v Kimberley Town		1-1			158	
Belper Town v Kimberley Town		0-0				189
Kimberley Town v Belper Town			1-3				56
Staveley Works v Long Eaton United	2-0			40		
Gainsborough Town v Radford	3-0			60		
Grimethorpe MW v Melton Town	1-3			20		
Louth United v Sheffield	3-0			40		
Yorkshire Amateur v Heanor Town	1-2			45		
Oakham United v Immingham Town	1-1			46		
Immingham Town v Oakham United		1-0			60	
Ilkeston Town v Liversedge	3-2			137		
Boston v Eccleshill United	0-4			56		
Wigston Fields v Ossett Albion	1-2			40		
Derby Prims v Brigg Town	0-4			64		
Maltby MW v Sutton Town	1-0			60		
Rossington Main v Denaby United	1-0			50		
Hallam v Ossett Town	0-3			105		
Kiveton Park v Arnold	1-0			25		
Harworth CI v Collingham	1-0			100		
Baker Perkins v Northfield Town	0-2			42		
Racing Club Warwick v Oldbury United	5-2			86		
Tividale v Harrisons	2-3			42		
Wednesfield Social v Walsall-Wood	3-2			47		
Paget Rangers v Mile Oak Rovers & Youth	1-1			82		
Mile Oak Rovers & Youth v Paget Ranger		1-2			79	
Hinckley Town v Rushall Olympic	2-1			73		
Spalding United v Solihull Borough	1-2			161		
Bilston Town v Anstey Nomads	0-1			82		
Hinckley Athletic v Chasetown	1-2			134		
Desborough Town v Ashtree Highfield	5-4			55		
West Midlands Police v Highgate United	3-0			65		
Lye Town v Evesham United	2-1			193		
Long Buckby v Kings Heath	1-0			35		
Malvern Town v Halesowen Harriers	0-1			75		
Brackley Town v Rushden Town	2-2			123		
Rushden Town v Brackley Town		3-0			302	
Boldmere St Michaels v Rothwell Town	1-0			62		
Bourne Town v Eynesbury Rovers	0-0			62		
Eynesbury Rovers v Bourne Town		2-1			100	
Sawbridgeworth Town v Chatteris Town	0-2			25		
Norwich United v Harlow Town	0-1			112		
Stansted v Downham Town	2-1			64		
LBC Ortonians v Saffron Walden Town	0-2			60		
Histon v Watton United	0-2			52		
Newmarket Town v Gorleston	1-2			46		
Holbeach United v Halstead Town	2-2			130		
Halstead Town v Holbeach United		0-3			180	
Great Yarmouth Town v Stowmarket Town	1-0			125		
Clacton Town v Tiptree United	0-1			50		

Match	Score	Replay	Att	Att (replay)
Thetford Town v Lowestoft Town	3-2		130	
Burnham Ramblers v Brightlingsea United	4-0		72	
St Ives Town v March Town United	1-5		100	
Brantham Athletic v Ely City	5-5		27	
Ely City v Brantham Athletic		4-2		42
Diss Town v Soham Rangers	3-2		292	
Wroxham v Canvey Island	4-2		78	
Felixstowe Town v Bowers United	6-2		45	
Hemel Hempstead v Flackwell Heath	0-2		72	
Maidenhead United v Wingate	4-0		65	
Feltham v Wolverton Town (MK)	2-1		34	
London Colney v Baldock Town	0-2		83	
Shillington v Ford United (London)	0-2		40	
Wootton Blue Cross v Cheshunt	2-2		68	
Cheshunt v Wootton Blue Cross		4-1		95
Berkhamsted Town v Edgware Town	3-3		53	
Edgware Town v Berkhamsted Town		1-4		91
Hornchurch v The 61	1-2		81	
Ruislip v Leighton Town	3-2		38	
Aveley v Ruislip Manor	0-3		51	
Hertford Town v Hanwell Town	2-1		52	
Totternhoe v Kempston Rovers	3-1		44	
Milton Keynes Borough v Clapton	1-0		24	
Welwyn GC v Beckton United	4-0		40	
Northwood v Letchworth GC	2-0		80	
Barkingside v Finchley	0-2		31	
Purfleet v Tring Town	0-1		84	
Hoddesdon Town v Pirton	2-0		74	
Selby v Langford	6-2		26	
Amersham Town v Rainham Town	2-0		29	
Arlesey Town v East Thurrock United	0-1		43	
Stotfold v Potton United	2-1		80	
Tilbury v Stevenage Borough	1-0		63	
Royston Town v Rayners Lane	1-1		64	
Rayners Lane v Royston Town		0-1		48
Southgate Athletic v Ware	1-2		32	
Three Bridges v Deal Town	3-1		71	
Bedfont v Faversham Town	3-1		40	
Hythe Town v Sittingbourne	2-0		200	
Eastbourne Town v Egham Town	2-2		99	
Egham Town v Eastbourne Town		1-2		53
Corinthian Casuals v Horsham YMCA	3-2		23	
Redhill v Darenth Heathside	0-3		69	
Peacehaven & Telscombe v Ringmer	1-2		68	
Molesey v Hastings Town	1-2		70	
Southwark Borough v Langney Sports	4-2		50	
Crockenhill v Banstead Athletic	2-3		29	
Lancing v Whitehawk	0-1		117	
Old Salesians v Wandsworth & Norwood	1-1		25	
Wandsworth & Norwood v Old Salesians		2-0		56
Cray Wanderers v Farnham Town	2-1		87	
Chipstead v Whitstable Town	0-2		72	
Chobham v Malden Vale	0-2		24	
Chatham Town v Epsom & Ewell	0-5		52	
Oakwood v Haywards Heath	2-1		29	
Burgess Hill Town v Canterbury City	1-0		121	
Pagham v Slade Green	4-1		126	
Beckenham Town v Littlehampton Town	1-0		80	
Herne Bay v Eastbourne United	2-7		50	
Shoreham v Hailsham Town	0-1		46	
Ramsgate v Tunbridge Wells	1-0		75	
West Wickham v Merstham	2-0		38	
Clanfield v Vale Recreation	7-4		63	
Horndean v Portfield	2-1		74	
Bournemouth v Portsmouth RN	2-2		51	
Portsmouth RN v Bournemouth		2-3		
Eastleigh v Bosham	3-1		72	
Thame United v Wick	0-2		78	

Gillette®

The Best a Man Can Get ™

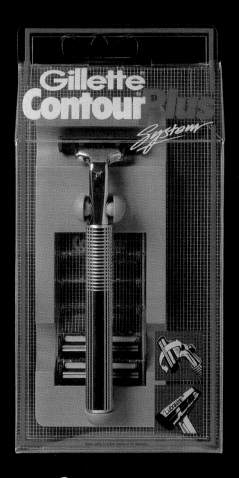

Gillette® Contour®Plus WITH LUBRASTRIP®
for a closer, smoother shave

What is Clubcall?

Clubcall is the football side of Supercall Sports' comprehensive cover of domestic and international sporting events. At the time of writing, Clubcall was associated with eighty-eight clubs, not to mention our non-league lines, the Jimmy Greaves line, and the flagship of them all, the England/F.A. line which updates daily with interviews from the England camp, and match day service that starts with early team news, follows the action with commentaries or regular reports from the ground and ends, as with all our Clubcall lines, with post match reactions from the players concerned.

We are particularly proud of our match service. Apart from informing fans unable to make it to the game how events are going (though it must be stressed we do spend all week encouraging fans to go to the match!) it enables those of you who have attended, to ring your club's line when you return home to see if those involved on the park saw things in the same light as you did!

The beauty of Clubcall, we feel, is that we provide a genuinely in-depth service for the true supporter. We keep you informed and entertained with fresh interviews daily, we provide a platform for a club's staff to air their views and enable a club to bridge the communications gap between players and fans, and in combining public relations with journalism we promote the club and provide them with much needed revenue.

Let's not forget that we are, in effect, a "silent sponsor" of football. A share of profits from each line goes to the club concerned, and this year Clubcall will have put themselves amongst, in financial terms, the leading sponsors of football. Clubs large and small appreciate that revenue, and give us their fullest co-operation to ensure that a first class service is provided.

The amount of technology involved in transmitting literally hundreds of thousands of words a week is phenomenal: British Telecom, however, has invested long-term in Supercall to ensure an even better service this season. We like to think we're first with the facts ... and that we separate it from the fiction. Everyone involved in football loves talking about the game of course – and we hope we provide an ideal platform; and as we always say: "You can't be misquoted on Clubcall!"

Whatever your involvement in the game – have a great season.

ENGLAND CLUBCALL

— PHONE NOW —
0898 12 11 96

☎ Live match commentary and match reports. ☎ Team selections and other news from the England squad, 24 hours <u>EVERY</u> day. ☎ It's all on England clubcall, the official F.A. telephone information service.

And you can catch up on all the latest news from your favourite league clubs. ☎ These are the <u>OFFICIAL</u> club telephone information services. ☎ Updated daily. ☎ Phone your Clubcall number now.

Dial 0898 121 – then add the number you want:–

ALDERSHOT	630	EXETER CITY	634	ROTHERHAM UNITED	637
ARSENAL	170	FULHAM	198	SCARBOROUGH	650
ASTON VILLA	148	GILLINGHAM	107	SCUNTHORPE UNITED	652
BARNSLEY	152	GRIMSBY TOWN	576	SHEFFIELD WEDNESDAY	186
BIRMINGHAM CITY	188	HARTLEPOOL UNITED	147	SHREWSBURY TOWN	194
BLACKBURN ROVERS	179	HEREFORD UNITED	645	SOUTHAMPTON	178
BLACKPOOL	648	HUDDERSFIELD TOWN	635	STOCKPORT COUNTY	638
BOLTON WANDERERS	164	LEEDS UNITED	180	SUNDERLAND	140
BOURNEMOUTH	163	LEICESTER CITY	185	SWANSEA CITY	639
BRENTFORD	108	LEYTON ORIENT	150	SWINDON TOWN	640
BRISTOL CITY	176	LINCOLN CITY	889	TORQUAY UNITED	641
BRISTOL ROVERS	631	LIVERPOOL	184	TRANMERE ROVERS	646
BURNLEY	153	MANCHESTER CITY	191	WALSALL	104
BURY	197	MANCHESTER UNITED	161	W.B.A.	193
CAMBRIDGE UNITED	141	MIDDLESBROUGH	181	WEST HAM UNITED	165
CARDIFF CITY	171	MILLWALL	143	WIMBLEDON	175
CARLISLE UNITED	632	NEWCASTLE UNITED	190	WOLVES	103
CHARLTON ATHLETIC	146	NORWICH CITY	144	WREXHAM	642
CHELSEA	159	NOTTINGHAM FOREST	174	YORK CITY	643
CHESTER CITY	633	NOTTS COUNTY	101		
CHESTERFIELD	573	OLDHAM ATHLETIC	142	CELTIC	888
COVENTRY CITY	166	OXFORD UNITED	172	DUNDEE	649
CREWE ALEXANDRA	647	PETERBOROUGH UNITED	654	DUNFERMLINE ATHLETIC	556
CRYSTAL PALACE	145	PLYMOUTH ARGYLE	688	HEARTS	183
DARLINGTON	149	PORTSMOUTH	182	HIBS	189
DERBY COUNTY	187	PORT VALE	636	KILMARNOCK	557
DONCASTER ROVERS	651	PRESTON NORTH END	173	RANGERS	555
EVERTON	199	Q.P.R.	162		

BEAZER HOMES LEAGUE 151   **SHOOT SOCCER NEWS 195**   **VAUXHALL OPEL LEAGUE 155**
HFS LOANS LEAGUE 157   G.M. VAUXHALL CONFERENCE 653

Clubcall is a Supercall Sport Service. Other services include:
CRICKETCALL — International and County cricket commentary and information. Call Cricketcall Index on 0898 12 14 10.
TURFCALL — Horse racing live commentary and information. Call 0898 121 121.
For details of many other services covering the world of sport, call the Supercall Sport Index on 0898 12 11 10.
For your Supercall Sport Directory, send a S.A.E. to Dept. WS, PO Box 111, Bracknell, Berks. RG12 1LE
(allow 28 days for delivery).

CLUBCALL. 24 HOURS EVERY DAY
Calls are charged at around 38p/min peak and 25p/min off-peak including VAT. ☎ Supercall Sport.

Imagine...

a new cruise control so smooth, it can make you believe the world is flat.

Now you can place your new vehicle design at the leading edge of engineering technology.

AC's *Electro-Motor Cruise System* is an all-new, all-electric, vacuum-independent system that delivers remarkably smooth acceleration and deceleration.

The controller electronics are combined with AC-developed stepper motor technology, so the complete system is contained in a single package that easily installs under the bonnet. Under-dash electronics are eliminated.

The unit can be adjusted for any vehicle design, and the built-in service diagnostic system virtually eliminates manufacturer and dealer diagnostic problems.

Specify AC cruise control...and put your new vehicle design on the path of least resistance.

AC

In a league of its own.

AC Rochester

Chichester City *v* AFC Totton	3-4	28
East Cowes Victoria Ath *v* Petersfield Utd	1-0	51
Didcot Town *v* Arundel	3-0	60
Newbury Town *v* Romsey Town	2-3	87
Brockenhurst *v* Abingdon United	2-4	54
Bicester Town *v* Hartley Wintney	2-0	30
Barnstaple Town *v* Odd Down	1-0	132
DRG (FP) *v* Calne Town	1-4	68
Sherborne Town *v* Paulton Rovers	1-3	50
Moreton Town *v* Fairford Town	2-1	82
Chard Town *v* Westbury Town	1-4	80
Radstock Town *v* Penhill	2-1	52
Welton Rovers *v* Glastonbury	3-1	68
St Blazey *v* Minehead	1-3	69
Melksham Town *v* Wellington	1-3	70
Chippenham Town *v* Pegasus Junior	2-1	125
Lawrence WH *v* Swanage Town & Herston	1-1	40

Swanage Town & Herston *v* Lawrence WH		1-2	80

Yate Town *v* Almondsbury Picksons	2-1	142
Larkhall Athletic *v* Tiverton Town	1-3	101
Harrow Hill *v* Clandown	4-1	40
Truro City *v* Wimborne Town	2-1	138
Bishops Cleeve *v* Bristol Manor Farm	1-0	52
Devizes Town *v* Brislington	2-1	53

First Round	Result				Attendance			
Saturday 5th November 1988	1st Tie	1st Rep	2nd Rep	3rd Rep	1st Tie	1st Rep	2nd Rep	3rd Rep
Cleator Moor Celtic *v* Clitheroe	0-1				82			
Rowntree Mackintosh *v* Northallerton Town	4-1				44			
Annfield Plain *v* Leyland Motors	1-4				37			
South Shields *v* Darwen	4-1				80			
Dunston FB *v* Ponteland United	1-0				102			
Whickham *v* Seaton Delaval ST	3-0				180			
Bridlington Town *v* Alnwick Town	3-1				160			
Billingham Town *v* West Allotment Celtic	0-2				54			
Harrogate RA *v* Harrogate Town	3-2				712			
Netherfield *v* Murton	0-2				80			
Hebburn Reyrolle *v* Consett	1-3				146			
Irlam Town *v* Newcastle Town	3-2				52			
Eastwood Hanley *v* Rocester	0-0				202			
(abandoned 97 mins fog)								
Rocester *v* Eastwood Hanley		0-1				209		
Merseyside Police *v* Vauxhall GM (Cheshire)	0-1				60			
Burscough *v* Rossendale United	1-6				107			
Droylsden *v* Salford	1-1				148			
Salford *v* Droylsden		1-2				110		
Maghull *v* Poulton Victoria	2-4				75			
Ashton United *v* General Chemicals	1-0				100			
Bootle *v* Curzon Ashton	0-1				28			
North Ferriby United *v* Melton Town	1-0				52			
Belper Town *v* Ossett Albion	5-2				113			
Thackley *v* Guiseley	0-3				350			
Kiveton Park *v* Hatfield Main	0-1				34			
Brigg Town *v* Lincoln United	0-0				61			
Lincoln United *v* Brigg Town		0-1				122		
Eccleshill United *v* Rossington Main	0-2				47			
Hucknall Town *v* Ilkeston Town	1-2				220			
Maltby MW *v* Borrowash Victoria	3-5				80			
Gainsborough Town *v* Stapenhill	2-1				30			
Heanor Town *v* Harworth CI	4-3				147			
Staveley Works *v* Louth United	1-2				50			
Ossett Town *v* Immingham Town	2-1				40			
Rushden Town *v* Wednesfield Social	4-0				203			
Buckingham Town *v* Hinckley Town	0-3				115			

Northampton Spencer v Racing Club Warwick	0-1		65	
Long Buckby v Boldmere St Michaels	1-2		70	
Lye Town v Stamford	1-2		128	
Chasetown v West Midlands Police	1-2		83	
Desborough Town v Anstey Nomads	5-0		87	
Harrisons v Paget Rangers	1-4		51	
Solihull Borough v Northfield Town	0-2		30	
Halesowen Harriers v Irthlingborough Diamonds	3-0		102	
Wroxham v Saffron Walden Town	2-1		150	
Eynesbury Rovers v Gorleston	3-1		120	
Harwich & Parkeston v Harlow Town	0-1		180	
Ely City v Felixstowe Town	3-3		56	
Felixstowe Town v Ely City		5-2		107
March Town United v Heybridge Swifts	2-1		175	
Tiptree United v Burnham Ramblers	0-2		63	
Thetford Town v Great Yarmouth Town	0-5		136	
Stansted v Watton United	5-3		72	
Holbeach United v Chatteris Town	1-0		129	
Diss Town v Bury Town	0-3		396	
Flackwell Heath v Milton Keynes Borough	4-0		65	
Amersham Town v Tilbury	0-1		41	
Totternhoe v East Thurrock United	0-1		78	
Baldock Town v Ruislip	3-3		158	
Ruislip v Baldock Town		0-4		58
Vauxhall Motors v Selby	1-1		75	
Selby v Vauxhall Motors		3-1		65
Hertford Town v Tring Town	1-3		100	
Welwyn GC v Ford United (London)	0-3		50	
Maidenhead United v Royston Town	2-5		75	
Hoddesdon Town v Feltham	2-0		70	
Ware v Berkhamsted Town	1-1		47	
Berkhamsted Town v Ware		2-0		65
Hounslow v Northwood	3-2		100	
Finchley v Stotfold	1-0		90	
The 61 v Ruislip Manor	1-0		31	
Cheshunt v Barton Rovers	2-0		85	
Yeading v Wandsworth & Norwood	2-1		54	
Pagham v Hailsham Town	2-4		151	
Whitehawk v Beckenham Town	0-1		82	
Hythe Town v Hastings Town	4-3		350	
Steyning Town v Burgess Hill Town	2-3		90	
Banstead Athletic v Epsom & Ewell	1-2		55	
Cray Wanderers v Eastbourne Town	3-3		111	
Eastbourne Town v Cray Wanderers		3-0		183
Three Bridges v Ramsgate	1-1		125	
Ramsgate v Three Bridges		0-0		89
Ramsgate v Three Bridges			0-2		121
Oakwood v Bedfont	0-2		26	
West Wickham v Darenth Heathside	0-1		39	
Dorking v Whitstable Town	0-1		195	
Malden Vale v Eastbourne United	1-0		51	
Ringmer v Southwark Borough	2-1		160	
Corinthian-Casuals v Camberley Town	1-6		25	
Wick v Eastleigh	2-0		107	
AFC Totton v Romsey Town	2-2		119	
Romsey Town v AFC Totton		3-0		177
Abingdon United v Clanfield	4-1		60	
Horndean v Thatcham Town	0-1		67	
Didcot Town v East Cowes Victoria Athletic	0-1		70	
Bournemouth v Bicester Town	0-2		73	
Tiverton Town v Minehead	2-0		184	
Torrington v 'Paulton Rovers	1-2		70	
Wellington v Chippenham Town	1-2		65	
Shortwood United v Yate Town	0-1		103	
Westbury United v Welton Rovers	0-2		99	
Sharpness v Radstock Town	1-4		133	
Lawrence Weston Hallen v Calne Town	4-1		80	
Truro City v Exmouth Town	0-2		189	

Barnstaple Town *v* Moreton Town	0-1				163			
Harrow Hill *v* Bridport	0-2				50			
Devizes Town *v* Bishops Cleeve	5-0				80			

Second Round — Result — Attendance

Saturday 26th November 1988	1st Tie	1st Rep	2nd Rep	3rd Rep	1st Tie	1st Rep	2nd Rep	3rd Rep
Harrogate RA *v* Rossington Main	5-1				90			
Garforth Town *v* Consett	1-0				153			
Rowntree Mackintosh *v* Dunston FB	0-1				59			
South Shields *v* Murton	3-4				350			
Leyland Motors *v* Bridlington Town	0-1				126			
Rossendale United *v* Farsley Celtic	3-2				376			
West Allotment Celtic *v* Ossett Town	0-2				150			
Colne Dynamoes *v* Emley	1-2				1416			
Clitheroe *v* Whickham	2-4				184			
Brigg Town *v* Droylsden	4-1				85			
Guiseley *v* Curzon Ashton	2-1				263			
Gainsborough Town *v* Borrowash Victoria	1-3				30			
Heanor Town *v* Hatfield Main	3-1				120			
Ilkeston Town *v* Belper Town	3-1				201			
Eastwood Hanley *v* St Helens Town	2-0				97			
Irlam Town *v* North Ferriby United	0-3				79			
Louth United *v* Wythenshawe Amateurs	2-2				58			
Wythenshawe Amateurs *v* Louth United		0-2				60		
Poulton Victoria *v* Ashton United	2-1				96			
Vauxhall GM (Cheshire) *v* Warrington Town	1-0				55			
Hinckley Town *v* Boldmere St Michaels	0-2				91			
Paget Rangers *v* Stamford	4-0				101			
Desborough Town *v* Halesowen Harriers	0-2				122			
West Midlands Police *v* Gresley Rovers	2-4				85			
Northfield Town *v* Racing Club Warwick	2-0				84			
Tamworth *v* Bridgnorth Town	2-1				783			
March Town United *v* Rainworth MW	5-2				250			
Wisbech Town *v* Rushden Town	2-1				575			
Hoddesdon Town *v* Holbeach United	0-2				84			
Braintree Town *v* Royston Town	3-1				236			
Tring Town *v* East Thurrock United	2-4				108			
Ford United (London) *v* Bury Town	0-2				63			
Great Yarmouth Town *v* Felixstowe Town	1-1				95			
Felixstowe Town *v* Great Yarmouth Town		2-4				62		
Burnham Ramblers *v* Eynesbury Rovers	3-0				111			
Sudbury Town *v* Baldock Town	2-0				456			
Stansted *v* Cheshunt	0-1				110			
Berkhamsted Town *v* Witham Town	3-2				62			
Harefield United *v* Harlow Town	1-6				52			
Wroxham *v* Finchley	0-1				140			
Tilbury *v* The 61	4-1				63			
Haverhill Rovers *v* Selby	1-1				99			
Selby *v* Haverhill Rovers		0-2				65		
Abingdon United *v* Bedfont	1-0				50			
Horsham *v* Eastbourne Town	1-4				40			
Ringmer *v* Hailsham Town	0-3				275			
Hounslow *v* Sholing Sports	4-0				130			
Bicester Town *v* Chertsey Town	0-3				123			
Romsey Town *v* Hythe Town	1-0				114			
Whitstable Town *v* Corinthian	2-3				163			
Havant Town *v* Flackwell Heath	1-0				100			
East Cowes Victoria *v* Thatcham Town	2-5				63			
Beckenham Town *v* Burgess Hill Town	0-3				125			
Whyteleafe *v* Hungerford Town	0-2				120			
Yeading *v* Bashley	1-2				220			
Wick *v* Abingdon Town	2-0				95			
Malden Vale *v* Darenth Heathside	1-3				54			
Epsom & Ewell *v* Three Bridges	6-2				139			
Newport IOW *v* Camberley Town	1-2				267			

	Result	Attendance
Falmouth Town v Bridport 0-3		205
Tiverton Town v Exmouth Town.................... 2-0		361
Welton Rovers v Old Georgians..................... 3-2		106
Radstock Town v Chippenham Town 3-3		83
Chippenham Town v Radstock Town	2-0	122
Clevedon Town v Devizes Town 2-2		70
Devizes Town v Clevedon Town	1-0	107
Lawrence Weston Hallen v Paulton Rovers 1-4		83
Mangotsfield United v Yate Town 1-1		317
Yate Town v Mangotsfield United	3-0	515
Moreton Town v Dawlish Town 4-2		88

Third Round	Result				Attendance			
Saturday 17th December 1988	1st Tie	1st Rep	2nd Rep	3rd Rep	1st Tie	1st Rep	2nd Rep	3rd Rep
Harrogate RA v Borrowash Victoria...............	6-3				125			
Whickham v Dunston FB	3-0				425			
Ossett Town v Bridlington Town....................	2-2				140			
Bridlington Town v Ossett Town		0-1				263		
Emley v Guiseley	4-0				773			
Garforth Town v Rossendale United...............	1-4				255			
North Ferriby United v Murton.....................	3-0				121			
Ilkeston Town v Northfield Town	4-2				269			
Paget Rangers v Louth United	3-1				126			
Halesowen Harriers v Heanor Town	0-1				136			
Gresley Rovers v Tamworth..........................	1-3				1186			
Eastwood Hanley v Poulton Victoria...............	3-1				115			
Vauxhall GM (Cheshire) v Holbeach United	1-2				72			
Brigg Town v Boldmere St Michaels...............	2-2				67			
Boldmere St Michaels v Brigg Town...............		0-1				341		
Braintree Town v Fichley	0-0				271			
Finchley v Braintree Town............................		0-2				70		
Cheshunt v Bury Town	1-3				150			
Berkhamsted Town v Wisbech Town	2-4				219			
Harlow Town v Tilbury................................	3-3				135			
Tilbury v Harlow Town								
(tie awarded to Tilbury as Harlow Town failed to fulfil fixture)								
East Thurrock United v Great Yarmouth Town	3-0				195			
Burnham Ramblers v Haverhill Rovers	6-0				182			
March Town United v Sudbury Town	1-2				575			
Hailsham Town v Darenth Heathside...............	1-0				191			
Burgess Hill Town v Chertsey Town................	1-1				180			
Chertsey Town v Burgess Hill Town................		3-1				185		
Hungerford Town v Eastbourne Town	5-1				99			
Wick v Epsom & Ewell	1-1				106			
Epsom & Ewell v Wick		4-2						
Hounslow v Corinthian................................	2-0				128			
Havant Town v Camberley Town	1-7				74			
Abingdon United v Thatcham Town	0-1				111			
Bashley v Moreton Town	4-1				320			
Paulton Rovers v Devizes Town	4-3				125			
Welton Rovers v Yate Town	5-1				155			
Romsey Town v Bridport	1-2				97			
Tiverton Town v Chippenham Town	3-0				296			

Fourth Round	Result				Attendance			
Saturday 21st January 1989	1st Tie	1st Rep	2nd Rep	3rd Rep	1st Tie	1st Rep	2nd Rep	3rd Rep
Ossett Town v Whickham.............................	1-0				430			
Rossendale United v Emley	3-1				1820			
Heanor Town v Eastwood Hanley	1-1				197			
Eastwood Hanley v Heanor Town		2-1				168		

North Ferriby United *v* Harrogate RA............. 2-2   186
Harrogate RA *v* North Ferriby United.............   1-3   319
Ilkeston Town *v* Tamworth........................... 1-2   1687
Brigg Town *v* Holbeach United..................... 3-5   234
Braintree Town *v* Bury Town 0-0   732
Bury Town *v* Braintree Town   2-1   980
Wisbech Town *v* Paget Rangers 1-0   1000
East Thurrock United *v* Chertsey Town 2-0   336
Hounslow *v* Sudbury Town 0-1   480
Epsom & Ewell *v* Hailsham Town 1-2   245
Tilbury *v* Burnham Ramblers 0-1   226
Camberley Town *v* Hungerford Town 0-1   112
Bridport *v* Welton Rovers 3-0   378
Tiverton Town *v* Thatcham Town.................. 1-2   665
Paulton Rovers *v* Bashley 1-3   410

Fifth Round	Result				Attendance			
Saturday 11th February 1989	*1st Tie*	*1st Rep*	*2nd Rep*	*3rd Rep*	*1st Tie*	*1st Rep*	*2nd Rep*	*3rd Rep*
Ossett Town *v* North Ferriby United 1-2					470			
Eastwood Hanley *v* Tamworth...................... 0-1					811			
Holbeach United *v* Wisbech Town................. 2-4					1578			
Rossendale United *v* Sudbury Town 0-1					1402			
Bury Town *v* Burnham Ramblers 2-0					1100			
Hailsham Town *v* Hungerford Town 2-3					914			
Bridport *v* Thatcham Town.......................... 0-2					736			
East Thurrock United *v* Bashley.................... 1-4					838			

Sixth Round	Result				Attendance			
Saturday 4th March 1989	*1st Tie*	*1st Rep*	*2nd Rep*	*3rd Rep*	*1st Tie*	*1st Rep*	*2nd Rep*	*3rd Rep*
Bury Town *v* North Ferriby United 1-2					1365			
Sudbury Town *v* Bashley 2-0					1956			
Tamworth *v* Wisbech Town 1-0					2362			
Hungerford Town *v* Thatcham Town 2-0					1501			

Semi-Final

First Leg – Saturday 25th March 1989

Tamworth *v* North Ferriby United................. 1-2   2575
Hungerford Town *v* Sudbury Town................ 0-0   1684

Second Leg – Saturday 1st April 1989

North Ferriby United *v* Tamworth................. 1-3   1435
Sudbury Town *v* Hungerford Town................ 6-0   4320

Tamworth won on aggregate 4-3
Sudbury Town won on aggregate 6-0

Final

Saturday 6th May 1989
Tamworth *v* Sudbury Town.......................... 1-1   26487
at Wembley Stadium

Replay – Wednesday 10th May 1989
Tamworth *v* Sudbury Town.......................... 3-0   11201
at Peterborough United FC

117

F.A. Challenge Vase Winners 1975-89

Year	Winners		Runners-up		Venue
1975	Hoddesdon Town	2	Epsom & Ewell	1	Wembley
1976	*Billericay Town	1	Stamford	0	Wembley
1977	Billericay Town	2	Sheffield	1	Nottingham
1978	Blue Star	2	Barton Rovers	1	Wembley
1979	Billericay Town	4	Almondsbury Greenway	1	Wembley
1980	Stamford	2	Guisborough Town	0	Wembley
1981	*Whickham	3	Willenhall Town	2	Wembley
1982	Forest Green Rovers	3	Rainworth Miners' Welfare	0	Wembley
1983	V. S. Rugby	1	Halesowen Town	0	Wembley
1984	Stansted	3	Stamford	2	Wembley
1985	Halesowen Town	3	Fleetwood Town	1	Wembley
1986	Halesowen Town	3	Southall	0	Wembley
1987	St. Helens Town	3	Warrington Town	2	Wembley
1988	*Colne Dynamoes	1	Emley	0	Wembley
1989	†Tamworth	3	Sudbury Town	0	Peterborough

* After extra time

†After 1-1 draw at Wembley

F.A. Challenge Vase Competition 1989-90

Exemptions

32 Clubs Exempt to the Second Round

Bashley	Eastwood Hanley	Holbeach United
Berkhamsted Town	Emley	Hounslow
Braintree Town	Falmouth Town	Hungerford Town
Bridgnorth Town	Farsley Celtic	March Town United
Bridlington Town	Garforth Town	North Ferriby United
Bridport	Great Yarmouth Town	Ossett Town
Burnham Ramblers	Gresley Rovers	Rosendale United
Chertsey Town	Guiseley	Sudbury Town
Clevedon Town	Hailsham Town	Thatcham Town
Corinthian	Havant Town	Wisbech Town
East Thurrock United	Haverhill Rovers	

32 Clubs Exempt to the First Round

Abingdon Town	Horsham	Stamford
Borrowash Victoria	Ilkeston Town	Tilbury
Brigg Town	Mangotsfield United	Tiverton Town
Camberley Town	Murton	Warrington Town
Dawlish Town	Newport IOW	Welton Rovers
Epsom & Ewell	Old Georgians	West Allotment Celtic
Exmouth Town	Paget Rangers	Whickham
Harefield United	Paulton Rovers	Witham Town
Harrogate RA	Rainworth MW	Wythenshawe Amateurs
Hatfield Main	St Helens Town	Yeading
Heanor Town	Sholing Sports	

FA/GM National School
International Youth Caps 1988-89

Under-16	Finland	Norway	Denmark	Iceland	Sweden	Israel	Spain	West Germany	Italy	Spain	Oman	Oman
J. Stanger (Manchester United)	1	1	1	1	1	1	1	1	1	1	*1	*1
D. Hancock (West Ham United)	2		2	2	2	2	2	*10	2	2		
K. Fowler (Arsenal)	3	**8	3		3	3	3	*9	3	3	3	3
P. Reed (West Ham United)	4	5	4	4	5	6	4	2	4	4	*6	2
R. Price (Oldham Athletic)	5	*4	5	*5	4	5	5			*5		
G. Flitcroft (Manchester City)	6	8	8	8	8	4	6	4	6	6	6	6
T. Sinclair (Blackpool)	7	*8		*11	*7	*7	*9	8	10	*10	7	*10
S. Clements (Arsenal)	8	6	6	6	6	8	7	5	7	7	8	8
O. Morah (Tottenham Hotspur)	9	*9	*9	*9	9	9	10	11	11	11	9	9
M. Joseph (Arsenal)	10	7	10	10	10	10	8	7	9	9	*10	7
M. Flatts (Arsenal)	11	11	11	11	11	11	9		*10	10	11	11
M. Foster	*1				*1							
D. Schonberger (Queen's Park Rangers)	*3	3	*3	3		*3		9			*3	*3
C. Gaunt (Arsenal)	*5	4	*5	5	*4	*5		3	5	5	5	5
A. Kenton (Oldham Athletic)	*9	9	9	9	*9	*9	11				10	10
C. Makin (Oldham Athletic)	*10	10	7	*3	*2	*2	*2	10		*2	2	*8
A. Fuller (Watford)		2	*8	7	7	7	*11	6	8	8	4	4
S. Sheppard (Watford)											1	1

*Substitute

FA/GM National School
International Matches 1988-89

Under-16

31.7.88	England	4	Finland	0	Vasteras
1.8.88	England	1	Norway	1	Vasteras
3.8.88	England	2	Denmark	2	Vasteras
5.8.88	England	2	Iceland	0	Vasteras
6.8.88	England	4	Sweden	0	Vasteras
20.8.88	England	1	Israel	1	Wembley
3.11.88	England	0	Spain	2	Chiavari
4.11.88	England	3	West Germany	2	Chiavari
7.11.88	England	2	Italy	1	Carlini
9.11.88	England	0	Spain	2	Carlini
15.2.89	Oman	2	England	0	Sohar
17.2.89	Oman	3	England	0	Muscat

119

F.A. Youth Challenge Cup Winners 1953-89

(AGGREGATE SCORES)

Year	Winners		Runners-up	
1953	Manchester United	9	Wolverhampton W	3
1954	Manchester United	5	Wolverhampton W	4
1955	Manchester United	7	West Bromwich Albion	1
1956	Manchester United	4	Chesterfield	3
1957	Manchester United	8	West Ham United	2
1958	Wolverhampton W	7	Chelsea	6
1959	Blackburn Rovers	2	West Ham United	1
1960	Chelsea	5	Preston North End	2
1961	Chelsea	5	Everton	3
1962	Newcastle United	2	Wolverhampton W	1
1963	West Ham United	6	Liverpool	5
1964	Manchester United	5	Swindon Town	2
1965	Everton	3	Arsenal	2
1966	Arsenal	5	Sunderland	3
1967	Sunderland	2	Birmingham City	0
1968	Burnley	3	Coventry City	2
1969	Sunderland	6	West Bromwich Albion	3
1970	Tottenham Hotspur	4	Coventry City	3
1971	Arsenal	2	Cardiff City	0
1972	Aston Villa	5	Liverpool	2
1973	Ipswich Town	4	Bristol City	1
1974	Tottenham Hotspur	2	Huddersfield Town	1
1975	Ipswich Town	5	West Ham United	1
1976	West Bromwich Albion	5	Wolverhampton W	0
1977	Crystal Palace	1	Everton	0
1978*	Crystal Palace	1	Aston Villa	0
1979	Millwall	2	Manchester City	0
1980	Aston Villa	3	Manchester City	2
1981	West Ham United	2	Tottenham Hotspur	1
1982	Watford	7	Manchester United	6
1983†	Norwich City	6	Everton	5
1984	Everton	4	Stoke City	2
1985	Newcastle United	4	Watford	1
1986	Manchester City	3	Manchester United	1
1987	Coventry City	2	Charlton Athletic	1
1988	Arsenal	6	Doncaster Rovers	1
1989	Watford	2	Manchester City	1

*One leg only   †After a replay

F.A. County Youth Challenge Cup
Winners 1945-89

(AGGREGATE SCORES)

Year	Winners		Runners-up	
1945	Staffordshire	3	Wiltshire	2
1946	Berks. & Bucks.	4	Durham	3
1947	Durham	4	Essex	2
1948	Essex	5	Liverpool	3
1949	Liverpool	4	Middlesex	3
1950	Essex	4	Middlesex	3
1951	Middlesex	3	Leics. & Rutland	1
1952	Sussex	3	Liverpool	1
1953	Sheffield & Hallam	5	Hampshire	3
1954	Liverpool	4	Gloucestershire	1
1955	Bedfordshire	2	Sheffield & Hallam	0
1956	Middlesex	3	Staffordshire	2
1957	Hampshire	4	Cheshire	3
1958	Staffordshire	8	London	0
1959	Birmingham	7	London	5
1960	London	6	Birmingham	4
1961	Lancashire	6	Nottinghamshire	3
1962	Middlesex	6	Nottinghamshire	3
1963	Durham	3	Essex	2
1964	Sheffield & Hallam	1	Birmingham	0
1965	Northumberland	7	Middlesex	4
1966	Leics. & Rutland	6	London	5
1967	Northamptonshire	5	Hertfordshire	4
1968	North Riding	7	Devon	4
1969	Northumberland	1	Sussex	0
1970*	Hertfordshire	2	Cheshire	1
1971*	Lancashire	2	Gloucestershire	0
1972*	Middlesex	2	Liverpool	0
1973*	Hertfordshire	3	Northumberland	0
1974*	Nottinghamshire	2	London	0
1975*	Durham	2	Bedfordshire	1
1976*	Northamptonshire	7	Surrey	1
1977*	Liverpool	3	Surrey	0
1978*	Liverpool	3	Kent	1
1979*	Hertfordshire	4	Liverpool	1
1980*	Liverpool	2	Lancashire	0
1981*	Lancashire	3	East Riding	2
1982*†	Devon	3	Kent	2
1983*	London	3	Gloucestershire	0
1984*	Cheshire	2	Manchester	1
1985*	East Riding	2	Middlesex	1
1986*	Hertfordshire	4	Manchester	0
1987*	North Riding	3	Gloucestershire	1
1988*‡	East Riding	5	Middlesex	3
1989*	Liverpool	2	Hertfordshire	1

*One leg only   †After a 0-0 draw   ‡After a 1-1 draw

F.A. Youth Challenge Cup Competition 1988-89

Preliminary Round	Result			Attendance		
	1st Tie	*1st Rep*	*2nd Rep*	*1st Tie*	*1st Rep*	*2nd Rep*
Stockton v Bedlington Terriers	1-2			27		
Billingham Synthonia v Shildon	2-1			35		
Guiseley v Carlisle United	1-2			63		
South Bank v Guisborough Town	0-5			35		
Chester-le-Street v Darlington....................	2-7			37		
Marske United v Billingham Town......................	2-0			51		
Preston North End v Blackburn Rovers	0-2			187		
South Liverpool v Atherton Collieries ....(walkover for Atherton Collieries)						
Chadderton v Rotherham United	1-10			70		
Marine v Bolton Wanderers	0-3			Nil		
Thackley v Atherton LR....................................	4-1			70		
Bootle v Rochdale	4-0			37		
Heanor Town v Bury ....(walkover for Bury)						
Formby v Halifax Town.....................................(walkover for Halifax Town)						
Chesterfield v Tranmere Rovers.........................	0-2			95		
Hinckley Town v Lincoln City............................	1-2			54		
Radford v Bilston Town	0-8			Nil		
Burton Albion v Scunthorpe United.....................	0-3			135		
Kettering Town v Walsall-Wood	5-1			32		
Nuneaton Borough v Alvechurch	1-1			34		
Alvechurch v Nuneaton Borough		1-3			36	
Tamworth v Mile Oak Rovers & Youth.................	0-3			44		
Rothwell Town v Kidderminster Harriers..............	0-7			27		
Banbury United v Oldswinford	4-2			26		
Corby Town v Rushall Olympic...........................	4-0			30		
Dunstable v Welwyn GC	1-1			27		
Welwyn GC v Dunstable		2-4			30	
Wisbech Town v Rushden Town...........................	1-4			70		
Stevenage Brough v Wellingborough Town	2-0			70		
Ruislip Manor v Bury Town	3-1			43		
Letchworth GC v St Albans City..........................	2-6			38		
Vauxhall Motors (Beds) v Clapton......................(walkover for Clapton)						
Billericay Town v Saffron Walden Town	2-2			Nil		
Saffron Walden Town v Billericay Town		0-4			95	
East Ham United v Collier Row ....(walkover for Collier Row)						
Welling United v Canvey Island	0-1			80		
Hampton v Hounslow..	3-0			45		
Uxbridge v Boreham Wood	5-0			55		
Brentford v Kingsbury Town	7-0			136		
Walton & Hersham v Burnham	1-0			7		
Slough Town v Maidenhead United	7-2			Nil		
Worthing v Marlow	1-1			19		
Marlow v Worthing		3-2			23	
Dover Athletic v Chatham Town ....(walkover for Dover)						
Egham Town v Carshalton Athletic	2-1			60		
Hailsham Town v Sheppey United	3-1			Nil		
Worthing United v Ringmer...............................	1-1			20		
Ringmer v Worthing United...............................		3-3			57	
Worthing United v Ringmer...............................			5-2			14
Banstead Athletic v Whitehawk	2-2			32		
Whitehawk v Banstead Athletic		2-0			88	
Bognor Regis Town v Hungerford Town	9-0			65		
Basingstoke Town v Newbury Town	1-2			183		
Yate Town v Cheltenham Town	2-4			41		
Weston-super-Mare v Hereford United	0-0			83		
Hereford United v Weston-super-Mare		2-0			82	
Worcester City v Mangotsfield United	0-3			42		
Dorchester Town v Torquay United.....................	0-3			37		
Romsey Town v Weymouth	3-1			64		
Trowbridge Town v Wimborne Town ....(walkover for Trowbridge Town)						

First Round Qualifying	Result			Attendance		
	1st Tie	1st Rep	2nd Rep	1st Tie	1st Rep	2nd Rep
Carlisle United *v* Billingham Synthonia.................	3-2			96		
York City *v* Bedlington Terriers	2-0			41		
Markse United *v* Darlington...............................	0-5			24		
Spennymoor United *v* Guisborough Town............	1-2			25		
Rotherham United *v* Atherton Collieries	8-1			86		
Rhyl *v* Blackburn Rovers................................(walkover for Blackburn Rovers)						
Bootle *v* Thackley..	1-0			43		
Huddersfield Town *v* Bolton Wanderers	1-1			231		
Bolton Wanderers *v* Huddersfield Town		1-2			169	
Tranmere Rovers *v* Halifax Town	5-1					
Garforth Town *v* Bury	1-7			61		
Scunthorpe United *v* Bilston Town	3-0			77		
Hinckley Athletic *v* Lincoln City	2-1			78		
Mile Oak Rovers & Youth *v* Nuneaton Borough	1-0			42		
Witney Town *v* Kettering Town	1-2			41		
Corby Town *v* Banbury United	7-0			24		
Lye Town *v* Kidderminster Harriers.....................	0-3			45		
Stevenage Borough *v* Rushden Town	1-2			124		
Peterborough United *v* Dunstable	1-1			85		
Dunstable *v* Peterborough United		2-3			68	
Clapton *v* St Albans City...................................	1-3					
Loughton *v* Ruislip Manor	1-5			39		
Canvey Island *v* Collier Row	0-1			60		
Royston Town *v* Billericay Town........................	3-7			76		
Brentford *v* Uxbridge	6-2			77		
Feltham *v* Hampton	1-3			35		
Marlow *v* Slough Town	1-5			30		
Whyteleafe *v* Walton & Hersham	1-1			20		
Walton & Hersham *v* Whyteleafe		0-4				
Thanet United *v* Egham Town ....(walkover for Egham Town)						
Southwick *v* Dover Athletic	1-1			Nil		
Dover Athletic *v* Southwick		3-1				
Whitehawk *v* Worthing United	4-2			48		
Horley Town *v* Hailsham Town..........................	3-2			14		
Aldershot *v* Newbury Town	0-0			97		
Newbury Town *v* Aldershot		4-2			51	
Havant Town *v* Bognor Regis Town	0-3			111		
Mangotsfield United *v* Hereford United................	1-2			73		
Wotton Rovers *v* Cheltenham Town	3-2			10		
Trowbridge Town *v* Romsey Town	0-3			22		
Gosport Borough *v* Torquay United....................	0-2			105		

Second Round Qualifying	Result			Attendance		
	1st Tie	1st Rep	2nd Rep	1st Tie	1st Rep	2nd Rep
Carlisle United *v* York City	2-1			75		
Darlington *v* Guisborough Town	4-0			93		
Rotherham United *v* Blackburn Rovers	0-1			102		
Bootle *v* Huddersfield Town...............................	1-0			55		
Tranmere Rovers *v* Bury	3-1			300		
Scunthorpe United *v* Hinckley Athletic................	4-0			123		
Mile Oak Rovers & Youth *v* Kettering Town	1-0			52		
Corby Town *v* Kidderminster Harriers.................	0-1			104		
Rushden Town *v* Peterborough United	2-4			105		
St Albans City *v* Ruislip Manor	3-2			49		
Collier Row *v* Billericay Town	0-2			82		
Brentford *v* Hampton	4-0			188		
Slough Town *v* Whyteleafe	2-2			60		
Whyteleafe *v* Slough Town		4-3			60	
Egham Town *v* Dover Athletic............................	4-1			62		
Whitehawk *v* Horley Town	0-0			39		

Horley Town v Whitehawk		6-0			32	
Newbury Town v Bognor Regis Town	4-0			104		
Hereford United v Wotton Rovers	6-1					
Romsey Town v Torquay United	0-4			79		

First Round Proper

	Result			Attendance		
	1st Tie	1st Rep	2nd Rep	1st Tie	1st Rep	2nd Rep
Carlisle United v Bootle	2-0			61		
Tranmere Rovers v Hull City	1-1			371		
Hull City v Tranmere Rovers		2-1			147	
Blackpool v Barnsley	2-0			50		
Hartlepool United v Burnley	0-3			54		
Blackburn Rovers v Oldham Athletic	1-1			188		
Oldham Athletic v Blackburn Rovers		1-0			176	
Wigan Athletic v Darlington	1-1			121		
Darlington v Wigan Athletic		4-0			90	
Sunderland v Bradford City	1-3			353		
West Bromwich Albion v Scunthorpe United	9-0			272		
Mile Oak Rovers & Youth v Hednesford Town	1-3			48		
Chester City v Aston Villa	0-2			190		
Grimsby Town v Derby County	0-3			137		
Wrexham v Port Vale	0-2			112		
Walsall v Wolverhampton Wanderers	3-2			417		
Shrewsbury Town v Crewe Alexandra	1-6			145		
Cambridge United v St Albans City	3-1			26		
Brentford v Wokingham Town	4-1			137		
Norwich City v Northampton Town	1-2			83		
Peterborough United v Billericay Town	6-0			199		
Hendon v Colchester United	1-4			128		
Kidderminster Harriers v West Ham United	1-2			681		
Millwall v Oxford United	0-0					
Oxford United v Millwall		4-4			224	
Millwall v Oxford United			4-0			
Epsom & Ewell v Erith & Belvedere	1-1			43		
Erith & Belvedere v Epsom & Ewell		0-1			45	
Horley Town v Queens Park Rangers	0-5			83		
Brighton & Hove Albion v Sutton United	5-0			143		
Staines Town v Reading	2-6			58		
Whyteleafe v Egham Town	5-1			80		
Newbury Town v Horndean	3-0			130		
Croydon v Gillingham	1-7			124		
AFC Bournemouth v Swansea City	1-1			134		
Swansea City v AFC Bournemouth		0-2			71	
Hereford United v Torquay United	2-0			96		
Exeter City v Cardiff City	0-0			310		
Cardiff City v Exeter City		3-1			82	
Portsmouth v Swindon Town	4-2			123		
Bristol Rovers v Bristol City	1-3			270		
Plymouth Argyle v Newport County	11-0			318		

Second Round Proper

	Result			Attendance		
	1st Tie	1st Rep	2nd Rep	1st Tie	1st Rep	2nd Rep
Bradford City v Port Vale	2-1			351		
Liverpool v Carlisle United	3-0			407		
Burnley v Leeds United	1-2			757		
Blackpool v Newcastle United	1-2			105		
Darlington v Manchester United	2-5			885		
Doncaster Rovers v Everton	1-1			784		
Everton v Doncaser Rovers		4-1			339	
Middlesbrough v Sheffield Wednesday	2-2			306		
Sheffield Wednesday v Middlesbrough		2-0			196	
Oldham Athletic v Sheffield United	1-2			190		
Mansfield Town v Manchester City	0-1			322		

	Result			Attendance		
	1st Tie	1st Rep	2nd Rep	1st Tie	1st Rep	2nd Rep
Crewe Alexandra v Hull City	1-4			1213		
Hednesford Town v Birmingham City	0-5			157		
Leicester City v Nottingham Forest	2-1			566		
Aston Villa v Luton Town	1-3			448		
Northampton Town v Walsall	0-3			52		
Colchester United v Southend United	2-3			59		
Derby County v Coventry City	1-1			179		
Coventry City v Derby County		3-1			510	
West Bromwich Albion v West Ham United	3-1			285		
Notts County v Ipswich Town	2-2			240		
Ipswich Town v Notts County		4-1			209	
Watford v Leyton Orient	1-1			169		
Leyton Orient v Watford		0-0			136	
Leyton Orient v Watford			1-2			171
Cambridge United v Stoke City	2-2			55		
Stoke City v Cambridge United		6-1			269	
Tottenham Hotspur v Peterborough United	7-1			154		
Epsom & Ewell v Arsenal	0-11			225		
Crystal Palace v Southampton	2-1			210		
Queens Park Rangers v Fulham	3-1					
Whyteleafe v Reading	1-5			150		
Newbury Town v Cardiff City	0-3			150		
Brighton & Hove Albion v Charlton Athletic	1-7			84		
Millwall v Hereford United	2-0			53		
Wimbledon v Chelsea	0-4			261		
Bristol City v Plymouth Argyle	2-3			106		
AFC Bournemouth v Brentford	2-3			106		
Portsmouth v Gillingham	1-0					

Third Round Proper

	Result			Attendance		
	1st Tie	1st Rep	2nd Rep	1st Tie	1st Rep	2nd Rep
Everton v Leicester City	0-0			533		
Leicester City v Everton		4-1			474	
Newcastle United v Walsall	4-3			241		
Coventry City v Liverpool	2-4			1253		
Leeds United v Birmingham City	0-0			201		
Birmingham City v Leeds United		1-1			323	
Leeds United v Birmingham City			2-4			186
Sheffield United v Bradford City	0-0			290		
Bradford City v Sheffield United		1-0			562	
Manchester City v Hull City	1-0			749		
Sheffield Wednesday v Manchester United	0-0			538		
Manchester United v Sheffield Wednesday		2-0			1550	
Chelsea v Ipswich Town	2-2			112		
Ipswich Town v Chelsea		2-1			481	
Millwall v Reading	4-2			287		
Plymouth Argyle v Portsmouth	0-6			613		
Charlton Athletic v Tottenham Hotspur	0-0			203		
Tottenham Hotspur v Charlton Athletic		2-0			120	
Cardiff City v Stoke City	0-1			219		
Brentford v Crystal Palace	1-0			210		
Watford v Queens Park Rangers	2-2			278		
Queens Park Rangers v Watford		0-2			152	
West Bromwich Albion v Southend United	3-2			378		
Arsenal v Luton Town	3-2			482		

Fourth Round Proper

	Result			Attendance		
	1st Tie	1st Rep	2nd Rep	1st Tie	1st Rep	2nd Rep
Brentford v Stoke City	1-1			722		
Stoke City v Brentford		1-2			1240	
Millwall v Liverpool	0-1			1076		
Manchester United v Ipswich Town	4-1			1834		
Bradford City v Manchester City	0-5			1254		

	Result			Attendance		
Leicester City *v* Newcastle United	1-3			992		
Portsmouth *v* Watford	1-1			471		
Watford *v* Portsmouth		5-2			149	
Arsenal *v* West Bromwich Albion........................	2-0			813		
Tottenham Hotspur *v* Birmingham City	2-1			159		

Fifth Round Proper	Result			Attendance		
	1st Tie	*1st Rep*	*2nd Rep*	*1st Tie*	*1st Rep*	*2nd Rep*
Tottenham Hotspur *v* Manchester City	0-2			501		
Newcastle United *v* Arsenal	1-0			1205		
Watford *v* Liverpool..	3-0			726		
Brentford *v* Manchester United	2-1			2567		

Semi-Final

1st Leg

Watford *v* Brentford...	2-1	1704
Manchester City *v* Newcastle United	2-1	2760

2nd Leg

Brentford *v* Watford...	2-2	1305
Newcastle United *v* Manchester City	0-1	2104

Watford won on aggregate 4-3
Manchester City won on aggregate 3-1

Final

1st Leg

Manchester City *v* Watford	1-0	4900

2nd Leg

Watford *v* Manchester City................................	2-0	5449

Watford won on aggregate 2-1

F.A. County Youth Challenge Cup Competition 1988-89

First Round

	1st Tie	1st Rep
Cumberland *v* Westmorland	2-0	
Durham *v* North Riding	3-1	
Liverpool *v* Manchester	1-0	
Cheshire *v* Nottinghamshire	3-4	
Derbyshire *v* Staffordshire	2-1	
Leicestershire & Rutland *v* Lincolnshire	0-1	
Norfolk *v* Cambridgeshire	3-1	
Suffolk *v* Hertfordshire	2-6	
Kent *v* Surrey	2-3	
Berks & Bucks *v* Royal Navy	1-3	
Oxfordshire *v* Worcestershire	2-0	
Devon *v* Dorset	4-0	
Cornwall *v* Somerset & Avon (South)	1-4	

Second Round

	1st Tie	1st Rep
Northumberland *v* East Riding	1-2	
Lancashire *v* Cumberland	1-2	
West Riding *v* Durham	3-1	
Sheffield & Hallamshire *v* Liverpool	1-3	
Birmingham *v* Nottinghamshire	3-1	
Shropshire *v* Derbyshire	0-1	
Bedfordshire *v* Lincolnshire	4-0	
Huntingdonshire *v* Northamptonshire	0-3	
Essex *v* Norfolk	2-1	
London *v* Hertfordshire	1-3	
Sussex *v* Middlesex	0-1	
Army *v* Surrey	2-6	
Hampshire *v* Royal Navy	1-0	
Herefordshire *v* Oxfordshire	2-1	
Gloucestershire *v* Devon	0-1	
Wiltshire *v* Somerset & Avon (South)	2-1	

Third Round

	1st Tie	1st Rep
West Riding *v* Cumberland	2-1	
East Riding *v* Liverpool	3-6	
Bedfordshire *v* Derbyshire	0-1	
Birmingham *v* Northamptonshire	1-4	
Middlesex *v* Hertfordshire	0-1	
Essex *v* Surrey	2-1	
Devon *v* Herefordshire	4-1	
Hampshire *v* Wiltshire	2-2	
Wiltshire *v* Hampshire		0-3

Fourth Round

Northamptonshire *v* West Riding	1-0	Hampshire *v* Hertfordshire	1-3
Derbyshire *v* Liverpool	1-3	Devon *v* Essex	3-1

Semi-Final

Liverpool *v* Northamptonshire	5-2	Devon *v* Hertfordshire	1-2

Final

Liverpool *v* Hertfordshire (at Boreham Wood FC) 2-1

England Youth Caps 1988-89

	Rep. of Ireland	Greece	France	Greece	Czechoslovakia
I. Walker (Tottenham Hotspur)	1	1	1	1	1
P. Towles (Watford)	2	2	2		2
A. McCarthy (Queens Park Rangers)	3				
P. Mitchell (Bournemouth)	4		*7	2	
J. Kavanagh (Derby County)	5	5	5	4	4
I. Hendon (Tottenham Hotspur)	6	6	6	5	5
N. Heaney (Arsenal)	7	7			
A. Cole (Arsenal)	8	8	8	9	9
A. Newhouse (Chester City)	9	9	9	10	8
M. Turner (Portsmouth)	10	10	10	*8	
C. Hartfield (Arsenal)	11	3		6	10
B. Small (Aston Villa)	*3		11	11	11
C. Halstead (Oldham Athletic)	*7				
B. Allen (Queens Park Rangers)	*9	*9	*9		
S. Walters (Crewe Alexandra)		4	4	8	6
A. Wright (Blackpool)		11	3	3	3
S. Houghton (Tottenham Hotspur)		*11		*7	*11
R. Jones (Crewe Alexandra)			7	7	
D. Sutch (Norwich City)					7

*Substitute

Watford – F.A. Youth Cup Winners 1989

Youth International Matches 1947-89

WYC **World Youth Championship**
IYT **International Youth Tournament**
*Qualifying Competition †Professionals ‡Abandoned

ENGLAND v. ALGERIA

			Goals	
Year	Date	Venue	Eng	Alg
†1984	April 22	Cannes	3	0

ENGLAND v. ARGENTINA

			Eng	Arg
†WYC1981	Oct. 5	Sydney	1	1

ENGLAND v. AUSTRALIA

			Eng	Aus
†WYC1981	Oct. 8	Sydney	1	1

ENGLAND v. AUSTRIA

			Eng	Aust
IYT1949	April 19	Zeist	4	2
IYT1952	April 17	Barcelona	5	5
IYT1957	April 16	Barcelona	0	3
1958	Mar. 4	Highbury	3	2
1958	June 1	Graz	4	3
IYT1960	April 20	Vienna	0	1
†IYT1964	April 1	Rotterdam	2	1
†1980	Sep. 6	Pazin	0	1
†IYT1981	May 29	Bonn	7	0
†1981	Sep. 3	Umag	3	0
†1984	Sep. 6	Izola	2	2

ENGLAND v. BELGIUM

			Eng	Belg
IYT1948	April 16	West Ham	3	1
IYT1951	Mar. 22	Cannes	1	1
IYT1953	Mar. 31	Brussels	2	0
‡1956	Nov. 7	Brussels	3	2
1957	Nov. 3	Sheffield	2	0
†IYT1965	April 15	Ludwigshafen	3	0
*IYT1969	Mar. 11	West Ham	1	0
*IYT1972	May 13	Palma	0	0
†IYT1973	June 4	Viareggio	0	0
†IYT1977	May 19	Lokeren	1	0
†1979	Jan 17	Brussels	4	0
†1980	Sep. 8	Labin	6	1
†1983	April 13	Birmingham	1	1
†1988	May 20	Chatel	0	0

ENGLAND v. BRAZIL

			Eng	Bra
†1986	Mar. 29	Cannes	0	0
†1986	May 13	Peking	1	2
†1987	June 2	Niteroi	0	2

ENGLAND v. BULGARIA

			Eng	Bulg
IYT1956	Mar. 28	Salgotarjan	1	2
IYT1960	April 16	Graz	0	1
IYT1962	April 24	Ploesti	0	0
†IYT1968	April 7	Nimes	0	0
†IYT1969	Mar. 26	Waregem	2	0
†IYT1972	May 13	Palma	0	0
†IYT1979	May 31	Vienna	0	1

ENGLAND v. CAMEROON

			Eng	Cam
†WYC1981	Oct. 3	Sydney	2	0
†1985	June 1	Toulon	1	0

ENGLAND v. CHINA

			Eng	China
†1983	Mar. 31	Cannes	5	1
†WYC1985	Aug. 26	Baku	0	2
†1986	May 5	Peking	1	0

ENGLAND v. CZECHOSLOVAKIA

			Goals	
Year	Date	Venue	Eng	Czech
IYT1955	April 7	Lucca	0	1
†IYT1966	May 21	Rijeka	2	3
†IYT1969	May 20	Leipzig	3	1
IYT1979	May 24	Bischofshofen	3	0
†1979	Sep. 8	Pula	1	2
†1982	April 11	Cannes	0	1
†IYT1983	May 20	Highbury	1	1
*†IYT1989	April 26	Bystrica	0	1

ENGLAND v. DENMARK

			Eng	Den
†1955	Oct. 1	Plymouth	9	2
1956	May 20	Esbjerg	2	1
*†IYT1979	Oct. 31	Esbjerg	3	1
*IYT1980	Mar. 26	Coventry	4	0
†1982	July 15	Stjordal	5	2
†1983	July 16	Holbeck	0	1
†1987	Feb. 16	Manchester	2	1

ENGLAND v. EGYPT

			Eng	Egypt
†WYC1981	Oct. 11	Sydney	4	2

ENGLAND v. FINLAND

			Eng	Fin
†IYT1975	May 19	Berne	1	0

ENGLAND v. FRANCE

			Eng	France
1957	Mar. 24	Fontainbleau	1	0
1958	Mar. 22	Eastbourne	0	1
†IYT1966	May 23	Rijeka	1	2
†IYT1967	May 11	Istanbul	2	0
†1968	Jan. 25	Paris	0	1
*IYT1978	Feb. 8	Crystal Palace	3	1
*IYT1978	Mar. 1	Paris	0	0
†IYT1979	June 2	Vienna	0	0
†1982	April 12	Cannes	0	1
†1983	April 2	Cannes	0	2
†1984	April 23	Cannes	1	2
†1985	June 7	Toulon	1	3
†1986	Mar. 31	Cannes	1	2
†1986	May 11	Peking	1	1
†1988	May 22	Monthey	1	2
*†IYT1988	Nov. 15	Bradford	1	1

ENGLAND v. GERMANY D.R.

			Eng	GDR
IYT1958	April 7	Neunkirchen	1	0
1959	Mar. 8	Zwickau	3	4
1960	April 2	Portsmouth	1	1
†IYT1965	April 25	Essen	2	3
†IYT1969	May 22	Magdeburg	0	4
†IYT1973	June 10	Florence	3	2
†IYT1984	May 25	Moscow	1	1
†1988	May 21	Monthey	1	0

ENGLAND v. GERMANY F.R.

			Eng	GFR
IYT1953	April 4	Boom	3	1
IYT1954	April 15	Gelsenkirchen	2	2
IYT1956	April 1	Sztalinvaros	2	1
1957	Mar. 31	Oberhausen	4	1
1958	Mar. 12	Bolton	1	2
1961	Mar. 12	Flensberg	0	2
†1962	Mar. 31	Northampton	1	0
†1967	Feb. 14	Moenchengladbach	1	0

			Eng	
†IYT1972	May	22	Barcelona ... 2	0
†1975	Jan.	25	Las Palmas ... 4	2
†1976	Nov.	14	Monte Carlo ... 1	1
†IYT1979	May	28	Salzburg ... 2	0
†1979	Sep.	1	Pula ... 1	1
†1983	Sep.	5	Pazin ... 2	0

ENGLAND v. GREECE

			Goals	
Year	Date	Venue	Eng	Greece
IYT1957	April 18	Barcelona ...	2	3
IYT1959	April 2	Dimitrovo ...	4	0
†IYT1977	May 23	Beveren ...	1	1
†1983	May 23	Puspokladany ...	1	0
*†IYT1988	Oct. 26	Birkenhead ...	5	0
*†IYT1989	Mar. 8	Xanthi ...	3	0

ENGLAND v. HUNGARY

			Eng	Hung
IYT1954	April 11	Dusseldorf ...	1	3
IYT1956	Mar. 31	Tatabanya ...	2	4
†1956	Oct. 23	Tottenham ...	2	1
†1956	Oct. 25	Sunderland ...	2	1
†IYT1965	April 21	Wuppertal ...	5	0
†IYT1975	May 16	Olten ...	3	1
†1977	Oct. 16	Las Palmas ...	3	0
†1979	Sep. 5	Pula ...	2	0
†1980	Sep. 11	Pula ...	1	2
†1981	Sep. 7	Porec ...	4	0
†1983	July 29	Debrecen ...	1	2
†1983	Sep. 3	Umag ...	3	2
†1986	Mar. 30	Cannes ...	2	0

ENGLAND v. ICELAND

			Eng	Ice
†IYT1973	May 31	Viareggio ...	2	0
†IYT1977	May 21	Turnhout ...	0	0
*†IYT1983	Oct. 12	Reykjavik ...	3	0
*†IYT1983	Nov. 1	Crystal Palace ...	3	0
*†IYT1984	Oct. 16	Manchester ...	5	3
*†IYT1985	Sep. 11	Reykjavik ...	5	0

ENGLAND v. IRELAND

			Eng	Ire
1948	May 15	Belfast ...	2	2
IYT1949	April 18	Haarlem ...	3	3
1949	May 14	Hull ...	4	2
1950	May 6	Belfast ...	0	1
1951	May 5	Liverpool ...	5	2
1952	April 19	Belfast ...	0	2
1953	April 11	Wolverhampton ...	0	0
IYT1954	April 10	Bruehl ...	5	0
1954	May 8	Newtonards ...	2	2
1955	May 14	Watford ...	3	0
1956	May 12	Belfast ...	0	1
1957	May 11	Leyton ...	6	2
1958	May 10	Bangor ...	2	4
1959	May 9	Liverpool ...	5	0
1960	May 14	Belfast ...	5	2
1961	May 13	Manchester ...	2	0
1962	May 12	Londonderry ...	1	2
†IYT1963	April 23	Wembley ...	4	0
1963	May 11	Oldham ...	1	1
1964	Jan. 25	Belfast ...	3	1
1965	Jan. 22	Birkenhead ...	2	3
1966	Feb. 26	Belfast ...	4	0
1967	Feb. 25	Stockport ...	3	0
1968	Feb. 23	Belfast ...	0	2
1969	Feb. 28	Birkenhead ...	0	2
1970	Feb. 28	Lurgan ...	1	3
1971	Mar. 6	Blackpool ...	1	1
1972	Mar. 11	Chester ...	1	1
1973	Mar. 24	Wellington ...	3	0
1974	April 19	Birkenhead ...	1	2

			Eng	
†IYT1975	May	13	Kriens ... 3	0
†IYT1983	May	16	Arnstadt ... 1	0
*†IYT1981	Feb.	11	Walsall ... 1	0
*†IYT1981	Mar.	11	Belfast ... 3	0

ENGLAND v. REP. OF IRELAND

				Goals Rep.
Year	Date	Venue	Eng	of Ire
IYT1953	April 5	Leuven ...	2	0
†IYT1964	Mar. 30	Middleburg ...	6	0
*†IYT1968	Feb. 7	Dublin ...	0	0
*†IYT1968	Feb. 28	Portsmouth ...	4	1
*†IYT1970	Jan. 14	Dublin ...	4	1
*†IYT1970	Feb. 4	Luton ...	10	0
†IYT1972	May 15	Sabadell ...	4	0
†IYT1975	May 9	Brunnen ...	1	0
*†IYT1985	Feb. 26	Dublin ...	0	1
*†IYT1986	Feb. 25	Leeds ...	2	0
†1988	Feb. 17	Stoke ...	2	0
†1988	Sep. 20	Dublin ...	2	0

ENGLAND v. ISRAEL

			Eng	Israel
†1962	May 20	Tel Aviv ...	3	1
†1962	May 22	Haifa ...	1	2

ENGLAND v. ITALY

			Eng	Italy
IYT1958	April 13	Luxembourg ...	0	1
IYT1959	Mar. 25	Sofia ...	1	3
IYT1961	April 4	Braga ...	2	3
†IYT1965	April 23	Marl-Huels ...	3	1
†IYT1966	May 25	Rijeka ...	1	1
†IYT1967	May 5	Izmir ...	1	1
†1973	Feb. 14	Cava Dei Tirreni ...	0	1
†1973	Mar. 14	Highbury ...	1	0
†IYT1973	June 7	Viareggio ...	1	0
†1978	Nov. 19	Monte Carlo ...	1	2
*†1979	Feb. 28	Rome ...	1	0
*†IYT1979	April 4	Birmingham ...	2	0
†IYT1983	May 22	Watford ...	1	1
†1984	April 20	Cannes ...	1	0
†1985	April 5	Cannes ...	2	2

ENGLAND v. LUXEMBOURG

			Eng	Lux
IYT1950	May 25	Vienna ...	1	2
IYT1954	April 17	Bad Neuenahr ...	0	2
1957	Feb. 2	West Ham ...	7	1
1957	Nov. 17	Luxembourg ...	3	0
IYT1958	April 9	Eschsalzett ...	5	0
†IYT1984	May 29	Moscow ...	2	0

ENGLAND v. MALTA

			Eng	Malta
†IYT1969	May 18	Wolfen ...	6	0
†IYT1979	May 26	Salzburg ...	3	0

ENGLAND v. MEXICO

			Eng	Mex
†1984	April 18	Cannes ...	4	0
†1985	June 5	Toulon ...	2	0
†WYC1985	Aug. 29	Baku ...	0	1

ENGLAND v. HOLLAND

			Eng	Hol
IYT1948	April 17	Tottenham ...	3	2
IYT1951	Mar. 26	Cannes ...	2	1
†1954	Nov. 21	Arnhem ...	2	3
†1955	Nov. 5	Norwich ...	3	1
1957	Mar. 2	Brentford ...	5	5

Year	Date		Venue	Goals Eng	Hol
IYT1957	April	14	Barcelona	1	2
1957	Oct.	2	Amsterdam	3	2
1961	Mar.	9	Utrecht	0	1
†1962	Jan.	31	Brighton	4	3
IYT1962	April	22	Ploesti	0	3
†IYT1963	April	13	Wimbledon	5	0
IYT1968	April	9	Nimes	1	0
*†IYT1974	Feb.	13	West Bromwich	1	1
*†IYT1974	Feb.	27	The Hague	1	0
†IYT1980	May	23	Halle	1	0
†1982	April	9	Cannes	1	0
†1985	April	7	Cannes	1	3
†1987	Aug.	1	Wembley	3	1

ENGLAND v. NORWAY

Year	Date		Venue	Goals Eng	Nor
†1982	July	13	Levanger	1	4
†1983	July	14	Korsor	1	0

ENGLAND v. PARAGUAY

				Eng	Par
†wycl985	Aug.	24	Baku	2	2

ENGLAND v. POLAND

				Eng	Pol
IYT1960	April	18	Graz	4	2
†IYT1964	Mar.	26	Breda	1	1
†IYT1971	May	26	Presnov	0	0
†IYT1972	May	20	Valencia	1	0
†1975	Jan.	21	Las Palmas	1	1
IYT1978	May	9	Chorzow	0	2
†1979	Sept.	3	Porec	0	1
†IYT1980	May	25	Leipzig	2	1
†1982	July	17	Steinkjer	3	2
†1983	July	12	Siagelse	1	0

ENGLAND v. PORTUGAL

				Eng	Port
IYT1954	April	18	Bonn	0	2
IYT1961	April	2	Lisbon	0	4
†IYT1964	April	3	The Hague	4	0
†IYT1971	May	30	Prague	3	0
†1978	Nov.	13	Monte Carlo	2	0
†IYT1980	May	18	Rosslau	1	1
†1982	April	7	Cannes	3	0

ENGLAND v. QATAR

				Eng	Qat
†wycl981	Oct.	14	Sydney	1	2
†1983	April	4	Cannes	1	1

ENGLAND v. RUMANIA

				Eng	Rum
1957	Oct.	15	Tottenham	4	2
IYT1958	April	11	Luxembourg	1	0
IYT1959	Mar.	31	Pazardijc	1	2
†IYT1963	April	15	Highbury	3	0
†wycl981	Oct.	17	Adelaide	0	1

ENGLAND v. SAAR

				Eng	Saar
IYT1954	April	13	Dortmund	1	1
IYT1955	April	9	Prato	3	1

ENGLAND v. SCOTLAND

				Eng	Sco
1947	Oct.	25	Doncaster	4	2
1948	Oct.	30	Aberdeen	1	3
IYT1949	April	21	Ultrecht	0	1

Year	Date		Venue	Goals Eng	Sco
1950	Feb.	4	Carlisle	7	1
1951	Feb.	3	Kilmarnock	6	1
1952	Mar.	15	Sunderland	3	1
1953	Feb.	7	Glasgow	4	3
1954	Feb.	6	Middlesbrough	2	1
1955	Mar.	5	Kilmarnock	3	4
1956	Mar.	3	Preston	2	2
1957	Mar.	9	Aberdeen	3	1
1958	Mar.	1	Hull	2	0
1959	Feb.	28	Aberdeen	1	1
1960	Feb.	27	Newcastle	1	1
1961	Feb.	25	Elgin	3	2
1962	Feb.	24	Peterborough	4	2
†IYT1963	April	19	White City	1	0
1963	May	18	Dumfries	3	1
1964	Feb.	22	Middlesbrough	1	1
1965	Feb.	27	Inverness	1	2
1966	Feb.	5	Hereford	5	3
1967	Feb.	4	Aberdeen	0	1
*†IYT1967	Mar.	1	Southampton	1	0
*†IYT1967	Mar.	15	Dundee	0	0
1968	Feb.	3	Walsall	0	5
1969	Feb.	1	Stranraer	1	1
1979	Jan.	31	Derby	1	2
1971	Jan.	30	Greenock	1	2
1972	Jan.	29	Bournemouth	2	0
1973	Jan.	20	Kilmarnock	3	2
1974	Jan.	26	Brighton	2	2
†IYT1981	May	27	Aachen	0	1
*†IYT1982	Feb.	23	Glasgow	0	1
*†IYT1982	Mar.	23	Coventry	2	2
†IYT1983	May	15	Birmingham	3	0
*†IYT1984	Nov.	27	Fulham	1	2
*1985	April	8	Cannes	1	0
*†IYT1986	Mar.	25	Aberdeen	1	4

ENGLAND v. SPAIN

				Eng	Spain
IYT1952	April	15	Barcelona	1	4
1957	Sept.	26	Birmingham	4	4
IYT1958	April	5	Saarbruecken	2	2
†1958	Oct.	8	Madrid	4	2
IYT1961	Mar.	30	Lisbon	0	0
†1964	Feb.	27	Murcia	2	1
†IYT1964	April	5	Amsterdam	4	0
†IYT1965	April	17	Heilbronn	0	0
†1966	Mar.	30	Swindon	3	0
†IYT1967	May	7	Manisa	2	1
†1971	Mar.	31	Pamplona	2	3
†1971	April	20	Luton	1	1
†1972	Feb.	9	Alicante	0	0
*†IYT1972	Mar.	15	Sheffield	4	1
*†IYT1975	Feb.	25	Bristol	1	1
*†IYT1975	Mar.	18	Madrid	1	0
†1976	Nov.	12	Monte Carlo	3	0
†IYT1978	May	7	Bukowas	1	0
†1978	Nov.	17	Monte Carlo	1	1
†IYT1981	May	25	Siegen	1	2
†IYT1983	May	13	Stoke	1	0

ENGLAND v. SWEDEN

				Eng	Swe
†IYT1971	May	24	Poprad	1	0
†1981	Sep.	5	Pazin	3	2
†1984	Sep.	10	Rovinj	1	1
†1986	Nov.	10	West Bromwich	3	3
†1988	May	19	Sion	2	0

ENGLAND v. SWITZERLAND

				Eng	Swit
IYT1950	May	26	Stockerau	2	1
IYT1951	Mar.	27	Nice	3	1
IYT1952	April	13	Barcelona	4	0
IYT1955	April	11	Florence	0	0
1956	Mar.	11	Schaffhausen	2	0
1956	Oct.	13	Brighton	2	2

ENGLAND v. SWITZERLAND (contd)

Year	Date		Venue	Eng	Swit
1958	May	26	Zurich	3	0
†1960	Oct.	8	Leyton	4	3
*1962	Nov.	22	Coventry	1	0
†1963	Mar.	21	Bienne	7	1
†IYT1973	June	2	Forte Dei Marmi	2	0
†IYT1975	May	11	Buochs	4	0
†1980	Sep.	4	Rovinj	3	0
†1982	Sep.	6	Porec	2	0
†1983	July	26	Hajduboszormeny	4	0
†1983	Sep.	1	Porec	4	2

ENGLAND v. THAILAND

Year	Date		Venue	Eng	Thai
†1986	May	7	Peking	1	2

ENGLAND v. TURKEY

Year	Date		Venue	Eng	Tur
IYT1959	Mar.	29	Dimitrovo	1	1
†IYT1978	May	5	Wodzislaw	1	1

ENGLAND v. U.S.S.R.

Year	Date		Venue	Eng	USSR
†IYT1963	April	17	Tottenham	2	0
†IYT1967	May	13	Istanbul	0	1
†IYT1968	April	11	Nimes	1	1
†IYT1971	May	28	Prague	1	1
†1978	Oct.	10	Las Palmas	1	0
†1982	Sep.	4	Umag	1	0
†1983	Mar.	29	Cannes	0	0
†IYT1983	May	17	Aston Villa	0	2
†IYT1984	May	27	Moscow	1	1
†1984	Sep.	8	Porec	1	0
†1985	April	3	Cannes	2	1
†1985	June	3	Toulon	0	2

ENGLAND v. URUGUAY

Year	Date		Venue	Eng	Uru
†1977	Oct.	9	Las Palmas	1	1
†1987	June	10	Montevideo	2	2

ENGLAND v. WALES

Year	Date		Venue	Eng	Wales
1948	Feb.	28	High Wycombe	4	3
IYT1948	April	15	London	4	0
1949	Feb.	26	Swansea	0	0
1950	Feb.	25	Worcester	1	0
1951	Feb.	17	Wrexham	1	1

ENGLAND v. WALES (contd)

Year	Date		Venue	Eng	Wales
1952	Feb.	23	Plymouth	6	0
1953	Feb.	21	Swansea	4	2
1954	Feb.	20	Derby	2	1
1955	Feb.	19	Milford Haven	7	2
1956	Feb.	18	Shrewsbury	5	1
1957	Feb.	9	Cardiff	7	1
1958	Feb.	15	Reading	8	2
1959	Feb.	14	Portmadoc	3	0
1960	Mar.	19	Canterbury	1	1
1961	Mar.	18	Newtown	4	0
1962	Mar.	17	Swindon	4	0
1963	Mar.	16	Haverfordwest	1	0
1964	Mar.	14	Leeds	2	1
1965	Mar.	20	Newport	2	2
1966	Mar.	19	Northampton	4	1
1967	Mar.	18	Cwmbran	3	3
1968	Mar.	16	Watford	2	3
1969	Mar.	15	Haverfordwest	3	1
*†IYT1970	Feb.	25	Newport	0	0
*†IYT1970	Mar.	18	Leyton	1	2
1970	April	20	Reading	0	0
1971	Feb.	20	Aberystwyth	1	2
1972	Feb.	19	Swindon	4	0
1973	Feb.	24	Portmadoc	4	1
*†IYT1974	Jan.	9	West Bromwich	1	0
1974	Mar.	2	Shrewsbury	2	1
*†IYT1974	Mar.	13	Cardiff	0	1
*†IYT1976	Feb.	11	Cardiff	1	0
*†IYT1976	Mar.	3	Manchester	2	3
*†IYT1977	Mar.	9	West Bromwich	1	0
*†IYT1977	Mar.	23	Cardiff	1	1

ENGLAND v. YUGOSLAVIA

Year	Date		Venue	Eng	Yugo
IYT1953	April	2	Liege	1	1
1958	Feb.	4	Chelsea	2	2
IYT1962	April	20	Ploesti	0	5
†IYT1967	May	9	Izmir	1	1
†IYT1971	May	22	Bardejov	1	0
†IYT1972	May	17	Barcelona	1	0
†1976	Nov.	16	Monte Carlo	0	3
†1978	May	20	Altenberg	2	0
†1981	Sep.	10	Pula	5	0
†1982	Sep.	9	Pula	1	0
†1983	July	25	Debrechen	4	4
†1983	Sep.	8	Pula	2	2
†1984	Sep.	12	Buje	1	4

Football League Champions 1888-1989

FIRST DIVISION 1888-1989

Season	Winners	Pts.	Max.	Season	Winners	Pts.	Max.
1888-89	Preston North End	40		1937-38	Arsenal	52	
1889-90	Preston North End	33	44	1938-39	Everton	59	
1890-91	Everton	29		1946-47	Liverpool	57	
1891-92	Sunderland	42	52	1947-48	Arsenal	59	
1892-93	Sunderland	48		1948-49	Portsmouth	58	
1893-94	Aston Villa	44		1949-50	*Portsmouth	53	
1894-95	Sunderland	47		1950-51	Tottenham Hotspur	60	
1895-96	Aston Villa	45	60	1951-52	Manchester United	57	
1896-97	Aston Villa	47		1952-53	*Arsenal	54	
1897-98	Sheffield United	42		1953-54	Wolverhampton Wanderers	57	
1898-99	Aston Villa	45		1954-55	Chelsea	52	
1899-1900	Aston Villa	50		1955-56	Manchester United	60	
1900-01	Liverpool	45		1956-57	Manchester United	64	
1901-02	Sunderland	44	68	1957-58	Wolverhampton Wanderers	64	
1902-03	Sheffield Wednesday	42		1958-59	Wolverhampton Wanderers	61	
1903-04	Sheffield Wednesday	47		1959-60	Burnley	55	
1904-05	Newcastle United	48		1960-61	Tottenham Hotspur	66	
1905-06	Liverpool	51		1961-62	Ipswich Town	56	84
1906-07	Newcastle United	51		1962-63	Everton	61	
1907-08	Manchester United	52		1963-64	Liverpool	57	
1908-09	Newcastle United	53		1964-65	*Manchester United	61	
1909-10	Aston Villa	53	76	1965-66	Liverpool	61	
1910-11	Manchester United	52		1966-67	Manchester United	60	
1911-12	Blackburn Rovers	49		1967-68	Manchester City	58	
1912-13	Sunderland	54		1968-69	Leeds United	67	
1913-14	Blackburn Rovers	51		1969-70	Everton	66	
1914-15	Everton	46		1970-71	Arsenal	65	
1919-20	West Bromwich Albion	60		1971-72	Derby County	58	
1920-21	Burnley	59		1972-73	Liverpool	60	
1921-22	Liverpool	57		1973-74	Leeds United	62	
1922-23	Liverpool	60		1974-75	Derby County	53	
1923-24	*Huddersfield Town	57		1975-76	Liverpool	60	
1924-25	Huddersfield Town	58		1976-77	Liverpool	57	
1925-26	Huddersfield Town	57		1977-78	Nottingham Forest	64	
1926-27	Newcastle United	56	84	1978-79	Liverpool	68	
1927-28	Everton	53		1979-80	Liverpool	60	
1928-29	Sheffield Wednesday	52		1980-81	Aston Villa	60	
1929-30	Sheffield Wednesday	60		1981-82	Liverpool	87	
1930-31	Arsenal	66		1982-83	Liverpool	82	
1931-32	Everton	56		1983-84	Liverpool	80	126
1932-33	Arsenal	58		1984-85	Everton	90	
1933-34	Arsenal	59		1985-86	Liverpool	88	
1934-35	Arsenal	58		1986-87	Everton	86	
1935-36	Sunderland	56		1987-88	Liverpool	90	120
1936-37	Manchester City	57		1988-89	Arsenal	76	114

SECOND DIVISION 1892-1989

Season	Winners	Pts.	Max.	Season	Winners	Pts.	Max.
1892-93	Small Heath	36	44	1913-14	Notts County	53	76
1893-94	Liverpool	50	56	1914-15	Derby County	53	
1894-95	Bury	48		1919-20	Tottenham Hotspur	70	
1895-96	*Liverpool	46	60	1920-21	Birmingham	58	
1896-97	Notts. County	42		1921-22	Nottingham Forest	56	
1897-98	Burnley	48		1922-23	Notts County	53	
1898-99	Manchester City	52		1923-24	Leeds United	54	
1899-1900	Sheffield Wednesday	54		1924-25	Leicester City	59	
1900-01	Grimsby Town	49		1925-26	Sheffield Wednesday	60	
1901-02	West Bromwich Albion	55	68	1926-27	Middlesbrough	62	
1902-03	Manchester City	54		1927-28	Manchester City	59	
1903-04	Preston North End	50		1928-29	Middlesbrough	55	
1904-05	Liverpool	58		1929-30	Blackpool	58	
1905-06	Bristol City	66		1930-31	Everton	61	
1906-07	Nottingham Forest	60		1931-32	Wolverhampton Wanderers	56	
1907-08	Bradford City	54		1932-33	Stoke City	56	
1908-09	Bolton Wanderers	52		1933-34	Grimsby Town	59	
1909-10	Manchester City	54	76	1934-35	Brentford	61	
1910-11	West Bromwich Albion	53		1935-36	Manchester United	56	
1911-12	Derby County	54		1936-37	Leicester City	56	
1012-13	Preston North End	53		1937-38	Aston Villa	57	

*Won on goal average/difference

No competition 1915-18 and 1939-46

SECOND DIVISION 1892-1989 (*contd*)

Season	Winners	Pts.	Max.	Season	Winners	Pts.	Max.
1938-39	Blackburn Rovers	55		1967-68	Ipswich Town	59	
1946-47	Manchester City	62		1968-69	Derby County	63	84
1947-48	Birmingham City	59	84	1969-70	Huddersfield Town	60	
1948-49	Fulham	57		1970-71	Leicester City	59	
1949-50	Tottenham Hotspur	61		1971-72	Norwich City	57	
1950-51	Preston North End	57		1972-73	Burnley	62	
1951-52	Sheffield Wednesday	53		1973-74	Middlesbrough	65	
1952-53	Sheffield United	60		1974-75	Manchester United	61	
1953-54	*Leicester City	56		1975-76	Sunderland	56	
1954-55	*Birmingham City	54		1976-77	Wolverhampton Wanderers	57	
1955-56	Sheffield Wednesday	55		1977-78	Bolton Wanderers	58	84
1956-57	Leicester City	61		1978-79	Crystal Palace	57	
1957-58	West Ham United	57		1979-80	Leicester City	55	
1958-59	Sheffield Wednesday	62		1980-81	West Ham United	66	
1959-60	Aston Villa	59		1981-82	Luton Town	88	
1960-61	Ipswich Town	59		1982-83	Queen's Park Rangers	85	
1961-62	Liverpool	62		1983-84	*Chelsea	88	126
1962-63	Stoke City	53		1984-85	Oxford United	84	
1963-64	Leeds United	63		1985-86	Norwich City	84	
1964-65	Newcastle United	57		1986-87	Derby County	84	
1965-66	Manchester City	59		1987-88	Millwall	82	132
1966-67	Coventry City	59		1988-89	Chelsea	99	138

THIRD DIVISION (S) 1920-58

Season	Winners	Pts.	Max.	Season	Winners	Pts.	Max.
1920-21	Crystal Palace	59		1936-37	Luton Town	58	
1921-22	*Southampton	61		1937-38	Millwall	56	
1922-23	Bristol City	59		1938-39	Newport County	55	
1923-24	Portsmouth	59		1946-47	Cardiff City	66	84
1924-25	Swansea Town	57		1947-48	Queen's Park Rangers	61	
1925-26	Reading	57		1948-49	Swansea Town	62	
1926-27	Bristol City	62		1949-50	Notts County	58	
1927-28	Millwall	65	84	1950-51	Nottingham Forest	70	
1928-29	*Charlton Athletic	54		1951-52	Plymouth Argyle	66	
1929-30	Plymouth Argyle	68		1952-53	Bristol Rovers	64	
1930-31	Notts County	59		1953-54	Ipswich Town	64	
1931-32	Fulham	57		1954-55	Bristol City	70	92
1932-33	Brentford	62		1955-56	Leyton Orient	66	
1933-34	Norwich City	61		1956-57	*Ipswich Town	59	
1934-35	Charlton Athletic	61		1957-58	Brighton and Hove Albion	60	
1935-36	Coventry City	57					

THIRD DIVISION (N) 1921-58

Season	Winners	Pts.	Max.	Season	Winners	Pts.	Max.
1921-22	Stockport County	56	76	1936-37	Stockport County	60	
1922-23	Nelson	51		1937-38	Tranmere Rovers	56	
1923-24	Wolverhampton Wanderers	63		1938-39	Barnsley	67	
1924-25	Darlington	58		1946-47	Doncaster Rovers	72	84
1925-26	Grimsby Town	61		1947-48	Lincoln City	60	
1926-27	Stoke City	63		1948-49	Hull City	65	
1927-28	Bradford	63	84	1949-50	Doncaster Rovers	55	
1928-29	Bradford City	63		1950-51	Rotherham United	71	
1929-30	Port Vale	67		1951-52	Lincoln City	69	
1930-31	Chesterfield	58		1952-53	Oldham Athletic	59	
1931-32	*Lincoln City	57	80	1953-54	Port Vale	69	
1932-33	Hull City	59		1954-55	Barnsley	65	92
1933-34	Barnsley	62		1955-56	Grimsby Town	68	
1934-35	Doncaster Rovers	57	84	1956-57	Derby County	63	
1935-36	Chesterfield	60		1957-58	Scunthorpe United	66	

THIRD DIVISION 1958-89

Season	Winners	Pts.	Max.	Season	Winners	Pts.	Max.
1958-59	Plymouth Argyle	62		1962-63	Northampton Town	62	
1959-60	Southampton	61		1963-64	*Coventry City	60	
1960-61	Bury	68		1964-65	Carlisle United	60	
1961-62	Portsmouth	65		1965-66	Hull City	69	

*Won on goal average   No competition 1939-46

Season	Winners	Pts.	Max.	Season	Winners	Pts.	Max.
1966-67	Queen's Park Rangers	67		1977-78	Wrexham	61	
1967-68	Oxford United	57		1978-79	Shrewsbury Town	61	
1968-69	*Watford	64		1979-80	Grimsby Town	62	
1969-70	Orient	62	92	1980-81	Rotherham United	61	
1970-71	Preston North End	61		1981-82	Burnley	80	
1971-72	Aston Villa	70		1982-83	Portsmouth	91	
1972-73	Bolton Wanderers	61		1983-84	Oxford United	95	
1973-74	Oldham Athletic	62		1984-85	Bradford City	94	138
1974-75	Blackburn Rovers	60		1985-86	Reading	94	
1975-76	Hereford United	63		1986-87	AFC Bournemouth	97	
1976-77	Mansfield Town	64		1987-88	Sunderland	93	
				1988-89	Wolverhampton Wanderers	92	

FOURTH DIVISION 1958-89

Season	Winners	Pts.	Max.	Season	Winners	Pts.	Max.
1958-59	Port Vale	64		1973-74	Peterborough United	65	
1958-60	Walsall	65	92	1974-75	Mansfield Town	68	
1960-61	Peterborough United	66		1975-76	Lincoln City	74	
1961-62	Millwall	56	88	1976-77	Cambridge United	65	
1962-63	Brentford	62		1977-78	Watford	71	
1963-64	*Gillingham	60		1978-79	Reading	65	
1964-65	Brighton and Hove Albion	63		1979-80	Huddersfield Town	66	
1965-66	Doncaster Rovers	59		1980-81	Southend United	67	
1966-67	Stockport County	64		1981-82	Sheffield United	96	
1967-68	Luton Town	66		1982-83	Wimbledon	98	
1968-69	Doncaster Rovers	59		1983-84	York City	101	
1969-70	Chesterfield	64		1984-85	Chesterfield	91	138
1970-71	Notts County	69	92	1985-86	Swindon Town	102	
1971-72	Grimsby Town	63		1986-87	Northampton Town	99	
1972-73	Southport	62		1987-88	Wolverhampton Wanderers	90	
				1988-89	Rotherham United	82	

Review of the Barclays League Season 1988-89

Football's most traumatic season ended with the most dramatic finale imaginable as Arsenal snatched the First Division championship from Liverpool against all the odds. When the two teams met at Anfield on the evening of 26 May, Liverpool needed only to avoid losing by two goals to be able to celebrate their second League and Cup "double" in four seasons.

A goal in the second minute of injury time by midfielder Michael Thomas, which gave the match its improbable final scoreline of 2-0 to Arsenal, brought the League title to Highbury for the first time since the London club's own "double" year of 1971. After nine months of First Division action Arsenal and Liverpool had finished the season with the same points total (76) and exactly similar goal differences (+37). Arsenal only became champions by virtue of having scored eight more goals. It was as close as that.

There was no lack of drama at the bottom of the First Division either. Newly-promoted Middlesbrough travelled to Sheffield Wednesday for their last match on 13 May knowing that defeat for either team would almost certainly consign them to the drop. Steve Whitton's 65th-minute effort for Wednesday relegated the second north-east side in this season, Newcastle having already known that fate for some weeks.

Luton Town pulled clear with their 1-0 home win against the First Division's revelation, Norwich City, on a day when Danny Wilson missed one spot-kick but converted another for a precious three points. Aston Villa's survival depended on West Ham United's failing to win their last two fixtures – away to Nottingham Forest and Liverpool. Plucky "Hammers", whose away record was reasonably good – they finished with more victories than any other team outside the top six – got the points at Forest's County Ground (2-1) but were finally overwhelmed at Anfield (1-5). Despite playing a two-hour Wembley final in ninety degrees only three days earlier, the Cup-winners had been in no mood to compromise their title ambitions.

Crystal Palace, with a late surge, were thought to be the only team capable of depriving Manchester City of the second automatic promotion spot behind Chelsea in Division 2. City certainly had their supporters living on their nerves when they blew a 3-0 lead against Bournemouth in the last fixture at Maine Road on 6 May, Luther Blissett equalising in the sixth minute of injury time. Palace though, were having problems of their own on that day as they surrendered a 2-1 lead at Leicester (both Madden penalties) with just three minutes remaining.

The two rivals went into their respective final matches on 13 May knowing that the combination of a 1-0 City defeat at Bradford City and a 4-0 win by Palace at home to doomed Birmingham City would take the Londoners up into the First Division. In a match interrupted for 26 minutes by a pitch invasion, Palace raced to a 4-0 lead before the heartbreaking news filtered through that Mel Machin's team had grabbed an 85th-minute equaliser at Valley Parade, thereby making Palace's scoring feats irrelevant. But the play-offs awaited the high-flying "Eagles".

Wolverhampton Wanderers, with their super marksmen Steve Bull and Andy Mutch, were Third Division champions by eight points and Sheffield United achieved second place on goal difference from Port Vale by virtue of their 2-2 draw at Molineux on 9 May. At the foot of the table Reading won 4-2 at Chesterfield after trailing 2-0 at half-time to rescue themselves and send their opponents down. Blackpool won 2-1 at Swansea City, thanks to an own goal, to avoid the drop and it was Southend United who became the unlucky seasiders, condemned even though they had beaten eighth-placed Chester City 1-0 at home.

Rotherham United made it back to Division 3 at the first attempt with a 3-1 win at Stockport County on 6 May and confirmed themselves as Fourth Division champions with a goalless draw at home to Cambridge United a week later, a result which deprived their visitors of a play-off spot. Tranmere Rovers' 1-1 draw with Crewe Alexandra, watched by the largest Prenton Park crowd since 1972, was enough for both clubs to go up automatically.

In the last few weeks of the season Darlington and Colchester United had been the two clubs which looked most likely to lose their Barclays League status. The latter's results improved under new boss Jock Wallace (with Alan Ball as coach) and Darlington found themselves having to win at Scunthorpe United on 6 May – or be playing in the GM Vauxhall Conference in three months' time. The home side were pushing hard for automatic promotion and Tony Daws scored a hat-trick in their 5-1 victory. Darlington manager Brian Little's last trip to Scunthorpe (as Wolves boss) had resulted in his being sacked! Their place in the League will now be taken by Maidstone United.

Barclays League Play-Offs

Division 2
Semi-Finals
Swindon Town v Crystal Palace 1-0, 0-2
Blackburn Rovers* v Watford 0-0, 1-1
Final
Blackburn Rovers v Crystal Palace 3-1, 0-3

Division 3
Semi-Finals
Preston North End v Port Vale 1-1, 1-3
Bristol Rovers v Fulham 1-0, 4-0
Final
Bristol Rovers v Port Vale 1-1, 0-1

Division 4
Semi-Finals
Scunthorpe United v Wrexham 1-3, 0-2
Leyton Orient v Scarborough 2-0, 0-1
Final
Wrexham v Leyton Orient 0-0, 1-2

* Won on away goals

First Division Results 1988-89

	Arsenal	Aston Villa	Charlton Athletic	Coventry City	Derby County	Everton	Liverpool	Luton Town	Manchester United	Middlesbrough	Millwall	Newcastle United	Norwich City	Nottingham Forest	Queens Park Rangers	Sheffield Wednesday	Southampton	Tottenham Hotspur	West Ham United	Wimbledon
Arsenal	—	2-3	2-2	2-0	2-1	1-3	1-1	1-1	1-1	0-1	0-2	1-0	5-0	1-1	2-1	1-0	1-0	2-0	1-1	2-2
Aston Villa	0-3	—	2-2	2-1	1-1	1-0	1-1	1-1	3-3	2-0	2-2	3-1	3-1	1-1	1-1	2-0	1-2	2-1	1-0	0-1
Charlton Athletic	2-3	1-2	—	3-0	0-2	3-2	2-0	5-2	3-0	1-0	0-2	2-2	1-2	0-1	1-1	2-0	2-1	2-2	0-0	1-0
Coventry City	1-0	2-1	3-0	—	0-0	1-2	1-0	1-0	0-1	0-0	3-0	2-0	2-1	2-2	0-3	5-1	1-1	1-1	1-2	2-1
Derby County	2-1	1-1	0-0	0-1	—	0-1	1-1	0-1	2-2	1-0	1-1	0-0	0-1	0-2	4-1	1-0	3-1	1-0	3-1	4-1
Everton	1-3	1-0	3-2	1-2	0-1	—	1-0	1-2	3-3	2-1	1-1	0-2	0-1	1-0	4-0	2-0	2-0	0-1	3-1	1-1
Liverpool	0-2	1-1	2-0	1-0	1-1	1-0	—	5-0	0-2	0-4	1-2	2-0	2-0	1-0	1-0	5-1	6-1	1-0	2-0	1-1
Luton Town	1-1	1-1	1-1	1-0	0-1	1-2	1-0	—	2-1	3-1	3-0	0-0	2-3	2-1	3-1	1-1	6-1	1-0	2-0	2-2
Manchester United	1-1	3-3	3-0	0-1	2-2	3-3	1-0	2-1	—	1-0	0-0	0-0	2-0	1-0	0-0	2-1	2-2	1-0	2-0	1-0
Middlesbrough	0-1	2-0	1-0	0-0	1-0	2-1	0-4	3-1	1-0	—	2-0	2-0	2-2	3-4	3-2	3-0	3-3	2-2	0-1	0-1
Millwall	1-2	2-2	0-2	3-0	1-1	1-1	1-2	3-0	0-0	2-1	—	3-2	2-2	2-2	3-2	1-3	3-3	2-1	1-0	2-1
Newcastle United	0-1	4-0	1-3	2-1	2-2	0-2	2-2	2-0	0-0	3-0	4-1	—	2-3	1-1	1-0	1-3	3-0	1-2	1-2	0-1
Norwich City	0-0	1-0	4-0	2-1	1-2	0-0	1-1	1-1	1-0	0-0	1-0	3-0	—	1-2	2-2	0-0	3-0	1-0	2-1	4-3
Nottingham Forest	1-4	2-2	1-0	2-1	0-2	1-1	4-1	1-0	3-2	2-2	3-0	3-0	0-0	—	2-1	2-3	3-1	0-2	2-1	1-1
Queens Park Rangers	0-0	4-0	3-1	1-0	1-0	2-1	0-1	2-1	0-2	0-0	2-0	1-0	2-2	1-2	—	0-0	3-1	3-2	0-1	0-0
Sheffield Wednesday	2-1	1-0	1-1	5-0	1-1	0-1	2-1	1-0	2-1	1-0	2-0	1-3	0-2	2-0	0-1	—	2-0	2-1	2-2	3-2
Southampton	1-3	3-1	1-3	0-1	3-1	1-1	1-2	1-1	2-2	3-2	3-0	4-1	2-2	3-3	3-1	1-0	—	2-2	0-1	1-2
Tottenham Hotspur	2-3	2-0	1-1	1-1	1-1	2-1	1-2	2-1	1-3	1-2	1-0	2-0	2-1	1-2	2-1	2-0	2-0	—	3-0	3-2
West Ham United	1-4	2-2	1-3	2-1	1-2	0-1	0-2	0-0	1-1	1-1	2-0	4-0	2-1	3-3	2-2	0-0	1-2	0-2	—	1-2
Wimbledon	1-5	1-0	1-1	2-1	4-1	1-1	1-1	4-0	1-1	1-1	1-0	0-1	0-2	4-1	1-0	1-0	2-1	1-2	0-1	—

138

First Division Final Positions 1988-89

		P	Home					Away					Total			
			W	D	L	F	A	W	D	L	F	A	F	A	GD	Pts
1.	Arsenal	38	10	6	3	35	19	12	4	3	38	17	73	36	+37	76
2.	Liverpool	38	11	5	3	33	11	11	5	3	32	17	65	28	+37	76
3.	Nottingham Forest	38	8	7	4	31	16	9	6	4	33	27	64	43	+21	64
4.	Norwich City	38	8	7	4	23	20	9	4	6	25	25	48	45	+3	62
5.	Derby County	38	9	3	7	23	18	8	4	7	17	20	40	38	+2	58
6.	Tottenham Hotspur	38	8	6	5	31	24	7	6	6	29	22	60	46	+14	57
7.	Coventry City	38	9	4	6	28	23	5	9	5	19	19	47	42	+5	55
8.	Everton	38	10	7	2	33	18	4	5	10	17	27	50	45	+5	54
9.	Queen's Park Rangers	38	9	5	5	23	16	5	6	8	20	21	43	37	+6	53
10.	Millwall	38	10	3	6	27	21	4	8	7	20	31	47	52	−5	53
11.	Manchester United	38	10	5	4	27	13	3	7	9	18	22	45	35	+10	51
12.	Wimbledon	38	10	3	6	30	19	4	6	9	20	27	50	46	+4	51
13.	Southampton	38	6	7	6	25	26	4	8	7	27	40	52	66	−14	45
14.	Charlton Athletic	38	6	7	6	25	24	4	5	10	19	34	44	58	−14	42
15.	Sheffield Wednesday	38	6	6	7	21	25	4	6	9	13	26	34	51	−17	42
16.	Luton Town	38	8	6	5	32	21	2	5	12	10	31	42	52	−10	41
17.	Aston Villa	38	7	6	6	25	22	2	7	10	20	34	45	56	−11	40
18.	Middlesbrough	38	6	7	6	28	30	3	5	11	16	31	44	61	−17	39
19.	West Ham United	38	3	6	10	19	30	7	2	10	18	32	37	62	−25	38
20.	Newcastle United	38	3	6	10	19	28	4	4	11	13	35	32	63	−31	31

Arsenal – First Division Champions

Second Division Results 1988-89

(Home) \ (Away)	West Bromwich Albion	Watford	Walsall	Swindon Town	Sunderland	Stoke City	Shrewsbury Town	Portsmouth	Plymouth Argyle	Oxford United	Oldham Athletic	Manchester City	Leicester City	Leeds United	Ipswich Town	Hull City	Crystal Palace	Chelsea	Brighton & Hove Albion	Bradford City	Bournemouth	Blackburn Rovers	Birmingham City	Barnsley
Barnsley	2-1	2-2	1-0	1-1	3-3	1-1	1-2	1-0	3-1	1-0	4-3	1-2	3-0	2-2	2-0	0-2	1-1	1-1	2-2	0-0	5-2	0-1	0-0	—
Birmingham City	1-4	2-3	0-0	1-2	2-2	0-1	2-1	0-0	1-1	0-1	0-0	0-2	2-3	0-0	1-0	2-0	1-4	1-4	1-2	1-0	0-1	2-0	—	3-5
Blackburn Rovers	1-2	2-1	3-1	1-0	0-1	4-3	1-1	3-1	1-2	1-1	3-1	0-4	2-1	0-0	2-2	1-1	5-4	1-1	2-1	—	1-0	—	2-0	2-1
Bournemouth	2-1	0-1	3-1	2-3	0-1	0-0	1-1	3-1	0-4	2-2	2-0	0-1	2-1	0-0	0-1	2-1	2-0	1-0	2-1	1-3	—	2-0	1-0	3-2
Bradford City	2-1	1-0	3-1	2-2	1-3	0-0	1-3	1-0	2-0	2-0	3-0	0-1	1-1	2-0	1-2	2-1	0-2	0-2	0-1	—	0-1	1-1	3-0	1-2
Brighton & Hove Alb.	2-0	1-0	2-0	2-2	1-1	2-1	2-0	5-2	2-0	2-2	2-0	1-1	2-1	1-1	2-1	1-1	0-1	0-2	—	1-3	2-0	2-0	4-0	1-2
Chelsea	1-1	1-0	4-0	3-2	1-1	2-1	3-0	3-2	5-0	1-0	2-2	1-3	4-2	1-0	3-0	2-1	1-0	—	2-0	2-0	2-3	2-2	1-1	5-3
Crystal Palace	1-0	0-2	0-0	2-1	0-0	1-1	1-1	0-1	4-1	1-1	2-0	0-0	2-1	0-1	2-0	3-1	—	1-0	2-3	2-0	4-0	2-1	1-1	1-1
Hull City	0-1	0-3	3-1	1-2	1-1	1-1	3-0	1-0	2-0	1-2	1-0	0-0	4-2	2-1	2-4	—	1-1	3-0	1-0	1-1	3-0	1-1	4-1	1-1
Ipswich Town	1-0	2-0	3-0	1-0	2-1	2-0	1-0	2-0	1-1	2-1	2-2	0-0	2-2	1-0	—	2-1	2-1	1-0	2-3	2-1	4-0	1-2	1-1	1-1
Leeds United	1-0	3-0	2-0	0-0	1-0	2-2	2-0	5-1	2-0	1-0	0-1	1-2	4-2	—	1-1	3-1	0-1	0-2	1-0	1-1	0-4	1-0	3-0	4-0
Leicester City	1-1	4-0	1-0	1-1	1-1	1-1	3-0	2-1	1-1	1-1	1-1	0-2	—	4-1	2-3	1-1	0-2	1-1	1-1	2-0	3-0	4-0	2-1	1-0
Manchester City	1-1	2-2	2-1	2-0	2-1	3-1	2-2	2-0	2-0	2-1	0-0	—	4-0	1-1	1-1	1-1	1-3	0-0	1-0	4-0	1-1	3-0	4-0	0-2
Oldham Athletic	3-1	2-0	3-1	1-1	1-1	1-0	4-1	3-0	2-2	2-1	—	0-0	3-0	2-0	4-0	1-2	2-1	4-1	1-0	0-3	3-0	1-1	0-0	0-3
Oxford United	3-1	4-0	1-3	1-1	1-3	2-1	4-2	5-1	0-2	—	1-1	0-1	0-3	2-3	4-4	4-1	2-2	0-0	1-3	0-1	0-2	1-1	1-0	0-1
Plymouth Argyle	2-2	3-0	2-1	1-0	0-2	2-2	2-2	3-5	—	1-0	2-2	1-0	1-1	2-0	3-4	4-1	2-1	2-0	1-0	1-1	1-1	0-1	1-2	1-3
Portsmouth	0-3	1-1	1-1	0-4	1-3	4-1	4-2	—	0-1	1-0	0-2	1-1	3-0	3-1	0-3	3-1	2-2	1-0	1-2	3-1	0-2	1-1	0-3	1-0
Shrewsbury Town	0-4	4-0	1-0	4-4	1-2	4-0	—	1-5	1-2	2-1	3-1	1-3	1-0	2-3	1-1	0-1	2-2	0-0	1-2	2-3	3-4	1-1	3-4	2-3
Stoke City	1-2	1-0	1-0	1-1	3-2	—	4-0	5-1	4-0	2-1	1-1	1-1	2-2	0-0	0-0	1-1	1-0	2-0	1-1	2-0	2-0	1-1	0-4	1-0
Sunderland	1-1	1-0	4-0	3-2	—	1-1	3-0	2-2	2-0	1-1	2-1	2-2	2-1	0-1	2-1	1-1	1-3	0-2	2-0	4-0	2-3	1-1	4-1	5-3
Swindon Town	1-1	1-1	2-0	—	1-0	1-0	1-1	2-0	1-0	0-0	1-1	0-1	3-3	1-1	0-0	0-3	1-2	3-0	1-0	4-1	4-0	1-0	2-0	1-0
Walsall	0-0	0-1	—	2-0	1-1	1-1	0-1	0-0	2-2	2-2	1-1	3-1	0-0	1-1	1-0	1-1	1-0	2-1	1-0	0-1	0-0	1-1	0-1	2-3
Watford	3-0	—	5-5	2-3	2-0	3-0	2-1	1-0	3-0	1-2	3-1	1-0	0-1	1-1	3-2	2-0	0-1	0-7	1-0	0-0	1-0	1-2	1-0	4-0
West Bromwich Albion	—	0-1	0-0	3-1	1-0	6-0	0-4	3-0	2-2	3-2	3-1	1-0	1-1	2-1	1-2	2-0	5-3	2-3	1-0	1-0	0-0	2-0	0-0	1-1

Second Division Final Positions 1988-89

		Home					Away					Total			
	P	**W**	**D**	**L**	**F**	**A**	**W**	**D**	**L**	**F**	**A**	**F**	**A**	**GD**	**Pts**
1. Chelsea.................46		15	6	2	50	25	14	6	3	46	25	96	50	+46	99
2. Manchester City 46		12	8	3	48	28	11	5	7	29	25	77	53	+24	82
3. Crystal Palace 46		15	6	2	42	17	8	6	9	29	32	71	49	+22	81 *
4. Watford..................46		14	5	4	41	18	8	7	8	33	30	74	48	+26	78
5. Blackburn Rovers 46		16	4	3	50	22	6	7	10	24	37	74	59	+15	77
6. Swindon Town 46		13	8	2	35	15	7	8	8	33	38	68	53	+15	76
7. Barnsley 46		12	8	3	37	21	8	6	9	29	37	66	58	+8	74
8. Ipswich Town...........46		13	3	7	42	23	9	4	10	29	38	71	61	+10	73
9. West Bromwich A.....46		13	7	3	43	18	5	11	7	22	23	65	41	+24	72
10. Leeds United 46		12	6	5	34	20	5	10	8	25	30	59	50	+9	67
11. Sunderland..............46		12	8	3	40	23	4	7	12	20	37	60	60	—	63
12. Bournemouth...........46		13	3	7	32	20	5	5	13	21	42	53	62	−9	62
13. Stoke City 46		10	9	4	33	25	5	5	13	24	47	57	72	−15	59
14. Bradford City..........46		8	11	4	29	22	5	6	12	23	37	52	59	−7	56
15. Leicester City..........46		11	6	6	31	20	2	10	11	25	43	56	63	−7	55
16. Oldham Athletic.......46		9	10	4	49	32	2	11	10	26	40	75	72	+3	54
17. Oxford United..........46		11	6	6	40	34	3	6	14	22	36	62	70	−8	54
18. Plymouth Argyle.......46		11	4	8	35	22	3	8	12	20	44	55	66	−11	54
19. Brighton & Hove A. 46		11	5	7	36	24	3	4	16	21	42	57	66	−9	51
20. Portsmouth.............46		10	6	7	33	21	3	6	14	20	41	53	62	−9	51
21. Hull City................46		7	9	7	31	25	4	5	14	21	43	52	68	−16	47
22. Shrewsbury Town 46		4	11	8	25	31	4	7	12	15	36	40	67	−27	42
23. Birmingham City 46		6	4	13	21	33	2	7	14	10	43	31	76	−45	35
24. Walsall 46		3	10	10	27	42	2	6	15	14	38	41	80	−39	31

*Promoted via the play-offs

Chelsea – Second Division Champions.

141

Third Division Results 1988-89

Home \ Away	Aldershot	Blackpool	Bolton Wanderers	Brentford	Bristol City	Bristol Rovers	Bury	Cardiff City	Chester City	Chesterfield	Fulham	Gillingham	Huddersfield Town	Mansfield Town	Northampton Town	Notts County	Port Vale	Preston North End	Reading	Sheffield United	Southend United	Swansea City	Wigan Athletic	Wolverhampton Wanderers
Aldershot	—	1-0	1-0	0-0	0-1	1-3	4-1	1-1	1-1	2-0	1-1	0-2	0-1	0-1	1-1	2-3	2-2	2-1	1-1	1-2	2-2	0-1	3-1	1-2
Blackpool	4-0	—	2-0	0-3	2-2	1-1	2-2	0-1	1-1	1-2	1-2	4-1	1-1	1-0	1-1	0-1	0-2	1-0	4-1	1-2	2-0	0-1	2-0	0-2
Bolton Wanderers	1-0	2-2	—	4-2	2-0	1-1	2-4	3-0	1-1	5-0	3-2	2-1	3-1	1-0	2-1	3-3	1-1	1-0	3-2	2-0	3-0	1-1	1-1	1-2
Brentford	2-1	1-0	3-0	—	0-1	2-1	2-2	1-2	0-1	1-4	0-1	1-0	0-1	2-0	2-1	4-0	2-1	0-2	0-1	1-4	4-0	1-1	0-1	2-2
Bristol City	1-1	1-2	2-0	0-1	—	0-0	3-0	4-1	4-1	2-1	1-5	1-2	5-1	2-0	3-1	4-0	1-0	0-1	2-1	1-3	2-2	2-1	3-2	0-0
Bristol Rovers	2-2	0-0	1-1	3-1	2-3	—	3-0	2-0	2-0	2-0	0-1	0-2	0-6	0-1	3-1	4-1	2-0	0-0	0-3	1-1	1-0	1-0	3-2	0-3
Bury	0-1	1-1	4-2	2-2	0-3	0-0	—	2-0	1-2	2-0	7-0	2-0	3-0	0-0	1-1	1-1	3-1	0-3	3-0	0-1	0-1	2-0	0-1	3-1
Cardiff City	3-2	0-1	0-3	2-1	1-4	2-2	0-3	—	1-2	0-1	4-1	1-2	1-1	1-3	2-1	1-0	2-1	0-3	2-4	0-1	2-1	3-0	1-0	1-1
Chester City	2-1	1-1	1-1	1-2	1-4	0-3	2-0	2-1	—	0-1	0-2	1-2	2-0	3-0	2-1	3-0	1-2	1-0	1-1	2-2	1-1	2-0	1-1	1-1
Chesterfield	2-1	0-2	5-0	4-0	2-1	2-0	0-1	3-1	2-1	—	0-1	3-0	3-0	5-0	6-0	0-0	1-3	3-0	3-3	1-4	1-0	0-2	1-0	0-3
Fulham	5-1	1-2	3-2	0-1	1-5	0-1	7-0	4-1	0-1	2-0	—	3-1	2-1	2-1	3-0	1-4	0-1	0-0	0-0	2-0	0-1	5-2	1-0	2-2
Gillingham	1-1	1-0	2-1	1-0	1-2	2-0	2-0	1-2	2-1	3-0	1-1	—	1-2	1-2	1-0	5-0	1-2	4-2	2-1	3-2	3-0	6-1	1-0	1-3
Huddersfield Town	1-1	1-1	3-1	0-1	5-1	0-6	3-0	3-0	1-2	1-2	0-1	3-0	—	1-0	3-0	2-0	1-0	5-1	2-4	1-0	0-2	4-1	0-1	0-1
Mansfield Town	1-1	0-1	0-0	1-0	2-0	0-1	0-0	1-3	1-3	3-0	2-1	1-2	1-2	—	2-1	1-2	2-0	1-2	1-1	3-1	0-1	6-2	1-0	3-1
Northampton Town	6-0	1-0	2-1	2-1	1-3	1-3	1-1	1-2	1-2	3-2	1-1	1-0	1-2	1-1	—	1-0	1-2	4-2	1-0	1-3	3-2	1-3	1-3	3-1
Notts County	4-1	1-0	3-3	0-4	0-4	1-4	1-1	0-1	0-3	0-0	4-1	0-5	0-2	2-1	0-1	—	1-0	3-0	1-1	1-1	2-0	0-1	0-1	1-0
Port Vale	3-0	1-0	1-1	1-2	0-1	0-2	1-3	1-2	2-1	3-1	1-0	2-1	0-1	0-2	2-1	1-0	—	0-1	3-3	2-0	5-3	0-2	2-1	3-3
Preston North End	2-2	2-1	0-1	2-0	1-0	0-0	3-0	3-0	0-1	0-3	0-0	2-4	1-5	2-1	2-4	0-3	1-0	—	2-1	2-0	3-1	1-1	1-1	0-2
Reading	3-1	4-1	3-2	0-1	2-1	0-3	0-3	4-2	1-1	3-3	0-0	1-2	2-4	1-1	0-1	3-0	3-3	1-2	—	1-1	2-0	2-0	3-0	3-1
Sheffield United	1-1	1-2	2-0	4-1	3-1	1-1	1-0	1-0	2-2	4-1	0-2	2-4	0-1	1-3	3-2	1-1	0-2	1-0	1-1	—	2-1	2-2	1-2	1-0
Southend United	2-2	0-2	0-3	0-4	2-2	0-1	1-0	1-2	1-1	2-3	1-0	2-1	2-0	0-1	4-1	1-2	3-2	4-0	1-2	2-0	—	2-0	3-0	3-0
Swansea City	0-1	1-0	1-1	2-1	1-2	0-1	0-2	0-3	3-1	1-1	1-3	1-1	1-0	1-2	2-0	1-1	2-1	5-1	0-2	2-0	1-2	—	1-2	1-1
Wigan Athletic	2-1	2-1	1-1	1-1	0-1	2-2	1-1	3-1	1-1	0-2	3-0	3-0	5-1	1-1	4-1	2-1	1-0	3-1	2-0	2-2	1-2	0-2	—	2-1
Wolverhampton Wdrs	1-0	2-1	1-2	2-0	0-0	0-1	4-0	1-1	3-1	1-0	2-2	6-1	4-1	6-2	3-2	1-0	3-3	6-0	2-1	2-2	3-0	1-1	2-1	—

Third Division Final Positions 1988-89

			Home					Away				Total			
	P	W	D	L	F	A	W	D	L	F	A	F	A	GD	Pts
1. Wolverhampton Wanderers	46	18	4	1	61	19	8	10	5	35	30	96	49	+47	92
2. Sheffield United	46	16	3	4	57	21	9	6	8	36	33	93	54	+39	84
3. Port Vale	46	15	3	5	46	21	9	9	5	32	27	78	48	+30	84 *
4. Fulham	46	12	7	4	42	28	10	2	11	27	39	69	67	+2	75
5. Bristol Rovers	46	9	11	3	34	21	10	6	7	33	30	67	51	+16	74
6. Preston North End	46	14	7	2	56	31	5	8	10	23	29	79	60	+19	72
7. Brentford	46	14	5	4	36	21	4	9	10	30	40	66	61	+5	68
8. Chester City	46	12	6	5	38	18	7	5	11	26	43	64	61	+3	68
9. Notts County	46	11	7	5	37	22	7	6	10	27	32	64	54	+10	67
10. Bolton Wanderers	46	12	8	3	42	23	4	8	11	16	31	58	54	+4	64
11. Bristol City	46	10	3	10	32	25	8	6	9	21	30	53	55	−2	63
12. Swansea City	46	11	8	4	33	22	4	8	11	18	31	51	53	−2	61
13. Bury	46	11	7	5	27	22	5	6	12	28	45	55	67	−12	61
14. Huddersfield Town	46	10	8	5	35	25	7	1	15	28	48	63	73	−10	60
15. Mansfield Town	46	10	8	5	32	22	4	9	10	16	30	48	52	−4	59
16. Cardiff City	46	10	9	4	30	16	4	6	13	14	40	44	56	−12	57
17. Wigan Athletic	46	9	5	9	28	22	5	9	9	27	31	55	53	+2	56
18. Reading	46	10	6	7	37	29	5	5	13	31	43	68	72	−4	56
19. Blackpool	46	10	6	7	36	29	4	7	12	20	30	56	59	−3	55
20. Northampton Town	46	11	2	10	41	34	5	4	14	25	42	66	76	−10	54
21. Southend United	46	10	9	4	33	26	3	6	14	23	49	56	75	−19	54
22. Chesterfield	46	9	5	9	35	35	5	2	16	16	51	51	86	−35	49
23. Gillingham	46	7	3	13	25	32	5	1	17	22	49	47	81	−34	40
24. Aldershot	46	7	6	10	29	29	1	7	15	19	49	48	78	−30	37

*Promoted via the play-offs

Wolverhampton Wanderers – Third Division Champions.

Fourth Division Results 1988-89

Home \ Away	Bur	Cam	Car	Col	Cre	Dar	Don	Exe	Gri	Hal	Har	Her	Ley	Lin	Pet	Roc	Rot	Sca	Scu	Sto	Tor	Tra	Wre	Yor
Burnley	—	2-0	0-2	2-1	4-0	1-1	1-0	3-0	1-0	1-2	2-2	0-0	3-0	2-3	3-0	2-1	2-1	1-0	2-1	0-0	3-1	2-1	4-2	0-0
Cambridge United	1-1	—	3-2	3-1	3-1	1-3	0-1	2-0	4-0	2-1	4-1	1-1	2-2	2-3	2-2	1-0	1-1	2-2	3-1	1-1	3-1	1-1	2-0	1-1
Carlisle United	0-0	1-1	—	1-2	2-0	1-2	0-1	0-1	1-0	3-1	2-0	3-0	2-1	1-3	2-2	1-0	0-2	1-1	2-2	1-1	2-2	2-3	1-2	0-1
Colchester United	2-2	1-2	1-0	—	3-1	1-2	4-2	2-2	3-2	2-1	1-1	8-0	1-1	3-0	1-2	0-0	2-3	1-3	1-0	2-2	2-0	2-1	2-1	1-2
Crewe Alexandra	4-0	2-0	0-3	3-1	—	2-1	1-3	4-1	2-2	2-2	3-0	0-0	1-3	2-0	1-2	3-1	1-1	1-1	2-1	1-4	0-0	2-1	2-2	2-2
Darlington	1-1	1-1	1-0	1-2	1-0	—	3-0	1-2	0-2	0-2	1-0	0-0	1-0	1-0	2-3	1-1	1-0	2-1	2-2	1-4	3-0	0-0	2-2	1-2
Doncaster Rovers	1-0	0-3	3-0	4-2	2-2	1-0	—	5-0	1-4	4-1	2-0	3-2	1-2	0-1	2-3	1-5	0-4	1-0	2-2	2-2	2-0	0-0	2-2	2-0
Exeter City	3-0	4-0	0-2	2-2	1-1	1-0	3-0	—	2-1	2-0	3-0	1-1	2-2	0-1	0-0	1-3	0-1	0-2	3-0	1-0	2-1	0-0	4-0	2-0
Grimsby Town	1-0	4-0	3-3	3-2	2-0	1-1	5-0	2-1	—	2-0	3-0	3-0	2-2	0-0	5-0	1-3	0-0	1-0	2-0	2-1	2-0	0-0	4-0	2-0
Halifax Town	1-0	3-2	0-2	2-1	1-1	4-1	2-1	1-0	0-1	—	2-0	3-1	2-0	2-1	2-1	0-0	1-1	0-2	2-0	3-0	2-0	0-0	3-0	5-3
Hartlepool United	2-2	4-2	2-1	1-1	3-2	0-0	1-0	2-1	1-0	2-0	—	2-0	4-3	0-1	0-0	4-0	1-1	3-0	2-1	2-1	1-1	2-2	4-3	2-3
Hereford United	0-0	1-1	4-0	3-2	1-1	2-0	1-0	1-0	1-0	1-0	1-0	—	1-3	2-2	1-1	3-1	1-1	1-1	0-0	1-1	1-1	0-0	1-0	4-1
Leyton Orient	3-0	1-1	2-1	2-1	1-1	3-2	2-1	4-0	0-1	3-1	0-1	1-3	—	2-2	1-1	3-0	1-0	1-1	0-0	1-1	2-0	2-0	1-0	4-0
Lincoln City	2-3	3-0	1-1	2-1	3-0	5-1	1-1	4-0	2-2	2-1	0-0	2-2	0-1	—	1-1	4-0	0-3	2-1	0-0	0-0	1-1	2-1	3-0	2-1
Peterborough United	3-0	1-5	3-0	1-1	0-0	1-2	2-0	4-1	0-2	0-2	3-1	1-2	2-1	1-2	—	0-1	1-1	0-3	1-2	1-1	1-0	1-0	1-1	5-1
Rochdale	2-1	2-1	0-0	0-0	2-0	3-0	3-0	2-0	1-2	2-1	0-0	2-3	1-3	1-0	0-1	—	1-3	3-3	4-0	1-0	2-0	2-0	2-3	3-3
Rotherham United	2-1	0-0	1-1	1-0	2-1	1-2	1-0	2-1	1-1	3-1	0-1	6-0	2-0	2-0	0-0	1-3	—	1-0	0-2	1-2	1-0	1-0	1-1	1-1
Scarborough	3-0	2-1	2-0	1-1	1-0	3-0	0-0	2-1	1-0	0-0	1-1	1-0	0-1	2-1	3-0	3-3	1-0	—	1-1	1-1	5-2	3-1	3-1	4-2
Scunthorpe United	1-0	1-3	0-1	1-0	2-1	1-2	3-0	2-0	3-0	1-0	3-0	1-0	2-2	0-0	1-2	0-0	1-2	1-3	—	1-1	0-0	0-0	0-0	0-0
Stockport County	2-1	0-0	1-1	1-3	3-1	1-0	1-1	1-0	3-0	0-2	3-0	1-0	3-0	1-1	1-1	1-1	0-1	2-2	1-1	—	2-1	1-0	2-0	2-0
Torquay United	4-2	3-1	1-0	1-0	0-0	2-0	2-0	1-1	1-1	1-1	1-1	1-1	1-0	2-0	2-2	1-0	0-0	1-0	0-0	1-1	—	3-0	1-0	1-1
Tranmere Rovers	2-1	1-1	0-1	2-1	1-2	0-0	0-1	0-0	2-3	2-2	2-1	2-1	3-1	2-1	0-0	0-0	3-1	0-0	0-0	1-1	3-0	—	3-3	0-1
Wrexham	4-2	3-1	1-0	2-2	2-0	3-3	1-1	3-0	1-2	3-0	2-1	1-0	1-0	3-0	0-0	2-0	0-0	1-1	3-1	1-0	3-0	3-3	—	2-1
York City	0-0	1-2	1-1	1-1	2-2	4-1	1-1	3-1	0-3	5-3	2-3	4-1	1-1	2-1	5-1	3-3	1-1	4-2	2-0	2-0	1-1	0-1	1-0	—

144

Fourth Division Final Positions 1988-89

		Home					Away					Total			
	P	W	D	L	F	A	W	D	L	F	A	F	A	GD	Pts
1. Rotherham United 46	46	13	6	4	44	18	9	10	4	32	17	76	35	+41	82
2. Tranmere Rovers 46	46	15	6	2	34	13	6	11	6	28	30	62	43	+19	80
3. Crewe Alexandra 46	46	13	7	3	42	24	8	8	7	25	24	67	48	+19	78
4. Scunthorpe United 46	46	11	9	3	40	22	10	5	8	37	35	77	57	+20	77
5. Scarborough 46	46	12	7	4	33	23	9	7	7	34	29	67	52	+15	77
6. Leyton Orient 46	46	16	2	5	61	19	5	10	8	25	31	86	50	+36	75 *
7. Wrexham 46	46	12	7	4	44	28	7	7	9	33	35	77	63	+14	71
8. Cambridge United.....46	46	13	7	3	45	25	5	7	11	26	37	71	62	+9	68
9. Grimsby Town 46	46	11	9	3	33	18	6	6	11	32	41	65	59	+6	66
10. Lincoln City............46	46	12	6	5	39	26	6	4	13	25	34	64	60	+4	64
11. York City...............46	46	10	8	5	43	27	7	5	11	19	36	62	63	−1	64
12. Carlisle United 46	46	9	6	8	26	25	6	9	8	27	27	53	52	+1	60
13. Exeter City.............46	46	14	4	5	46	23	4	2	17	19	45	65	68	−3	60
14. Torquay United........46	46	15	2	6	32	23	2	6	15	13	37	45	60	−15	59
15. Hereford United.......46	46	11	8	4	40	27	3	8	12	26	45	66	72	−6	58
16. Burnley 46	46	12	6	5	35	20	2	7	14	17	41	52	61	−9	55
17. Peterborough Utd. 46	46	10	3	10	29	32	4	9	10	23	42	52	74	−22	54
18. Rochdale 46	46	10	10	3	32	26	3	4	16	24	56	56	84	−26	53
19. Hartlepool United.....46	46	10	6	7	33	33	4	4	15	17	45	50	78	−28	52
20. Stockport County......46	46	8	10	5	31	20	2	11	10	23	32	54	52	+2	51
21. Halifax Town 46	46	10	7	6	42	27	3	4	16	27	48	69	75	−6	50
22. Colchester United 46	46	8	7	8	35	30	4	7	12	25	48	60	78	−18	50
23. Doncaster Rovers 46	46	9	6	8	32	32	4	4	15	17	46	49	78	−29	49
24. Darlington...............46	46	3	12	8	28	38	5	6	12	25	38	53	76	−23	42

*Promoted via the play-offs

Rotherham United – Fourth Division Champions.

145

Football League/Milk/Littlewoods Cup Winners 1961-89

Year	Winners	Runners-up	Score	Venue
1961	*Aston Villa	Rotherham United	3-2	
1962	*Norwich City	Rochdale	4-0	
1963	*Birmingham City	Aston Villa	3-1	
1964	*Leicester City	Stoke City	4-3	
1965	*Chelsea	Leicester City	3-2	
1966	*West Bromwich Albion	West Ham United	5-3	
1967	Queen's Park Rangers	West Bromwich Albion	3-2	Wembley
1968	Leeds United	Arsenal	1-0	Wembley
1969	†Swindon Town	Arsenal	3-1	Wembley
1970	†Manchester City	West Bromwich Albion	2-1	Wembley
1971	Tottenham Hotspur	Aston Villa	2-0	Wembley
1972	Stoke City	Chelsea	2-1	Wembley
1973	Tottenham Hotspur	Norwich City	1-0	Wembley
1974	Wolverhampton Wanderers	Manchester City	2-1	Wembley
1975	Aston Villa	Norwich City	1-0	Wembley
1976	Manchester City	Newcastle United	2-1	Wembley
1977	‡Aston Villa	Everton	3-2	Wembley
1978	¶Nottingham Forest	Liverpool	1-0	Manchester
1979	Nottingham Forest	Southampton	3-2	Wembley
1980	Wolverhampton Wanderers	Nottingham Forest	1-0	Wembley
1981	§Liverpool	West Ham United	2-1	Birmingham
1982	†Liverpool	Tottenham Hotspur	3-1	Wembley
1983	†Liverpool	Manchester United	2-1	Wembley
1984	¶Liverpool	Everton	1-0	Manchester
1985	Norwich City	Sunderland	1-0	Wembley
1986	Oxford United	Queen's Park Rangers	3-0	Wembley
1987	Arsenal	Liverpool	2-1	Wembley
1988	Luton Town	Arsenal	3-2	Wembley
1989	Nottingham Forest	Luton Town	3-1	Wembley

*Aggregate score †After extra time ‡After 0-0 and 1-1 draws at Wembley and Sheffield ¶After 0-0 draw at Wembley §After 1-1 draw at Wembley

Littlewoods Challenge Cup 1988-89

First Round (Two Legs)

Bolton Wanderers	1:1	Chester City	0:3
Bournemouth	1:0	Bristol Rovers	0:0
Bristol City	1:1	Exeter City	0:0
Bury	2:2	Wrexham	1:2
Cambridge United	1:1	Gillingham	2:3
Cardiff City	0:2	Swansea City	1:0
Carlisle United	1:0	Blackpool	1:3
Colchester United	0:0	Northampton Town	0:5
Crewe Alexandra	1:1	Lincoln City	1:2
Doncaster Rovers	1:0	Darlington	1:2
Fulham	2:0	Brentford	2:1
Grimsby Town	0:0	Rotherham United	1:1
Hartlepool United	2:0	Sheffield United	2:2
Hereford United	0:2	Plymouth Argyle	3:3
Leyton Orient	2:0	Aldershot	0:0
Notts County	5:0	Mansfield Town	0:1
Port Vale	3:1	Chesterfield	2:1
Rochdale	3:1	Burnley	3:2
Scarborough	1:2*	Halifax Town	1:2
Scunthorpe United	3:2	Huddersfield Town	2:2
Shrewsbury Town	2:0	Walsall	2:3
Southend United	2:1	Brighton & Hove Albion	0:0
Stockport County	0:1	Tranmere Rovers	1:1
Torquay United	0:1	Reading	1:3
West Bromwich Albion	0:2	Peterborough United	3:0
Wigan Athletic	0:0	Preston North End	0:1
Wolverhampton Wanderers	3:0	Birmingham City	2:1*
York City	0:0	Sunderland	0:4

*Won on away goals

Littlewoods Challenge Cup Competition 1988-89

2nd Round (2 Legs)		3rd Round	4th Round	5th Round	Semi-Final (2 Legs)	Final

Nottingham Forest — 6:4
Chester City — 0:3
> *Nottingham Forest — 3
Bournemouth — 0:1
Coventry City — 4:3
> Coventry City — 2
>> Nottingham Forest — 0:2

Leicester City — 4:2
Watford — 1:2
> *Leicester City — 2
Norwich City — 2:3
Preston North End — 0:0
> Norwich City — 0
>> *Leicester City — 0:1
>>> *Nottingham Forest — 5

Queens Park Rgrs — 3:4
Cardiff City — 0:1
> *Queens Park Rgrs — 2
Northampton Town — 1:1
Charlton Athletic — 1:2
> Charlton Athletic — 1
>> *Queens Park Rgrs — 0:1
>>> Queens Park Rgrs — 2

>>>> Nottingham Forest — 1:1

Barnsley — 0:1
Wimbledon — 2:0
> *Wimbledon — 2
Rotherham United — 0:0
Manchester United — 1:5
> Manchester United — 1
>> Wimbledon — 0:0

Reading — 1:1
Bradford City — 1:2
> *Bradford City — 1:1
Scunthorpe United — 4:2
Chelsea — 1:2
> Scunthorpe United — 1:0
>> *Bradford City — 3
>>> *Bradford City — 0

Everton — 3:2
Bury — 0:2
> *Everton — 1:2
Darlington — 2:0
Oldham Athletic — 0:4
> Oldham Athletic — 1:0
>> Everton — 1

>>> Bristol City — 1:0

First leg in Nottingham
Second leg in Bristol

Oxford United — 2:0
Bristol City — 4:2
> *Bristol City — 4
Swindon Town — 1:0
Crystal Palace — 2:2
> Crystal Palace — 1
>> *Bristol City — 1
>>> Bristol City — 1

Middlesbrough — 0:0
Tranmere Rovers — 0:1
> *Tranmere Rovers — 1
Blackpool — 2:1†
Sheffield Wednesday — 0:3
> Blackpool — 0
>> Tranmere Rovers — 0

At Wembley

Sunderland — 0:1
West Ham United — 3:2
> *West Ham United — 5
Derby County — 1:2
Southend United — 0:1
> Derby County — 0
>> *West Ham United — 4
>>> *West Ham United — 2

Liverpool — 1:3
Walsall — 0:1
> *Liverpool — 1:0:2
Hull City — 1:0
Arsenal — 2:3
> Arsenal — 1:0:1
>> Liverpool — 1

>>> West Ham United — 0:0

Birmingham City — 0:0
Aston Villa — 2:5
> *Aston Villa — 3
Millwall — 3:3
Gillingham — 0:1
> Millwall — 1
>> *Aston Villa — 6
>>> Aston Villa — 1

Port Vale — 1:0
Ipswich Town — 0:3
> *Ipswich Town — 2
Leyton Orient — 1:2‡
Stoke City — 2:1
> Leyton Orient — 0
>> Ipswich Town — 2

First leg at West Ham
Second leg at Luton

Portsmouth — 2:1
Scarborough — 2:3
> *Scarborough — 2:0
Southampton — 1:3
Lincoln City — 1:1
> Southampton — 2:1
>> *Southampton — 2
>>> Southampton — 1:1

Notts County — 1:1
Tottenham Hotspur — 1:2
> *Tottenham Hotspur — 0:2
Blackburn Rovers — 3:3
Brentford — 1:4
> Blackburn Rovers — 0:1
>> Tottenham Hotspur — 1

>>> Luton Town — 3:2

Manchester City — 1:6
Plymouth Argyle — 0:3
> *Manchester City — 4
Sheffield United — 3:0
Newcastle United — 0:2
> Sheffield United — 2
>> Manchester City — 1
>>> *Luton Town — 1:2

Peterborough United — 1:1
Leeds United — 2:3
> *Leeds United — 0
Burnley — 1:0
Luton Town — 1:1
> Luton Town — 2
>> *Luton Town — 3

Nottingham Forest — 3

Luton Town — 1

*Denotes home club   † Won on away goals rule   ‡ Won on penalty-kicks

Sherpa Van Trophy Competition 1988-89

Preliminary Round

Northern Section:

Bury	1	Bolton Wanderers	0
Bolton Wanderers	1	Preston North End	0
Preston North End	4	Bury	0
Doncaster Rovers	1	Grimsby Town	1
Grimsby Town	1	Rotherham United	0
Rotherham United	2	Doncaster Rovers	1
Tranmere Rovers	2	Stockport County	1
Stockport County	1	Crewe Alexandra	1
Crewe Alexandra	1	Tranmere Rovers	1
York City	0	Burnley	2
Burnley	3	Hartlepool United	0
Hartlepool United	0	York City	2
Darlington	3	Carlisle United	2
Carlisle United	1	Scarborough	1
Scarborough	4	Darlington	0
Scunthorpe United	1	Halifax Town	2
Halifax Town	1	Huddersfield Town	0
Huddersfield Town	1	Scunthorpe United	0
Wigan Athletic	1	Blackpool	2
Blackpool	2	Rochdale	0
Rochdale	0	Wigan Athletic	2
Chester City	1	Wrexham	2
Wrexham	1	Sheffield United	1
Sheffield United	2	Chester City	2

Southern Section:

Leyton Orient	1	Reading	1
Reading	5	Aldershot	2
Aldershot	1	Leyton Orient	3
Cardiff City	2	Swansea City	0
Swansea City	1	Torquay United	0
Torquay United	3	Cardiff City	1
Fulham	0	Brentford	2
Brentford	2	Gillingham	0
Gillingham	2	Fulham	1
Southend United	2	Lincoln City	1
Lincoln City	1	Colchester United	2
Colchester United	2	Southend United	1
Mansfield Town	1	Notts County	1
Notts County	1	Chesterfield	1
Chesterfield	2	Mansfield Town	1
Port Vale	1	Hereford United	1
Hereford United	2	Wolverhampton Wanderers	5
Wolverhampton Wanderers	5	Port Vale	1
Northampton Town	1	Cambridge United	1
Cambridge United	2	Peterborough United	2
Peterborough United	0	Northampton Town	2
Bristol Rovers	1	Bristol City	0
Bristol City	2	Exeter City	0
Exeter City	1	Bristol Rovers	1

First Round

Northern Section:

Blackpool	4	Rotherham United	3
Burnley	1	Crewe Alexandra	1*
Grimsby Town	1	Huddersfield Town	3
Halifax Town	3	Darlington	0
Preston North End	0	Bolton Wanderers	1
Scarborough	3	York City	1
Tranmere Rovers	0	Wigan Athletic	1
Wrexham	2	Sheffield United	1

Southern Section:

Brentford	2	Notts County	0
Bristol Rovers	0	Cardiff City	1
Chesterfield	4	Cambridge United	3
Colchester United	1	Leyton Orient	0
Northampton Town	3	Southend United	1
Reading	2	Hereford United	3
Torquay United	3	Gillingham	0
Wolverhampton Wanderers	3	Bristol City	0

Quarter-Final

Northern Section:

Bolton Wanderers	3	Wrexham	1
Halifax Town	0	Blackpool	2
Huddersfield Town	1	Scarborough	2
Wigan Athletic	0	Crewe Alexandra	1

Southern Section:

Bristol Rovers	0	Torquay United	1
Chesterfield	0	Brentford	1
Colchester United	0	Hereford United	1
Wolverhampton Wanderers	3	Northampton Town	1

Semi-Final

Northern Section:

Blackpool	1	Scarborough	0
Crewe Alexandra	1	Bolton Wanderers	2

Southern Section:

Brentford	0	Torquay United	1
Hereford United	0	Wolverhampton Wanderers	2

Final

Northern Section
First Leg:

Bolton Wanderers	1	Blackpool	0

Second Leg:

Blackpool	1	Bolton Wanderers	1

Southern Section
First Leg:

Torquay United	1	Wolverhampton Wanderers	2

Second Leg:

Wolverhampton Wanderers	0	Torquay United	2

Play-Off Final (at Wembley Stadium)

Bolton Wanderers	4	Torquay United	1

*Won on penalty-kicks

"Every facet of the game was mastered by the most perfect player ever to grace an English pitch. He had immense athleticism, was majestic in the air and possessed clinical finishing power.

If all the brains in the game sat in committee to design the perfect player then they would come up with a reincarnation of Tom Finney."

The official biography of Tom Finney is published on 15 September

Tom Finney was probably the greatest all-round footballer ever – more versatile and effective even than the legendary Stanley Matthews. For fourteen seasons, he was the mainstay and inspiration of Preston North End. He was capped for England 76 times, showing his mastery by playing in three positions – on both wings and at centre forward.

New and exciting information. 240 pages, 110 photographs, beautifully produced in hardback. Available from all good bookshops.

Carnegie Press, 125 Woodplumpton Road, Preston PR2 2LS. Tel (0772) 728868.
ISBN 0 948789 29 8

Bolton Wanderers – Sherpa Van Trophy Winners 1989

Freight Rover/Sherpa Van Trophy Winners 1985-89

Year	Winners		Runners-up		Venue
1985	Wigan Athletic	3	Brentford	1	Wembley
1986	Bristol City	3	Bolton Wanderers	0	Wembley
1987	Mansfield Town	1*	Bristol City	1	Wembley
1988	Wolverhampton Wanderers	2	Burnley	0	Wembley
1989	Bolton Wanderers	4	Torquay United	1	Wembley

*Won on penalty-kicks

Full Members'/Simod Cup Winners 1986-89

Year	Winners		Runners-up		Venue
1986	Chelsea	5	Manchester City	4	Wembley
1987	Blackburn Rovers	1	Charlton Athletic	0	Wembley
1988	Reading	4	Luton Town	1	Wembley
1989	Nottingham Forest	4	Everton	3	Wembley

Simod Cup Competition 1988-89

First Round

Aston Villa	6	Birmingham City	0
Blackburn Rovers	3	Manchester City	2
Bradford City	3	Brighton & Hove Albion	1
Charlton Athletic	0	Sunderland	1
Chelsea	6	Plymouth Argyle	2
Crystal Palace	4	Walsall	2
Derby County	1	Bournemouth	0
Leeds United	3	Shrewsbury Town	1
Middlesbrough	1	Oldham Athletic	0
Millwall	1*	Barnsley	1
Norwich City	2	Swindon Town	1
Oxford United	2	Ipswich Town	3
Portsmouth	2	Hull City	1
Southampton	3	Stoke City	0
Watford	2	Leicester City	0
West Ham United	5	West Bromwich Albion	2

Second Round

Blackburn Rovers	2	Sunderland	1
Bradford City	2	Chelsea	3
Derby County	2	Aston Villa	1
Ipswich Town	1	Norwich City	0
Middlesbrough	2	Portsmouth	1
Millwall	2	Leeds United	0
Southampton	1	Crystal Palace	2
Watford	1*	West Ham United	1

Third Round

Chelsea	1	Nottingham Forest	4
Crystal Palace	4	Luton Town	1
Everton	2	Millwall	0
Ipswich Town	1	Blackburn Rovers	0
Middlesbrough	1	Coventry City	0
Sheffield Wednesday	0	Queens Park Rangers	1
Watford	2	Newcastle United	1
Wimbledon	0*	Derby County	0

Fourth Round

Ipswich Town	1	Nottingham Forest	3
Middlesbrough	2	Crystal Palace	3
Watford	1	Queens Park Rangers	1*
Wimbledon	1	Everton	2

Semi-Final

Nottingham Forest	3	Crystal Palace	1
Everton	1	Queens Park Rangers	0

Final

Nottingham Forest	4	Everton	3
(at Wembley Stadium)			

*Won on penalty-kicks

F.A. Sunday Cup Winners 1965-89

Year	Winners		Runners-up		Venue
1965	*London	6	Staffordshire	2	
1966	Unique United	1	Aldridge Fabrications	0	Dudley
1967	Carlton United	2	Stoke Works	0	Hendon
1968	Drovers	2	Brook United	0	Cambridge
1969	Leigh Park	3	Loke United	1	Romford
1970	Vention United	1	Unique United	0	Corby
1971	Beacontree Rovers	2	Saltley United	0	Leamington
1972	Newtown Unity	4	Springfield Colts	0	Dudley
1973	†Carlton United	2	Wear Valley	1	Spennymoor
1974	Newtown Unity	3	Brentford East	0	Birmingham
1975	Fareham Town Centipedes	1	Players Ath Engineers	0	High Wycombe
1976	Brandon United	2	Evergreen	1	Spennymoor
1977	Langley Park R.H.	2	Newtown Unity	0	Spennymoor
1978	Arras	2	Lion Rangers	1	Bishop's Stortford
	(After 2-2 draw at Nuneaton)				
1979	Lobster	3	Carlton United	2	Southport
1980	Fantail	1	Twin Foxes	0	Letchworth
1981	Fantail	1	Mackintosh	0	Birkenhead
1982	Dingle Rail	2	Twin Foxes	1	Hitchin
1983	Eagle	2	Lee Chapel North	1	Walthamstow
1984	†Lee Chapel North	4	Eagle	3	Dagenham
	(After 1-1 draw at Runcorn)				
1985	Hobbies	2	Avenue	1	Nuneaton
	(After 1-1 draw at Norwich and 2-2 draw at Birkenhead)				
1986	Avenue	1	Glenn Sports	0	Birkenhead
1987	†Lodge Cottrell	1	Avenue	0	Birmingham
1988	Nexday	2	Sunderland Humb Plains	0	Newcastle
1989	Almethak	3	East Levenshulme	1	Stockport

*Aggregate score
†After extra time

F.A. Sunday Cup Competition 1988-89

	First Round	Result

	Sunday 9th October 1988	1st Tie	1st Rep
Dudley & Weetslade v Almethak		1-1	
Almethak v Dudley & Weetslade			3-0
Kent v Blackhall WMC		1-3	
Blyth Waterloo SC v Nenthead		0-3	
Boundary v Royal Oak		1-0	
Carnforth v Lynemouth Inn		1-2	
Croxteth & Gillmoss RBL v Overpool United		4-2	
East Levenshulme v Britannia		2-1	
East & West Toxteth v Oakenshaw		0-1	
FC Nirvana v Harrows		4-0	
AD Bulwell v FC Coachman		0-3	
Hoval Farrar v Rose United		3-0	
Brereton Town v Darchem SM		8-1	
B.R.J. v Dereham Hobbies United		3-3	
Dereham Hobbies United v B.R.J.			3-1
Shouldham Sunday v Kettering Odyssey		1-2	
Bulmers v Girton Eagles		1-3	
Greenleys v Mackintosh		2-1	
Colne Hammers v Evergreen		1-0	
Trinity v Brimsdown Rovers		0-2	

Scott v H.S.C. 0-6
Hallen Sunday v AFC Bishopstoke 3-1
Sheffield House Rangers v Inter Royalle 2-0
Port of Bristol v Horndean................................... 2-3
Chequers v Sanco .... (walkover for Chequers)
Sartan United v Dee Roof Vikings............................ 2-1
Oxford Road Social v Sheerness East 4-1
Artois United v Essex Sports................................. 5-2

Second Round

Result

Sunday 13th November 1988

1st   1st
Tie   Rep

Oakenshaw v Blackhall WMC.............................. 1-5
Nenthead v Sunderland Humbledon Plains 1-1
Sunderland Humbledon Plains v Nenthead   3-0
Almethak v Eagle 2-1
Morrison Sports v Lynemouth Inn......................... 2-0
East Bowling Unity v Cleator Moor WMC 2-5
Boundary v Croxteth & Gillmoss RBL 1-3
Northwood v Whetley Lane WMC 3-0
Deborah United v Woodpecker............................ 1-4
East Levenshulme v Nicosia 3-2
Hoval Farrar v Railway Hotel 5-1
Fantail v Lodge Cottrell 0-2
Avenue Victoria Lodge v FC Coachman 1-1
FC Coachman v Avenue Victoria Lodge   1-2
Iron Bridge v Slade Celtic 0-1
Chuckery WMC v Brereton Town 2-3
Greenleys v Lion Rangers .... (walkover for Greenleys)
FC Nirvana v Birmingham Celtic 1-0
Verulam Arms Athletic v Sandwell......................... 4-3
Girton Eagles v Dereham Hobbies United 3-1
Grosvenor Park v Kettering Odyssey 5-1
Hazel Tennants v Leyton Argyle 2-1
Halesowen Harriers v Brimsdown Rovers................... 4-0
Newey Goodman v Leggatts Athletic....................... 1-0
Inter Volante v H.S.C. 3-2
Ford Basildon v Colne Hammers 3-1
Sheffield House Rangers v Santogee 66 2-3
Nexday v Rolls Royce Sunday 1-0
Hallen Sunday v St Josephs (South Oxhey).................. 5-4
Oxford Road Social v Lee Chapel North 0-2
Artois United v Chequers.................................. 0-1
Cabot Towers v Horndean.................................. 4-1
Broad Plain House v Ranelagh Sports 1-0
Sartan United v Watford Labour Club....................... 2-2
Watford Labour Club v Sartan United.......................   1-2

Third Round

Result

Sunday 18th December 1988

1st   1st
Tie   Rep

Woodpecker v Cleator Moor WMC.......................... 3-0
Avenue Victoria Lodge v Morrison Sports 5-1
Blackhall WMC v Croxteth & Gillmoss RBL .... 3-1 *
Almethak v Northwood.................................... 2-0
Humbledon Plains v East Levenshulme 0-2
Hoval Farrar v Slade Celtic 0-3
Girton Eagles v FC Nirvana 4-1
Lodge Cottrell v Verulam Arms Athletic 1-0
Hazel Tennants v Brereton Town............................ 4-2
Grosvenor Park v Greenleys 0-1
Halesowen Harriers v Broad Plain House 0-8

Newey Goodman v Hallen Sunday 2-0
Chequers v Nexday.. 0-4
Cabot Towers v Inter Volante 2-2
Inter Volante v Cabot Towers   4-1
Ford Basildon v Santogee 66 4-1
Sartan United v Lee Chapel North... 0-2

*Blackhall WMC FC removed from the Competition due to the conduct of their supporters

Fourth Round	Result	
Sunday 22nd January 1989	*1st Tie*	*1st Rep*

East Levenshulme v Avenue Victoria Lodge................................... 3-2
Blackhall WMC v Woodpecker .... (walkover for Woodpecker FC)
Almethak v Slade Celtic.. 3-0
Ford Basildon v Hazel Tennants 5-1
Nexday v Girton Eagles 4-0
Greenleys v Lodge Cottrell... 0-3
Lee Chapel North v Broad Plain House 2-0
Inter Volante v Newey Goodman... 2-2
Newey Goodman v Inter Volante... 2-1

Fifth Round	Result	
Sunday 19th February 1989	*1st Tie*	*1st Rep*

Almethak v Newey Goodman 2-1
Woodpecker v East Levenshulme 0-3
Lee Chapel North v Lodge Cottrell... 2-3
Nexday v Ford Basildon... 3-2

Semi-Final	Result	
Sunday 19th March 1989	*1st Tie*	*1st Rep*

East Levenshulme v Lodge Cottrell 4-1
at Warrington Town FC
Nexday v Almethak 0-1
at Irthlingborough Diamonds FC

Final	Result	
Sunday 14th May 1989	*1st Tie*	*1st Rep*

Almethak v East Levenshulme 3-1
at Stockport County FC

Other Leagues' Tables 1988-89

GM VAUXHALL CONFERENCE

	P	W	D	L	F	A	Pts
Maidstone United	40	25	9	6	92	46	84
Kettering Town	40	23	7	10	56	39	76
Boston United	40	22	8	10	61	51	74
Wycombe Wanderers	40	20	11	9	68	52	71
Kidderminster Harriers...	40	21	6	13	68	57	69
Runcorn	40	19	8	13	77	53	65
Macclesfield Town	40	17	10	13	63	57	61
Barnet......................	40	18	7	15	64	69	61
Yeovil Town	40	15	11	14	68	67	56
Northwich Victoria	40	14	11	15	64	65	53
Welling United.............	40	14	11	15	45	46	53
Sutton United	40	12	15	13	64	54	51
Enfield	40	14	8	18	62	67	50
Altrincham.................	40	13	10	17	51	61	49
Cheltenham Town	40	12	12	16	55	58	48
Telford United	40	13	9	18	37	43	48
Chorley	40	13	6	21	57	71	45
Fisher Athletic	40	10	11	19	55	65	41
Stafford Rangers	40	11	7	22	49	74	40
Aylesbury United	40	9	9	22	43	71	36
Weymouth	40	7	10	23	37	70	31

HFS LOANS LEAGUE

Premier Division

	P	W	D	L	F	A	Pts
Barrow......................	42	26	9	7	69	35	87
Hyde United................	42	24	8	10	77	44	80
Witton Albion..............	42	22	13	7	67	39	79
Bangor City................	42	22	10	10	77	48	76
Marine	42	23	7	12	69	48	76
Goole Town	42	22	7	13	75	60	73
Fleetwood Town...........	42	19	16	7	53	44	73
Rhyl	42	18	10	14	75	65	64
Frickley Athletic...........	42	17	10	15	64	53	61
Mossley....................	42	17	9	16	56	58	60
South Liverpool	42	15	13	14	65	57	58
Caernarfon Town	42	15	10	17	49	63	55
Matlock Town..............	42	16	5	21	65	73	53
Southport	42	13	12	17	66	52	51
Buxton	42	12	14	16	61	63	50
Morecambe.................	42	13	9	20	55	60	47 *
Gainsborough Town........	42	12	11	19	56	73	47
Shepshed Charterhouse...	42	14	8	20	49	60	44 *
Stalybridge C...............	42	9	13	20	46	81	40
Harwich	42	7	14	21	42	70	35
Gateshead..................	42	7	13	22	36	70	34
Worksop Town	42	6	5	31	42	103	23

*Points deducted

BEAZER HOMES LEAGUE

Premier Division

	P	W	D	L	F	A	Pts
Merthyr Tydfil	42	26	7	9	104	58	85
Dartford.....................	42	25	7	10	79	33	82
V.S. Rugby	42	24	7	11	64	43	79
Worcester City.............	42	20	13	9	72	49	73
Cambridge City............	42	20	10	12	72	51	70
Dover Athletic.............	42	19	12	11	65	47	69
Gosport Borough..........	42	18	12	12	73	57	66
Burton Albion	42	18	10	14	79	68	64
Bath City	42	15	13	14	66	51	58
Bromsgrove Rovers........	42	14	16	12	68	56	58
Wealdstone	42	16	10	16	60	53	58
Crawley Town..............	42	14	16	12	61	56	58
Dorchester Town...........	42	14	16	12	56	61	58
Alvechurch	42	16	8	18	56	59	56
Moor Green	42	14	13	15	58	70	55
Corby Town	42	14	11	17	55	59	53
Waterlooville...............	42	13	13	16	61	63	52
Ashford Town..............	42	13	13	16	59	76	52
Fareham Town.............	42	15	6	21	43	68	51
Leicester United...........	42	6	11	25	46	84	29
Redditch United............	42	5	7	30	36	105	22
Bedworth United..........	42	4	7	31	36	102	19

Midland Division

	P	W	D	L	F	A	Pts
Gloucester City	42	28	8	6	95	37	92
Atherstone United	42	26	9	7	85	38	87
Tamworth	42	26	9	7	85	45	87
Halesowen Town...........	42	25	10	7	85	42	85
Grantham Town	42	23	11	8	66	37	80
Nuneaton Borough	42	19	9	14	71	58	66
Rushden Town.............	42	19	8	15	71	50	65
Spalding United	42	17	13	12	72	64	64
Dudley Town...............	42	16	13	13	73	62	61
Sutton Coldfield Town	42	18	7	17	56	56	61
Willenhall Town............	42	16	12	14	65	71	60
Forest Green Rovers	42	12	16	14	64	67	52
Bilston Town	42	15	7	20	63	71	52
Ashtree Highfield	42	12	15	15	57	62	51
Hednesford Town	42	12	15	15	49	57	51
Banbury United	42	10	14	18	53	74	44
Bridgnorth Town	42	12	7	23	59	77	43
Stourbridge	42	11	10	21	37	65	43
King's Lynn................	42	7	13	22	31	67	34
Coventry Sporting..........	42	6	13	23	39	91	31
Wellingborough Town	42	5	15	22	39	72	30
Mile Oak Rovers	42	5	10	27	46	98	25

Southern Division

	P	W	D	L	F	A	Pts
Chelmsford City	42	30	5	7	106	38	95
Gravesend & Northfleet	42	27	6	9	70	40	87
Poole Town	42	24	11	7	98	48	83
Bury Town	42	25	7	10	75	34	82
Burnham	42	22	13	7	78	47	79
Baldock Town..............	42	23	5	14	69	40	74
Hastings Town	42	21	11	10	75	48	74
Hounslow	42	21	6	15	75	60	69
Salisbury...................	42	20	5	17	79	58	65
Trowbridge Town	42	19	7	16	59	52	64
Folkestone	42	17	8	17	62	65	59
Corinthian	42	13	13	16	59	69	52
Canterbury City	42	14	8	20	52	60	50
Witney Town...............	42	13	11	18	61	71	50
Dunstable	42	11	14	17	42	57	47
Buckingham Town	42	12	10	20	56	79	46
Erith & Belvedere..........	42	11	10	21	48	63	43
Andover	42	11	9	22	56	90	42
Sheppey United............	42	10	8	24	50	90	38
Thanet United	42	7	15	20	47	95	36
Tonbridge A.F.C...........	42	7	6	29	50	98	27
Ruislip	42	6	8	28	47	112	26

156

VAUXHALL-OPEL LEAGUE

Premier Division

	P	W	D	L	F	A	Pts
Leytonstone Ilford	40	26	11	5	76	36	89
Farnborough Town	40	24	9	9	85	61	81
Slough Town	40	24	6	12	72	42	78
Carshalton Athletic	40	19	15	8	59	36	72
Grays Athletic	40	19	13	10	62	47	70
Kingstonian	40	19	11	12	54	37	68
Bishop's Stortford	40	20	6	16	70	56	66
Hayes	40	18	12	12	61	47	66
Bognor Regis Town	40	17	11	14	38	49	62
Barking	40	16	13	13	49	45	61
Wokingham Town	40	15	11	16	60	54	56
Hendon	40	13	17	12	51	68	56
Windsor & Eton	40	14	13	15	52	50	55
Bromley	40	13	15	14	61	48	54
Leyton-Wingate	40	13	15	14	55	56	54
Dulwich Hamlet	40	12	12	18	58	57	48
St. Albans City	40	12	9	21	51	59	45
Dagenham	40	11	12	19	53	68	45
Harrow Borough	40	9	13	20	53	75	40
Marlow	40	9	11	22	48	83	38
Tooting & Mitcham Utd	40	10	6	26	41	81	36
Croydon	40	4	9	29	27	81	21

Division One

	P	W	D	L	F	A	Pts
Staines Town	40	26	9	5	79	29	87
Basingstoke Town	40	25	8	7	85	36	83
Woking	40	24	10	6	72	30	82
Hitchin Town	40	21	11	8	60	32	74
Wivenhoe Town	40	22	6	12	62	44	72
Lewes	40	21	8	11	72	54	71
Walton & Hersham	40	21	7	12	56	36	70
Kingsbury Town	40	20	7	13	65	41	67
Uxbridge	40	19	7	14	60	54	64
Wembley	40	18	6	16	45	58	60
Boreham Wood	40	16	9	15	57	52	57
Leatherhead	40	14	8	18	56	58	50
Metropolitan Police	40	13	9	18	52	68	48
Chesham United	40	12	9	19	54	67	45
Southwick	40	9	15	16	44	58	42
Chalfont St. Peter	40	11	9	20	56	82	42
Hampton	40	7	14	19	37	62	35
Worthing	40	8	10	22	49	80	32*
Collier Row	40	8	7	25	37	82	31
Bracknell Town	40	8	6	26	38	70	30
Basildon United	40	6	7	27	34	77	25

*2 pts deducted

Division Two North

	P	W	D	L	F	A	Pts
Harlow Town	40	27	9	6	83	38	90
Purfleet	40	22	12	8	60	42	78
Tring Town	40	22	10	10	65	44	76
Stevenage Borough	40	20	13	9	84	55	73
Heybridge Swifts	40	21	9	12	64	43	72
Billericay Town	40	19	11	12	65	52	68
Clapton	40	18	11	13	65	56	65
Barton Rovers	40	18	11	13	58	50	65
Aveley	40	18	10	14	54	52	64
Hertford Town	40	16	13	13	62	49	59*
Ware	40	17	8	17	60	65	59
Hemel Hempstead	40	16	11	16	55	59	59
Witham Town	40	16	7	19	69	67	55
Vauxhall Motors	40	15	9	18	53	57	54
Berkhamsted Town	40	14	10	18	57	70	52
Hornchurch	40	11	16	15	59	61	49
Tilbury	40	13	10	19	53	60	49
Royston Town	40	12	7	23	46	72	43
Rainham Town	40	9	15	18	49	62	42
Saffron Walden Town	40	8	16	18	54	72	40
Letchworth Garden City	40	4	18	20	34	71	30
Wolverton Town	40	5	7	30	42	95	13**

*2 pts deducted
**9 pts deducted

Division Two South

	P	W	D	L	F	A	Pts
Dorking	40	32	4	4	109	35	100
Whyteleafe	40	25	9	6	86	41	84
Finchley	40	21	9	10	70	45	72
Molesey	40	19	13	8	58	42	70
Harefield United	40	19	7	14	56	45	64
Hungerford Town	40	17	13	10	55	45	64
Ruislip Manor	40	16	9	15	56	43	57
Feltham	40	16	9	15	58	53	57
Epsom & Ewell	40	16	8	16	55	55	56
Egham Town	40	16	7	17	54	58	55
Eastbourne United	40	15	9	16	68	61	54
Chertsey Town	40	13	14	13	55	58	53
Flackwell Heath	40	13	11	16	51	49	50
Camberley Town	40	15	5	20	51	71	50
Yeading	40	13	9	18	47	63	46*
Banstead Athletic	40	12	8	20	50	65	44
Maidenhead United	40	10	13	17	44	61	43
Southall	40	11	10	19	41	73	43
Newbury Town	40	11	8	21	47	65	41
Horsham	40	7	14	19	36	68	35
Petersfield United	40	5	7	28	36	87	22

*2 pts deducted

A Hundred Years of the Northern League

By Brian Hunt and Arthur Clark

Formed in 1889, only one year after The Football League, the Northern League pioneered football in the North-East and can be justifiably proud to be celebrating a succession of Centenary events during 1989. The name of Charles Samuel Craven will ever be remembered by Northern League clubs. It was he who called the seven founder clubs to an inaugural meeting in the Three Tuns Hotel in Durham City on March 25th 1889 to "form the Northern League".

Incredibly, the place, date and even the hour were identical exactly one hundred years later when the League held its Centenary Dinner – an unforgettably nostalgic and historic event – but only one part of a busy and successful year of sporting and social celebrations.

The League's early days were difficult; times were hard, life was grim and there was economic depression and social strife. But football was a unifying factor and the football field became a community focal point, particularly in the small towns and villages of the steel making and mining areas. There was little else. Arthur Hopcraft wrote – "the working classes saw football as an escape out of drudgery and claimed it as their own." This is still partly true today.

Over the past 100 years there have been more highs than lows. The 1928 Crook – Bishop Auckland "expenses" saga resulting in 341 suspensions in the North-East was a body blow, but the Northern League quickly recovered.

Clubs strove for F.A. Amateur Cup glory. In 1895 Northern League club Middlesbrough won the second F.A. Amateur Cup Competition and the League's clubs appeared in 19 of the 22 F.A. Amateur Cup finals prior to the First World War. In 1939 Bishop Auckland and Willington, only five miles apart and both League members, met in the Final at Sunderland where Bishops won 3-0 after extra time. In 1950 the same two clubs nearly filled Wembley for a reputedly classic final of finals. A shocked Bishops played well but lost 4-0 to a super footballing team intent on avenging 1939.

The soccer revival after the Second World War became a relief valve for the many amateur club supporters. Crowds flocked to almost every game and the Northern League again dominated the F.A. Amateur Cup throughout the '50s. Two more Northern League clubs contested an epic marathon final in 1954. Almost 200,000 watched Crook Town beat Bishop Auckland by a single goal at the third attempt. But the Bishops won the cup back in 1955 and again in 1956 and 1957 when the greatest amateur player of all time, British Olympic captain Bob Hardisty, announced his retirement. Crook Town won it again in 1959, 1962 and 1964 with left-winger Jimmy McMillan picking up his fourth winner's medal – a record.

For many years the 14-club Northern League had operated a "closed shop" policy. Then in 1958 the League was extended to take in Whitley Bay; later Spennymoor United, North Shields, Blyth Spartans, Consett and Ashington, and others followed. After a while the new clubs did well and the Bishops/Crook dominance faded. Blyth Spartans won the championship ten times, 5 times in succession, Spennymoor United 6 times, and North Shields surprised everyone with an F.A. Amateur Cup victory in 1969.

The F.A. Amateur Cup, the "owd pot" was put into cold storage in 1974-5 when the F.A. removed the distinction between amateur and professional, replacing the Cup with the F.A. Trophy. The inclusion of semi-professionals inevitably created stronger opposition and since 1975 no Northern League club has appeared at Wembley, a disappointment to many as the League's clubs had held the F.A. Amateur Cup a total of 24 times.

In 1982 the League again opened its doors to admit more clubs from the four Northern counties. Some good clubs joined, spending nearly £2 million to improve their grounds and facilities to meet the Northern League standards, and now in the current season, 1988-89, there are 40 member clubs in two divisions.

In the early years personalities were abundant. In 1906 Ernest B. Proud, Bishop Auckland's solicitor goalkeeper and later the League's President, played against France in the inaugural Amateur International, the first of 82 league players to win caps. Jack Coulthard set the League's goal scoring record with 10 in South Bank's 13-0 win of Ferryhill in 1936. One Rev. Robert Ferry "Hill" Drury, a Middlesbrough, Darlington and Bishops player in the early 1900s, was a true "Blue" amateur. He not only paid at the gate to play, but also insisted in joining the queue!

In the 1890s Northern League clubs were F.A. Cup rivals with Football League clubs and sometimes attracted bigger gates. Tours abroad were common. In 1909 and 1911 Northern League West Auckland twice won the Sir Thomas Lipton Trophy – the "first World Cup" – in Italy, beating Juventus 6-1 the second time. In 100 years exactly 100 clubs have played in the Northern League, which has a reputation for having produced some outstanding players and referees. 27 full English Internationals played in the League as youngsters.

The League has had only two secretaries and three chairmen since 1945, and in recent years has attracted valuable sponsorships. Rothmans, Drybroughs and now Skol have been sponsors for 13 years.

The League's most famous club, Bishop Auckland, shocked the football world when, along with Whitley Bay, they left the League in June 1988 to join the Northern Premier League, members of the Non-League Pyramid of Football which Northern League clubs had steadfastly resisted joining because of geography and economics. In consequence, its status threatened, the League is currently looking anew at the possibility of linking into the national set-up. Opinion is now divided and it is an emotive issue.

The North East has always been renowned for football fervour and the quality football by players known for their toughness and determination, as well as for their skill. Anxious to preserve its good image, the League sets high standards. It demands responsible behaviour, both on and off the field, and promotes rewarding good conduct schemes. Good sportsmanship and self control is a must for players and officials alike. The League's slogan "The Alternative Face of Football" has caught on, and more families have been attracted to watch matches in its Centenary season.

Renamed the "Skol Northern League" in 1988, League officials have set an exciting programme of Centenary celebrations. The match on May 16th against Barclays Football League was outstandingly successful, ending in a 2-2 draw. England Internationals Bryan Robson and Chris Waddle, both local boys, returned to their home territory, and players from Newcastle United, Sunderland and Middlesbrough and others made formidable opposition. An old-time fun game is arranged for Beamish Open Air Museum and Italian giants Juventus will play against the League side at Newcastle in the final Centenary game.

Northern Arts are joining with the League in promoting a touring play entitled "Northern Glory", depicting the colourful 100-year history of the League – a story full of laughs, tears, conflict, drama, music and songs with a professional cast – an ambitious undertaking.

Also ambitious is the League's 500-page Centenary book "Northern Goalfields", complete with records, results, tables, honours, stories, pictures and innumerable facts. A fascinating history containing the full story of the survival of the Northern League and its people.

The celebrations will culminate in a final Centenary Dinner in Newcastle for over a thousand enthusiasts and guests which will be a fitting climax to an exciting and memorable year, indeed the end of a century of fine tradition and outstanding football achievement. From that moment the Northern League will look forward to its second hundred years of progress and success with confidence, expectation and promise. There will be more champions, more personalities, more heroes, more passions and still more glory, and there will be even greater competition, new challenges, inevitable changes, maybe bitter disappointments, but the survival of the traditions of the second oldest league in the world is a certainty.

THE COCA-COLA FOOTBALL ASSOCIATION
SOCCER ST★R SCHEME

How the new Soccer Star Scheme can help every teacher and youth manager

"The Soccer Star Scheme is a unique soccer education programme developed by the F.A. with the support of the E.S.F.A. The Scheme assists boys and girls to enjoy and improve their football whilst reinforcing attitudes of behaviour."

Over 4,000 teachers and youth leaders have already registered into the Scheme as they have appreciated the following benefits for their schools and clubs:

1. All teachers and youth leaders receive a complimentary start pack with free posters, free books including the 64 page Instructional F.A. Soccer Star Book. A voucher to receive the Soccer Star Video at one-third discount is also included.

2. The Scheme focuses on 6 challenges which test the young players' ability in the most important soccer techniques.

3. The tests are relevant, valid, easy to administer. They require a minimum of equipment and facilities, are quickly organised and simple to record.

4. The Scheme is open to all teachers or youth managers regardless of their previous football experience or coaching qualifications.

5. The free F.A. Soccer Star Book outlines the tests and simple practices for boys and girls to master the techniques and score highly on the tests.

6. On completion of the tests the results are sent to the F.A. who return to the teacher/coach a computerised graph of the group's performance.

7. The youngsters receive individualised graphs, reports, badges, certificates, pennants and a free sportsmanship booklet.

Acclaimed as a major contribution to the soccer education of all youngsters you can obtain details of the Soccer Star Scheme by telephoning: Joan, Jean or Bettine on 0707 51840, 0707 50057 (24hr ansaphone); or writing to Joan Pritchard, Awards Organiser at: The Coca-Cola Football Association Soccer Star Scheme, 22-24A The Broadway, Darkes Lane, Potters Bar, Herts EN6 2HH.

The Football Association Fixture Programme 1989-90

AUGUST 1989

Sat 5	Official Opening of Season
Sat 12	Tennent's F.A. Charity Shield
Sat 19	Football League Season Starts
Wed 23	Littlewoods Cup (1) 1st Leg
Wed 30	Littlewoods Cup (1) 2nd Leg

SEPTEMBER 1989

Sat 2	F.A. Cup (P)
Wed 6	Sweden v England (WC)
	Finland v Wales (WC)
	Yugoslavia v Scotland (WC)
Sat 9	F.A. Vase (EP)
	F.A. Youth Cup (p)*
Wed 13	European Cups (1) 1st Leg
Sat 16	F.A. Cup (IQ)
Wed 20	Littlewoods Cup (2) 1st Leg
Sat 23	F.A. Trophy (1Q)
Wed 27	European Cups (1) 2nd Leg
Sat 30	F.A. Cup (2Q)
	F.A. Youth Cup (1Q)*

OCTOBER 1989

Wed 4	Littlewoods Cup (2) 2nd Leg
Sat 7	F.A. Vase (P)
Sun 8	F.A. Sunday Cup (1)
Wed 11	Poland v England (WC)
	Wales v Holland (WC)
	France v Scotland (WC)
	Rep. of Ireland v N. Ireland (WC)
Sat 14	F.A. Cup (3Q)
	F.A. Youth Cup (2Q)*
Wed 18	European Cups (2) 1st Leg
Sat 21	F.A. Trophy (2Q)
	F.A. County Youth Cup (1)*
Wed 25	Littlewoods Cup (3)
Sat 28	F.A. Cup (4Q)

NOVEMBER 1989

Wed 1	European Cups (2) 2nd Leg
Sat 4	F.A. Vase (1)
Sat 11	F.A. Youth Cup (1)*
Sun 12	F.A. Sunday Cup (2)
Wed 15	England v Italy (F)
	West Germany v Wales (WC)
	Scotland v Norway (WC)
Sat 18	F.A. Cup (1)
Wed 22	U.E.F.A. Cup (3) 1st Leg
Sat 25	F.A. Vase (2)
Wed 29	Littlewoods Cup (4)

DECEMBER 1989

Sat 2	F.A. Trophy (3Q)
	F.A. County Youth Cup (2)*
Wed 6	U.E.F.A. Cup (3) 2nd Leg
Sat 9	F.A. Cup (2)
	F.A. Youth Cup (2)*
Sun 10	F.A. Sunday Cup (3)
Wed 13	Holland v England (F)
Sat 16	F.A. Vase (3)

JANUARY 1990

Sat 6	F.A. Cup (3)
Sat 13	F.A. Trophy (1)
	F.A. Youth Cup (3)*
Wed 17	Littlewoods Cup (5)
Sat 20	F.A. Vase (4)
	F.A. County Youth Cup (3)*
Sun 21	F.A. Sunday Cup (4)
Sat 27	F.A. Cup (4)

FEBRUARY 1990

Sat 3	F.A. Trophy (2)
Sat 10	F.A. Vase (5)
	F.A. Youth Cup (4)*
Wed 14	Littlewoods Cup (SF) 1st Leg
Sat 17	F.A. Cup (5)
Sun 18	F.A. Sunday Cup (5)
Sat 24	F.A. Trophy (3)
	F.A. County Youth Cup (4)*
Wed 28	Littlewoods Cup (SF) 2nd Leg

MARCH 1990

Sat 3	F.A. Vase (6)
	F.A. Youth Cup (5)*
Wed 7	European Cups (QF) 1st Leg
Sat 10	F.A. Cup (6)
	England v France (Schoolboys)
Sat 17	F.A. Trophy (4)
Sun 18	F.A. Sunday Cup (SF)
Wed 21	European Cups (QF) 2nd Leg
Sat 24	F.A. Vase (SF) 1st Leg
	F.A. County Youth Cup (SF)*
Wed 28	International date
Sat 31	F.A. Vase (SF) 2nd Leg
	F.A. Youth Cup (SF)*

APRIL 1990
Wed 4	European Cups (SF) 1st Leg
Sat 7	F.A. Cup (SF)
	F.A. Trophy (SF) 1st Leg
Sat 14	F.A. Trophy (SF) 2nd Leg
Wed 18	European Cups (SF) 2nd Leg
Wed 25	International date
Sat 28	F.A. County Youth Cup Final
Sun 29	Littlewoods Cup Final
	F.A. Sunday Cup Final

MAY 1990
Wed 2	U.E.F.A. Cup Final 1st Leg

Sat 5	F.A. Vase Final
	F.A. Youth Cup Final*
Wed 9	European Cup Winners' Cup Final
Sat 12	F.A. Cup Final
Wed 16	U.E.F.A. Cup Final 2nd Leg
Sat 19	F.A. Trophy Final
Wed 23	European Champion Clubs' Cup Final

JUNE 1990
Sat 2	England v Holland (Schoolboys)
Fri 8	World Cup Finals (end 8th July)

P = Preliminary Round   WC = World Cup   EP = Extra Preliminary Round
1Q = First Qualifying Round   F = Friendly   QF = Quarter-Final   SF = Semi-Final
* = Closing date for round

163

Barclays League
FIXTURE LIST

Season 1989-90
© The Football League 1989

Sat. 19th August

Charlton Athletic v Derby County ....
Coventry City v Everton ....
Liverpool v Manchester City ....
Manchester United v Arsenal ....
Nottingham Forest v Aston Villa ....
Queens Park Rangers v Crystal Palace ....
Sheffield Wednesday v Norwich City ....
Southampton v Millwall ....
Tottenham Hotspur v Luton Town ....
Wimbledon v Chelsea ....

SECOND DIVISION
Blackburn Rovers v Oldham Athletic...............................
Bradford City v Port Vale ....
Brighton & Hove Albion v AFC Bournemouth ....
Hull City v Leicester City ....
Ipswich Town v Barnsley ....
Middlesbrough v Wolverhampton Wanderers....................
Newcastle United v Leeds United....................................
Plymouth Argyle v Oxford United...................................
Stoke City v West Ham United ....
Swindon Town v Sunderland ....
Watford v Portsmouth...
West Bromwich Albion v Sheffield United ....

THIRD DIVISION
Birmingham City v Crewe Alexandra...............................
Blackpool v Wigan Athletic ....
Bristol Rovers v Brentford ....
Bury v Bristol City..
Cardiff City v Bolton Wanderers ....
Chester City v Mansfield Town ....
Fulham v Tranmere Rovers...
Huddersfield Town v Swansea City ....
Leyton Orient v Notts County ....
Reading v Shrewsbury Town ....
Rotherham United v Preston North End...........................
Walsall v Northampton Town ....

FOURTH DIVISION
Chesterfield v Colchester United.....................................
Exeter City v Doncaster Rovers ....
Gillingham v Aldershot..
Grimsby Town v Cambridge United ....
Halifax Town v Hartlepool United ....
Hereford United v Carlisle United...................................
Lincoln City v Scunthorpe United ....
Peterborough United v Maidstone United.........................
Rochdale v Burnley..
Scarborough v Wrexham..
Southend United v York City ....
Stockport County v Torquay United ....

Tues. 22nd August

FIRST DIVISION
Arsenal v Coventry City ....

Chelsea v Queens Park Rangers......................................
Crystal Palace v Manchester United................................
Everton v Tottenham Hotspur ....
Luton Town v Sheffield Wednesday ....
Millwall v Charlton Athletic ....

SECOND DIVISION
AFC Bournemouth v West Bromwich Albion....................
Barnsley v Stoke City..
Oldham Athletic v Watford...
Sunderland v Ipswich Town ....

Wed. 23rd August

FIRST DIVISION
Aston Villa v Liverpool ....
Derby County v Wimbledon..
Manchester City v Southampton ....
Norwich City v Nottingham Forest ....

SECOND DIVISION
Leeds United v Middlesbrough ....
Leicester City v Blackburn Rovers...................................
West Ham United v Bradford City...................................

Fri. 25th August

THIRD DIVISION
Crewe Alexandra v Reading...

Sat. 26th August

FIRST DIVISION
Arsenal v Wimbledon ....
Aston Villa v Charlton Athletic......................................
Chelsea v Sheffield Wednesday ....
Crystal Palace v Coventry City.......................................
Derby County v Manchester United ....
Everton v Southampton ....
Luton Town v Liverpool...
Manchester City v Tottenham Hotspur ....
Millwall v Nottingham Forest ....
Norwich City v Queens Park Rangers...............................

SECOND DIVISION
AFC Bournemouth v Hull City ....
Barnsley v Brighton & Hove Albion ....
Leeds United v Blackburn Rovers ....
Leicester City v Newcastle United ....
Oldham Athletic v Swindon Town ....
Oxford United v Watford ....
Port Vale v West Bromwich Albion ....
Portsmouth v Stoke City..
Sheffield United v Ipswich Town ....
Sunderland v Middlesbrough ....
West Ham United v Plymouth Argyle ....
Wolverhampton Wanderers v Bradford City ....

Bolton Wanderers v Fulham...
Brentford v Chester City ....
Bristol City v Birmingham City ....
Mansfield Town v Bristol Rovers.....................................
Notts County v Blackpool ....
Preston North End v Bury ....
Shrewsbury Town v Leyton Orient ....
Swansea City v Northampton Town ....
Tranmere Rovers v Cardiff City ....
Walsall v Huddersfield Town ....
Wigan Athletic v Rotherham United................................

FOURTH DIVISION
Aldershot v Lincoln City ....
Burnley v Stockport County ....
Cambridge United v Hereford United ....
Carlisle United v Chesterfield ....
Colchester United v Halifax Town...................................
Doncaster Rovers v Gillingham ....
Hartlepool United v Exeter City ....
Maidstone United v Scarborough ....
Scunthorpe United v Rochdale ....
Torquay United v Grimsby Town ....
Wrexham v Southend United ....
York City v Peterborough United.....................................

Tues. 29th August

FIRST DIVISION
Charlton Athletic v Chelsea ....
Southampton v Aston Villa ....
Wimbledon v Millwall..

Wed. 30th August

FIRST DIVISION
Coventry City v Manchester City......................................
Liverpool v Crystal Palace ....
Manchester United v Norwich City ....
Nottingham Forest v Derby County ....
Queens Park Rangers v Luton Town ....
Sheffield Wednesday v Everton ....

Fri. 1st September

FOURTH DIVISION
Southend United v Hartlepool United................................
Stockport County v York City ....

Sat. 2nd September

SECOND DIVISION
Blackburn Rovers v Oxford United ....
Bradford City v Portsmouth ....
Brighton & Hove Albion v Port Vale ....
Hull City v West Ham United..
Ipswich Town v AFC Bournemouth..................................
Middlesbrough v Sheffield United....................................
Newcastle United v Oldham Athletic ....
Plymouth Argyle v Barnsley ....
Stoke City v Leeds United ....
Watford v Leicester City..
West Bromwich Albion v Sunderland...............................

THIRD DIVISION
Birmingham City v Swansea City.....................................
Blackpool v Shrewsbury Town..
Bristol Rovers v Notts County ....
Bury v Wigan Athletic...
Cardiff City v Brentford ....

Chester City v Crewe Alexandra ....
Fulham v Mansfield Town...
Huddersfield Town v Bolton Wanderers ....
Leyton Orient v Preston North End ....
Northampton Town v Bristol City ....
Reading v Tranmere Rovers ....
Rotherham United v Walsall ....

FOURTH DIVISION
Chesterfield v Burnley..
Exeter City v Carlisle United...
Gillingham v Scunthorpe United......................................
Grimsby Town v Colchester United ....
Halifax Town v Torquay United.......................................
Hereford United v Maidstone United................................
Lincoln City v Doncaster Rovers ....
Peterborough United v Aldershot ....
Rochdale v Wrexham...
Scarborough v Cambridge United ....

Sun. 3rd September

SECOND DIVISION
Swindon Town v Wolverhampton Wanderers ....

Fri. 8th September

FOURTH DIVISION
Colchester United v Hereford United ....

Sat. 9th September

FIRST DIVISION
Arsenal v Sheffield Wednesday..
Aston Villa v Tottenham Hotspur ....
Chelsea v Nottingham Forest..
Crystal Palace v Wimbledon...
Derby County v Liverpool ....
Everton v Manchester United..
Luton Town v Charlton Athletic ....
Manchester City v Queens Park Rangers ....
Millwall v Coventry City..
Norwich City v Southampton..

SECOND DIVISION
AFC Bournemouth v Newcastle United.............................
Barnsley v Middlesbrough ....
Leeds United v Ipswich Town..
Leicester City v West Bromwich Albion ....
Oldham Athletic v Plymouth Argyle ....
Oxford United v Bradford City ....
Port Vale v Blackburn Rovers ....
Portsmouth v Hull City ....
Sheffield United v Brighton & Hove Albion ....
Sunderland v Watford ....
West Ham United v Swindon Town ....
Wolverhampton Wanderers v Stoke City ....

THIRD DIVISION
Bolton Wanderers v Bristol Rovers...................................
Brentford v Bury ....
Bristol City v Blackpool ....
Crewe Alexandra v Fulham...
Mansfield Town v Cardiff City ....
Notts County v Reading ....
Preston North End v Huddersfield Town ....
Shrewsbury Town v Birmingham City ....
Swansea City v Chester City ....
Tranmere Rovers v Rotherham United ....
Walsall v Leyton Orient ....
Wigan Athletic v Northampton Town ....

FOURTH DIVISION
Aldershot v Southend United ....

Burnley v Exeter City ....
Cambridge United v Chesterfield ....
Carlisle United v Grimsby Town ....
Doncaster Rovers v Peterborough United.........................
Hartlepool United v Gillingham....................................
Maidstone United v Stockport County ....
Scunthorpe United v Scarborough ....
Torquay United v Lincoln City ....
Wrexham v Halifax Town ....
York City v Rochdale ....

Tues. 12th September

SECOND DIVISION
Portsmouth v Plymouth Argyle......................................
Port Vale v Hull City ....
Sheffield United v Swindon Town..................................
Wolverhampton Wanderers v Brighton & Hove Albion.......

Wed. 13th September

SECOND DIVISION
Oxford United v Newcastle United ....

Fri. 15th September

THIRD DIVISION
Chester City v Notts County...
Halifax Town v Carlisle United....................................
Southend United v Torquay United ....
Stockport County v Hartlepool United...........................

Sat. 16th September

FIRST DIVISION
Charlton Athletic v Everton ....
Coventry City v Luton Town ....
Liverpool v Norwich City..
Manchester United v Millwall.......................................
Nottingham Forest v Arsenal...
Queens Park Rangers v Derby County ....
Sheffield Wednesday v Aston Villa ....
Southampton v Crystal Palace ....
Tottenham Hotspur v Chelsea ....
Wimbledon v Manchester City......................................

SECOND DIVISION
Blackburn Rovers v Sunderland.....................................
Bradford City v Leicester City ....
Brighton & Hove Albion v West Ham United..................
Hull City v Leeds United ....
Ipswich Town v Wolverhampton Wanderers ....
Middlesbrough v AFC Bournemouth...............................
Newcastle United v Portsmouth.....................................
Plymouth Argyle v Sheffield United..............................
Stoke City v Oldham Athletic.......................................
Swindon Town v Barnsley..
Watford v Port Vale ....
West Bromwich Albion v Oxford United ....

THIRD DIVISION
Birmingham City v Tranmere Rovers..............................
Blackpool v Crewe Alexandra ....
Bristol Rovers v Preston North End...............................
Bury v Mansfield Town ....
Cardiff City v Bristol City ....
Fulham v Swansea City ....
Huddersfield Town v Brentford ....
Leyton Orient v Wigan Athletic....................................
Northampton Town v Shrewsbury Town..........................
Reading v Walsall ....
Rotherham United v Bolton Wanderers ....

FOURTH DIVISION
Chesterfield v Aldershot..
Exeter City v Cambridge United ....
Gillingham v Burnley..
Grimsby Town v Maidstone United ....
Hereford United v Wrexham ....
Lincoln City v York City..
Peterborough United v Scunthorpe United ....
Rochdale v Colchester United ....
Scarborough v Doncaster Rovers ....

Fri. 22nd September

THIRD DIVISION
Tranmere Rovers v Huddersfield Town ....

FOURTH DIVISION
Cambridge United v Halifax Town ....
Doncaster Rovers v Southend United ....

Sat. 23rd September

FIRST DIVISION
Arsenal v Charlton Athletic ....
Aston Villa v Queens Park Rangers ....
Chelsea v Coventry City ....
Crystal Palace v Nottingham Forest ....
Derby County v Southampton ....
Everton v Liverpool ....
Luton Town v Wimbledon ....
Manchester City v Manchester United............................
Millwall v Sheffield Wednesday ....
Norwich City v Tottenham Hotspur ....

SECOND DIVISION
AFC Bournemouth v Blackburn Rovers ....
Barnsley v Bradford City ....
Leeds United v Swindon Town ....
Leicester City v Brighton & Hove Albion ....
Oldham Athletic v West Bromwich Albion ....
Oxford United v Ipswich Town ....
Port Vale v Stoke City ....
Portsmouth v Middlesbrough ....
Sheffield United v Hull City ....
Sunderland v Newcastle United ....
West Ham United v Watford ....
Wolverhampton Wanderers v Plymouth Argyle ....

THIRD DIVISION
Bolton Wanderers v Leyton Orient................................
Brentford v Birmingham City ....
Bristol City v Bristol Rovers...
Crewe Alexandra v Northampton Town ....
Mansfield Town v Blackpool ....
Notts County v Rotherham United ....
Preston North End v Chester City ....
Shrewsbury Town v Bury ....
Swansea City v Reading ....
Walsall v Fulham ....
Wigan Athletic v Cardiff City ....

FOURTH DIVISION
Aldershot v Stockport County ....
Burnley v Hereford United ....
Carlisle United v Gillingham ....
Colchester United v Scarborough ....
Hartlepool United v Peterborough United ....
Maidstone United v Chesterfield....................................
Scunthorpe United v Exeter City....................................
Torquay United v Rochdale ....
Wrexham v Lincoln City...
York City v Grimsby Town ....

Tues. 26th September

SECOND DIVISION
AFC Bournemouth v Port Vale......................................
Barnsley v Wolverhampton Wanderers ....
Portsmouth v West Ham United ....
Sheffield United v Oldham Athletic ....
Stoke City v Bradford City..
Swindon Town v Plymouth Argyle................................

THIRD DIVISION
Birmingham City v Walsall...
Bristol City v Shrewsbury Town ....
Bury v Rotherham United ....
Cardiff City v Northampton Town ....
Crewe Alexandra v Brentford......................................
Fulham v Huddersfield Town ....
Leyton Orient v Bristol Rovers ....
Notts County v Bolton Wanderers ....
Preston North End v Blackpool....................................
Reading v Chester City ....
Wigan Athletic v Tranmere Rovers...............................

FOURTH DIVISION
Burnley v York City ....
Cambridge United v Carlisle United ....
Colchester United v Maidstone United..........................
Doncaster Rovers v Aldershot ....
Gillingham v Southend United......................................
Rochdale v Hartlepool United ....
Scunthorpe United v Torquay United ....
Wrexham v Stockport County......................................

Wed. 27th September

SECOND DIVISION
Brighton & Hove Albion v Ipswich Town ....
Leeds United v Oxford United......................................
Leicester City v Sunderland ....
Middlesbrough v Hull City ....
Newcastle United v Watford ....
West Bromwich Albion v Blackburn Rovers.....................

FOURTH DIVISION
Exeter City v Grimsby Town ....
Hereford United v Chesterfield.....................................
Lincoln City v Peterborough United ....
Scarborough v Halifax Town ....

Fri. 29th September

THIRD DIVISION
Tranmere Rovers v Bristol City.....................................

Sat. 30th September

FIRST DIVISION
Aston Villa v Derby County ....
Chelsea v Arsenal...
Crystal Palace v Everton...
Liverpool v Manchester United ....
Manchester City v Luton Town ....
Millwall v Norwich City..
Nottingham Forest v Charlton Athletic...........................
Sheffield Wednesday v Coventry City............................
Southampton v Wimbledon..
Tottenham Hotspur v Queens Parks Rangers ....

SECOND DIVISION
Blackburn Rovers v Barnsley ....
Bradford City v Swindon Town.....................................
Hull City v Newcastle United ....
Ipswich Town v Stoke City..

Oldham Athletic v Leicester City ....
Oxford United v AFC Bournemouth ....
Plymouth Argyle v Brighton & Hove Albion ....
Port Vale v Leeds United...
Sunderland v Sheffield United ....
Watford v Middlesbrough ....
West Ham United v West Bromwich Albion.....................
Wolverhampton Wanderers v Portsmouth ....

THIRD DIVISION
Blackpool v Birmingham City..
Bolton Wanderers v Mansfield Town ....
Brentford v Wigan Athletic ....
Bristol Rovers v Reading...
Chester City v Fulham..
Huddersfield Town v Leyton Orient ....
Northampton Town v Bury ....
Rotherham United v Cardiff City ....
Shrewsbury Town v Crewe Alexandra...........................
Swansea City v Notts County......................................
Walsall v Preston North End ....

FOURTH DIVISION
Aldershot v Scunthorpe United ....
Carlisle United v Colchester United...............................
Chesterfield v Rochdale ....
Grimsby Town v Hereford United ....
Halifax Town v Exeter City ....
Hartlepool United v Doncaster Rovers...........................
Maidstone United v Cambridge United ....
Peterborough United v Gillingham ....
Southend United v Lincoln City ....
Stockport County v Scarborough..................................
Torquay United v Burnley ....
York City v Wrexham ....

Fri. 6th October

THIRD DIVISION
Blackpool v Reading...

FOURTH DIVISION
Halifax Town v Gillingham ....

Sat. 7th October

SECOND DIVISION
Blackburn Rovers v Middlesbrough................................
Bradford City v Brighton & Hove Albion ....
Hull City v Swindon Town ....
Ipswich Town v Newcastle United ....
Oldham Athletic v Barnsley ....
Oxford United v Portsmouth ....
Plymouth Argyle v Stoke City.......................................
Port Vale v Leicester City ....
Sunderland v AFC Bournemouth ....
Watford v West Bromwich Albion..................................
West Ham United v Leeds United ....
Wolverhampton Wanderers v Sheffield United ....

THIRD DIVISION
Bolton Wanderers v Wigan Athletic ....
Brentford v Bristol City...
Bristol Rovers v Fulham ....
Chester City v Bury ....
Huddersfield Town v Cardiff City...................................
Northampton Town v Preston North End ....
Rotherham United v Birmingham City............................
Shrewsbury Town v Mansfield Town ....
Swansea City v Crewe Alexandra ....
Tranmere Rovers v Leyton Orient ....
Walsall v Notts County..

FOURTH DIVISION
Aldershot v Colchester United......................................
Carlisle United v Wrexham...
Chesterfield v Lincoln City...
Grimsby Town v Rochdale...

Hartlepool United v Scunthorpe United ....
Maidstone United v Burnley ....
Peterborough United v Exeter City.................................
Southend United v Scarborough ....
Stockport County v Hereford United ....
Torquay United v Doncaster Rovers ....
York City v Cambridge United ....

Fri. 13th October

Cambridge United v Torquay United ....
Colchester United v York City..

Sat. 14th October

FIRST DIVISION
Arsenal v Manchester City ....
Charlton Athletic v Tottenham Hotspur ....
Coventry City v Nottingham Forest ....
Derby County v Crystal Palace ....
Everton v Millwall ....
Luton Town v Aston Villa ....
Manchester United v Sheffield Wednesday.....................
Norwich City v Chelsea ....
Queens Park Rangers v Southampton ....
Wimbledon v Liverpool..

SECOND DIVISION
AFC Bournemouth v Oldham Athletic............................
Barnsley v Port Vale ....
Brighton & Hove Albion v Watford ....
Leeds United v Sunderland ....
Leicester City v Oxford United ....
Middlesbrough v Plymouth Argyle ....
Newcastle United v Bradford City ....
Portsmouth v Blackburn Rovers ....
Sheffield United v West Ham United ....
Stoke City v Hull City ....
Swindon Town v Ipswich Town ....
West Bromwich Albion v Wolverhampton Wanderers.........

THIRD DIVISION
Birmingham City v Northampton Town............................
Bristol City v Swansea City ....
Bury v Bristol Rovers..
Cardiff City v Chester City ....
Crewe Alexandra v Bolton Wanderers ....
Fulham v Rotherham United...
Leyton Orient v Blackpool ....
Mansfield Town v Walsall ....
Notts County v Tranmere Rovers ....
Preston North End v Brentford.......................................
Reading v Huddersfield Town ....
Wigan Athletic v Shrewsbury Town ....

FOURTH DIVISION
Burnley v Hartlepool United ....
Doncaster Rovers v Carlisle United ....
Exeter City v Chesterfield ....
Gillingham v Stockport County......................................
Hereford United v Southend United ....
Lincoln City v Halifax Town..
Rochdale v Peterborough United ....
Scarborough v Grimsby Town ....
Scunthorpe United v Maidstone United...........................
Wrexham v Aldershot ....

Mon. 16th October

THIRD DIVISION
Tranmere Rovers v Mansfield Town ....

FOURTH DIVISION
Stockport County v Southend United...............................

Tues. 17th October

SECOND DIVISION
Barnsley v Sheffield United..
Hull City v Oldham Athletic..
Plymouth Argyle v Leicester City ....
Portsmouth v Leeds United ....
Stoke City v West Bromwich Albion ....
Swindon Town v Oxford United.....................................
Watford v AFC Bournemouth ....
Wolverhampton Wanderers v Port Vale ....

THIRD DIVISION
Brentford v Bolton Wanderers..
Bristol City v Notts County ....
Bury v Swansea City ....
Cardiff City v Bristol Rovers ....
Chester City v Birmingham City....................................
Huddersfield Town v Wigan Athletic ....
Northampton Town v Blackpool.....................................
Preston North End v Crewe Alexandra............................
Reading v Fulham ....
Rotherham United v Leyton Orient.................................
Walsall v Shrewsbury Town ....

FOURTH DIVISION
Burnley v Peterborough United ....
Cambridge United v Doncaster Rovers ....
Carlisle United v Scunthorpe United...............................
Chesterfield v Halifax Town ....
Colchester United v Wrexham ....
Grimsby Town v Gillingham ....
Rochdale v Exeter City ....
Torquay United v Hartlepool United ....
York City v Aldershot...

Wed. 18th October

FIRST DIVISION
Tottenham Hotspur v Arsenal ....

SECOND DIVISION
Bradford City v Ipswich Town ....
Middlesbrough v Brighton & Hove Albion......................
Newcastle United v Blackburn Rovers ....
West Ham United v Sunderland ....

FOURTH DIVISION
Hereford United v Scarborough ....
Maidstone United v Lincoln City....................................

Fri. 20th October

THIRD DIVISION
Swansea City v Tranmere Rovers ....

Sat. 21st October

FIRST DIVISION
Coventry City v Manchester United ....
Crystal Palace v Millwall ....
Derby County v Chelsea..
Everton v Arsenal ....
Luton Town v Norwich City ....
Manchester City v Aston Villa ....
Queens Park Rangers v Charlton Athletic........................
Southampton v Liverpool ....
Tottenham Hotspur v Sheffield Wednesday.....................
Wimbledon v Nottingham Forest ....

SECOND DIVISION
AFC Bournemouth v Portsmouth....................................
Blackburn Rovers v Watford ....

168

Brighton & Hove Albion v Newcastle United ....
Ipswich Town v Plymouth Argyle ....
Leeds United v Wolverhampton Wanderers ....
Leicester City v Swindon Town ....
Oldham Athletic v Middlesbrough......................................
Oxford United v Barnsley ....
Port Vale v West Ham United ....
Sheffield United v Stoke City..
Sunderland v Bradford City ....
West Bromwich Albion v Hull City....................................

THIRD DIVISION

Birmingham City v Huddersfield Town..............................
Blackpool v Cardiff City ....
Bolton Wanderers v Chester City ....
Bristol Rovers v Northampton Town ....
Crewe Alexandra v Rotherham United ....
Fulham v Bury..
Leyton Orient v Reading ....
Mansfield Town v Bristol City..
Notts County v Preston North End ....
Shrewsbury Town v Brentford ....
Wigan Athletic v Walsall ....

FOURTH DIVISION

Aldershot v Torquay United ....
Doncaster Rovers v Burnley ....
Exeter City v Hereford United..
Gillingham v Chesterfield ....
Halifax Town v Rochdale ....
Hartlepool United v York City ....
Lincoln City v Grimsby Town
Peterborough United v Stockport County ....
Scarborough v Carlisle United ....
Scunthorpe United v Colchester United............................
Southend United v Maidstone United ....
Wrexham v Cambridge United ....

Tues. 24th October

THIRD DIVISION

Mansfield Town v Swansea City ....

Fri. 27th October

THIRD DIVISION

Tranmere Rovers v Crewe Alexandra ....

Sat. 28th October

FIRST DIVISION

Arsenal v Derby County..
Aston Villa v Crystal Palace ....
Charlton Athletic v Coventry City ....
Chelsea v Manchester City ....
Liverpool v Tottenham Hotspur..
Manchester United v Southampton....................................
Millwall v Luton Town ....
Norwich City v Everton..
Nottingham Forest v Queens Park Rangers ....
Sheffield Wednesday v Wimbledon....................................

SECOND DIVISION

Barnsley v Leicester City..
Bradford City v Leeds United..
Hull City v Brighton & Hove Albion ....
Middlesbrough v West Bromwich Albion..........................
Newcastle United v Port Vale ....
Plymouth Argyle v Blackburn Rovers ....
Portsmouth v Ipswich Town ....
Stoke City v Sunderland ....
Swindon Town v AFC Bournemouth ....
Watford v Sheffield United ....
West Ham United v Oxford United ....

Wolverhampton Wanderers v Oldham Athletic..................

THIRD DIVISION

Brentford v Fulham ....
Bristol City v Wigan Athletic..
Bury v Birmingham City..
Cardiff City v Leyton Orient ....
Chester City v Bristol Rovers ....
Huddersfield Town v Shrewsbury Town............................
Northampton Town v Notts County ....
Prston North End v Bolton Wanderers ....
Reading v Mansfield Town..
Rotherham United v Blackpool ....
Walsall v Swansea City

FOURTH DIVISION

Burnley v Aldershot ....
Cambridge United v Scunthorpe United ....
Carlisle United v Hartlepool United ....
Chesterfield v Southend United ....
Colchester United v Peterborough United ....
Grimsby Town v Halifax Town ....
Hereford United v Lincoln City ....
Maidstone United v Wrexham ....
Rochdale v Scarborough..
Stockport County v Exeter City ....
Torquay United v Gillingham ....
York City v Doncaster Rovers ....

Mon. 30th October

SECOND DIVISION

Port Vale v Middlesbrough ....

Tues. 31st October

SECOND DIVISION

AFC Bournemouth v West Ham United ....
Blackburn Rovers v Hull City..
Ipswich Town v Watford..
Oldham Athletic v Bradford City ....
Sheffield United v Portsmouth..
Sunderland v Barnsley ....

THIRD DIVISION

Birmingham City v Cardiff City..
Blackpool v Bury ....
Bolton Wanderers v Walsall ....
Crewe Alexandra v Bristol City..
Fulham v Northampton Town..
Leyton Orient v Chester City..
Mansfield Town v Preston North End................................
Notts County v Brentford ....
Shrewsbury Town v Tranmere Rovers................................
Swansea City v Rotherham United ....
Wigan Athletic v Reading..

FOURTH DIVISION

Aldershot v Carlisle United..
Doncaster Rovers v Maidstone United ....
Gillingham v Rochdale..
Halifax Town v Hereford United..
Hartlepool United v Cambridge United............................
Scunthorpe United v York City..
Southend United v Burnley..
Wrexham v Torquay United...

Wed. 1st November

SECOND DIVISION

Brighton & Hove Albion v Swindon Town ....
Leeds United v Plymouth Argyle ....
Leicester City v Wolverhampton Wanderers ....
Oxford United v Stoke City..

West Bromwich Albion v Newcastle United ....

THIRD DIVISION
Bristol Rovers v Huddersfield Town ....

FOURTH DIVISION
Exeter City v Colchester United....................................
Lincoln City v Stockport County ....
Peterborough United v Grimsby Town ....
Scarborough v Chesterfield ....

Fri. 3rd November

THIRD DIVISION
Cardiff City v Bury..

FOURTH DIVISION
Stockport County v Halifax Town ....

Sat. 4th November

FIRST DIVISION
Arsenal v Norwich City ....
Aston Villa v Everton ....
Charlton Athletic v Manchester United ....
Chelsea v Millwall ....
Liverpool v Coventry City..
Luton Town v Derby County..
Manchester City v Crystal Palace ....
Nottingham Forest v Sheffield Wednesday ....
Southampton v Tottenham Hotspur..................................
Wimbledon v Queens Park Rangers.................................

SECOND DIVISION
Barnsley v Portsmouth ....
Brighton & Hove Albion v Blackburn Rovers....................
Hull City v Watford ....
Ipswich Town v West Bromwich Albion ....
Leeds United v AFC Bournemouth ....
Newcastle United v Middlesbrough ....
Oldham Athletic v Sunderland.......................................
Plymouth Argyle v Bradford City ....
Port Vale v Oxford United ....
Sheffield United v Leicester City ....
Swindon Town v Stoke City ....
Wolverhampton Wanderers v West Ham United...............

THIRD DIVISION
Bolton Wanderers v Swansea City ....
Brentford v Tranmere Rovers...
Bristol Rovers v Blackpool...
Chester City v Huddersfield Town ....
Leyton Orient v Fulham ....
Mansfield Town v Notts County ....
Northampton Town v Rotherham United ....
Preston North End v Shrewsbury Town ....
Reading v Birmingham City ....
Walsall v Bristol City ....
Wigan Athletic v Crewe Alexandra................................

FOURTH DIVISION
Burnley v Colchester United ....
Cambridge United v Aldershot ....
Carlisle United v Maidstone United ....
Doncaster Rovers v Scunthorpe United...........................
Exeter City v Lincoln City..
Gillingham v Scarborough ....
Grimsby Town v Chesterfield ....
Hartlepool United v Wrexham.......................................
Hereford United v Rochdale ....
Southend United v Peterborough United ....
York City v Torquay United...

Fri. 10th November

THIRD DIVISION
Crewe Alexandra v Mansfield Town ....
Tranmere Rovers v Walsall ....

FOURTH DIVISION
Colchester United v Cambridge United ....
Halifax Town v Southend United ....

Sat. 11th November

FIRST DIVISION
Coventry City v Southampton...
Crystal Palace v Luton Town ....
Derby County v Manchester City ....
Everton v Chelsea ....
Manchester United v Nottingham Forest ....
Millwall v Arsenal ....
Norwich City v Aston Villa ....
Queens Park Rangers v Liverpool ....
Sheffield Wednesday v Charlton Athletic..........................
Tottenham Hotspur v Wimbledon ....

SECOND DIVISION
AFC Bournemouth v Sheffield United ....
Blackburn Rovers v Ipswich Town..................................
Bradford City v Hull City...
Leicester City v Leeds United ....
Middlesbrough v Swindon Town ....
Oxford United v Oldham Athletic ....
Portsmouth v Port Vale ....
Stoke City v Brighton & Hove Albion ....
Sunderland v Wolverhampton Wanderers.........................
Watford v Plymouth Argyle ....
West Bromwich Albion v Barnsley ....
West Ham United v Newcastle United ....

THIRD DIVISION
Birmingham City v Leyton Orient ....
Blackpool v Brentford...
Bristol City v Bolton Wanderers ....
Bury v Reading ....
Fulham v Cardiff City ....
Huddersfield Town v Northampton Town ....
Notts County v Wigan Athletic ....
Rotherham United v Chester City ....
Shrewsbury Town v Bristol Rovers ....
Swansea City v Preston North End ....

FOURTH DIVISION
Aldershot v Hartlepool United ....
Chesterfield v Stockport County ....
Lincoln City v Gillingham ....
Maidstone United v York City ....
Peterborough United v Hereford United ....
Rochdale v Doncaster Rovers..
Scarborough v Exeter City ....
Scunthorpe United v Burnley ....
Torquay United v Carlisle United....................................
Wrexham v Grimsby Town ....

Sat. 18th November

FIRST DIVISION
Arsenal v Queens Park Rangers......................................
Aston Villa v Coventry City ....
Chelsea v Southampton...
Crystal Palace v Tottenham Hotspur ....
Derby County v Sheffield Wednesday ....
Everton v Wimbledon...
Luton Town v Manchester United ....
Manchester City v Nottingham Forest ....
Millwall v Liverpool ....
Norwich City v Charlton Athletic ....

AFC Bournemouth v Stoke City ....
Barnsley v Newcastle United...
Leeds United v Watford ....
Leicester City v Ipswich Town ....
Oldham Athletic v Brighton & Hove Albion......................
Oxford United v Hull City ....
Port Vale v Swindon Town..
Portsmouth v West Bromwich Albion ....
Sheffield United v Bradford City ....
Sunderland v Plymouth Argyle ....
West Ham United v Middlesbrough ....
Wolverhampton Wanderers v Blackburn Rovers................

Fri. 24th November

THIRD DIVISION
Chester City v Walsall...

FOURTH DIVISION
Gillingham v Colchester United ....
Scarborough v York City ....
Southend United v Cambridge United.............................

Sat. 25th November

FIRST DIVISION
Charlton Athletic v Manchester City...............................
Coventry City v Norwich City ....
Liverpool v Arsenal..
Manchester United v Chelsea ....
Nottingham Forest v Everton ....
Queens Park Rangers v Millwall ....
Sheffield Wednesday v Crystal Palace ....
Southampton v Luton Town...
Tottenham Hotspur v Derby County................................
Wimbledon v Aston Villa ....

SECOND DIVISION
Blackburn Rovers v West Ham United ....
Bradford City v AFC Bournemouth..................................
Brighton & Hove Albion v Sunderland.............................
Hull City v Barnsley ....
Ipswich Town v Oldham Athletic ....
Middlesbrough v Oxford United ....
Newcastle United v Sheffield United...............................
Plymouth Argyle v Port Vale ....
Stoke City v Leicester City ....
Watford v Wolverhampton Wanderers ....
West Bromwich Albion v Leeds United ....

THIRD DIVISION
Birmingham City v Bolton Wanderers..............................
Blackpool v Tranmere Rovers ....
Bristol Rovers v Swansea City ....
Bury v Crewe Alexandra ....
Cardiff City v Preston North End ....
Fulham v Wigan Athletic ....
Huddersfield Town v Notts County..................................
Leyton Orient v Mansfield Town.....................................
Northampton Town v Brentford ....
Reading v Bristol City...
Rotherham United v Shrewsbury Town ....

FOURTH DIVISION
Chesterfield v Hartlepool United ....
Exeter City v Wrexham ....
Grimsby Town v Aldershot ....
Halifax Town v Maidstone United ....
Hereford United v Doncaster Rovers...............................
Lincoln City v Burnley ....
Peterborough United v Torquay United ....
Rochdale v Carlisle United ....
Stockport County v Scunthorpe United ....

Sun. 26th November

SECOND DIVISION
Swindon Town v Portsmouth..

Wed. 29th November

FIRST DIVISION
Sheffield Wednesday v Liverpool ....

Fri. 1st December

SECOND DIVISION
Oldham Athletic v Blackburn Rovers................................

THIRD DIVISION
Wigan Athletic v Birmingham City ....

Sat. 2nd December

FIRST DIVISION
Arsenal v Manchester United ....
Aston Villa v Nottingham Forest.....................................
Chelsea v Wimbledon ....
Crystal Palace v Queens Park Rangers ....
Derby County v Charlton Athletic....................................
Everton v Coventry City..
Luton Town v Tottenham Hotspur ....
Manchester City v Liverpool ....
Millwall v Southampton ....
Norwich City v Sheffield Wednesday...............................

SECOND DIVISION
AFC Bournemouth v Brighton & Hove Albion ....
Barnsley v Ipswich Town ....
Leeds United v Newcastle United...................................
Leicester City v Hull City...
Oxford United v Plymouth Argyle....................................
Port Vale v Bradford City ....
Portsmouth v Watford...
Sheffield United v West Bromwich Albion ....
Sunderland v Swindon Town ....
West Ham United v Stoke City ....
Wolverhampton Wanderers v Middlesbrough...................

THIRD DIVISION
Bolton Wanderers v Northampton Town ....
Bristol City v Rotherham United.....................................
Crewe Alexandra v Cardiff City ....
Mansfield Town v Huddersfield Town ....
Notts County v Fulham ....
Preston North End v Reading ....
Shrewsbury Town v Chester City....................................
Swansea City v Blackpool ....
Tranmere Rovers v Bury ....
Walsall v Bristol Rovers ....

FOURTH DIVISION
Aldershot v Halifax Town...
Burnley v Grimsby Town..
Cambridge United v Rochdale ....
Carlisle United v Peterborough United.............................
Colchester United v Lincoln City ....
Doncaster Rovers v Stockport County.............................
Hartlepool United v Hereford United ....
Maidstone United v Exeter City......................................
Scunthorpe United v Southend United ....
Torquay United v Scarborough ....
Wrexham v Chesterfield ....
York City v Gillingham ....

Sun. 3rd December

THIRD DIVISION
Brentford v Leyton Orient ....

Sat. 9th December

FIRST DIVISION
Charlton Athletic v Millwall ....
Coventry City v Arsenal ....
Liverpool v Aston Villa ....
Manchester United v Crystal Palace..................................
Nottingham Forest v Norwich City ....
Queens Park Rangers v Chelsea.......................................
Sheffield Wednesday v Luton Town ....
Southampton v Manchester City ....
Tottenham Hotspur v Everton ....
Wimbledon v Derby County..

SECOND DIVISION
Blackburn Rovers v Leicester City....................................
Bradford City v West Ham United.....................................
Brighton & Hove Albion v Wolverhampton Wanderers.......
Hull City v Port Vale ....
Ipswich Town v Sunderland ....
Middlesbrough v Leeds United ....
Newcastle United v Oxford United ....
Stoke City v Barnsley...
Watford v Oldham Athletic...
West Bromwich Albion v AFC Bournemouth....................

Sun. 10th December

SECOND DIVISION
Plymouth Argyle v Portsmouth ....
Swindon Town v Sheffield United....................................

Fri. 15th December

THIRD DIVISION
Tranmere Rovers v Chester City ....

FOURTH DIVISION
Halifax Town v Doncaster Rovers ....

Sat. 16th December

FIRST DIVISION
Arsenal v Luton Town ....
Charlton Athletic v Crystal Palace ....
Chelsea v Liverpool ....
Coventry City v Wimbledon ....
Everton v Manchester City...
Manchester United v Tottenham Hotspur ....
Millwall v Aston Villa ....
Norwich City v Derby County...
Sheffield Wednesday v Queens Park Rangers ....

SECOND DIVISION
AFC Bournemouth v Barnsley...
Blackburn Rovers v Stoke City ....
Hull City v Ipswich Town..
Leeds United v Brighton & Hove Albion ....
Middlesbrough v Leicester City ....
Newcastle United v Plymouth Argyle................................
Oxford United v Wolverhampton Wanderers ....
Port Vale v Sheffield United...
Portsmouth v Sunderland ....
Watford v Bradford City..
West Ham United v Oldham Athletic.................................

THIRD DIVISION
Birmingham City v Preston North End ....
Blackpool v Fulham...
Bristol City v Leyton Orient ....
Bury v Walsall ....
Cardiff City v Notts County...
Crewe Alexandra v Bristol Rovers...................................
Rotherham United v Huddersfield Town ....
Shrewsbury Town v Bolton Wanderers.............................
Wigan Athletic v Swansea City ....

FOURTH DIVISION
Chesterfield v York City ....
Colchester United v Torquay United ....
Exeter City v Gillingham ....
Grimsby Town v Southend United....................................
Hereford United v Scunthorpe United ....
Maidstone United v Hartlepool United ....
Rochdale v Lincoln City ....
Scarborough v Aldershot ....
Wrexham v Burnley..

Sun. 17th December

FIRST DIVISION
Nottingham Forest v Southampton ....

SECOND DIVISION
West Bromwich Albion v Swindon Town ....

THIRD DIVISION
Brentford v Mansfield Town ....
Northampton Town v Reading...

FOURTH DIVISION
Cambridge United v Peterborough United.........................
Carlisle United v Stockport County ....

Tues. 26th December

FIRST DIVISION
Aston Villa v Manchester United ....
Crystal Palace v Chelsea ....
Derby County v Everton ....
Liverpool v Sheffield Wednesday ....
Luton Town v Nottingham Forest.....................................
Manchester City v Norwich City......................................
Queens Park Rangers v Coventry City...............................
Southampton v Arsenal ....
Tottenham Hotspur v Millwall ....
Wimbledon v Charlton Athletic ....

SECOND DIVISION
Barnsley v Watford ....
Bradford City v Middlesbrough ....
Brighton & Hove Albion v Portsmouth ....
Ipswich Town v West Ham United....................................
Leicester City v AFC Bournemouth..................................
Oldham Athletic v Port Vale ....
Plymouth Argyle v West Bromwich Albion ....
Sheffield United v Leeds United ....
Stoke City v Newcastle United..
Sunderland v Oxford United ....
Swindon Town v Blackburn Rovers ....
Wolverhampton Wanderers v Hull City.............................

THIRD DIVISION
Bolton Wanderers v Blackpool ....
Bristol Rovers v Birmingham City ....
Chester City v Wigan Athletic ....
Fulham v Bristol City ....
Huddersfield Town v Bury ....
Leyton Orient v Northampton Town..................................
Mansfield Town v Rotherham United ....
Notts County v Shrewsbury Town ....

172

Preston North End v Tranmere Rovers............................
Reading v Brentford ....
Swansea City v Cardiff City ....
Walsall v Crewe Alexandra ....

Aldershot v Exeter City..
Burnley v Carlisle United ....
Doncaster Rovers v Wrexham ....
Gillingham v Maidstone United ....
Hartlepool United v Scarborough....................................
Lincoln City v Cambridge United ....
Peterborough United v Chesterfield.................................
Scunthorpe United v Grimsby Town ....
Southend United v Colchester United ....
Stockport County v Rochdale ....
Torquay United v Hereford United ....
York City v Halifax Town ....

Fri. 29th December

SECOND DIVISION
Plymouth Argyle v Hull City ....

FOURTH DIVISION
Stockport County v Cambridge United.............................

Sat. 30th December

FIRST DIVISION
Aston Villa v Arsenal...
Crystal Palace v Norwich City ....
Derby County v Coventry City.......................................
Liverpool v Charlton Athletic..
Luton Town v Chelsea ....
Manchester City v Millwall ....
Queens Park Rangers v Everton ....
Southampton v Sheffield Wednesday ....
Tottenham Hotspur v Nottingham Forest ....
Wimbledon v Manchester United ....

SECOND DIVISION
Barnsley v Leeds United..
Bradford City v West Bromwich Albion ....
Brighton & Hove Albion v Oxford United ....
Ipswich Town v Middlesbrough ....
Leicester City v West Ham United..................................
Oldham Athletic v Portsmouth ....
Sheffield United v Blackburn Rovers ....
Stoke City v Watford ....
Sunderland v Port Vale ....
Swindon Town v Newcastle United.................................
Wolverhampton Wanderers v AFC Bournemouth ....

THIRD DIVISION
Bolton Wanderers v Bury ....
Bristol Rovers v Tranmere Rovers...................................
Chester City v Blackpool ....
Fulham v Shrewsbury Town ....
Huddersfield Town v Bristol City ....
Leyton Orient v Crewe Alexandra...................................
Mansfield Town v Northampton Town ....
Notts County v Birmingham City ....
Preston North End v Wigan Athletic...............................
Reading v Rotherham United...
Swansea City v Brentford ....
Walsall v Cardiff City...

FOURTH DIVISION
Aldershot v Rochdale ....
Burnley v Halifax Town ....
Doncaster Rovers v Colchester United ....
Gillingham v Wrexham ....
Hartlepool United v Grimsby Town.................................
Lincoln City v Carlisle United..

Peterborough United v Scarborough................................
Scunthorpe United v Chesterfield....................................
Southend United v Exeter City ....
Torquay United v Maidstone United................................
York City v Hereford United

Mon. 1st January

FIRST DIVISION
Arsenal v Crystal Palace..
Charlton Athletic v Southampton....................................
Chelsea v Aston Villa ....
Coventry City v Tottenham Hotspur ....
Everton v Luton Town ....
Manchester United v Queens Park Rangers.......................
Millwall v Derby County ....
Norwich City v Wimbledon ....
Nottingham Forest v Liverpool ....
Sheffield Wednesday v Manchester City ....

SECOND DIVISION
AFC Bournemouth v Plymouth Argyle ....
Blackburn Rovers v Bradford City...................................
Hull City v Sunderland ....
Leeds United v Oldham Athletic.....................................
Middlesbrough v Stoke City ....
Newcastle United v Wolverhampton Wanderers ....
Oxford United v Sheffield United ....
Port Vale v Ipswich Town ....
Portsmouth v Leicester City ....
Watford v Swindon Town ....
West Bromwich Albion v Brighton & Hove Albion............
West Ham United v Barnsley ....

THIRD DIVISION
Birmingham City v Fulham ....
Blackpool v Huddersfield Town ....
Brentford v Walsall ....
Bristol City v Preston North End ....
Bury v Leyton Orient ....
Cardiff City v Reading ....
Crewe Alexandra v Notts County ....
Northampton Town v Chester City ....
Rotherham United v Bristol Rovers.................................
Shrewsbury Town v Swansea City ....
Tranmere Rovers v Bolton Wanderers ....
Wigan Athletic v Mansfield Town...................................

FOURTH DIVISION
Cambridge United v Burnley..
Carlisle United v York City...
Chesterfield v Doncaster Rovers ....
Colchester United v Hartlepool United ....
Exeter City v Torquay United..
Grimsby Town v Stockport County.................................
Halifax Town v Peterborough United..............................
Hereford United v Gillingham ....
Maidstone United v Aldershot.......................................
Rochdale v Southend United ....
Scarborough v Lincoln City ....
Wrexham v Scunthorpe United......................................

Fri. 5th January

THIRD DIVISION
Tranmere Rovers v Northampton Town ....

FOURTH DIVISION
Colchester United v Stockport County ....

Sat. 6th January

Bolton Wanderers v Reading...
Brentford v Rotherham United.....................................
Bristol City v Chester City ....
Crewe Alexandra v Huddersfield Town ....
Mansfield Town v Birmingham City ....
Notts County v Bury ....
Preston North End v Fulham ....
Shrewsbury Town v Cardiff City ....
Swansea City v Leyton Orient....................................
Walsall v Blackpool ....
Wigan Athletic v Bristol Rovers ....

FOURTH DIVISION

Aldershot v Hereford United ....
Burnley v Scarborough...
Cambridge United v Gillingham ....
Carlisle United v Southend United ....
Doncaster Rovers v Grimsby Town ....
Hartlepool United v Lincoln City ....
Maidstone United v Rochdale ....
Scunthorpe United v Halifax Town...............................
Torquay United v Chesterfield....................................
Wrexham v Peterborough United.................................
York City v Exeter City ....

Fri. 12th January

THIRD DIVISION

Chester City v Brentford ....

FOURTH DIVISION

Halifax Town v Colchester United................................
Southend United v Wrexham ....

Sat. 13th January

FIRST DIVISION

Charlton Athletic v Aston Villa....................................
Coventry City v Crystal Palace....................................
Liverpool v Luton Town..
Manchester United v Derby County ....
Nottingham Forest v Millwall ....
Queens Park Rangers v Norwich City............................
Sheffield Wednesday v Chelsea ....
Southampton v Everton ....
Tottenham Hotspur v Manchester City...........................
Wimbledon v Arsenal ....

SECOND DIVISION

Blackburn Rovers v Leeds United ....
Bradford City v Wolverhampton Wanderers ....
Brighton & Hove Albion v Barnsley ....
Hull City v AFC Bournemouth ....
Ipswich Town v Sheffield United ....
Middlesbrough v Sunderland ....
Newcastle United v Leicester City ....
Plymouth Argyle v West Ham United ....
Stoke City v Portsmouth..
Swindon Town v Oldham Athletic ....
Watford v Oxford United ....
West Bromwich Albion v Port Vale ....

THIRD DIVISION

Birmingham City v Bristol City ....
Blackpool v Notts County..
Bristol Rovers v Mansfield Town..................................
Bury v Preston North End..
Cardiff City v Tranmere Rovers ....
Fulham v Bolton Wanderers..
Huddersfield Town v Walsall.......................................
Leyton Orient v Shrewsbury Town ....
Reading v Crewe Alexandra..
Rotherham United v Wigan Athletic..............................

Chesterfield v Carlisle United ....
Exeter City v Hartlepool United ....
Gillingham v Doncaster Rovers ....
Grimsby Town v Torquay United ....
Hereford United v Cambridge United ....
Lincoln City v Aldershot ....
Peterborough United v York City ....
Rochdale v Scunthorpe United ....
Scarborough v Maidstone United ....
Stockport County v Burnley ....

Sun. 14th January

THIRD DIVISION

Northampton Town v Swansea City ....

Fri. 19th January

THIRD DIVISION

Tranmere Rovers v Fulham..

Sat. 20th January

FIRST DIVISION

Arsenal v Tottenham Hotspur ....
Aston Villa v Southampton ....
Chelsea v Charlton Athletic ....
Crystal Palace v Liverpool ....
Derby County v Nottingham Forest ....
Everton v Sheffield Wednesday ....
Luton Town v Queens Park Rangers ....
Manchester City v Coventry City..................................
Millwall v Wimbledon ....
Norwich City v Manchester United ....

SECOND DIVISION

AFC Bournemouth v Ipswich Town................................
Barnsley v Plymouth Argyle ....
Leeds United v Stoke City ....
Leicester City v Watford ....
Oldham Athletic v Newcastle United ....
Oxford United v Blackburn Rovers ....
Port Vale v Brighton & Hove Albion ....
Portsmouth v Bradford City ....
Sheffield United v Middlesbrough ....
Sunderland v West Bromwich Albion.............................
West Ham United v Hull City ....
Wolverhampton Wanderers v Swindon Town ....

THIRD DIVISION

Bolton Wanderers v Cardiff City ....
Brentford v Bristol Rovers ....
Bristol City v Bury...
Crewe Alexandra v Birmingham City.............................
Mansfield Town v Chester City ....
Notts County v Leyton Orient ....
Preston North End v Rotherham United...........................
Shrewsbury Town v Reading ....
Wigan Athletic v Blackpool ....

FOURTH DIVISION

Aldershot v Gillingham ....
Burnley v Rochdale ....
Cambridge United v Grimsby Town ....
Carlisle United v Hereford United.................................
Colchester United v Chesterfield..................................
Doncaster Rovers v Exeter City ....
Hartlepool United v Halifax Town ....
Maidstone United v Peterborough United........................
Scunthorpe United v Lincoln City ....
Torquay United v Stockport County ....
Wrexham v Scarborough ....
York City v Southend United ....

Sun.21st January

THIRD DIVISION
Swansea City v Huddersfield Town ....

Fri. 26th January

THIRD DIVISION
Chester City v Swansea City ....

FOURTH DIVISION
Halifax Town v Wrexham ....

Sat. 27th January

THIRD DIVISION
Birmingham City v Shrewsbury Town ....
Blackpool v Bristol City ....
Bristol Rovers v Bolton Wanderers...............................
Bury v Brentford...
Cardiff City v Mansfield Town ....
Fulham v Crewe Alexandra...
Huddersfield Town v Preston North End ....
Leyton Orient v Walsall ....
Reading v Notts County ....
Rotherham United v Tranmere Rovers ....

FOURTH DIVISION
Chesterfield v Cambridge United ....
Exeter City v Burnley ....
Gillingham v Hartlepool United...................................
Grimsby Town v Carlisle United ....
Hereford United v Colchester United ....
Lincoln City v Torquay United ....
Peterborough United v Doncaster Rovers.......................
Rochdale v York City ....
Scarborough v Scunthorpe United ....
Southend United v Aldershot ....
Stockport County v Maidstone United ....

Sun. 28th January

THIRD DIVISION
Northampton Town v Wigan Athletic ....

Fri. 2nd February

FOURTH DIVISION
Halifax Town v Cambridge United ....
Southend United v Doncaster Rovers ....

Sat. 3rd February

FIRST DIVISION
Charlton Athletic v Arsenal ....
Coventry City v Chelsea ....
Liverpool v Everton ....
Manchester United v Manchester City...........................
Nottingham Forest v Crystal Palace ....
Queens Park Rangers v Aston Villa ....
Sheffield Wednesday v Millwall ....
Southampton v Derby County ....
Tottenham Hotspur v Norwich City ....
Wimbledon v Luton Town ....

SECOND DIVISION
Blackburn Rovers v AFC Bournemouth ....
Bradford City v Barnsley ....
Brighton & Hove Albion v Leicester City ....

Hull City v Sheffield United ....
Ipswich Town v Oxford United ....
Middlesbrough v Portsmouth ....
Newcastle United v Sunderland ....
Plymouth Argyle v Wolverhampton Wanderers ....
Stoke City v Port Vale ....
Watford v West Ham United ....
West Bromwich Albion v Oldham Athletic ....

THIRD DIVISION
Birmingham City v Brentford ....
Blackpool v Mansfield Town ....
Bristol Rovers v Bristol City..
Bury v Shrewsbury Town..
Cardiff City v Wigan Athletic ....
Chester City v Preston North End ....
Fulham v Walsall ....
Huddersfield Town v Tranmere Rovers ....
Leyton Orient v Bolton Wanderers................................
Northampton Town v Crewe Alexandra ....
Reading v Swansea City ....
Rotherham United v Notts County ....

FOURTH DIVISION
Chesterfield v Maidstone United ....
Exeter City v Scunthorpe United..................................
Gillingham v Carlisle United ....
Grimsby Town v York City ....
Hereford United v Burnley ....
Lincoln City v Wrexham ....
Peterborough United v Hartlepool United ....
Rochdale v Torquay United ....
Scarborough v Colchester United ....
Stockport County v Aldershot ....

Sun. 4th February

SECOND DIVISION
Swindon Town v Leeds United ....

Fri. 9th February

THIRD DIVISION
Tranmere Rovers v Birmingham City.............................

Sat. 10th February

FIRST DIVISION
Arsenal v Nottingham Forest.......................................
Aston Villa v Sheffield Wednesday ....
Chelsea v Tottenham Hotspur ....
Crystal Palace v Southampton ....
Derby County v Queens Park Rangers ....
Everton v Charlton Athletic ....
Luton Town v Coventry City ....
Manchester City v Wimbledon.....................................
Millwall v Manchester United......................................
Norwich City v Liverpool..

SECOND DIVISION
AFC Bournemouth v Middlesbrough ....
Barnsley v Swindon Town ....
Leeds United v Hull City ....
Leicester City v Bradford City ....
Oldham Athletic v Stoke City ....
Oxford United v West Bromwich Albion ....
Port Vale v Watford ....
Portsmouth v Newcastle United ....
Sheffield United v Plymouth Argyle...............................
Sunderland v Blackburn Rovers ....
West Ham United v Brighton & Hove Albion....................
Wolverhampton Wanderers v Ipswich Town ....

Bolton Wanderers v Rotherham United ....
Brentford v Huddersfield Town ....
Bristol City v Cardiff City ....
Crewe Alexandra v Blackpool ....
Mansfield Town v Bury ....
Notts County v Chester City ....
Preston North End v Bristol Rovers ....
Shrewsbury Town v Northampton Town...........................
Swansea City v Fulham ....
Walsall v Reading ....
Wigan Athletic v Leyton Orient ....

FOURTH DIVISION
Aldershot v Chesterfield..
Burnley v Gillingham..
Cambridge United v Exeter City ....
Carlisle United v Halifax Town ....
Colchester United v Rochdale ....
Doncaster Rovers v Scarborough ....
Hartlepool United v Stockport County ....
Maidstone United v Grimsby Town ....
Scunthorpe United v Peterborough United ....
Torquay United v Southend United ....
Wrexham v Hereford United...
York City v Lincoln City..

Mon. 12th February

THIRD DIVISION
Tranmere Rovers v Reading..

Tues. 13th February

THIRD DIVISION
Bolton Wanderers v Huddersfield Town ....
Brentford v Cardiff City ....
Bristol City v Northampton Town ....
Crewe Alexandra v Chester City ....
Mansfield Town v Fulham..
Notts County v Bristol Rovers ....
Preston North End v Leyton Orient ....
Shrewsbury Town v Blackpool..
Swansea City v Birmingham City....................................
Walsall v Rotherham United ....
Wigan Athletic v Bury ....

FOURTH DIVISION
Aldershot v Peterborough United ....
Burnley v Chesterfield...
Cambridge United v Scarborough ....
Carlisle United v Exeter City ....
Colchester United v Grimsby Town ....
Doncaster Rovers v Lincoln City ....
Hartlepool United v Southend United..............................
Scunthorpe United v Gillingham ....
Torquay United v Halifax Town......................................
Wrexham v Rochdale...
York City v Stockport County ....

Wed. 14th February

FOURTH DIVISION
Maidstone United v Hereford United...............................

Fri. 16th February

FOURTH DIVISION
Stockport County v Doncaster Rovers..............................

Sat. 17th February

FIRST DIVISION
Charlton Athletic v Luton Town ....
Coventry City v Millwall...
Liverpool v Derby County ....
Manchester United v Everton..
Nottingham Forest v Chelsea..
Queens Park Rangers v Manchester City ....
Sheffield Wednesday v Arsenal.......................................
Southampton v Norwich City..
Tottenham Hotspur v Aston Villa ....
Wimbledon v Crystal Palace ....

SECOND DIVISION
Blackburn Rovers v Port Vale ....
Bradford City v Oxford United ....
Brighton & Hove Albion v Sheffield United ....
Hull City v Portsmouth ....
Ipswich Town v Leeds United...
Middlesbrough v Barnsley ....
Newcastle United v AFC Bournemouth............................
Plymouth Argyle v Oldham Athletic ....
Stoke City v Wolverhampton Wanderers ....
Swindon Town v West Ham United ....
Watford v Sunderland..
West Bromwich Albion v Leicester City ....

THIRD DIVISION
Birmingham City v Wigan Athletic ....
Blackpool v Swansea City ....
Bristol Rovers v Walsall ....
Bury v Tranmere Rovers ....
Cardiff City v Crewe Alexandra ....
Chester City v Shrewsbury Town....................................
Fulham v Notts County ....
Huddersfield Town v Mansfield Town ....
Leyton Orient v Brentford ....
Northampton Town v Bolton Wanderers ....
Reading v Preston North End ....
Rotherham United v Bristol City.....................................

FOURTH DIVISION
Chesterfield v Wrexham ....
Exeter City v Maidstone United......................................
Gillingham v York City ....
Grimsby Town v Burnley..
Halifax Town v Aldershot..
Hereford United v Hartlepool United ....
Lincoln City v Colchester United ....
Peterborough United v Carlisle United.............................
Rochdale v Cambridge United ....
Scarborough v Torquay United ....
Southend United v Scunthorpe United ....

Tues. 20th February

THIRD DIVISION
Northampton Town v Walsall ....

Fri. 23rd February

THIRD DIVISION
Tranmere Rovers v Blackpool ....

FOURTH DIVISION
Colchester United v Gillingham ....

Sat. 24th February

FIRST DIVISION
Arsenal v Liverpool...
Aston Villa v Wimbledon ....

Chelsea v Manchester United ....
Crystal Palace v Sheffield Wednesday ....
Derby County v Tottenham Hotspur................................
Everton v Nottingham Forest ....
Luton Town v Southampton ....
Manchester City v Charlton Athletic...............................
Millwall v Queens Park Rangers ....
Norwich City v Coventry City ....

SECOND DIVISION
AFC Bournemouth v Bradford City...................................
Barnsley v Hull City ....
Leeds United v West Bromwich Albion..............................
Leicester City v Stoke City ....
Oldham Athletic v Ipswich Town ....
Oxford United v Middlesbrough ....
Port Vale v Plymouth Argyle ....
Portsmouth v Swindon Town ....
Sheffield United v Newcastle United................................
Sunderland v Brighton & Hove Albion ....
West Ham United v Blackburn Rovers ....
Wolverhampton Wanderers v Watford ....

THIRD DIVISION
Bolton Wanderers v Birmingham City..............................
Bristol City v Reading ....
Crewe Alexandra v Bury ....
Mansfield Town v Leyton Orient.....................................
Notts County v Huddersfield Town..................................
Preston North End v Cardiff City ....
Shrewsbury Town v Rotherham United...........................
Swansea City v Bristol Rovers ....
Walsall v Chester City ....
Wigan Athletic v Fulham ....

FOURTH DIVISION
Aldershot v Grimsby Town ....
Burnley v Lincoln City ....
Carlisle United v Rochdale ....
Hartlepool United v Chesterfield ....
Maidstone United v Halifax Town ....
Scunthorpe United v Stockport County ....
Torquay United v Peterborough United ....
Wrexham v Exeter City ....
York City v Scarborough ....

Sun. 25th February

THIRD DIVISION
Brentford v Northampton Town ....

FOURTH DIVISION
Cambridge United v Southend United..............................
Doncaster Rovers v Hereford United...............................

Fri. 2nd March

THIRD DIVISION
Cardiff City v Shrewsbury Town ....

FOURTH DIVISION
Stockport County v Colchester United ....

Sat. 3rd March

FIRST DIVISION
Charlton Athletic v Norwich City ....
Coventry City v Aston Villa ....
Liverpool v Millwall ....
Manchester United v Luton Town....................................
Nottingham Forest v Manchester City ....
Queens Park Rangers v Arsenal ....
Sheffield Wednesday v Derby County ....
Southampton v Chelsea...
Tottenham Hotspur v Crystal Palace ....
Wimbledon v Everton...

SECOND DIVISION
Blackburn Rovers v Wolverhampton Wanderers................
Bradford City v Sheffield United.....................................
Brighton & Hove Albion v Oldham Athletic......................
Hull City v Oxford United ....
Ipswich Town v Leicester City ....
Middlesbrough v West Ham United ....
Newcastle United v Barnsley..
Plymouth Argyle v Sunderland ....
Stoke City v AFC Bournemouth ....
Swindon Town v Port Vale ....
Watford v Leeds United ....
West Bromwich Albion v Portsmouth ....

THIRD DIVISION
Birmingham City v Mansfield Town ....
Blackpool v Walsall ....
Bristol Rovers v Wigan Athletic ....
Bury v Notts County ....
Chester City v Bristol City ....
Fulham v Preston North End ....
Huddersfield Town v Crewe Alexandra ....
Leyton Orient v Swansea City..
Northampton Town v Tranmere Rovers ....
Reading v Bolton Wanderers...
Rotherham United v Brentford.......................................

FOURTH DIVISION
Chesterfield v Torquay United ....
Exeter City v York City..
Gillingham v Cambridge United ....
Grimsby Town v Doncaster Rovers ....
Halifax Town v Scunthorpe United..................................
Hereford United v Aldershot ....
Lincoln City v Hartlepool United ....
Peterborough United v Wrexham....................................
Rochdale v Maidstone United ....
Scarborough v Burnley..
Southend United v Carlisle United ....

Tues. 6th March

SECOND DIVISION
AFC Bournemouth v Oxford United ....
Barnsley v Blackburn Rovers ....
Portsmouth v Wolverhampton Wanderers ....
Sheffield United v Sunderland ....
Stoke City v Ipswich Town ....
Swindon Town v Bradford City.......................................

THIRD DIVISION
Birmingham City v Blackpool...
Bristol City v Tranmere Rovers.......................................
Bury v Northampton Town ....
Cardiff City v Rotherham United ....
Crewe Alexandra v Shrewsbury Town.............................
Fulham v Chester City...
Leyton Orient v Huddersfield Town ....
Mansfield Town v Bolton Wanderers ....
Notts County v Swansea City ....
Preston North End v Walsall ....
Reading v Bristol Rovers ....
Wigan Athletic v Brentford..

FOURTH DIVISION
Burnley v Torquay United ....
Cambridge United v Maidstone United ....
Colchester United v Carlisle United.................................
Doncaster Rovers v Hartlepool United.............................
Gillingham v Peterborough United ....
Rochdale v Chesterfield ....
Scunthorpe United v Aldershot ....
Wrexham v York City ....

Wed. 7th March

Brighton & Hove Albion v Plymouth Argyle ....
Leeds United v Port Vale..
Leicester City v Oldham Athletic ....
Middlesbrough v Watford ....
Newcastle United v Hull City ....
West Bromwich Albion v West Ham United......................

FOURTH DIVISION
Exeter City v Halifax Town...
Hereford United v Grimsby Town ....
Lincoln City v Southend United ....
Scarborough v Stockport County.....................................

Fri. 9th March

THIRD DIVISION
Chester City v Reading
Tranmere Rovers v Wigan Athletic.................................

FOURTH DIVISION
Southend United v Gillingham...
Stockport County v Wrexham..

Sat. 10th March

FIRST DIVISION
Aston Villa v Luton Town..
Chelsea v Norwich City..
Crystal Palace v Derby County ....
Liverpool v Wimbledon...
Manchester City v Arsenal...
Millwall v Everton..
Nottingham Forest v Coventry City ....
Sheffield Wednesday v Manchester United......................
Southampton v Queens Park Rangers ....
Tottenham Hotspur v Charlton Athletic ....

SECOND DIVISION
Blackburn Rovers v West Bromwich Albion.....................
Bradford City v Stoke City...
Hull City v Middlesbrough..
Ipswich Town v Brighton & Hove Albion ....
Oldham Athletic v Sheffield United ....
Oxford United v Leeds United..
Plymouth Argyle v Swindon Town...................................
Port Vale v AFC Bournemouth.......................................
Sunderland v Leicester City ....
Watford v Newcastle United ....
West Ham United v Portsmouth ....
Wolverhampton Wanderers v Barnsley ....

THIRD DIVISION
Blackpool v Preston North End.......................................
Bolton Wanderers v Notts County ....
Brentford v Crewe Alexandra...
Bristol Rovers v Leyton Orient ....
Huddersfield Town v Fulham ....
Northampton Town v Cardiff City ....
Rotherham United v Bury ....
Shrewsbury Town v Bristol City ....
Swansea City v Mansfield Town ....
Walsall v Birmingham City...

FOURTH DIVISION
Aldershot v Doncaster Rovers ....
Carlisle United v Cambridge United ....
Chesterfield v Hereford United.......................................
Grimsby Town v Exeter City ....
Halifax Town v Scarborough ....
Hartlepool United v Rochdale ....
Maidstone United v Colchester United.............................
Peterborough United v Lincoln City ....

Torquay United v Scunthorpe United ....
York City v Burnley ....

Fri. 16th March

THIRD DIVISION
Wigan Athletic v Bolton Wanderers ....

FOURTH DIVISION
Cambridge United v York City ....
Gillingham v Halifax Town ....

Sat. 17th March

FIRST DIVISION
Arsenal v Chelsea ....
Charlton Athletic v Nottingham Forest............................
Coventry City v Sheffield Wednesday..............................
Derby County v Aston Villa ....
Everton v Crystal Palace ....
Luton Town v Manchester City ....
Manchester United v Liverpool ....
Norwich City v Millwall..
Queens Park Rangers v Tottenham Hotspur.....................
Wimbledon v Southampton ....

SECOND DIVISION
AFC Bournemouth v Sunderland ....
Barnsley v Oldham Athletic ....
Brighton & Hove Albion v Bradford City ....
Leeds United v West Ham United ....
Leicester City v Port Vale ....
Middlesbrough v Blackburn Rovers.................................
Newcastle United v Ipswich Town ....
Portsmouth v Oxford United ....
Sheffield United v Wolverhampton Wanderers ....
Stoke City v Plymouth Argyle...
Swindon Town v Hull City ....
West Bromwich Albion v Watford....................................

THIRD DIVISION
Birmingham City v Rotherham United ....
Bristol City v Brentford...
Bury v Chester City ....
Cardiff City v Huddersfield Town....................................
Crewe Alexandra v Swansea City ....
Fulham v Bristol Rovers...
Leyton Orient v Tranmere Rovers..................................
Mansfield Town v Shrewsbury Town ....
Notts County v Walsall...
Preston North End v Northampton Town ....
Reading v Blackpool..

FOURTH DIVISION
Burnley v Maidstone United ....
Colchester United v Aldershot...
Doncaster Rovers v Torquay United................................
Exeter City v Peterborough United..................................
Hereford United v Stockport County ....
Lincoln City v Chesterfield...
Rochdale v Grimsby Town ....
Scarborough v Southend United ....
Scunthorpe United v Hartlepool United ....
Wrexham v Carlisle United...

Mon. 19th March

SECOND DIVISION
Port Vale v Barnsley...

THIRD DIVISION
Tranmere Rovers v Notts County ....

FOURTH DIVISION
Stockport County v Gillingham.......................................

Tues. 20th March

SECOND DIVISION
Blackburn Rovers v Portsmouth ....
Hull City v Stoke City ....
Ipswich Town v Swindon Town ....
Oldham Athletic v AFC Bournemouth............................
Plymouth Argyle v Middlesbrough ....
Sunderland v Leeds United ....
Watford v Brighton & Hove Albion ....
Wolverhampton Wanderers v West Bromwich Albion.........

THIRD DIVISION
Blackpool v Leyton Orient..
Bolton Wanderers v Crewe Alexandra ....
Brentford v Preston North End ....
Chester City v Cardiff City..
Huddersfield Town v Reading ....
Northampton Town v Birmingham City...........................
Rotherham United v Fulham...
Shrewsbury Town v Wigan Athletic ....
Swansea City v Bristol City ....
Walsall v Mansfield Town ....

FOURTH DIVISION
Aldershot v Wrexham...
Carlisle United v Doncaster Rovers ....
Chesterfield v Exeter City ....
Grimsby Town v Scarborough ....
Halifax Town v Lincoln City...
Hartlepool United v Burnley ....
Southend United v Hereford United ....
Torquay United v Cambridge United ....
York City v Colchester United......................................

Wed. 21st March

SECOND DIVISION
Bradford City v Newcastle United ....
Oxford United v Leicester City ....
West Ham United v Sheffield United ....

THIRD DIVISION
Bristol Rovers v Bury...

FOURTH DIVISION
Maidstone United v Scunthorpe United...........................
Peterborough United v Rochdale ....

Fri. 23rd March

THIRD DIVISION
Swansea City v Bury ....

FOURTH DIVISION
Southend United v Stockport County..............................

Sat. 24th March

FIRST DIVISION
Coventry City v Charlton Athletic ....
Crystal Palace v Aston Villa ....
Derby County v Arsenal...
Everton v Norwich City ....
Luton Town v Millwall..
Manchester City v Chelsea ....
Queens Park Rangers v Nottingham Forest ....
Southampton v Manchester United.................................
Tottenham Hotspur v Liverpool.....................................
Wimbledon v Sheffield Wednesday................................

SECOND DIVISION
AFC Bournemouth v Watford ....
Blackburn Rovers v Newcastle United ....
Brighton & Hove Albion v Middlesbrough........................
Ipswich Town v Bradford City ....
Leeds United v Portsmouth ....
Leicester City v Plymouth Argyle ....
Oldham Athletic v Hull City..
Oxford United v Swindon Town.....................................
Port Vale v Wolverhampton Wanderers ....
Sheffield United v Barnsley ....
Sunderland v West Ham United.....................................
West Bromwich Albion v Stoke City ....

THIRD DIVISION
Birmingham City v Chester City.....................................
Blackpool v Northampton Town ....
Bolton Wanderers v Brentford......................................
Bristol Rovers v Cardiff City ....
Crewe Alexandra v Preston North End............................
Fulham v Reading ....
Leyton Orient v Rotherham United ....
Mansfield Town v Tranmere Rovers ....
Notts County v Bristol City ....
Shrewsbury Town v Walsall ....
Wigan Athletic v Huddersfield Town ....

FOURTH DIVISION
Aldershot v York City..
Exeter City v Rochdale ....
Gillingham v Grimsby Town ....
Halifax Town v Chesterfield ....
Hartlepool United v Torquay United ....
Peterborough United v Burnley ....
Scarborough v Hereford United ....
Scunthorpe United v Carlisle United...............................
Wrexham v Colchester United ....

Sun. 25th March

FOURTH DIVISION
Doncaster Rovers v Cambridge United ....
Lincoln City v Maidstone United....................................

Fri. 30th March

THIRD DIVISION
Tranmere Rovers v Swansea City ....

FOURTH DIVISION
Cambridge United v Wrexham ....
Stockport County v Peterborough United ....

Sat. 31st March

FIRST DIVISION
Arsenal v Everton ....
Aston Villa v Manchester City ....
Charlton Athletic v Queens Park Rangers........................
Chelsea v Derby County..
Liverpool v Southampton ....
Manchester United v Coventry City................................
Millwall v Crystal Palace...
Norwich City v Luton Town ....
Nottingham Forest v Wimbledon ....
Sheffield Wednesday v Tottenham Hotspur......................

SECOND DIVISION
Barnsley v Oxford United ....
Bradford City v Sunderland ....
Hull City v West Bromwich Albion ....
Middlesbrough v Oldham Athletic..................................
Newcastle United v Brighton & Hove Albion ....
Plymouth Argyle v Ipswich Town ....

Portsmouth v AFC Bournemouth.....................................
Stoke City v Sheffield United...
Swindon Town v Leicester City.......................................
Watford v Blackburn Rovers..
West Ham United v Port Vale ....
Wolverhampton Wanderers v Leeds United ....

THIRD DIVISION
Brentford v Shrewsbury Town ....
Bristol City v Mansfield Town..
Bury v Fulham...
Cardiff City v Blackpool..
Chester City v Bolton Wanderers ....
Huddersfield Town v Birmingham City............................
Northampton Town v Bristol Rovers ....
Preston North End v Notts County ....
Reading v Leyton Orient ....
Rotherham United v Crewe Alexandra ....
Walsall v Wigan Athletic ....

FOURTH DIVISION
Burnley v Doncaster Rovers...
Carlisle United v Scarborough ....
Chesterfield v Gillingham ....
Colchester United v Scunthorpe United...........................
Grimsby Town v Lincoln City ....
Hereford United v Exeter City..
Maidstone United v Southend United ....
Rochdale v Halifax Town ....
Torquay United v Aldershot ....
York City v Hartlepool United ....

Fri. 6th April

SECOND DIVISION
Brighton & Hove Albion v Hull City...............................
Oldham Athletic v Wolverhampton Wanderers.................

THIRD DIVISION
Crewe Alexandra v Tranmere Rovers ....

FOURTH DIVISION
Aldershot v Burnley ....

Sat. 7th April

FIRST DIVISION
Arsenal v Aston Villa..
Charlton Athletic v Liverpool..
Chelsea v Luton Town ....
Coventry City v Derby County.......................................
Everton v Queens Park Rangers.....................................
Manchester United v Wimbledon ....
Millwall v Manchester City..
Norwich City v Crystal Palace..
Nottingham Forest v Tottenham Hotspur ....
Sheffield Wednesday v Southampton ....

SECOND DIVISION
AFC Bournemouth v Swindon Town ....
Blackburn Rovers v Plymouth Argyle ....
Leeds United v Bradford City...
Leicester City v Barnsley ....
Oxford United v West Ham United ....
Port Vale v Newcastle United ....
Portsmouth v Sheffield United.......................................
Sunderland v Stoke City ....
Watford v Ipswich Town ....
West Bromwich Albion v Middlesbrough.........................

THIRD DIVISION
Birmingham City v Bury..
Blackpool v Rotherham United ....
Bolton Wanderers v Preston North End...........................
Brentford v Notts County ....
Bristol Rovers v Chester City ....

Leyton Orient v Cardiff City ....
Mansfield Town v Reading...
Northampton Town v Fulham...
Shrewsbury Town v Huddersfield Town...........................
Swansea City v Walsall ....
Wigan Athletic v Bristol City...

FOURTH DIVISION
Doncaster Rovers v York City ....
Exeter City v Stockport County ....
Gillingham v Torquay United ....
Halifax Town v Grimsby Town ....
Hartlepool United v Carlisle United ....
Lincoln City v Hereford United ....
Peterborough United v Colchester United ....
Scarborough v Rochdale..
Scunthorpe United v Cambridge United ....
Southend United v Chesterfield ....
Wrexham v Maidstone United ....

Mon. 9th April

THIRD DIVISION
Tranmere Rovers v Shrewsbury Town..............................

FOURTH DIVISION
Stockport County v Lincoln City ....

Tues. 10th April

SECOND DIVISION
Barnsley v Sunderland ....
Bradford City v Oldham Athletic ....
Hull City v Blackburn Rovers ....
Ipswich Town v Portsmouth ....
Plymouth Argyle v Leeds United ....
Sheffield United v Watford ....
Stoke City v Oxford United..
Swindon Town v Brighton & Hove Albion ....
Wolverhampton Wanderers v Leicester City ....

THIRD DIVISION
Bristol City v Crewe Alexandra......................................
Bury v Blackpool ....
Cardiff City v Birmingham City......................................
Chester City v Leyton Orient...
Fulham v Brentford ....
Huddersfield Town v Bristol Rovers ....
Notts County v Northampton Town ....
Preston North End v Mansfield Town..............................
Reading v Wigan Athletic ....
Rotherham United v Swansea City ....
Walsall v Bolton Wanderers ....

FOURTH DIVISION
Burnley v Southend United ....
Cambridge United v Hartlepool United............................
Carlisle United v Aldershot..
Chesterfield v Scarborough ....
Colchester United v Exeter City......................................
Grimsby Town v Peterborough United ....
Rochdale v Gillingham ....
Torquay United v Wrexham ....
York City v Scunthorpe United.......................................

Wed. 11th April

SECOND DIVISION
Middlesbrough v Port Vale ....
Newcastle United v West Bromwich Albion ....
West Ham United v AFC Bournemouth ....

FOURTH DIVISION
Hereford United v Halifax Town.....................................
Maidstone United v Doncaster Rovers ....

Fri. 13th April

SECOND DIVISION
Oldham Athletic v Leeds United ....

Sat. 14th April

FIRST DIVISION
Aston Villa v Chelsea...
Crystal Palace v Arsenal ....
Derby County v Millwall ....
Liverpool v Nottingham Forest ....
Luton Town v Everton ....
Manchester City v Sheffield Wednesday ....
Queens Park Rangers v Manchester United......................
Southampton v Charlton Athletic...................................
Tottenham Hotspur v Coventry City ....
Wimbledon v Norwich City ....

SECOND DIVISION
Barnsley v West Ham United ....
Bradford City v Blackburn Rovers...................................
Brighton & Hove Albion v West Bromwich Albion.............
Ipswich Town v Port Vale ....
Leicester City v Portsmouth ....
Plymouth Argyle v AFC Bournemouth ....
Sheffield United v Oxford United ....
Stoke City v Middlesbrough ....
Sunderland v Hull City ....
Swindon Town v Watford ....
Wolverhampton Wanderers v Newcastle United ....

THIRD DIVISION
Bolton Wanderers v Tranmere Rovers ....
Bristol Rovers v Rotherham United.................................
Chester City v Northampton Town ....
Fulham v Birmingham City ....
Huddersfield Town v Blackpool ....
Leyton Orient v Bury ....
Mansfield Town v Wigan Athletic...................................
Notts County v Crewe Alexandra ....
Preston North End v Bristol City....................................
Reading v Cardiff City ....
Swansea City v Shrewsbury Town...................................
Walsall v Brentford ....

FOURTH DIVISION
Aldershot v Maidstone United.......................................
Burnley v Cambridge United ....
Doncaster Rovers v Chesterfield ....
Gillingham v Hereford United ....
Hartlepool United v Colchester United ....
Lincoln City v Scarborough ....
Peterborough United v Halifax Town................................
Scunthorpe United v Wrexham ....
Southend United v Rochdale ....
Stockport County v Grimsby Town..................................
Torquay United v Exeter City..
York City v Carlisle United ....

Mon. 16th April

FIRST DIVISION
Arsenal v Southampton...
Charlton Athletic v Wimbledon ....
Chelsea v Crystal Palace ....
Coventry City v Queens Park Rangers..............................
Everton v Derby County ....
Manchester United v Aston Villa ....
Millwall v Tottenham Hotspur ....
Norwich City v Manchester City.....................................
Nottingham Forest v Luton Town...................................

SECOND DIVISION
Blackburn Rovers v Swindon Town ....

Hull City v Wolverhampton Wanderers...........................
Leeds United v Sheffield United ....
Middlesbrough v Bradford City ....
Newcastle United v Stoke City.......................................
Oxford United v Sunderland ....
Port Vale v Oldham Athletic ....
Portsmouth v Brighton & Hove Albion ....
West Bromwich Albion v Plymouth Argyle ....

THIRD DIVISION
Birmingham City v Bristol Rovers ....
Blackpool v Bolton Wanderers ....
Brentford v Reading ....
Bristol City v Fulham ....
Bury v Huddersfield Town ....
Cardiff City v Swansea City ....
Crewe Alexandra v Walsall ....
Northampton Town v Leyton Orient................................
Rotherham United v Mansfield Town ....
Tranmere Rovers v Preston North End.............................
Wigan Athletic v Chester City ....

FOURTH DIVISION
Carlisle United v Burnley ....
Chesterfield v Peterborough United.................................
Colchester United v Southend United ....
Exeter City v Aldershot ....
Grimsby Town v Scunthorpe United ....
Halifax Town v York City ....
Hereford United v Torquay United ....
Maidstone United v Gillingham ....
Rochdale v Stockport County ....
Scarborough v Hartlepool United....................................
Wrexham v Doncaster Rovers ....

Tues. 17th April

SECOND DIVISION
AFC Bournemouth v Leicester City..................................
Watford v Barnsley ....
West Ham United v Ipswich Town...................................

THIRD DIVISION
Shrewsbury Town v Notts County ....

FOURTH DIVISION
Cambridge United v Lincoln City.....................................

Fri. 20th April

THIRD DIVISION
Chester City v Tranmere Rovers ....

FOURTH DIVISION
Southend United v Grimsby Town....................................
Stockport County v Carlisle United ....

Sat. 21st April

FIRST DIVISION
Aston Villa v Millwall ....
Crystal Palace v Charlton Athletic...................................
Derby County v Norwich City...
Liverpool v Chelsea..
Luton Town v Arsenal ....
Manchester City v Everton..
Queens Park Rangers v Sheffield Wednesday ....
Southampton v Nottingham Forest ....
Tottenham Hotspur v Manchester United..........................
Wimbledon v Coventry City ....

SECOND DIVISION
Barnsley v AFC Bournemouth...
Bradford City v Watford...
Brighton & Hove Albion v Leeds United ....

Ipswich Town v Hull City..
Leicester City v Middlesbrough ....
Oldham Athletic v West Ham United.................................
Plymouth Argyle v Newcastle United..............................
Sheffield United v Port Vale ....
Stoke City v Blackburn Rovers ....
Sunderland v Portsmouth ....
Swindon Town v West Bromwich Albion ....
Wolverhampton Wanderers v Oxford United ....

THIRD DIVISION
Bolton Wanderers v Shrewsbury Town...........................
Bristol Rovers v Crewe Alexandra.................................
Fulham v Blackpool...
Huddersfield Town v Rotherham United ....
Leyton Orient v Bristol City ....
Mansfield Town v Brentford...
Notts County v Cardiff City...
Preston North End v Birmingham City ....
Reading v Northampton Town...
Swansea City v Wigan Athletic ....
Walsall v Bury ....

FOURTH DIVISION
Aldershot v Scarborough...
Burnley v Wrexham..
Doncaster Rovers v Halifax Town ....
Gillingham v Exeter City ....
Hartlepool United v Maidstone United ....
Lincoln City v Rochdale..
Peterborough United v Cambridge United ....
Scunthorpe United v Hereford United ....
Torquay United v Colchester United ....
York City v Chesterfield ....

Mon. 23rd April

SECOND DIVISION
Port Vale v Sunderland ....

THIRD DIVISION
Tranmere Rovers v Bristol Rovers...................................

Tues. 24th April

SECOND DIVISION
AFC Bournemouth v Wolverhampton Wanderers ....
Blackburn Rovers v Sheffield United ....
Hull City v Plymouth Argyle ....
Portsmouth v Oldham Athletic ....
Watford v Stoke City ....

THIRD DIVISION
Birmingham City v Notts County ....
Blackpool v Chester City ....
Brentford v Swansea City ....
Bristol City v Huddersfield Town ....
Bury v Bolton Wanderers ....
Cardiff City v Walsall...
Crewe Alexandra v Leyton Orient...................................
Northampton Town v Mansfield Town ....
Rotherham United v Reading ....
Shrewsbury Town v Fulham ....
Wigan Athletic v Preston North End...............................

FOURTH DIVISION
Cambridge United v Stockport County............................
Carlisle United v Lincoln City.......................................
Chesterfield v Scunthorpe United...................................
Colchester United v Doncaster Rovers............................
Grimsby Town v Hartlepool United................................
Halifax Town v Burnley ....
Rochdale v Aldershot ....
Wrexham v Gillingham ....

Wed. 25th April

SECOND DIVISION
Leeds United v Barnsley...
Middlesbrough v Ipswich Town ....
Newcastle United v Swindon Town.................................
Oxford United v Brighton & Hove Albion ....
West Bromwich Albion v Bradford City ....
West Ham United v Leicester City..................................

FOURTH DIVISION
Exeter City v Southend United ....
Hereford United v York City..
Maidstone United v Torquay United................................
Scarborough v Peterborough United................................

Fri. 27th April

FOURTH DIVISION
Southend United v Halifax Town ....

Sat. 28th April

FIRST DIVISION
Arsenal v Millwall ....
Aston Villa v Norwich City ....
Charlton Athletic v Sheffield Wednesday.......................
Chelsea v Everton ....
Liverpool v Queens Park Rangers ....
Luton Town v Crystal Palace ....
Manchester City v Derby County ....
Nottingham Forest v Manchester United ....
Southampton v Coventry City...
Wimbledon v Tottenham Hotspur ....

SECOND DIVISION
Barnsley v West Bromwich Albion ....
Brighton & Hove Albion v Stoke City ....
Hull City v Bradford City..
Ipswich Town v Blackburn Rovers..................................
Leeds United v Leicester City...
Newcastle United v West Ham United ....
Oldham Athletic v Oxford United ....
Plymouth Argyle v Watford ....
Port Vale v Portsmouth ....
Sheffield United v AFC Bournemouth ....
Swindon Town v Middlesbrough ....
Wolverhampton Wanderers v Sunderland.........................

THIRD DIVISION
Bolton Wanderers v Bristol City ....
Brentford v Blackpool...
Bristol Rovers v Shrewsbury Town ....
Cardiff City v Fulham...
Chester City v Rotherham United...................................
Leyton Orient v Birmingham City ....
Mansfield Town v Crewe Alexandra................................
Northampton Town v Huddersfield Town ....
Preston North End v Swansea City ....
Reading v Bury ....
Walsall v Tranmere Rovers ....
Wigan Athletic v Notts County ....

FOURTH DIVISION
Burnley v Scunthorpe United ....
Carlisle United v Torquay United....................................
Doncaster Rovers v Rochdale...
Exeter City v Scarborough ....
Gillingham v Lincoln City ....
Grimsby Town v Wrexham ....
Hartlepool United v Aldershot ....
Hereford United v Peterborough United ....
Stockport County v Chesterfield ....
York City v Maidstone United..

Sun. 29th April

FOURTH DIVISION

Cambridge United v Colchester United ....

Sat. 5th May

FIRST DIVISION

Coventry City v Liverpool...
Crystal Palace v Manchester City ....
Derby County v Luton Town..
Everton v Aston Villa ....
Manchester United v Charlton Athletic...........................
Millwall v Chelsea ....
Norwich City v Arsenal ....
Queens Park Rangers v Wimbledon................................
Sheffield Wednesday v Nottingham Forest ....
Tottenham Hotspur v Southampton.................................

SECOND DIVISION

AFC Bournemouth v Leeds United ....
Blackburn Rovers v Brighton & Hove Albion....................
Bradford City v Plymouth Argyle ....
Leicester City v Sheffield United ....
Middlesbrough v Newcastle United ....
Oxford United v Port Vale ....
Portsmouth v Barnsley...
Stoke City v Swindon Town ....
Sunderland v Oldham Athletic.......................................

Watford v Hull City ....
West Bromwich Albion v Ipswich Town ....
West Ham United v Wolverhampton Wanderers................

THIRD DIVISION

Birmingham City v Reading ....
Blackpool v Bristol Rovers..
Bristol City v Walsall ....
Bury v Cardiff City ....
Crewe Alexandra v Wigan Athletic.................................
Fulham v Leyton Orient ....
Huddersfield Town v Chester City ....
Notts County v Mansfield Town ....
Rotherham United v Northampton Town ....
Shrewsbury Town v Preston North End ....
Swansea City v Bolton Wanderers ....
Tranmere Rovers v Brentford..

FOURTH DIVISION

Aldershot v Cambridge United ....
Chesterfield v Grimsby Town ....
Colchester United v Burnley ....
Halifax Town v Stockport County ....
Lincoln City v Exeter City...
Maidstone United v Carlisle United.................................
Peterborough United v Southend United ....
Rochdale v Hereford United ....
Scarborough v Gillingham ....
Scunthorpe United v Doncaster Rovers............................
Torquay United v York City...
Wrexham v Hartlepool United..

B & Q LEAGUE FIXTURES 1989-90

© Scottish Football League 1989

Sat. 12th August

PREMIER DIVISION

Aberdeen v Hibernian ....
Dundee United v Motherwell ....
Dunfermline Athletic v Dundee ....
Heart of Midlothian v Celtic ....
Rangers v St. Mirren ....

FIRST DIVISION

Albion Rovers v Ayr United ....
Alloa v St. Johnstone ....
Clyde v Airdrieonians ....
Clydebank v Partick Thistle ....
Forfar Athletic v Falkirk ....
Hamilton Academical v Meadowbank Thistle ....
Raith Rovers v Morton ....

SECOND DIVISION

Berwick Rangers v Cowdenbeath ....
Dumbarton v Queen of the South ....
East Stirlingshire v East Fife ....
Kilmarnock v Brechin City ....
Montrose v Stranraer ....
Stenhousemuir v Queen's Park ....
Stirling Albion v Arbroath ....

Sat. 19th August

PREMIER DIVISION

Celtic v Dunfermline Athletic......................................
Dundee v Dundee United ....
Hibernian v Rangers ....
Motherwell v Aberdeen ....
St. Mirren v Heart of Midlothian.................................

FIRST DIVISION

Airdrieonians v Hamilton Academical ....
Ayr United v Forfar Athletic ....
Falkirk v Raith Rovers ....
Meadowbank Thistle v Alloa..
Morton v Clyde ....
Partick Thistle v Albion Rovers ....
St. Johnstone v Clydebank ....

SECOND DIVISION

Arbroath v Kilmarnock ....
Brechin City v Dumbarton ....
Cowdenbeath v Montrose ....
East Fife v Stenhousemuir ....
Queen of the South v Berwick Rangers...........................
Queen's Park v East Stirlingshire................................
Stranraer v Stirling Albion ....

Sat. 26th August

PREMIER DIVISION

Aberdeen v Dundee ....
Celtic v Rangers...
Dundee United v Dunfermline Athletic...........................
Heart of Midlothian v Hibernian ....
Motherwell v St. Mirren ....

FIRST DIVISION

Airdieonians v Albion Rovers ....
Alloa v Falkirk ....
Ayr United v Hamilton Academical................................

Clydebank v Morton..
Meadowbank Thistle v Raith Rovers ....
Partick Thistle v Clyde ....
St. Johnstone v Forfar Athletic ....

SECOND DIVISION

Arbroath v Stenhousemuir...
Berwick Rangers v Stirling Albion................................
Cowdenbeath v East Fife ....
East Stirlingshire v Dumbarton ....
Montrose v Brechin City..
Queen of the South v Stranraer ....
Queen's Park v Kilmarnock ....

Sat. 2nd September

FIRST DIVISION

Albion Rovers v Clydebank ....
Clyde v Ayr United ....
Falkirk v Meadowbank Thistle......................................
Forfar Athletic v Partick Thistle ....
Hamilton Academical v Alloa.......................................
Morton v Airdrieonians..
Raith Rovers v St. Johnstone ....

SECOND DIVISION

Brechin City v Arbroath ....
Dumbarton v Berwick Rangers.....................................
East Fife v Queen's Park ....
Kilmarnock v East Stirlingshire....................................
Stenhousemuir v Montrose ....
Stirling Albion v Queen of the South.............................
Stranraer v Cowdenbeath ....

Tues. 5th September

FIRST DIVISION

Airdrieonians v Falkirk ....
Alloa v Albion Rovers ....
Ayr United v Morton ....
Clydebank v Clyde ....
Meadowbank Thistle v Forfar Athletic ....
Partick Thistle v Raith Rovers ....
St. Johnstone v Hamilton Academical............................

Sat. 9th September

PREMIER DIVISION

Dundee v Heart of Midlothian ....
Dunfermline Athletic v Motherwell ....
Hibernian v Dundee United ....
Rangers v Aberdeen ....
St. Mirren v Celtic ....

FIRST DIVISION

Albion Rovers v St. Johnstone......................................
Clyde v Alloa ....
Falkirk v Ayr United ....
Forfar Athletic v Clydebank ....
Hamilton Academical v Partick Thistle...........................
Morton v Meadowbank Thistle ....
Raith Rovers v Airdrieonians ....

SECOND DIVISION

Berwick Rangers v East Fife...

184

Dumbarton v Stranraer ....
East Stirlingshire v Stenhousemuir ....
Kilmarnock v Cowdenbeath ....
Montrose v Queen's Park ....
Queen of the South v Arbroath ....
Stirling Albion v Brechin City ....

Sat. 16th September

PREMIER DIVISION
Aberdeen v Dunfermline Athletic ....
Dundee United v Celtic ....
Hibernian v St. Mirren ....
Motherwell v Heart of Midlothian ....
Rangers v Dundee ....

FIRST DIVISION
Airdrieonians v St. Johnstone ....
Ayr United v Clydebank ....
Clyde v Forfar Athletic ....
Falkirk v Hamilton Academical ....
Meadowbank Thistle v Partick Thistle ....
Morton v Alloa ....
Raith Rovers v Albion Rovers ....

SECOND DIVISION
Arbroath v Montrose ....
Brechin City v Queen of the South ....
Cowdenbeath v Stirling Albion ....
East Fife v Dumbarton ....
Queen's Park v Berwick Rangers ....
Stenhousemuir v Kilmarnock ....
Stranraer v East Stirlingshire ....

Sat. 23rd September

PREMIER DIVISION
Celtic v Motherwell ....
Dundee v Hibernian ....
Dunfermline Athletic v Rangers ....
Heart of Midlothian v Dundee United ....
St. Mirren v Aberdeen ....

FIRST DIVISION
Albion Rovers v Clyde ....
Alloa v Ayr United ....
Clydebank v Meadowbank Thistle ....
Forfar Athletic v Raith Rovers ....
Hamilton Academical v Morton ....
Partick Thistle v Airdrieonians ....
St. Johnstone v Falkirk ....

SECOND DIVISION
Dumbarton v Stirling Albion ....
East Fife v Brechin City ....
East Stirlingshire v Arbroath ....
Kilmarnock v Berwick Rangers ....
Montrose v Queen of the South ....
Queen's Park v Cowdenbeath ....
Stenhousemuir v Stranraer ....

Sat. 30th September

PREMIER DIVISION
Aberdeen v Celtic ....
Dundee United v St. Mirren ....
Hibernian v Dunfermline Athletic ....
Motherwell v Dundee ....
Rangers v Heart of Midlothian ....

FIRST DIVISION
Airdrieonians v Alloa ....
Ayr United v Partick Thistle ....
Clyde v Hamilton Academical ....

Falkirk v Albion Rovers ....
Meadowbank Thistle v St. Johnstone ....
Morton v Forfar Athletic ....
Raith Rovers v Clydebank ....

SECOND DIVISION
Arbroath v Queen's Park ....
Berwick Rangers v Montrose ....
Brechin City v Stenhousemuir ....
Cowdenbeath v Dumbarton ....
Queen of the South v East Stirlingshire ....
Stirling Albion v Kilmarnock ....
Stranraer v East Fife ....

Tues. 3rd October

PREMIER DIVISION
Motherwell v Rangers ....

Wed. 4th October

PREMIER DIVISION
Celtic v Hibernian ....
Dundee United v Aberdeen ....
Heart of Midlothian v Dunfermline Athletic ....
St. Mirren v Dundee ....

Sat. 7th October

FIRST DIVISION
Albion Rovers v Forfar Athletic ....
Alloa v Raith Rovers ....
Ayr United v Airdrieonians ....
Clydebank v Hamilton Academical ....
Meadowbank Thistle v Clyde ....
Partick Thistle v Falkirk ....
St. Johnstone v Morton ....

SECOND DIVISION
Arbroath v Dumbarton ....
Cowdenbeath v Brechin City ....
East Fife v Queen of the South ....
East Stirlingshire v Berwick Rangers ....
Montrose v Kilmarnock ....
Queens Park v Stranraer ....
Stenhousemuir v Stirling Albion ....

Sat. 14th October

PREMIER DIVISION
Aberdeen v Heart of Midlothian ....
Dundee v Celtic ....
Dunfermline Athletic v St. Mirren ....
Hibernian v Motherwell ....
Rangers v Dundee United ....

FIRST DIVISION
Airdrieonians v Meadowbank Thistle ....
Clyde v St. Johnstone ....
Falkirk v Clydebank ....
Forfar Athletic v Alloa ....
Hamilton Academical v Albion Rovers ....
Morton v Partick Thistle ....
Raith Rovers v Ayr United ....

SECOND DIVISION
Berwick Rovers v Stenhousemuir ....
Brechin City v East Stirlingshire ....
Dumbarton v Queen's Park ....
Kilmarnock v East Fife ....
Queen of the South v Cowdenbeath ....
Stirling Albion v Montrose ....
Stranraer v Arbroath ....

Sat. 21st October

PREMIER DIVISION
Celtic v Heart of Midlothian.......................................
Dundee v Dunfermline Athletic....................................
Hibernian v Aberdeen..
Motherwell v Dundee United ....
St. Mirren v Rangers...

FIRST DIVISION
Albion Rovers v Meadowbank Thistle...........................
Ayr United v St. Johnstone ....
Clydebank v Airdrieonians ....
Falkirk v Morton...
Forfar Athletic v Hamilton Academical ....
Partick Thistle v Alloa..
Raith Rovers v Clyde..

SECOND DIVISION
Berwick Rangers v Brechin City...................................
Cowdenbeath v Arbroath..
Dumbarton v Stenhousemuir..
Montrose v East Stirlingshire......................................
Queen of the South v Queen's Park ....
Stirling Albion v East Fife...
Stranraer v Kilmarnock ....

Sat. 28th October

PREMIER DIVISION
Aberdeen v Motherwell ....
Dundee United v Dundee ....
Dunfermline Athletic v Celtic......................................
Heart of Midlothian v St. Mirren..................................
Rangers v Hibernian...

FIRST DIVISION
Airdrieonians v Forfar Athletic....................................
Alloa v Clydebank ....
Clyde v Falkirk...
Hamilton Academical v Raith Rovers ....
Meadowbank Thistle v Ayr United ....
Morton v Albion Rovers...
St. Johnstone v Partick Thistle ....

SECOND DIVISION
Arbroath v Berwick Rangers..
Brechin City v Stranraer ....
East Fife v Montrose...
East Stirlingshire v Cowdenbeath ....
Kilmarnock v Dumbarton ....
Queen's Park v Stirling Albion.....................................
Stenhousemuir v Queen of the South ....

Sat. 4th November

PREMIER DIVISION
Dundee v Aberdeen ....
Dunfermline Athletic v Dundee United...........................
Hibernian v Heart of Midlothian ....
Rangers v Celtic..
St. Mirren v Motherwell ....

FIRST DIVISION
Albion Rovers v Alloa ....
Clyde v Clydebank ....
Falkirk v Airdrieonians ....
Forfar Athletic v Meadowbank Thistle ....
Hamilton Academical v St. Johnstone ....
Morton v Ayr United ....
Raith Rovers v Partick Thistle ....

SECOND DIVISION
Brechin City v Queen's Park ....
Dumbarton v Montrose...
East Fife v Arbroath ....

Kilmarnock v Queen of the South..................................
Stenhousemuir v Cowdenbeath ....
Stirling Albion v East Stirlingshire ....
Stranraer v Berwick Rangers ....

Sat. 11th November

PREMIER DIVISION
Aberdeen v Rangers..
Celtic v St. Mirren...
Dundee United v Hibernian ....
Heart of Midlothian v Dundee ....
Motherwell v Dunfermline Athletic ....

FIRST DIVISION
Airdrieonians v Raith Rovers ....
Alloa v Clyde ....
Ayr Unitd v Falkirk..
Clydebank v Forfar Athletic..
Meadowbank Thistle v Morton ....
Partick Thistle v Hamilton Academical...........................
St. Johnstone v Albion Rovers.....................................

SECOND DIVISION
Arbroath v Brechin City ....
Berwick Rangers v Dumbarton ....
Cowdenbeath v Stranraer ....
East Stirlingshire v Kilmarnock ....
Montrose v Stenhousemuir ....
Queen of the South v Stirling Albion..............................
Queen's Park v East Fife ....

Sat. 18th November

PREMIER DIVISION
Celtic v Dundee United..
Dundee v Rangers..
Dunfermline Athletic v Aberdeen ....
Heart of Midlothian v Motherwell ....
St. Mirren v Hibernian...

FIRST DIVISION
Albion Rovers v Raith Rovers ....
Alloa v Morton..
Clydebank v Ayr United...
Forfar Athletic v Clyde..
Hamilton Academical v Falkirk ....
Partick Thistle v Meadowbank Thistle ....
St. Johnstone v Airdrieonians ....

SECOND DIVISION
Dumbarton v Cowdenbeath ....
East Fife v Stranraer ....
East Stirlingshire v Queen of the South...........................
Kilmarnock v Stirling Albion..
Montrose v Berwick Rangers ....
Queen's Park v Arbroath ....
Stenhousemuir v Brechin City ....

Sat. 25th November

PREMIER DIVISION
Aberdeen v St. Mirren ....
Dundee United v Heart of Midlothian..............................
Hibernian v Dundee ....
Motherwell v Celtic..
Rangers v Dunfermline Athletic ....

FIRST DIVISION
Airdrieonians v Partick Thistle ....
Ayr United v Alloa ....
Clyde v Albion Rovers ....
Falkirk v St. Johnstone..

Meadowbank Thistle v Clydebank ....
Morton v Hamilton Academical ....
Raith Rovers v Forfar Athletic ....

SECOND DIVISION
Arbroath v East Stirlingshire ....
Berwick Rangers v Kilmarnock ....
Brechin City v East Fife ....
Cowdenbeath v Queen's Park ....
Queen of the South v Montrose ....
Stirling Albion v Dumbarton ....
Stranraer v Stenhousemuir...

Sat. 2nd December

PREMIER DIVISION
Celtic v Aberdeen ....
Dundee v Motherwell ....
Dunfermline Athletic v Hibernian ....
Heart of Midlothian v Rangers..
St. Mirren v Dundee United ....

FIRST DIVISION
Albion Rovers v Falkirk ....
Alloa v Airdrieonians ....
Clydebank v Raith Rovers ....
Forfar Athletic v Morton ....
Hamilton Academical v Clyde ....
Partick Thistle v Ayr United ....
St. Johnstone v Meadowbank Thistle ....

SECOND DIVISION
Berwick Rangers v East Stirlingshire................................
Brechin City v Cowdenbeath ....
Dumbarton v Arbroath ....
Kilmarnock v Montrose...
Queen of the South v East Fife ....
Stirling Albion v Stenhousemuir ....
Stranraer v Queen's Park ....

Sat. 9th December

PREMIER DIVISION
Aberdeen v Dundee United ....
Dundee v St. Mirren ....
Dunfermline Athletic v Heart of Midlothian......................
Hibernian v Celtic ....
Rangers v Motherwell..

FIRST DIVISION
Airdrieonians v Ayr United ....
Clyde v Meadowbank Thistle ....
Falkirk v Partick Thistle ....
Forfar Athletic v Albion Rovers......................................
Hamilton Academical v Clydebank...................................
Morton v St. Johnstone ....
Raith Rovers v Alloa ....

Sat. 16th December

PREMIER DIVISION
Celtic v Dundee ....
Dundee United v Rangers..
Heart of Midlothian v Aberdeen ....
Motherwell v Hibernian ....
St. Mirren v Dunfermline Athletic...................................

FIRST DIVISION
Albion Rovers v Hamilton Academical ....
Alloa v Forfar Athletic...
Ayr United v Raith Rovers ....
Clydebank v Falkirk ....
Meadowbank Thistle v Airdrieonians...............................
Partick Thistle v Morton...
St. Johnstone v Clyde...

SECOND DIVISION
Arbroath v Stranraer ....
Cowdenbeath v Queen of the South ....
East Fife v Kilmarnock...
East Stirlingshire v Brechin City.....................................
Montrose v Stirling Albion..
Queen's Park v Dumbarton...
Stenhousemuir v Berwick Rangers ....

Sat. 23rd December

PREMIER DIVISION
Dundee United v Motherwell ....
Rangers v St. Mirren..

FIRST DIVISION
Meadowbank Thistle v Hamilton Academical......................
Morton v Raith Rovers ....

SECOND DIVISION
Berwick Rangers v Queen of the South.............................
Dumbarton v Brechin City...
East Stirlingshire v Queen's Park ....
Kilmarnock v Arbroath...
Montrose v Cowdenbeath ....
Stenhousemuir v East Fife ....
Stirling Albion v Stranraer ....

Tues. 26th December

PREMIER DIVISION
Aberdeen v Hibernian ....
Dunfermline Athletic v Dundee ....
Heart of Midlothian v Celtic ....

FIRST DIVISION
Airdrieonians v Clyde ....
Ayr United v Albion Rovers ....
Falkirk v Forfar Athletic...
Partick Thistle v Clydebank ....
St. Johnstone v Alloa ....

SECOND DIVISION
Arbroath v Stirling Albion ....
Brechin City v Kilmarnock...
Cowdenbeath v Berwick Rangers....................................
East Fife v East Stirlingshire..
Queen of the South v Dumbarton ....
Queen's Park v Stenhousemuir ....
Stranraer v Montrose ....

Sat. 30th December

PREMIER DIVISION
Celtic v Dunfermline Athletic...
Dundee v Dundee United ....
Hibernian v Rangers..
Motherwell v Aberdeen ....
St. Mirren v Heart of Midlothian.....................................

FIRST DIVISION
Albion Rovers v Partick Thistle ....
Alloa v Meadowbank Thistle ....
Clyde v Morton ....
Clydebank v St. Johnstone ....
Forfar Athletic v Ayr United ....
Hamilton Academical v Airdrieonians ....
Raith Rovers v Falkirk ....

Mon. 1st January

PREMIER DIVISION
Heart of Midlothian v Hibernian ....

SECOND DIVISION
Brechin City v Montrose..

Tues. 2nd January

PREMIER DIVISION
Aberdeen v Dundee ....
Celtic v Rangers..
Motherwell v St. Mirren ....

FIRST DIVISION
Albion Rovers v Airdrieonians ....
Clyde v Partick Thistle ....
Falkirk v Alloa ....
Forfar Athletic v St. Johnstone ....
Hamilton Academical v Ayr United.................................
Raith Rovers v Meadowbank Thistle ....

SECOND DIVISION
Dumbarton v East Stirlingshire ....
East Fife v Cowdenbeath ....
Kilmarnock v Queen's Park ....
Stenhousemuir v Arbroath ....
Stirling Albion v Berwick Rangers..................................
Stranraer v Queen of the South ....

Wed. 3rd January

PREMIER DIVISION
Dundee United v Dunfermline Athletic.............................

FIRST DIVISION
Morton v Clydebank...

Sat. 6th January

PREMIER DIVISION
Dundee v Heart of Midlothian ....
Dunfermline Athletic v Motherwell ....
Hibernian v Dundee United ....
Rangers v Aberdeen ....
St. Mirren v Celtic ....

FIRST DIVISION
Airdrieonians v Morton...
Alloa v Hamilton Academical...
Ayr United v Clyde ....
Clydebank v Albion Rovers ....
Meadowbank Thistle v Falkirk..
Partick Thistle v Forfar Athletic ....
St. Johnstone v Raith Rovers..

SECOND DIVISION
Arbroath v East Fife ....
Berwick Rangers v Stranraer ....
Cowdenbeath v Stenhousemuir.......................................
East Stirlingshire v Stirling Albion..................................
Montrose v Dumbarton ....
Queen of the South v Kilmarnock....................................
Queen's Park v Brechin City ....

Sat. 13th January

PREMIER DIVISION
Aberdeen v Dunfermline Athletic ....
Dundee United v Celtic..

Hibernian v St. Mirren ....
Motherwell v Heart of Midlothian ....
Rangers v Dundee ....

FIRST DIVISION
Albion Rovers v Morton...
Ayr United v Meadowbank Thistle ....
Clydebank v Alloa ....
Falkirk v Clyde ....
Forfar Athletic v Airdrieonians.......................................
Partick Thistle v St. Johnstone ....
Raith Rovers v Hamilton Academical ....

SECOND DIVISION
Arbroath v Queen of the South ....
Brechin City v Stirling Albion..
Cowdenbeath v Kilmarnock ....
East Fife v Berwick Rangers...
Queen's Park v Montrose ....
Stenhousemuir v East Stirlingshire ....
Stranraer v Dumbarton ....

Sat. 20th January

SECOND DIVISION
Berwick Rangers v Queen's Park ....
Dumbarton v East Fife ....
East Stirlingshire v Stranraer ....
Kilmarnock v Stenhousemuir ....
Montrose v Arbroath ....
Queen of the South v Brechin City...................................
Stirling Albion v Cowdenbeath ....

Sat. 27th January

PREMIER DIVISION
Celtic v Motherwell ....
Dundee v Hibernian ....
Dunfermline Athletic v Rangers ....
Heart of Midlothian v Dundee United..............................
St. Mirren v Aberdeen ....

FIRST DIVISION
Airdrieonians v Clydebank ....
Alloa v Partick Thistle..
Clyde v Raith Rovers ....
Hamilton Academical v Forfar Athletic.............................
Meadowbank Thistle v Albion Rovers...............................
Morton v Falkirk..
St. Johnstone v Ayr United ....

SECOND DIVISION
Arbroath v Cowdenbeath ....
Brechin City v Berwick Rangers......................................
East Fife v Stirling Albion ....
East Stirlingshire v Montrose..
Kilmarnock v Stranraer ....
Queen's Park v Queen of the South ....
Stenhousemuir v Dumbarton...

Sat. 3rd February

PREMIER DIVISION
Aberdeen v Heart of Midlothian ....
Dundee v Celtic...
Dunfermline Athletic v St. Mirren...................................
Hibernian v Motherwell ....
Rangers v Dundee United...

FIRST DIVISION
Albion Rovers v Falkirk ....
Ayr United v Partick Thistle...
Clyde v Airdrieonians ....
Forfar Athletic v Raith Rovers..

Hamilton Academical v Clydebank.................................
Morton v Alloa...
St. Johnstone v Meadowbank Thistle ....

SECOND DIVISION

SECOND DIVISION
Berwick Rangers v Arbroath..
Cowdenbeath v East Stirlingshire.................................
Dumbarton v Kilmarnock..
Montrose v East Fife..
Queen of the South v Stenhousemuir ....
Stirling Albion v Queen's Park.....................................
Stranraer v Brechin City...

Sat. 10th February

PREMIER DIVISION
Celtic v Hibernian ....
Dundee United v Aberdeen ....
Heart of Midlothian v Dunfermline Athletic...................
Motherwell v Rangers...
St. Mirren v Dundee ....

FIRST DIVISION
Airdrieonians v Ayr United ....
Alloa v Clyde ....
Clydebank v Forfar Athletic...
Falkirk v St. Johnstone...
Meadowbank Thistle v Hamilton Academical..................
Partick Thistle v Morton...
Raith Rovers v Albion Rovers ....

SECOND DIVISION
Berwick Rangers v Stenhousemuir ....
Brechin City v Cowdenbeath.......................................
East Fife v Queen's Park ....
East Stirlingshire v Arbroath.......................................
Kilmarnock v Stirling Albion.......................................
Queen of the South v Dumbarton..................................
Stranraer v Montrose ....

Sat. 17th February

PREMIER DIVISION
Aberdeen v Celtic ....
Dundee United v St. Mirren...
Hibernian v Dunfermline Athletic.................................
Motherwell v Dundee ....
Rangers v Heart of Midlothian.....................................

FIRST DIVISION
Airdrieonians v Partick Thistle ....
Alloa v Albion Rovers ....
Ayr United v Forfar Athletic..
Clyde v Hamilton Academical ....
Falkirk v Clydebank..
Morton v St. Johnstone ....
Raith Rovers v Meadowbank Thistle ....

SECOND DIVISION
Arbroath v Kilmarnock ....
Cowdenbeath v East Fife...
Dumbarton v East Stirlingshire....................................
Montrose v Berwick Rangers.......................................
Queen's Park v Stranraer...
Stenhousemuir v Brechin City ....
Stirling Albion v Queen of the South............................

Sat. 24th February

SECOND DIVISION
Arbroath v Brechin City ....
Berwick Rangers v Kilmarnock....................................
Cowdenbeath v Queen of the South...............................
East Stirlingshire v Stirling Albion...............................

Montrose v Dumbarton...
Queen's Park v Stenhousemuir ....
Stranraer v East Fife..

Sat. 3rd March

PREMIER DIVISION
Celtic v Dundee United...
Dundee v Rangers..
Dunfermline Athletic v Aberdeen ....
Heart of Midlothian v Motherwell ....
St. Mirren v Hibernian ....

FIRST DIVISION
Albion Rovers v Airdrieonians ....
Clydebank v Ayr United..
Forfar Athletic v Alloa ....
Hamilton Academical v Falkirk ....
Meadowbank Thistle v Morton ....
Partick Thistle v Clyde ....
St. Johnstone v Raith Rovers.......................................

SECOND DIVISION
Brechin City v Queen's Park ....
Dumbarton v Stranraer...
East Fife v Arbroath ....
Kilmarnock v East Stirlingshire....................................
Queen of the South v Berwick Rangers..........................
Stenhousemuir v Cowdenbeath.....................................
Stirling Albion v Montrose..

Sat. 10th March

PREMIER DIVISION
Celtic v Heart of Midlothian..
Dundee v Dunfermline Athletic....................................
Hibernian v Aberdeen ....
Motherwell v Dundee United ....
St. Mirren v Rangers..

FIRST DIVISION
Albion Rovers v St. Johnstone......................................
Alloa v Falkirk ....
Ayr United v Clyde ....
Clydebank v Meadowbank Thistle.................................
Forfar Athletic v Airdrieonians.....................................
Partick Thistle v Hamilton Academical..........................
Raith Rovers v Morton ....

SECOND DIVISION
Berwick Rangers v East Fife..
Cowdenbeath v Stirling Albion ....
Dumbarton v Arbroath ....
East Stirlingshire v Stranraer.......................................
Kilmarnock v Queen's Park ....
Montrose v Stenhousemuir ....
Queen of the South v Brechin City................................

Sat. 17th March

FIRST DIVISION
Airdrieonians v Clydebank ....
Clyde v Raith Rovers...
Falkirk v Partick Thistle ....
Hamilton Academical v Ayr United...............................
Meadowbank Thistle v Forfar Athletic ....
Morton v Albion Rovers...
St. Johnstone v Alloa ....

SECOND DIVISION
Arbroath v Montrose..
Brechin City v Dumbarton...
East Fife v East Stirlingshire.......................................
Queen's Park v Cowdenbeath.......................................

Stenhousemuir v Kilmarnock ....
Stirling Albion v Berwick Rangers...............................
Stranraer v Queen of the South ....

Sat. 24th March

PREMIER DIVISION
Aberdeen v Motherwell ....
Dundee United v Dundee ....
Dunfermline Athletic v Celtic.....................................
Heart of Midlothian v St. Mirren..................................
Rangers v Hibernian...

FIRST DIVISION
Airdrieonians v Alloa ....
Ayr United v Falkirk ....
Clyde v Albion Rovers ....
Clydebank v Raith Rovers ....
Hamilton Academical v St. Johnstone ....
Meadowbank Thistle v Partick Thistle ....
Morton v Forfar Athletic ....

SECOND DIVISION
Arbroath v Queen's Park ....
Brechin City v Montrose..
Cowdenbeath v Berwick Rangers ....
Dumbarton v Kilmarnock ....
East Fife v Queen of the South......................................
East Stirlingshire v Stenhousemuir ....
Stirling Albion v Stranraer ....

Sat. 31st March

PREMIER DIVISION
Dundee v Aberdeen ....
Dunfermline Athletic v Dundee United............................
Hibernian v Heart of Midlothian ....
Rangers v Celtic...
St. Mirren v Motherwell ....

FIRST DIVISION
Albion Rovers v Meadowbank Thistle............................
Alloa v Hamilton Academical.......................................
Falkirk v Morton...
Forfar Athletic v Clyde ....
Partick Thistle v Clydebank ....
Raith Rovers v Ayr United ....
St. Johnstone v Airdrieonians.......................................

SECOND DIVISION
Berwick Rangers v Dumbarton......................................
Kilmarnock v Brechin City...
Montrose v East Fife...
Queen of the South v East Stirlingshire...........................
Queen's Park v Stirling Albion......................................
Stenhousemuir v Arbroath ....
Stranraer v Cowdenbeath ....

Sat. 7th April

PREMIER DIVISION
Aberdeen v Rangers..
Celtic v St. Mirren ....
Dundee United v Hibernian ....
Heart of Midlothian v Dundee ....
Motherwell v Dunfermline..

FIRST DIVISION
Albion Rovers v Forfar Athletic....................................
Clydebank v Clyde ....
Falkirk v Airdrieonians ....
Meadowbank Thistle v Alloa ....
Morton v Ayr United ....
Partick Thistle v St. Johnstone ....
Raith Rovers v Hamilton Academical ....

SECOND DIVISION
Arbroath v Queen of the South ....
Berwick Rangers v Stranraer ....
Brechin City v Stirling Albion.......................................
Cowdenbeath v Montrose ....
Kilmarnock v East Fife..
Queen's Park v East Stirlingshire ....
Stenhousemuir v Dumbarton...

Sat. 14th April

PREMIER DIVISION
Aberdeen v Dundee United ....
Dundee v St. Mirren ....
Dunfermline Athletic v Heart of Midlothian.....................
Hibernian v Celtic ....
Rangers v Motherwell ....

FIRST DIVISION
Airdrieonians v Meadowbank Thistle...............................
Alloa v Raith Rovers ....
Ayr United v Albion Rovers ....
Clyde v Falkirk ....
Forfar Athletic v Partick Thistle ....
Hamilton Academical v Morton ....
St. Johnstone v Clydebank ....

SECOND DIVISION
Dumbarton v Cowdenbeath ....
East Fife v Brechin City...
East Stirlingshire v Berwick Rangers..............................
Montrose v Queen's Park ....
Queen of the South v Stenhousemuir ....
Stirling Albion v Arbroath ....
Stranraer v Kilmarnock...

Sat. 21st April

PREMIER DIVISION
Celtic v Dundee ....
Dundee United v Rangers...
Heart of Midlothian v Aberdeen ....
Motherwell v Hibernian ....
St. Mirren v Dunfermline Athletic..................................

FIRST DIVISION
Airdrieonians v Raith Rovers ....
Clydebank v Morton..
Falkirk v Forfar Athletic..
Hamilton Academical v Albion Rovers ....
Meadowbank Thistle v Ayr United ....
Partick Thistle v Alloa...
St. Johnstone v Clyde ....

SECOND DIVISION
Arbroath v Cowdenbeath ....
Brechin City v Stranraer ....
East Fife v Dumbarton ....
East Stirlingshire v Montrose..
Kilmarnock v Queen of the South...................................
Queen's Park v Berwick Rangers ....
Stirling Albion v Stenhousemuir ....

Sat. 28th April

PREMIER DIVISION
Aberdeen v St. Mirren ....
Dundee United v Heart of Midlothian..............................
Hibernian v Dundee ....
Motherwell v Celtic ....
Rangers v Dunfermline Athletic ....

FIRST DIVISION
Albion Rovers v Partick Thistle ....

Alloa v Clydebank ....
Ayr United v St. Johnstone ....
Clyde v Meadowbank Thistle ....
Forfar Athletic v Hamilton Academical ....
Morton v Airdrieonians..
Raith Rovers v Falkirk ....

SECOND DIVISION
Berwick Rangers v Brechin City......................................
Cowdenbeath v East Stirlingshire ....
Dumbarton v Stirling Albion ....
Montrose v Kilmarnock...
Queen of the South v Queen's Park ....
Stenhousemuir v East Fife ....
Stranraer v Arbroath ....

Sat. 5th May

PREMIER DIVISION
Celtic v Aberdeen ....

Dundee v Motherwell ....
Dunfermline Athletic v Hibernian ....
Heart of Midlothian v Rangers...
St. Mirren v Dundee United..

FIRST DIVISION
Airdrieonians v Hamilton Academical ....
Albion Rovers v Clydebank ....
Alloa v Ayr United..
Meadowbank Thistle v Falkirk...
Morton v Clyde ....
Partick Thistle v Raith Rovers ....
St. Johnstone v Forfar Athletic ....

SECOND DIVISION
Berwick Rangers v Arbroath ....
Brechin City v East Stirlingshire.....................................
Kilmarnock v Cowdenbeath ....
Montrose v Queen of the South......................................
Queen's Park v Dumbarton..
Stirling Albion v East Fife...
Stranraer v Stenhousemuir..